GOD THE CREATOR

WHAT THE BIBLE SAYS ABOUT

GOD THE CREATOR

Wipf and Stock Publishers
EUGENE, OREGON

Wipf and Stock Publishers
199 West 8th Avenue, Suite 3
Eugene, Oregon 97401

What the Bible Says About God the Creator
By Cottrell, Jack

ISBN: 1-57910-525-4
Publication date 10/24/2000
Previously published by College Press Publishing Company, 1983

Table of Contents

Preface

> . . . The doctrine of God, it need scarcely be said, lies at the foundation of all right thinking in religion. In strictness, theology is just the doctrine of God. That is the meaning of the word. God is the Alpha and Omega of theological study, for as a man thinks about his God so will his theology be all through. It is not too strong to say that, in principle, every question of importance which arises in theology is already practically settled in the doctrine of God and His attributes. So essential is it to begin with Scripturally right thoughts about God. (James Orr, *Sidelights on Christian Doctrine*; London: Marshall Brothers, 1909; p. 8)

In these words James Orr articulates very well my own conviction concerning the fundamental nature of the study of the doctrine of God. This conviction causes me to feel an overwhelming sense of inadequacy to produce a work such as this, but at the same time I am very thankful to have the privilege of doing it.

This study has been long in gestation. My formal introduction to the biblical doctrine of God was in 1957, in Professor George Mark Elliott's course in Biblical Theology at The Cincinnati Bible Seminary. At Westminster Theological Seminary the course in "theology proper" was taught by the late Dr. Edwin H. Palmer, while courses by John Murray and Edward J. Young made their contribution to the overall subject. At Princeton Theological Seminary I audited Dr. George S. Hendry's course on "The First Article." These three academic experiences, from three different theological perspectives, provided stimulus and breadth; and I am grateful for each of them.

Unquestionably, though, my most important preparation for this study has been the course I have taught on "The Doctrine of God" at Cincinnati Christian Seminary since 1967. I remember very well the first time I taught it. There were three students; and in the very first class session one of them asked very innocently, "What *is* the doctrine of God, anyway?" I need not elaborate on all the thoughts that went through my mind when this question was asked, but I can say that I took it as a challenge to give this subject special attention both outside and inside the classroom. It might be said that this present work is an attempt to answer the question, "What *is* the doctrine of God, anyway?"

I should note that when I began actually to write this study, it was intended to be just one volume. As the work progressed it became obvious either that it would be a very large volume or that it would have to be published as a multivolume work. Because the material is organized into three major parts, the decision to produce three volumes instead of one was natural. Thus this book, the first of a trilogy, deals only with the doctrine of God as our Creator. The next volume will deal with the doctrine of providence: the work of God as the Sovereign Lord of nature and history, and his nature as manifested in this work. The final volume will deal with the doctrine of God as our Redeemer.

A word of explanation concerning Scripture quotations is in order. The New American Standard Bible has been used in every case except where noted, but I have made a few modifications in the printed form. The NASB prints much of the Old Testament in poetic form, but in most cases I have turned it into prose (without changing the words). Also, I have not used all capital letters for the word *Lord* where it represents "Yahweh" in the original text, though the NASB does. Likewise I have not used all capital letters when citing passages from the New Testament which are quotations from the Old Testament.

I want to thank College Press for providing the occasion to produce this work, and for agreeing to publish it in three volumes instead of one. Also I want to thank Cincinnati Christian Seminary for the half-year sabbatical which provided extra time to devote to the project, as well as the CCS secretaries for typing the manuscript. Finally I want to thank my longsuffering family for adjusting to the schedule and lifestyle of an author working to meet a deadline. I am especially grateful to my wife, Barbara, to whom this volume is dedicated.

Chapter One

INTRODUCTION

THE CONCEPT OF GOD

Brahman. Ahura Mazda. Shiva. Vishnu. Zeus. Thor. Ra. Isis. Cagn. Bumba. Zambe. Akongo. Allah. Nous. Odin. Krishna. Io. Marduk. Tezcatlipoca. Karusakaibo. Gainji. Aganua. Djanggawul. Tangaroa. Ndengei. Ta'aroa. Utu. Qat. Hainuwele. Horus. Hecate. Jove. Shang Ti. Hermes. Thoth. Apis. Ishtar. Hercules. T'ien. Venus. Xochiquetzal. Rhea. Tenga. Tanit. Selene. Wanga. Nyakala. Shimunenga. Unkulunkulu. Na Vahine. Frey. Jupiter. Ea. Dagon. Mawu. Ngai. Nzambi. Mwari. Mithra. Katonda. Marzyana. Moira. Dionysos. Apollo. Maat. Mictlancihuatl. Asklepios. Ixchel. Kaun Yin. Juno. Mars. Sul. Kali. Kattahha. Minerva. Nebo. Bel. Baal. Diana. Grannos. Hera. Varuna. Ceres. Chicomecohuatl. Anu. Eostre. Demeter. Cybele. Lowa. Napioa. Dzydzilelya. Athena. Kiho. Brigit. Aphrodite. Taiowa. Kumpara. Amaterasu. Awonawilona. Akka. Tepeu. Kumpara. Tammuz. Frija.

These are but a few of the many names which human beings have given to their gods. The names are both ancient and contemporary, and they come from all over the globe. This brief list illustrates the fact that the concept of deity is universal. All peoples of the earth have the idea of a higher being or higher beings on whom they depend, to whom they are responsible and/or who in some way affect or control their destiny. Even the denial of the existence of such a being demonstrates the presence of the concept.

The generic word for deity is found in most languages. This is the English word *god* and its equivalents, such as *gott, kami, dieu, deus, theos, elohim, goth, dios,* and *dio.* Descriptive appellations are also commonly used in referring to deity. These include "Father," "First Cause," "Unmoved Mover," "Supreme Being," "the Absolute," "the Infinite," "the ONE," "Great Spirit," "Creator," and "Lord."

Sometimes a more complete definition of God is offered. For instance, deity has been defined as "infinite spiritual essence," or "the one supreme being, the creator and ruler of the universe," or "a superhuman or supernatural being that controls the world." Other definitions are more lengthy and detailed. "God is the being who exists necessarily by himself, comprising all the attributes of perfection." "God is a spirit, infinite, eternal, and unchangeable, in his being, wisdom, power, holiness, justice, goodness, and truth." "God is a spiritual essence, intelligent, eternal, true, pure, just, merciful, most free, of vast power and wisdom, the eternal Father who begat the Son, his own image, from eternity, and the Son, the co-eternal image of the Father, and the Holy Spirit, proceeding from the Father and the Son."[1]

Definitions of deity will vary, of course, because the concept of the divine being differs widely from culture to culture and from religion to religion. The names applied to the gods of mankind are even more diverse, as the list above shows; and the list could be expanded indefinitely. Islamic tradition lists 99 names for the one god Allah, from "al-'Adl, the Just," to "al-Zahir, the Outward."[2] A

1. For some other definitions of God see H. Orton Wiley, *Christian Theology*(Kansas City, Mo.: Beacon Hill Press, 1940) I:218-20.

2. James Robson, "God, Concept of (Islam)," *A Dictionary of Comparative Religion,* ed. S.G.F. Brandon (London: Weidenfeld and Nicolson, 1970), pp. 306-7.

formal estimate of the number of gods in the many cults of Hinduism is 330,000,000.[3] These are all just manifestations of the one divine being Brahman; whether each has a separate name is uncertain. Arthur C. Clarke wrote a fictional story of a group of Tibetan monks who undertook the task of writing each of the nine billion names of the Supreme Being, going programatically through the alphabet from AAAAAAA . . . to ZZZZZZZ . . . . At first they figured the task would take 15,000 years; but when computers became available they were able to complete the job in just one hundred days. As soon as they finished, the universe came to an end.[4]

Usually such concepts, definitions, names, and speculations stand in sharp contrast to the One True God, the God of the Hebrews, the God of our Lord Jesus Christ, the God of the Bible. They are either totally false or woefully inadequate when compared with the biblical concept of God. Only God Himself can reveal his name and describe his nature. Even then we can formulate no definition of God as such, since God is not part of a category who can be defined in relation to the other members of that category. God is unique; he is the only member of his genus, so to speak. In a sense, everything we can say about God is a part of the definition of God. Even if we were to attempt such a description-definition, it would be only partial and incomplete, since man's mind will never grasp the fullness of God's being.

---

3. Ninian Smart, "Gods, Hindu," *A Dictionary of Comparative Religion*, ed. S.G.F. Brandon, p. 308.

4. Arthur C. Clarke, "The Nine Billion Names of God," *Science Fiction Hall of Fame*, ed. Robert Silverberg (Garden City, N.Y.: Doubleday, 1970). I:424-30.

THE STUDY OF GOD

Even though a complete understanding of God is beyond our finite capacities, the study of God is both possible and necessary. The specific term for such study is *theology.* This English word comes from two Greek words: *theos,* which means "God," and *logos,* which (in this combination) means "the study of."

Actually the word *theology* is used in a number of ways. In the most general sense it refers to the whole scope of religious studies included in a seminary curriculum; thus many such institutions are called "theological seminaries." In a narrower sense it refers to the field of theology as distinguished from the biblical, historical, and practical fields in a seminary curriculum. In this sense it usually includes the study of systematic theology, ethics, apologetics, and history of doctrine. In a third sense the word *theology* is often limited to the specific area of systematic or doctrinal theology, including the study of God, man, sin, salvation, the church, and last things. This is probably the most common use of the term.[5]

The fourth and most precise use of the term *theology* is the study of God himself, which is literally what the term means. Because of the other senses in which the term is used, however, the study of God is usually called "theology proper." This does not mean that theology in the other senses is improper, but that this is the most proper use of the term. This book is an exercise in "theology proper"; it is a study of God.

---

5. For a more complete discussion of these uses of the term *theology,* especially the third use, see Jack Cottrell, "Theology and the Church," *Christian Standard* (February 7, 1982), 117:4-5.

The Basis of Piety

The study of God must always be one of a Christian's top priorities, since the knowledge of God is one of the main pillars in a life of piety. When Jesus prayed for his disciples, he said, "And this is eternal life, that they may know Thee, the only true God, and Jesus Christ whom Thou hast sent" (John 17:3). Eternal life depends upon knowing God. This includes knowing about God, but it also includes knowing God existentially and personally. That is, we must make the facts about God determinative for our whole life and thought. We must embrace the truth about God with our whole hearts and mold our lives around it. We must live as though God is truly real; we must take his reality seriously.

For example, *worship* that is satisfying to ourselves and pleasing to God must be grounded in a true knowledge of God. Kierkegaard, the champion of subjectivism, once said that passionate worship of an idol is better than a cold, formal worship of the true God.[6] Even if this were true, it is no comfort to the idolater, since God does not accept either one. Subjective intensity does not make up for lack of knowledge of the truth about God. Jesus said those who worship God "must worship in spirit and truth" (John 4:24). He said this while rebuking the Samaritan woman for her ignorance of the true nature of God: "You worship that which you do not know; we worship that which we know; for salvation is from the Jews" (John 4:22). Likewise in Athens the Apostle Paul called attention to the Athenians' altar "To an Unknown God" among their other objects of worship. "What therefore you worship in ignorance, this I proclaim to you," he said. He then proceeded

6. Soren Kierkegaard, *Concluding Unscientific Postscript*, tr. David Swenson and Walter Lowrie (Princeton: Princeton University Press, 1941), pp. 179-80.

to give a mini-lesson on theology proper, providing them and us with one of the most sublime and succinct statements on the doctrine of God to be found anywhere (Acts 17:22-31). Without such truth our worship is no more than idolatry.

For another example, *morality* is also dependent upon a knowledge of God. The basic elements of right character and conduct are in the final analysis an imitation of the character of God, in whose image we are made. "But like the Holy One who called you, be holy yourselves also in all your behavior; because it is written, 'You shall be holy, for I am holy'" (I Peter 1:15-16). John shows how this applies to the commandment to love one another: "The one who does not love does not know God, for God is love" (I John 4:8). The more we know of the nature of God, the more we know about right and wrong conduct. Good ethics presupposes good theology.

Clement of Rome, in his post-apostolic letter "To the Corinthians," gives a good illustration of this point. Even though we are justified by faith, he says, we should still do good works just because God himself works, thus providing a pattern for us.

> What then must we do, brethren? Must we idly abstain from doing good, and forsake love? May the Master never allow this to befall us at least; but let us hasten with instancy and zeal to accomplish every good work. For the Creator and Master of the universe Himself rejoiceth in His works. For by His exceeding great might He established the heavens, and in His incomprehensible wisdom He set them in order. . . . We have seen that all the righteous were adorned in good works. Yea, and the Lord Himself having adorned Himself with works rejoiced. Seeing then that we have this pattern, let us conform ourselves with all diligence to His

will; let us with all our strength work the work of righteousness.[7]

The Current Theological Vacuum

In addition to the positive benefits gained from the study of God, there are always some negative factors that make this study even more imperative. That is to say, a study of the true God is necessary to combat and offset the atheism, false doctrine, ignorance, and indifference that exist to some degree in every age and culture. This has never been more true than it is now in twentieth century America. The mind-set of our culture has never been more hostile to or in greater need of a true knowledge of the true God.

Denial of God

Several factors have helped to create our current theological wasteland. One is the widespread denial of God and of the supernatural in general. There have always been atheists, of course. As the inspired psalmist says, "The fool has said in his heart, 'There is no God'" (Psalms 14:1; 53:1). If there were such fools in David's day, there are no doubt a proportionately much greater number today. Under the influence of evolutionism and scientism, and encouraged by a strong moral rebelliousness, the modern mind has become increasingly secularized. The recent "death of God" phenomenon was but the theological expression of a cultural fact, namely, that much of our current Western society has given up the idea of God and has affirmed that the natural universe alone is all that exists.

---

7. Clement of Rome, "To the Corinthians," 33, *The Apostolic Fathers*, ed. J.B. Lightfoot and J.R. Harmer (Grand Rapids: Baker, 1962), pp. 26-27.

Here we will call attention to two very different expressions of contemporary anti-supernaturalism, each of which exerts considerable influence in the direction of atheism. The first is secular humanism. We are aware, of course, that anyone who attempts to call attention to the spiritual danger of secular humanism will be accused of fundamentalist paranoia. Nevertheless we must emphasize the fact that this philosophy of "respectable" atheism is much more influential than we would like to think.

There is no question that secular humanism is a true atheism, even though in its first manifesto (1933) it designated itself as "religious humanism." This manifesto made the following statements:

> Religious humanists regard the universe as self-existing and not created.
>
> Humanism believes that man is a part of nature and that he has emerged as the result of a continuous process. . . .
>
> We are convinced that the time has passed for theism, deism, modernism, and the several varieties of "new thought."[8]

The second manifesto, published in 1973, is much more explicit in its denial of God. Here are some of its declarations:

> As in 1933, humanists still believe that traditional theism, especially faith in the prayer-hearing God, assumed to love and care for persons, to hear and understand their prayers, and to be able to do something about them, is an unproved and outmoded faith. . . .[9]
>
> . . . We find insufficient evidence for belief in the existence of a supernatural; it is either meaningless or irrelevant

---

8. *Humanist Manifestos I and II* (Buffalo: Prometheus Press, 1973), p. 8.
9. *Ibid.*, p. 13.

> to the question of the survival and fulfillment of the human race. As nontheists, we begin with humans not God, nature not deity. Nature may indeed be broader and deeper than we now know; any new discoveries, however, will but enlarge our knowledge of the natural.[10]
>
> . . . But we can discover no divine purpose or providence for the human species. While there is much that we do not know, humans are responsible for what we are or will become. No deity will save us; we must save ourselves.[11]

In the recent "Secular Humanist Declaration" (1980) the same theme is reiterated:

> As secular humanists, we are generally skeptical about supernatural claims. . . . We are doubtful of traditional views of God and divinity. . . . We consider the universe to be a dynamic scene of natural forces that are most effectively understood by scientific inquiry. We are always open to the discovery of new possibilities and phenomena in nature. However, we find that traditional views of the existence of God either are meaningless, have not yet been demonstrated to be true, or are tyrannically exploitative. Secular humanists may be agnostics, atheists, rationalists, or skeptics, but they find insufficient evidence for the claim that some divine purpose exists for the universe. They reject the idea that God has intervened miraculously in history or revealed himself to a chosen few, or that he can save or redeem sinners.[12]

---

10. *Ibid.*, p. 16.

11. *Ibid.*

12. *A Secular Humanist Declaration* (n.p., 1980), pp. 17-18. First printed in *Free Inquiry* (volume one, Winter 1980), a magazine promoting humanism and attacking religion—especially Christianity.

The humanist Gardner Williams points out that some humanists are reluctant to give up the term *God,* even though they no longer believe in religion or the supernatural. They are afraid of social rejection, and they do see a need for cultivating "a passionate devotion to the great ideal of man's highest good." Thus Williams, following a suggestion by George Santayana, offers a redefinition of terms. "I suggest," he says, "that we call the basic physical substance of the cosmos the *supreme being,* and save the word God for the ideal of man's highest good." Since man never really attains this ideal, God (as thus defined) "exists" only in potential and never in actuality. "Nevertheless He is a real fact. . . . So God must be a real, factual nonexistent potential."[13]

This suggestion by Williams, as incredible as it may seem to most of us, is offered seriously and is a good example of why there is so much confusion in the knowledge of God today. We must not underestimate the influence this kind of thinking is having on our society.[14]

Another example of the growth of anti-supernaturalism is the increasing popularity of science fiction. In one sense we may think of science fiction as a neutral and harmless genre of literature, one which many of us enjoy reading. I confess that I have read a moderate amount of it myself. But over the years, as I have read more and more in this area, I have become impressed with this fact: despite the fact that God or gods sometimes figure in a science fiction plot, there is absolutely no place for a truly supernatural,

---

13. Gardner Williams, "Humanistic Theism," *The Humanist Alternative,* ed. Paul Kurtz (Buffalo: Prometheus Press, 1973), pp. 67-68.

14. For more information on humanism's influence, see the following books by Tim LaHaye, all published by Revell: *The Battle for the Mind* (1980), *The Battle for the Family* (1981), and *The Battle for the Public Schools* (1982).

transcendent God in the universes created by most science fiction writers. What gods there are turn out to be just older, wiser, stronger beings who are part of the natural universe. In fact, some would suggest that science fiction has helped to condition us to substitute a kind of faith in alien but purely naturalistic superbeings for belief in God.[15]

This can be illustrated in a number of ways. For instance, Erich von Däniken in his books *Chariots of the Gods?* and *Gods from Outer Space* has suggested that mankind's god-myths are based on actual visits to Earth by alien astronauts whose super-powers worked wonders and even originated the human race, all within the purely naturalistic framework of advanced science, of course.[16] Whereas von Däniken has attempted to interpret the past via this hypothesis, science fiction writers are teaching us to place our hope for the future in possible visits from extra-terrestrials. This is seen in the tremendous success of 1982's most popular movie, "E.T.: The Extra-Terrestrial." It was also obvious in the closing scenes of the movie, "Close Encounters of the Third Kind." The human audience stood in awe and rapture as the benevolent and vastly superior aliens revealed themselves to their worshipers. The background music was strikingly and pointedly intended to create the mood of religious worship.

Thus science fiction is helping to relativize and naturalize the concept of God, and it is doing so within the boundaries allowed by the second humanist manifesto as quoted above: "Nature may indeed be broader and deeper than we now

---

15. See the August 1977 issue of the *SCP Journal*, "UFO's: Is Science Fiction Coming True?" (Available from Spiritual Counterfeits Project, P.O. Box 2418, Berkeley, Cal. 94702.)

16. See the critique of von Däniken by Clifford Wilson in his books *Crash Go the Chariots* (New York: Lancer Books, 1972), *The Chariots Still Crash* (Old Tappan, N.J.: Revell, 1975), and *Gods in Chariots and Other Fantasies* (San Diego: Creation-Life, 1975).

know; any new discoveries, however, will but enlarge our knowledge of the natural." Anything supernatural is already ruled out *a priori.*

Just how influential is science fiction? Probably much more than we care to think. Within the past year (roughly 1982) at least five science fiction books have been on the top ten best-seller list: *Foundation's Edge* by Isaac Asimov (a signer of "Humanist Manifesto II" and the "Secular Humanist Declaration"), *2010: Odyssey Two* by Arthur C. Clarke, *Friday* by Robert Heinlein, *White Plague* by Frank Herbert, and *Battlefield Earth* by L. Ron Hubbard (founder of the Scientology cult). Also, science fiction themes abound in the visual media and have immense popularity, e.g., "Star Trek," the "Star Wars" saga, and "E.T."

The point is that we should not be surprised at the widespread denial of God in our society, with influences such as these shaping our thought. They make us even more aware of the need for the study of God.

False Gods

A second element in the contemporary confusion about God is the abundance of false deities that are vying for allegiance today. The most significant factor here is the growing religious pluralism in the Western world and especially in the United States. There has been a considerable influx of anti-Christian cults and religions into the U.S., particularly from the Orient.[17] A large number of these (e.g.,

17. See, for instance, Peter Rowley, *New Gods in America* (New York: David Mackay, 1971); William J. Petersen, *Those Curious New Cults*, 2 ed. (New Canaan, Conn.: Keats, 1975); William J. Whalen, *Strange Gods: Contemporary Religious Cults in America* (Huntington, Ind.: Our Sunday Visitor, 1981); Robert S. Ellwood, Jr., *Alternative Altars* (Chicago: University of Chicago Press, 1979); Walter Martin, *The New Cults* (Santa Ana, Cal.: Vision House, 1980); and Margot Adler, *Drawing Down the Moon: Witches, Druids, Goddess-Worshippers, and Other Pagans in America Today* (Boston: Beacon Press, 1979).

Hare Krishna, TM, and the Divine Light Mission) are derived from Hinduism. Thus the Hindu concept of God, which is generally a form of pantheistic monism, is being accepted by more and more Westerners. Islam is also becoming more militantly evangelistic in the West. Older cults such as Mormonism continue to grow. Though each of these groups says a lot about the divine being, their gods are not the God of the Bible.

The modern pantheon is also populated by false gods created by both science and philosophy. Many scientists are atheists, and many are Bible-believers who accept the God of the Bible. But there are many others who believe in a Supreme Being who is far different from the True God. Some portray God as an impersonal cosmic force or as Supreme Intelligence. The British scientist Sir James Jeans pictured God as "the Great Architect of the Universe" who is "a pure mathematician."[18] Einstein sometimes spoke of God; but, as one of his biographers said, "Einstein's God was not the God of most other men."[19] Einstein is often quoted as saying, "I believe in Spinoza's God, who reveals himself in the harmony of all that exists, not in God who concerns himself with the fate and actions of men."[20] It should be noted, as Hocking points out, that Spinoza's God is not a being separate from the world but is identical with Nature, the very substance of the world itself. "To believe in Nature is to believe in God."[21] Thus "Einstein's God

18. James Jeans, *The Mysterious Universe* (New York: Macmillan, 1930), p. 144.

19. Ronald W. Clark, *Einstein: The Life and Times* (New York: World Publishing Company, 1971), p. 19.

20. *Ibid.*; see also William E. Hocking, *Science and the Idea of God* (Chapel Hill: University of North Carolina Press, 1944), p. 15.

21. Hocking, *Science and the Idea of God*, p. 14.

appears as the physical world itself, with its infinitely marvelous structure operating at atomic level with the beauty of a craftsman's wristwatch, and at stellar level with the majesty of a massive cyclotron."[22]

Philosophers also speak of God,[23] as the book edited by Charles Hartshorne and William Reese indicates; but their deities are too often man-made and false. Modern philosophical views of God, as classified by Hartshorne and Reese, include *Modern Panentheism* (God as Eternal-Temporal Consciousness, Knowing and Including the World in His own Actuality «but Not in His Essence»), *Limited Panentheism* (God as Eternal-Temporal Consciousness, Knowing or Partially Knowing, and Partially Including the World), *Extreme Temporalistic Theism* (God as Purely Temporal Consciousness, Knowing or Partially Knowing the World), and *Extreme Temporalistic Theism* (God as Purely Temporal but Not Conscious and Not Knowing the World).

Probably the most influential philosophical view of God today is Alfred North Whitehead's version of panentheism. Whitehead's system is known as process philosophy. He pictures everything that exists, including God, as being part of an eternal process. God himself is relative and mutable as he grows and changes along with the universe. Preeminent among Whitehead's philosophical followers is Charles Hartshorne.[24]

---

22. Ronald Clark, *Einstein*, p. 19.

23. Charles Hartshorne and William L. Reese, eds. *Philosophers Speak of God* (Chicago: University of Chicago Press, 1953).

24. See Alfred North Whitehead, *Process and Reality* (New York: Macmillan, 1929); Charles Hartshorne, *The Divine Relativity* (New Haven: Yale, 1948). See the complete bibliographical information in the volumes listed in the next footnote.

Process philosophy has had considerable influence on modern theology, having spawned a school of thought called process theology (naturally enough). This is one of the few really serious attempts to rework classical Christianity into a full-scaled theological system consistent with modern presuppositions. It appears to be gaining more and more adherents and is not likely to be just a fad. Some of its leading proponents are John B. Cobb, Jr., Schubert M. Ogden, W. Norman Pittenger, Bernard Meland, Henry N. Weiman, and Daniel Day Williams.[25]

Our culture abounds with false gods, whether created by religion, science, or philosophy. The imperative for a study of the True God has never been stronger.

Ignorance of God

Another factor calling for the study of God is an inexcusable ignorance of the true nature of God within the Christian community itself. This usually takes the form of a simple absence of knowledge, which is due to a failure to give any serious study to the subject. I say this is inexcusable because we have ample resources for a study of God (i.e., the Bible), and because of Paul's words in I Corinthians 15:34, "Some have no knowledge of God. I speak this to your shame."

Ignorance of God may also take the form of false ideas about God or false conceptions of God. This includes the inadequate but common ideas of God discussed by J.B. Phillips in his little book, *Your God Is Too Small.*[26] He

25. See the expositions and bibliographies in the following: John B. Cobb, Jr., and David Ray Griffin, eds., *Process Theology: An Introductory Exposition* (Philadelphia: Westminster, 1976); Ewert H. Cousins, ed., *Process Theology: Basic Writings* (New York: Newman Press, 1971); and Robert Mellert, *What Is Process Theology?* (New York: Paulist Press, 1975).

26. J.B. Phillips, *Your God Is Too Small* (New York: Macmillan, 1961).

shows how the following puny notions of God are popularly held by Christian people: Resident Policeman, Parental Hangover, Grand Old Man, Meek-and-Mild, God-in-a-Box, Heavenly Bosom, Managing Director, Second-hand God, Perennial Grievance, Pale Galilean, Projected Image, and Absolute Perfection. Langdon Gilkey describes "the most usual picture of God in our culture" as "a large, powerful, kindly elder statesman who treats us much as a doting grandfather might do, with occasional moods of needed judgment but with a balance of indulgence."[27]

Such ignorance of the true nature of God is serious. Isaiah 32:6 says, "For a fool speaks nonsense, and his heart inclines toward wickedness, to practice ungodliness and to speak error against the Lord." In the May 1976 issue of his periodical called *The Witness,* Curtis Dickinson asks, "What's Happened to God?" He laments the fact that "even among people who regularly attend church there is little understanding of God."

> . . . They are engaged in "church activities," given pep talks, how-to-do-it lectures and conversion sermons; they are encouraged to pray to God, to be godly, and to win others to God; they are to give to God, serve God, and desire to see Him and spend eternity with Him; but seldom if ever are they taught anything about Him, His nature and His attributes. It is no wonder that many churches have to give prizes to get people to ride their buses to the church house.

Brother Dickinson concludes that "without some knowledge of God's nature and attributes it is impossible to have faith in Him," and "there can hardly be any true concern for reflecting His image and obeying his commandments."[28]

---

27. Langdon Gilkey, *Maker of Heaven and Earth* (Garden City, N.Y.: Doubleday Anchor, 1965), p. 81.

28. Curtis Dickinson, "What's Happened to God? *The Witness* (May 1976), 16:1-2.

Neglect of God

One other factor that makes the need for the study of God acute today is the general neglect of God. This is not necessarily a denial of God nor an espousal of false gods. It is not so much an ignorance of God as an *ignoring* of God. As Psalm 10:4 says, "In his pride the wicked does not seek him; in all his thoughts there is no room for God" (NIV). Many have simply forgotten God, says Klaus Bockmühl. "Today we see God made practically redundant in theology and the church. He becomes the 'forgotten factor.' This forgetting of God in our generation is the reverse side of our overall worship of man." Paul's description fits exactly: "For even though they knew God, they did not honor Him as God, or give thanks" (Romans 1:21); "there is none who understands, there is none who seeks for God" (Romans 3:11). "Forgetfulness concerning God is the signature of our time," says Bockmühl.[29]

Let us not forget that when the Lord Jesus "shall be revealed from heaven with His mighty angels in flaming fire," he will be "dealing out retribution to those who do not know God" (II Thess. 1:7-8).

Thus the study of God is needed, both to offset the negative factors of atheism, false gods, ignorance, and neglect, as well as to provide the foundation for solid Christian faith and Christian living.

> Thus says the Lord, "Let not a wise man boast of his wisdom, and let not the mighty man boast of his might, let not a rich man boast of his riches; but let him who boasts boast of this, that he understands and knows Me (Jeremiah 9:23-24).

---

29. Klaus Bockmühl, "God and Other 'Forgotten Factors' in Theology," *Christianity Today* (February 19, 1982), 26:48.

> . . . We have not ceased to pray for you . . . that you may walk in a manner worthy of the Lord, to please Him in all respects, bearing fruit in every good work and increasing in the knowledge of God (Colossians 1:9-10).

THE NATURE OF GOD

Theology proper usually deals with both the *works* of God and the *nature* of God, and properly so. Both are described to some degree in Scripture, and an understanding of one is necessary for an understanding of the other.

To most of us the propriety of the study of the nature of God would not be questioned. However, in the latter part of the twentieth century this is by no means self-evident. This is the case because we are living in the midst of a considerable antimetaphysical bias, i.e., there are many who think it is improper to study the *nature* of anything.

The Modern Aversion to Metaphysics

Metaphysics has been one of the basic areas of philosophical study from the beginning. As the name indicates, it attempts to go beyond the study of the outward physical properties of material objects to a consideration of the very nature of being as such. (Cf. *ontology*, "the study of being.")

> . . . In modern philosophical usage "metaphysics" refers generally to the field of philosophy dealing with questions about the kinds of things there are and their modes of being. Its subject matter includes the concepts of existence, thing, property, event; the distinctions between particulars and universals, individuals and classes; the nature of relations, change, causation; and the nature of mind, matter, space, and time.[30]

---

30. Roger Hancock, "Metaphysics, History of," *The Encyclopedia of Philosophy*, ed. Paul Edwards (New York: Macmillan, 1967), V:289-90.

As thus understood metaphysics has usually dealt with the nature of *spiritual* as well as physical reality, especially the existence and nature of God. Traditional theology has assumed the validity of metaphysics in the sense that it has believed in the possibility and propriety of understanding something about the essence or nature of God. As H. M. Kuitert puts it, we have labored under

> . . . the conviction that we are not only part of a tangible world that lies before us, a world we can see and grasp, but that we are part of an invisible world, a world that lies in our background, the world of God as He exists in His own way. We are referring to the conviction that we can make universally valid statements about this invisible world just as we can make universally valid statements about the visible world. This conviction about the existence of another world and about our ability to talk common sense about it is the backbone of metaphysical theology.
>
> . . . For example, do dogmatic formulas and concepts about God and His essence, His works, and His words, answer to objective reality? Can we have any genuine knowledge of these things? . . .[31]

Traditional theology has said yes. In modern times, however, we have witnessed a growing repudiation of metaphysics as a valid branch of study. This can be traced in large measure to the philosophy of Immanuel Kant (1714-1804). Kant declared that we can have absolutely no knowledge about God, the universe as a whole, our essential selves, and things-in-themselves: all of which constitute the heart of the subject matter of metaphysics. This does not mean that we deny their existence, says Kant.

31. H. M. Kuitert, *The Reality of Faith*, tr. Lewis B. Smedes (Grand Rapids: Eerdmans, 1968), p. 23.

Indeed, certain aspects of our experience require us to postulate their reality. But we can have no real *knowledge* about them, since knowledge is derived from sense experience, and these items are not open to such contact.

The epistemological vacuum with reference to God cannot be overcome by divine revelation, says Kant, since there can be absolutely no intrusion into the world of physical phenomena from God's side. This excludes all forms of revelation.

Under the influence of Kant and other philosophers such as David Hume (1711-1776) and Soren Kierkegaard (1813-1855), twentieth-century philosophy has for the most part been "fiercely antimetaphysical," possessed of a "virtually monolithic opposition of the metaphysical," as R. C. Sproul says.[32] This includes the schools of philosophy which have dominated the modern scene: existentialism, pragmatism, logical positivism, and analytical philosophy. (Process philosophy is an exception.) Some have used the term *post-metaphysical* to refer to our age.[33]

This antimetaphysical bias has seriously affected theology, especially the study of God. Kant's dicta of no knowledge of the divine and no intervention into this world by the divine have taken their toll. The absence of revelation means that all statements about God are to some degree speculative and relative. Many of those who do not rule out revelation altogether still deny the possibility of *word* revelation. I.e., God may intervene in history in the form of acts or events, but he does not and cannot actually speak to us in human language. Thus any statements about God

---

32. R. C. Sproul, "The Relativity Blitz and Process Theology," *Christianity Today* (April 23, 1982), 26:50.

33. Kuitert, *The Reality of Faith*, p. 33; Harvey Cox, *The Secular City*, revised ed. (New York: Macmillan, 1966), p. 221.

are still just human interpretations about God and lack any absolute character. Kuitert describes it thus:

> The crux of the matter is rather whether we can formulate statements about God and His revelation that are universally valid. The antimetaphysical theologians . . . deny this possibility with one accord.
>
> Being antimetaphysical means to reject as a pretension the belief that theology works with concepts, ideas, or notions that make sense not only for the believer who makes use of them for himself, but for all believers, indeed for all men everywhere.[34]

What is at stake, he says, is "the *is*-character of theological, or dogmatical, statements about God and His acts."[35]

Beginning with the theology of Friedrich Schleiermacher (1768-1834),[36] and continuing with Albrecht Ritschl (1822-1889),[37] the antimetaphysical trend in theology continues into the twentieth century. Kuitert says, "The fear of making general statements that carry the pretension of being *ontological* judgments is more prevalent today than it was in Ritschl's time."[38]

We may cite for an example the theology of Emil Brunner (1889-1966). Brunner rejects the idea of God as a Being or a "substance" like "the Godhead of metaphysical speculation." "The idea of God of faith is only gained in the sphere of faith, not in that of metaphysical, neutral thinking."[39]

---

34. Kuitert, *The Reality of Faith*, pp. 24-25.
35. *Ibid.*, p. 14.
36. *Ibid.*, p. 15.
37. *Ibid.*, pp. 11ff. Kuitert calls Ritschl "the textbook example of antimetaphysical theology" (p. 11).
38. *Ibid.*, p. 13.
39. Emil Brunner, *The Christian Doctrine of God: Dogmatics, Volume I*, tr. Olive Wyon (Philadelphia: Westminster, 1950), pp. 139, 141.

For instance, the concept of omnipotence is to be rejected as unbiblical; it is "derived from the speculative ontological starting-point, *God = Being.*"[40]

Another example is Nels Ferre, whose book *The Living God of Nowhere and Nothing* expresses this idea. Ferre says, "I am with the 'death of God' theologians completely in their rejection of the Western tradition of substance," and in their "wrecking of the false Western metaphysics that has carried the Christian faith."[41] He denies that God is being, a being, or the Supreme Being. "I reject the theism that defines God in terms of being." This would only make God a finite object among other finite objects, a thing among other things.[42]

> The living God of the Christian faith . . . is precisely nowhere. The living God is the God of the spatial nowhere. But then how can anything at all be "there" if it is nowhere at all? That is the point. God is not anything. He is precisely no thing. Therefore he exists nowhere. . . .
>
> God is no thing, in this sense, literally nothing; and he is no where, in this sense, nowhere. . . .[43]

Another example is found in the book *The Later Heidegger and Theology.*[44] Martin Heidegger (1889-1976) held that the epoch of metaphysics, lasting from Plato to Nietzsche, was an "error" in which thinking was led astray by giving

40. *Ibid.*, p. 248.

41. Nels F. S. Ferre, *The Living God of Nowhere and Nothing* (Philadelphia: Westminster, 1966), p. 1.

42. *Ibid.*, pp. 11-12.

43. *Ibid.*, p. 15.

44. James M. Robinson and John B. Cobb, Jr. ed., *The Later Heidegger and Theology,* "New Frontiers in Theology," Volume I (New York: Harper and Row, 1963).

too much prominence to *being*. He announced the end of metaphysics and called for "a nonmetaphysical God."[45] God must be understood in existential and historical terms; his "being" is actually an occurrence or an event of unveiling and encounter.[46]

In the same volume Carl Michalson says that Heidegger and Edmund Husserl (1859-1938) have paved the way for converting theology from an ontological discipline to an historical discipline. "Husserl showed how it is possible to bracket out the question of being in order to give the question of meaning priority." Being is but a derivative of history.

> The Bible, for instance, does not ask the question of being but of historic meaning and act. To be sure, Exodus names God the "I am who I am." But the Hebrew expression "to be" . . . embraces the connotations given it not by ontology but by the history of Israel's responses to the acts of God.

Also, "New Testament faith is eschatological and not ontological."[47] Thus the old ontological hermeneutic must be replaced by an historical hermeneutic.[48]

Oscar Cullmann has developed his *heilsgeschichtliche* theology from this starting point: "It cannot be stressed enough that the Bible is not occupied with the 'Being' of God, but with his saving activity." "The whole content of the New Testament (and of the Old as well) is God's acting, not his being."[49] He attempts to clarify this with the following statement: "While the Bible from the beginning to the end

---

45. James M. Robinson, "The German Discussion of the Later Heidegger," *The Later Heidegger and Theology*, pp. 5, 9, 12.

46. *Ibid.*, pp. 22, 40-42.

47. Carl Michalson, "Theology as Ontology and as History," *The Later Heidegger and Theology*, pp. 146-147.

48. *Ibid.*, pp. 155-56.

49. Oscar Cullmann, *Salvation in History*, tr. Sidney Sowers et al. (New York: Harper and Row, 1967), pp. 177, 277.

speaks of God's *activity,* and not the *being* of God the Father, Son, and Holy Spirit, nevertheless a being is revealed *in* this activity *as* an activity."[50]

The result of this whole way of thinking is that God is not a being but is an act or an event or a relationship. "I am that I am" becomes "I will do what I will do." "He who is" becomes "He who comes." God is not a noun but a verb, as in the following comment by Nancy Hardesty as she reviews the work of a fellow feminist:

> . . . In speaking of God as a "dynamic verb" and the "Verb of Verbs" rather than as a "static noun," I think she is coming closer to an articulation of the meaning of God's revelation as "I am" to Moses at the burning bush than do most theologians who concentrate on such masculine images as "Father" and "King." . . .[51]

A very common way of justifying this antimetaphysical shift is to cite an alleged distinction between Hebrew and Greek thought forms. Metaphysical thinking, it is said, follows the Greek pattern, which is invalid and villainous. Theology has too long been in bondage to this error. The Hebrew pattern, derived from an analysis of the Old Testament, is just the opposite of the Greek and must be our model for all theology. The elements of the alleged contrast include the following:[52]

---

50. *Ibid.*, p. 16.

51. Nancy Hardesty, book review section, *Christianity Today* (June 6, 1975), 19:40-41. She is reviewing *Sexist Religion and Women in the Church,* ed. Alice Hageman (New York: Association, 1974), and is commenting specifically on Mary Daly's essay, "Theology After the Demise of God the Father: A Call for the Castration of Sexist Religion."

52. Adapted from "Greek vs. Hebraic Concepts," *Journal of the American Scientific Affiliation* (June 1979), 31:128, taken from Matthew Fox, "Elements of a Biblical Creation-Centered Spirituality," *Spirituality Today* (December 1978), pp. 368-69. See also James Barr, *Old and New in Interpretation* (New York: Harper and Row, 1966), p. 34.

GREEK	HEBRAIC
logical thinking	psychological thinking
spatial thinking	time thinking
eye people	ear people
freezes objects	welcomes movement
objective, impersonal	subjective, personal
distant, abstract	near, concrete
history as what is past	history as altering the future
seeks being	seeks becoming
being is static	being is dynamic, active
creation as origin of world	creation as inauguration of salvation history
word as ordering reason	word as deed
matter as object	matter as energy
dualistic	holistic
emphasizes distinctions	emphasizes wholeness
the timeless is central	the historical is central
redemption as perfection	redemption as liberation for the oppressed

Contemporary Antimetaphysical Theologies

In the present theological potpourri we can see many forms of the flight from metaphysics, some of which are no doubt at times espoused without a consciousness of their philosophical moorings. We must first call attention to the continuing denial of word revelation, which is both a cause and a continuing expression of this way of thinking. It is almost axiomatic in non-evangelical theology that the only form in which God can possibly reveal himself is through historical events, his actions in history. Word revelation is impossible and has never occurred. The Bible therefore is not revelation nor do its words constitute revelation; at best it is an historical, human witness to revelation.[53] The implications of this view for biblical authority and sound doctrine are disastrous.

A second example is the political or liberation theology which dominates so much of the religious world today. Harvey Cox declared nearly twenty years ago in *The Secular City* that the inexorable force of secularization has now made it impossible to speak of God in any metaphysical or ontological sense.[54] Instead, he says, *in the interest of social change,* we must begin speaking in political terms rather than metaphysical.[55] "The mode of theology which must replace metaphysical theology is the *political* mode. . . . The way we talk about God in a secular fashion is to talk about him politically."[56] Here the word *political* is used to refer to the process of change and revolution in human society which serves to bring about social justice. As long as that process is heading in the direction of socialistic and (usually) Marxist goals, it is interpreted by liberation theologians as evidence of the activity of God.

In his book *Marx and the Bible* Jose Miranda demonstrates this way of thinking perfectly. God does not have an objective ontological existence, he says; to think in terms of *being* is to fall into the error of Greek philosophy and replace the true God with an idol.[57] It is not possible to contemplate God directly or to think about him as he exists

---

53. John Baillie, *The Idea of Revelation in Recent Thought* (New York: Columbia University Press, 1956).

54. Harvey Cox, *The Secular City,* pp. 211-217.

55. *Ibid.*, p. 218.

56. *Ibid.*, p. 223.

57. Jose P. Miranda, *Marx and the Bible: A Critique of the Philosophy of Oppression,* tr. John Eagleson (Maryknoll, NY: Orbis Books, 1974), pp. 48-49, 58.

"in himself." "The God of the Bible . . . withdraws in the measure that my consciousness approaches him."[58] Rather, God exists *only* in other people, specifically in the poor and oppressed. Only when my conscience is touched by the plight of the poor, and only when I engage in the fight for social justice, do I know the true God, because there alone is he real. "The God of the Bible is known in the implacable moral imperative of justice."[59] God is God only in the revealing of himself in our needy neighbors, thereby commanding our conscience. The revelation and command are not direct, however; "God is knowable only through one's neighbor."[60]

> . . . The God who does not allow himself to be objectified, because only in the immediate command of conscience is he God, clearly specifies that he is knowable exclusively in the cry of the poor and the weak who seek justice. To know God directly is impossible, not because of the limitations of human understanding but rather, on the contrary, because Yahweh's total transcendence, his irreducible and unconfused otherness, would thereby disappear. Our ability to accept him in man goes beyond any comprehension which can thematize and encompass its object. Transcendence does not mean only an unimaginable and inconceivable God, but a God who is accessible only in the act of justice.[61]

Another antimetaphysical approach to God is found in relational theology. This view says that "the Bible defines God and man not in the abstract terms of 'nature' but in terms of their *relationship* to each other." The former is allegedly the Greek way; only the latter is true to Hebrew

58. *Ibid.*, pp. 49, 66.
59. *Ibid.*, p. 60.
60. *Ibid.*, p. 64.
61. *Ibid.*, p. 48.

thought forms. What are some implications of this assumption? One example is the common reinterpretation of creation as a relationship between God and the world *rather than* as an explanation of the origin of the world. (This will be discussed later.) Another example is the fragmenting of biblical authority, with the gospels being elevated to a level of authority above the rest of the Bible. This is because God relates to us preeminently through Jesus Christ rather than through Moses or Paul. As Michalson explains,

> . . . Theology is unwarranted in affirming that the God we meet in the Old Testament is the same God we meet in the New Testament. That is not to say there are two Gods but only that the Testaments are conceived not on the basis of one being of God but on the basis of two historically distinct modes of relationship to God. Inasmuch as Christians are those related to God on the basis of his covenant in Christ, the Old Testament does not have the same status as revelation as the New Testament, the analysis of being notwithstanding.[62]

Harold B. Kuhn notes that "many are accepting uncritically the so-called relational theology." We must agree with him when he says that "relational theology strikes squarely at the heart of important theological matters."[63] Kuhn discusses specifically the relational view of man, the atonement (cf. "interpersonal" versus substitutionary), and ethics. The doctrine of God is equally affected.

A final example of the antimetaphysical trend is the "experiential theology" which permeates Christendom today.

62. Carl Michalson, "Theology as Ontology and As History," p. 149.

63. Harold B. Kuhn, "Relationalism: Principle or Slogan?" *Christianity Today* (February 28, 1975), 19:49.

It is seen, for instance, in the renewed emphasis on religious experience. A focal point for this new "spirituality" is *meditation,* often interpreted not in the biblical sense of thinking about God, his words and his works, but rather in the sense of Eastern mysticism—a mentally-passive, non-rational openness to the "Divine."

Experiential theology is also seen in the nearly exclusive emphasis in some circles on methods and results, with little attention to sound doctrine. As one TV evangelist has said, "I've never had much interest in doctrine; all I want to do is save souls." His doctrinal shifting over the years has proved the truth of at least the first part of this statement. Others are willing to sacrifice biblical church polity on the altar of pragmatism: it "works better" another way.

Experiential theology is seen finally in the reduction of faith to the subjective experience of "believing *in*" God or Christ, while ignoring the importance of "believing *that*" certain doctrinal affirmations are true.[64] The element of assent is removed from faith, with only trust or personal commitment remaining. "Belief is personal not doctrinal."[65] In classical terms, as Kuitert point out, faith is seen exclusively as the *fides quae,* not the *fides qua.* That is, what matters is the faith *by which* one believes—the subjective experience of believing, not "the faith which was once for all delivered to the saints" (Jude 3) in the sense of *what* is believed. The "reality of faith" lies in the believing subject, not in the object or focus of the faith.[66] E.g., whether Jesus

---

64. See Jack Cottrell, *The Authority of the Bible* (Grand Rapids: Baker, 1979), pp. 76-77.

65. An example of this view is H. Eugene Johnson, *Simple Principles* (Tampa: author, 1977), pp. 7, 19, 37.

66. Kuitert, *The Reality of Faith,* pp. 9, 14-15.

actually rose from the dead is irrelevant as long as the story of the resurrection creates within me a new self-understanding (Bultmann). E.g., whether there really was a creation as described in Genesis 1, 2 is unimportant as long as I gain from these chapters a sense of dependence on God ("story theology"—which takes these "stories" *seriously* without necessarily taking them *literally*).[67] E.g., "what the Bible means *to me*" is more important than "what the Bible actually means."

Experiential theology reaches its nadir when "God is interpreted on the basis of experience rather than experience being interpreted on the basis of God," as Curtis Dickinson puts it. (Jose Miranda's description of God, cited above, is a good example of this methodology.) Dickinson sums it up this way:

> This is the way of 20th Century Religion. Each person places his own value on his separate experience, and out of it tries to derive some concept of what he calls God. Some of the worst perpetrators of this philosophy are religious leaders themselves. Experiences, with emotional vibrations, which set them apart from ordinary routine actions, have become the center of attraction both in and out of the church, taking the place of the worship of God. Preaching is aimed at producing an inner emotional experience, not at exalting God. The apostles preached that which was pleasing to God. Modern preachers make a survey to see what is most pleasing to men, then preach accordingly. The apostles

67. For more on "Story Theology," see the July 1975 issue of *Theology Today* (vol. 32), especially Hugh T. Kerr, "What's the Story?" p. 130; George W. Stroup, III, "A Bibliographical Critique," p. 142; and James H. Cone, "The Story Context of Black Theology," p. 148.

> took pains to explain God's person and purpose, to bring men to respond to God; modern evangelists take pains to explain men's experiences to bring about a response to their manipulations.[68]

All in all we see that the modern aversion to metaphysics and metaphysical thinking about God has had considerable influence in Christendom. We see that it has had serious implications about how one thinks about the "nature" of God. In brief, it brings into question even whether it is possible or appropriate to think in terms of God's nature or essence or being.

Is the Bible Antimetaphysical?

In response to these antimetaphysical tendencies we must say several things. On the one hand we would note that some aspects of the objection to metaphysics are quite sound. If metaphysics is interpreted mainly in terms of philosophical speculation (which seems to be the case with Brunner), then we agree that such metaphysics ought to be abandoned in favor of biblical thinking. Or if metaphysics is interpreted mainly in terms of pagan substance philosophy (which seems to be the case with Ferre), then we agree that it must be rejected.

On the other hand, however, we must say that this trend goes much too far when it tries to tell us we cannot speak certainly or even at all of God's nature or essence or being. We can reject certain types or excesses of metaphysics without rejecting metaphysics as such. Metaphysics per se is not cultural or relative, though certain approaches to it may

68. Curtis Dickinson, "What's Happened to God?" p. 1.

well be—*including the current antimetaphysical bias itself*, which is no more than a part of the mythology of our relativistic, secular age.

One of the aspects of this mythology is the neat but arbitrary contrast between Greek and Hebrew thinking.[69] Obviously there are many aspects of Greek thinking that are wrong, especially in its concept of God. (The same applies to ancient non-biblical Semitic thinking and to the Oriental mind as well.) But this does not justify a blanket indictment of everything found in the Greek world of thought. There were, after all, a number of Greek traditions, some of which contradicted each other. There are also areas where Greek and biblical thought forms parallel one another. This is particularly true in the New Testament, which is why the advocates of this myth tend to ignore John and Paul (*Hebrew* thinkers!) and concentrate on the Old Testament.[70]

But in Old Testament and New Testament alike we must recognize that there is no aversion to metaphysical concepts such as the nature of man, the nature of Christ, and

69. See James Barr's penetrating critique of this dichotomy in chapter 2 of *Old and New in Interpretation*, "Athens or Jerusalem? The Question of Distinctiveness." He says, "It is possible to argue that the Hebrew-Greek thought contrast serves as the historical-cultural projection of a particular ideal in theological interpretation" (p. 40). The strident opposition to Greek thought "is an intrusion from a modern consciousness" (p. 58). In Barr's judgment, "the intellectual status of this procedure may be said to have collapsed; and a main reason for the collapse has been the exaggeration and immoderation with which the contrast was applied" (p. 46).

70. See Barr's analysis again, especially his statement on p. 58: "In drawing up a fierce alignment against the categories and mental patterns of the Greeks modern purist theology has radically departed from the position of the New Testament itself, and thereby also contradicted itself very seriously. The New Testament itself gives very little footing for a theological emphasis on the Greek-Hebrew contrast, and gives us no reason to take the latter as a basic guide to interpretation."

the nature of God. The antimetaphysical crusade is an example of that ubiquitous theological demon, the *false choice*. One does not have to choose between the acting of God and the being of God (Cullmann), or God in relation and God in himself, or God as subject and God as object of thought. *These are not either-or choices.* That God is a subject/person does not exclude the fact that he has essential being and exists in terms of his own nature quite independent of any relationship to his creatures.

We need not fear that such thinking will relativize or finitize God. To say that God has being or even that he is "a being" does not relegate him to the same category of being shared by all other existent entities. This would give the term *being* a much too concrete and specific meaning, i.e., a specific *kind* of being. It is definitely true that God does not (indeed, cannot) share his kind of being with anything else. The fact of creation with the resulting Creator/creature distinction is an absolute barrier to any kind of shared being. The Creator's being and mode of being are of necessity different from that of all creatures. He alone is the Creator, existing in splendid majesty as uncreated being. This should still the fears of those who are concerned about substance philosophy: we need only to reserve the concept of *substance* for the category of created being, and perhaps for just part of it at that. (I.e., is created spiritual being "substance"?)

The main reason why we feel comfortable talking about the nature of God in ontological terms is that the Bible itself does so, and because the Bible is the word—even *words*—of God. Those who deny word revelation have limited their source of the knowledge of God to certain events of nature and history which they interpret to be acts of God.

Thus any statement about God's nature is merely a human conclusion drawn from reflection on these events. We are not surprised that they feel reluctant to speak confidently about God's nature. But if God himself has told us that he is spirit, or that he is immortal, or that he is all-powerful, we need not feel that we are treading on impossible or forbidden ground.

We conclude this section with the words of Langdon Gilkey: "A good ontology is a bulwark, not an enemy, of a sound Gospel theology."[71]

THE ATTRIBUTES OF GOD

We have concluded that it is proper to discuss the nature or essence of God. This is usually done in terms of God's *attributes,* referred to variously as characteristics, perfections, virtues, excellencies, properties, qualities, descriptions, definitives, and predicates. None of these words is ideal for the present purpose. Some prefer the term *perfections*[72] since it seems to avoid certain undesirable connotations in the other words. It is also a possible translation of the Greek word *aretē* in I Peter 2:9, also translated "excellencies" and "virtues." As the NASB has it, "But you are a chosen race . . . , that you may proclaim the excellencies of Him who has called you out of darkness into His marvelous light."

Some object to the term *attributes* because its Latin root means "to allot, to assign to." Thus Louis Berkhof says it is "not ideal, since it conveys the notion of adding or assigning something to one, and is therefore apt to create the

71. Langdon Gilkey, *Maker of Heaven and Earth*, p.86.

72. See, for instance, Karl Barth, *Church Dogmatics, Vol. II: The Doctrine of God, Part 1*, tr. T.H.L. Parker et al. (Edinburgh: T. & T. Clark, 1957), pp. 322ff.

impression that something is added to the divine Being."[73] Nevertheless Berkhof continues to use this term because it is traditional; we will do the same.

Attributes and Essence

What is the relation between God, his essence, and his attributes? The answer is that they are all the same. God *is* his essence, and his essence *is* his attributes.

It is proper to refer to God's essence, since this term is used for the mode in which any existing being exists. God *does* exist—objectively, in reality, as uncreated Spirit. Therefore he has an essence, a mode of being. We should note, however, that this language is imprecise. God does not *have* an essence; he *is* his essence. We cannot think of God in terms of the "body-soul" model, as if somehow the "soul" of God could be separated from his essence and still exist as God.

In the same way we must recognize that there is no distinction between God's essence (i.e., God himself) and his attributes. His essence is not some neutral substance which can be separated from or even conceived of separately from his attributes. We cannot strip away all the attributes from God and wind up with some pure, attributeless substance—"God as he *really* is." When we know the attributes of God, we known him as he really is, insofar as our finite minds are able to know him at all.

Every attribute of God bears this relation to the divine essence. God's nature in its entirety partakes of the quality described by each attribute, and does so necessarily. In this

73. Louis Berkhof, *Systematic Theology* (London: Banner of Truth Trust, 1939), p. 52; cf. p. 45.

sense God is different from creatures, in which we distinguish between accidental and essential characteristics. A ball, for instance, has the essential qualities of mass and spherical shape. But its other characteristics are accidental and may vary: it may be rubber or clay; it may be red or yellow; it may be heavy or light. For another example, a human being has the essential characteristic of personhood made in God's image, but other characteristics are quite contingent, e.g., height, weight, skin color, hair color, disposition, intelligence. All a man's accidental properties could be taken away or changed, and he would still be a man.

God's attributes, however, are inseparable from his essence; God could exist in no other way. An essence with *any* other qualities would not be the divine essence. I.e., there is no such thing as a mean God, a weak God, a sinful God, an ignorant God, or an indifferent God. God has no accidental, acquired, dispensable, contingent, or changeable attributes.

It is important to understand this especially in relation to the incarnation of God the Logos (John 1:1,14) in the human person of Jesus of Nazareth. Some have interpreted the *kenosis* of Philippians 2:7 (*ekenōsen*, he "made himself nothing," NIV) as an *emptying* in the sense that God the Logos divested himself of some or all of his divine attributes. But this is an impossibility! God *is* his attributes; he cannot separate himself from them and still be God. Thus Paul must say of Jesus Christ, "In Him all the *fulness* of Deity dwells in bodily form" (Col. 2:9). It could not be any other way!

> "Veiled in flesh the Godhead see;
> Hail, incarnate Deity!"

The Simplicity of God

The concept of the simplicity of God is an aspect of his *unity:* "Hear, O Israel! The Lord is our God, the Lord is one!" (Deuteronomy 6:4). He is one in the sense that he is the one and only true God; this is the unity of singularity. But he is one also in the sense that he is one indivisible being, not composed of parts; this is the unity of *simplicity*. He is simple as opposed to compound.

What does all this have to do with the attributes of God? Basically it raises the question of the degree to which the attributes correspond to the reality of God. Are the attributes truly distinct aspects of God's essence? If so, does this mean that God's nature is somehow divided into parts? If not, are the attributes merely illusionary?

In seeking to resolve this issue we must avoid two extremes. One is the philosophical concept of the *absolute* simplicity of God, the idea that God is one in the purest sense of the word. This is essentially a pagan idea, grounded in the assumption that the more nearly perfect a being is, the more simple it is. The absolutely perfect being (whether called God or not) is thus totally undifferentiated and is usually described simply as the ONE.

This concept of the highest being is found in a number of Eastern philosophies, e.g., Taoism and some forms of Hinduism.[74] It is also found in many of the classical Greek philosophies, being developed most fully by Plotinus the Neo-Platonist. According to Plotinus the ONE is completely qualityless and without multiplicity.[75]

---

74. See Frederick Copleston, *Religion and the One: Philosophies East and West* (New York: Crossroad, 1982), chapters 3 and 4.

75. Philip Merlan, "Plotinus," *The Encyclopedia of Philosophy*, VI:353.

From the second century onward those Christian theologians most influenced by Greek philosophy have tended to describe God in a similar way. Brunner notes this tendency with chagrin:

> Anyone who knows the history of the development of the doctrine of God in "Christian" theology, and especially the doctrine of the Attributes of God, will never cease to marvel at the unthinking way in which theologians adopted the postulates of philosophical speculation on the Absolute, and the amount of harm this has caused in the sphere of the "Christian" doctrine of God. . . .[76]

Examples may be found in Justin Martyr, Augustine, medieval nominalism, and protestant scholasticism.

Those who take this position often describe God in terms of negative attributes. When positive attributes are mentioned, they are not qualities that truly correspond to God's reality; they only describe our subjective perception of God. In reality each attribute is identical with all the others. The following statement by Augustine suggests this view:

> God is truly called in manifold ways, great, good, wise, blessed, true, and whatsoever other thing seems to be said of Him not unworthily; but His greatness is the same as His wisdom . . . ; and His goodness is the same as His wisdom and His greatness, and His truth the same as all those things; and in Him it is not one thing to be blessed, and another to be great, or wise, or true, or good, or in a word to be Himself.[77]

---

76. Emil Brunner, *The Christian Doctrine of God*, p. 242.

77. Augustine, "On the Trinity," Book IV, chapter vii, *The Works of Aurelius Augustine*, Vol. VII, ed. Marcus Dods, tr. A.W. Haddan (Edinburgh: T. & T. Clark, 1878), pp. 173-74.

As Heinrich Heppe describes the view of seventeenth-century Reformed scholasticism, "No elements in God are distinguished essentially. All the things in God are one indivisible and most single essence." As an example he cites Hottinger: "'The attributes are distinguished neither from the essence nor from each other but only by our conceiving.'" Also, from Braun, "'God's righteousness is His goodness, is His knowledge, is His will; or His mercy is His righteousness, etc.'"[78]

Such a concept can lead to some quite unscriptural notions of God. E.g., it can lead to agnosticism about God's nature. If the attributes have no real basis in God but are merely differentiations within our perception, then we really do not know anything about God himself. Also, it can lead to the merging of all the attributes into just one, such as love or power. Thus it is no wonder that this concept has been rejected as an extreme view.

Also to be rejected is the other extreme of a God who can be divided into parts. Such a view is seen in the application of the substance-accidents philosophy to God, as if God's essence were distinct from his attributes. It is also seen in the idea that God's being is somehow spread out over space, and that one part of his being can be "cut off" and spatially separated from the rest. This latter idea is represented by some emanationist and pantheistic concepts of God. It is also assumed by those who think of the human soul as a little "part" of God.

The biblical doctrine of the simplicity of God rules out both of these extremes. To say that God is one rules out

78 Heinrich Heppe, *Reformed Dogmatics*, ed. Ernst Bizer, tr. G. T. Thomson (London: Allen and Unwin, 1950), pp. 58-59.

divisions within the divine essence. God is truly uncompounded, not compounded of parts, not composite. The various attributes do not refer to different parts of God. "The whole of the divine essence is in each attribute and the attribute belongs to the whole essence."[79] God in his fullness *is* love; God in his fullness *is* justice.

Divisions are ruled out, but not distinctions. The attributes are real distinctions within God. As Karl Barth says, "He is in essence not only one, but multiple, individual and diverse."[80] Augustus Strong denies the pagan concept of oneness by asserting that the more nearly perfect a being is, the more *complex* it is! "We infer that God, the highest of all, instead of being simple force, is infinitely complex, that he has an infinite variety of attributes and powers."[81] In fact, there is no reason to exclude from the very nature of God characteristics that are basically opposites (though not contradictories), such as grace and justice, or love and wrath.

We should also note here that the concept of the unity of God does not rule out the reality of the Trinity. This will be discussed later.

Classification of Attributes

An effort is usually made to analyze the various attributes of God and to divide them into appropriate categories. There is no consensus of opinion as to how this should be done, however.

79. Lewis Sperry Chafer, *Systematic Theology* (Dallas: Dallas Seminary Press, 1947), I:191.

80. Karl Barth, *Church Dogmatics* II/1, p. 331. Barth also says, somewhat puzzlingly, "Each of the divine perfections is materially identical with each of the others and with the fulness of them all" (*ibid.*, p. 335).

81. Augustus H. Strong, *Systematic Theology*, 3 volumes in 1 (Valley Forge: Judson Press, 1907), p. 245.

The attributes are most commonly divided into two groups, though the rationale for the division and the terminology for the groups differ from theologian to theologian. Probably the most widely accepted division is between (1) attributes which describe the nature of God as he exists in himself, with no reference to any external actions or relationships to any other beings, and (2) attributes which describe the nature of God as he manifests himself in outward operations and relationships toward other beings. Examples of the former are aseity, eternity, and infinity; examples of the latter are love, wisdom, wrath, and goodness. Various sets of terms have been employed for these groups: absolute and relative, internal and external, primary and derived, quiescent and operative, intransitive and transitive (transient), immanent and emanent (transcendent), passive and active, God in himself and God in relation, divine freedom and divine love. H. O. Wiley discerns three categories: the absolute (God in himself), the relative (relative to creatures in general), and the moral (relative to moral creatures).[82] It is apparent that the last two groups are merely subdivisions of the second category above.

Other suggestions of dual groupings render approximately the same results. Some suggest a negative-positive distinction. Negative attributes are those which deny something about God (e.g., he is *not* limited, not dependent, not subject to change); positive ones affirm something about him (he *is* good, just, merciful). The resulting lists are similar to those drawn up according to the previous rationale.

Another method of categorizing the attributes separates the incommunicable from the communicable ones. The

82. H. Orton Wiley, *Christian Theology*, I:329.

former are those which belong only to God and in no sense to creatures (e.g., aseity, infinity); the latter are those which the Creator has shared or communicated in a finite degree with his moral creatures (e.g., love, wisdom). Again the lists differ little from those derived from the above methods. (Note: in this context the word *communication* does not mean the simple imparting of *information* about the attribute, but the imparting of the attribute itself.)

Finally, some would distinguish the natural or metaphysical attributes from the ethical or moral ones (still without much variation in the final lists). If this is meant to distinguish the essence of God from his character, it may be misleading, since *all* of God's attributes are a description of his essence.

None of these methods of analyzing the divine attributes is absolutely proper; the categories are not so neatly exclusive. For instance, *all* of God's attributes are truly descriptive of God as he is in himself, even if some are not expressed except in relation to creatures. Also, as Bavinck notes, even the "negative attributes furnish us with a very important positive knowledge concerning God."[83] That is to say, the distinctions are not absolute.

Still, the fact that the attributes of God seem to fall naturally into two broad groups, and that these groups are approximately the same no matter what labels are applied, would suggest that there is an appropriateness in making such a distinction. Bavinck provides an insight into this appropriateness when he remarks concerning the incommunicable (absolute, metaphysical) attributes that "these are really descriptions of the unique, absolute, divine manner in which

83. Herman Bavinck, *The Doctrine of God,* ed. and tr. William Hendriksen (Grand Rapids: Eerdmans, 1951), p. 139.

the other attributes (viz., those of essence, life, and spirit, mind and will, love and righteousness, etc.,) exist in God."[84] In this sense the latter are the actual character of God, and the former are descriptions or predicates of this character. The incommunicable or absolute attributes, says Bavinck, are self-existence, immutability, infinity, and oneness.[85] These four attributes apply equally to each of the others, and as such these are the attributes that make God *God*. E.g., God is good; and his goodness is self-existent, immutable, infinite, and one. God is holy; and his holiness is self-existent, immutable, infinite, and one. God is wise; and his wisdom is self-existent, immutable, infinite, and one. In other words, the communicable attributes are (so to speak) the essence of God's essence, and the incommunicable attributes are characteristics of this essence.

There seems to be no one method of classifying God's attributes which is flawless. Each seems to leave some loose ends. This does not affect our procedure in this study one way or another, since we do not intend to discuss the attributes in one separate and distinct section. Thus we will not use any of the suggested classifications.

METHODOLOGY AND PRESUPPOSITIONS

This leads us to an explanation of the methodology to be used in this study of the doctrine of God. A common procedure is to divide the subject matter into the *nature* of God and the *works* of God, and then to discuss these separately. (The works of God include such things as predestination,

84. *Ibid.*, p. 141.
85. *Ibid.*

creation, providence, and redemption.) Usually the nature of God is presented first, then the works. Examples of this methodology are found in Charles Hodge, William G. T. Shedd, Augustus Strong, Louis Berkhof, and Francis Pieper.[86]

The procedure here will be somewhat different. Our opinion is that the best way to understand the nature of God is not to study it in the abstract, in isolation from a consideration of his works, but rather to study his nature *in the light of* his works. For instance, how can we understand the transcendence of God, apart from a knowledge of the fact of creation *ex nihilo*? Does not the magnitude of God's providence illuminate for us the sovereignty of God? And how can we appreciate the righteousness or the faithfulness of God except in the light of his work of redemption?

Our plan is as follows. The material is divided into three major sections corresponding to the three major works of God in relation to the world: creation, providence, and redemption. First we will discuss God as Creator: his work of creation, and his nature as it is most specifically displayed in that work. Then we will discuss God as Sovereign: his work of providence, and his nature as it is illuminated by this aspect of his work. Finally we will study God as Redeemer: his work of redemption, and his nature as seen in his response to sin both for judgment and for salvation.

The main drawback of this method of study is that the attributes of God are not presented systematically and completely in any one section. Instead, the attributes which are

86. Charles Hodge, *Systematic Theology* (Grand Rapids: Eerdmans, n.d.); William G. T. Shedd, *Dogmatic Theology* (Grand Rapids: Zondervan, 1969 reprint); Augustus H. Strong, *Systematic Theology* (Valley Forge, PA: Judson, 1907); Louis Berkhof, *Systematic Theology (London: Banner of Truth Trust,* 1939); Francis Pieper, *Christian Dogmatics* (St. Louis: Concordia, 1950).

logically related to the creation are studied at that point, with the same applying to providence and redemption. Since some of the attributes are eminently displayed in more than one of God's works, they are discussed in more than one place. For instance, material on the *power* of God appears in all three sections. Our conclusion, though, is that the benefits gained by this procedure far outweigh such minor violations of neatness.

We must make it clear that our understanding of both the works and the nature of God is grounded in the special revelation of Scripture. This distinguishes our method from that of modern liberal theology, which also begins with the works of God and proceeds to his nature. Liberal theology is forced to use this method because of its view of revelation, which, if accepted at all, is in the form of events not words. On this presupposition, certain great events of history (or even all events of history) are perceived to be the locus of divine activity. God reveals himself through these events; the theologian then draws conclusions concerning the nature of God by reflecting on these events. Knowledge of the nature of God is thus an *inference* from his works. As one writer puts it, activity precedes ontology: "We have to try to understand who God *is* in terms of what he *does*."[87] This is *not* the rationale behind the methodology of this work, however. We simply believe it is easier to explain and to understand the various aspects of God's nature as revealed in Scripture, when the works of God have been explained first.

87. Shirley C. Guthrie, Jr., "Theology and Metaphysics," *America and the Future of Theology*, ed. William A. Beardslee (Philadelphia: Westminster, 1967), p. 131.

At this point we will set forth the three main assumptions on which this study of God is based. The first of these is that the primary source for the knowledge of God is God himself, via word revelation as recorded in the Bible. It is crucial that we understand the alternative. If our knowledge of God is not "from above," then it must be "from below," i.e., from our own finite and fallible minds. Gordon Kaufman probes the latter possibility in a study called "Constructing the Concept of God."[88] Having rejected the Bible as God's revelation, Kaufman says that all theology is the product of "the constructive powers of the imagination." With regard to God, "all speech and ideas about such (a) being are grounded in our own imaginative powers and . . . even claims about 'God's revelation' . . . are thus our own construction."[89] This is indeed the only alternative once we surrender the reality of a verbal revelation from God.

Our second assumption is that the Bible is the inspired and infallible word of God. All the special revelation which we have from God is contained in it. Strictly speaking everything in the Bible is not a revelation from God, but even that which is not revealed is nevertheless fully inspired (2 Tim. 3:16). Thus every part of the biblical text as penned by its original authors is completely trustworthy and inerrant.

Our final assumption is that the Bible can be understood. To be sure, some parts are more perspicuous than others,

88. Gordon D. Kaufman, "Constructing the Concept of God," *Is God GOD?* ed. Axel D. Steuer and James McClendon, Jr. (Nashville: Abingdon, 1981), pp. 111-43. See also his full-length study, *The Religious Imagination: Constructing the Concept of God* (Philadelphia: Westminster, 1981). See Clark H. Pinnock's comments on the latter in "God Made in the Image of Man," *Christianity Today* (September 3, 1982), 26:35.

89. Kaufman, "Constructing the Concept of God," pp. 112, 136.

and we may not at this moment possess all the necessary data for understanding some of the more difficult parts. But this does not negate the basic clarity of Scripture. God's revealing work is futile if the one for whom it is intended —man himself—cannot understand it. We must forcefully reject all subjectivistic and relativistic approaches to the study of God's word.

With these presuppositions in mind, we now proceed to a study of the biblical teaching about God.

Chapter Two

PAGAN ALTERNATIVES TO CREATION

Creation is the primary work of God. It is primary in the sense that it is his first work with respect to his creatures. (We do not consider the "eternal decree," however understood, to be an actual work of God; it is rather a preparation for his work.) Creation is primary also in the sense that it is foundational for everything else that occurs, i.e., for the other works of God and for all the works of man. It is the starting point for our understanding of everything relating to God and man.

We need to explain briefly what we mean by the concept of creation. (A more complete discussion follows in the next chapter.) Often the term is used to refer to the whole process or series of events which brought the human race into existence, or the whole scope of God's creative activity as described in the first chapter of Genesis. As such it is compared or contrasted with evolution, as in the "creation-evolution controversy" and "creationism." This is a proper use of the term, but we are not using it here in that general sense. Instead we are thinking *only* of the *initial act* of creation, when God brought the materials of the universe into existence out of nothing. We are focusing only on their first moment of existence, not on the subsequent ordering and organizing of these materials. We are concerned only with Genesis 1:1, and with it only insofar as it refers to that first single event of initial creation. We are not unconcerned about the creative activity which follows in Genesis 1:2-31, nor are we denying this phase of creation in favor of evolution. The fact is simply that the crucial point for the Christian doctrine of God is that primal act of the *ex nihilo* origination of all created materials. That will be the focus of our attention.

We believe that the Christian doctrine of creation gives us the true picture of how God and the universe are related to each other. Resting upon the fact of creation are a large number of other truths about God, man, and the universe. Hence when the biblical doctrine of creation is unknown or denied, the consequences are serious indeed. But this is precisely the case for most of the world: there is no understanding or acceptance of the concept of creation *ex nihilo*. Offered instead are a wide array of alternative explanations of the origin of the world or of the God-world relationship.

In this chapter we will present the basic alternatives to the Christian doctrine of creation. It is important to do this so that we will better understand what is at stake in the choice between the Bible and paganism.

DUALISTIC THEORIES

How one explains the origin and general structure of the universe (cosmos) is called his *cosmology*. The term *cosmogony* may be used if one is referring specifically to a theory of origins. The cosmologies of most pagan world views may be divided into two broad categories, namely, dualisms and monisms. These terms have other connotations, such as anthropological dualism (man is body and spirit, or body and mind); but we will be using them here in the broad cosmological or metaphysical sense.

Examples of Dualism

In a dualistic cosmos all reality is reducible to two ultimate ingredients or principles. "Any philosophical system that divides the world into two categories or types of thing, or uses two ultimate principles of explanation, or insists that there are two substances or kinds of substance is a form of dualism."[1] The two sides may be explained in different ways, e.g., God and matter, good and evil, heaven and earth, yang and yin. Here we will present some of the main examples.

Primitive Mythology

Practically every culture adopts some explanation of the origin of the universe, or at least the origin of mankind. In many cultures these explanations take the form of myth. Barbara Sproul has collected a considerable number of creation myths and creation accounts in a book called *Primal Myths: Creating the World.*[2] Many of these are examples of dualism. As Sproul notes,

> . . . Throughout the world, creation myths express and dramatize this primary religious proclamation of the absolute reality in its dual form of being and not-being. Eternal gods of every kind reach out over the equally eternal chaos of not-being and distinguish within it all the forces and realities of the world: light is separated from darkness, heaven from earth, water from land, good from bad, masculine from feminine, matter from spirit, life from death, being from not-being . . . .[3]

The order-versus-chaos format is quite common, with the unformed material being confronted by the principle of order (usually the deity).

> . . . Often identified as good, this sort of god takes on chaos (evil) as a challenge and, like any of us trying to get our houses in shape, begins by establishing basic principles.

1. Roland Hall, "Monism and Pluralism," *The Encyclopedia of Philosophy*, ed. Paul Edwards (New York: Macmillan, 1967), V:364.

2. Barbara Sproul, ed., *Primal Myths: Creating the World* (San Francisco: Harper and Row, 1979). See also Charles H. Long, *Alpha: The Myths of Creation* (New York: Collier Books, 1969).

3. Barbara Sproul, *Primal Myths*, p. 10.

> Light over here, dark there; solids in this place, liquids in that; and thus day and night, earth and water, come into being. Occasionally in such myths a part of chaos . . . is symbolized as a terrible monster, and the dragon or snake, like the bull in the china shop, has to be slain or at least sufficiently controlled. All over the world . . . valiant defenders of the principles of being and order do fierce battle with the forces of not-being and chaos and finally subdue them so that order and life can be established.[4]

In some dualistic myths an effort is made to trace the origins of the two opposing principles to some other source, perhaps even a common source. In such cases the thinking is still dualistic if it is clear that the primordial source is merely a stylistic device which immediately drops out of the picture or becomes subordinated to one or the other of the two opposing forces. In any case the two forces are looked upon as the ultimate powers of the cosmos.

One widely-known myth is the Babylonian creation epic, called the *Enuma Elish*. This myth begins with the gods coming forth out of the primeval waters, personified as Apsu (male) and Tiamat (female).

> When on high the heaven had not been named,
> Firm ground below had not been called by name,
> Naught but primordial Apsu, their begetter,
> (And) Mummu-Tiamat, she who bore them all,
> Their waters commingling as a single body; . . .
> Then it was that the gods were formed within them.[5]

---

4. *Ibid.*, p. 18.

5. Here we are following the translation in Charles Long, *Alpha*, pp. 83-95, taken from James B. Pritchard, ed., *Ancient Near Eastern Texts Relating to the Old Testament* (Princeton: Princeton University Press, 1950), pp. 60-72. For another translation see Barbara Sproul, *Primal Myths*, pp. 91-113. See also the summary in C. F. von Weizsäcker, *The Relevance of Science: Creation and Cosmogony* (London: Collins, 1964), pp. 27-30.

But the boisterous ways of the younger gods annoyed Apsu and Tiamat, and Apsu determined to kill them. But the plot was known, and one of the gods, Ea, killed Apsu instead. Some of the gods loyal to Tiamat urged her to take revenge. She agreed, and brought into existence a set of monsters to aid her.

> She set up the Viper, the Dragon, and the Sphinx,
> The Great-Lion, the Mad-Dog, and the Scorpion-Man,
> Mighty lion-demons, the Dragon-fly, the Centaur—
> Bearing weapons that spare not, fearless in battle.

When the rebel-gods heard that Tiamat and her monsters were coming to destroy them, they appointed the greatest among them, Marduk (the Babylonian champion), to meet her in combat. Agreeing, he went forth to meet Tiamat, accompanied by his weapons and allies: a bow and arrows, a mace, lightning, a net, and a company of evil, vicious winds. When they met in battle Tiamat opened her mouth to consume Marduk, and he directed the fierce winds down her throat so that her belly became distended. Then he loosed an arrow that rent her belly and split her heart.

At this point in the story comes the creation of the world, Marduk bringing all things into existence out of the dead bodies of his enemies.

> The lord trod on the legs of Tiamat,
> With his unsparing mace he crushed her skull.
> When the arteries of her blood he had severed,
> The North Wind bore (it) to places undisclosed. . . .
> Then the lord paused to view her dead body,
> That he might divide the monster and do artful works.
> He split her like a shellfish into two parts:
> Half of her he set up and ceiled it as sky . . . .

Other details of the creation are given, concluding with the slaying of Tiamat's new consort, Kingu, from whose body mankind was made by Ea, slayer of Apsu and father of Marduk.

In this myth, of course, Tiamat represents chaos, the evil side of the dualism, while Marduk the god-hero represents the good side.

From the other side of the world comes another dualistic myth, that of the Jicarilla Apache Indians. It begins with only the primal materials and the god-figures in existence:

> In the beginning nothing was here where the world now stands; there was no ground, no earth,—nothing but Darkness, Water, and Cyclone. There were no people living. Only the Hactcin [personifications of the powers of objects and natural forces] existed. It was a lonely place. There were no fishes, no living things.
>
> All the Hactcin were here from the beginning. They had the material out of which everything was created. They made the world first, the earth, the underworld, and then they made the sky. . . .[6]

In the Maori myth the god Io exists passively in the midst of the unformed waters until he begins to create:

> Io dwelt within breathing-space of immensity.
> The Universe was in darkness, with water everywhere.
> There was no glimmer of dawn, no clearness, no light.
> And he began by saying these words, . . .
> "Darkness, become a light-possessing darkness."
> And at once light appeared.

Two other commandments relating to light and darkness follow.

6. Barbara Sproul, *Primal Myths*, p. 263.

(Io) then looked to the waters which compassed him about
and spake a fourth time, saying:
"Ye waters of Tai-kama, be ye separate.
Heaven, be formed." Then the sky became suspended.
"Bring-forth thou Tupua-horo-nuku."
And at once the moving earth lay stretched abroad.[7]

A final example of dualistic mythology comes from the Roman poet Ovid. He, too, posits a mass of eternal, unformed matter brought under control by an organizer-god.

Before the ocean was, or earth, or heaven,
Nature was all alike, a shapelessness,
Chaos, so-called, all ruse and lumpy matter,
Nothing but bulk, inert, in whose confusion
Discordant atoms warred . . . .
Air without light, substance forever changing,
Forever at war: within a single body
Heat fought with cold, wet fought with dry, the hard
Fought with the soft, things having weight contended
With weightless things.
Till God, or kindlier Nature
Settled all argument, and separated
Heaven from earth, water from land, our air
From the high stratosphere, a liberation
So things evolved, and out of blind confusion
Found each its place, bound in eternal order. . . .
Whatever god it was, who out of chaos
Brought order to the universe, and gave it
Division, subdivision, he molded earth,
In the beginning, into a great globe . . . .[8]

---

7. *Ibid.*, p. 345.
8. *Ibid.*, p. 170.

The essence of these primitive creation myths is well summed up by Claude Tresmontant in the following quotation:

> We know that in the ancient mythologies, Assyro-Babylonian as well as Indian and Hellenic, chaos preceded the formation of the world. Chaos comes first. It is from a pre-existing chaos that the demiurge or the god fashions or sets in order the world. In fact it is thus the chaos which is the absolute, the first principle, the eternal uncreated. The gods in these mythologies often issue from the chaos by a tragic theogony . . . .[9]

Plato

Although Greek philosophy in general tended to be monistic, its outstanding representative was a dualist. We are speaking, of course, of Plato (428-348 B.C.). The "Platonic dualism" is a standard feature in the history of philosophy. Plato taught the existence of two ultimate kinds of reality: the unchanging world of being and the changing physical world of becoming. Both have existed eternally.

The realm of unchanging being is the world of forms or ideas, a kind of heavenly museum in which exists a perfect, ideal specimen of every kind of object or concept. These "ideas" are not just mental constructs in someone's mind, but have an independent ontological reality.

The realm of becoming, on the other hand, is this changing physical world of nature and history. It is the world known to us through sense perception, the world of matter. It has genuine reality, but has a lower ontological status than the realm of *being*.

In his dialogue known as the *Timaeus* Plato gave an account of how the physical universe as we know it came to

9. Claude Tresmontant, *The Origins of Christian Philosophy*, tr. Mark Pontifex (New York: Hawthorn Books, 1963), p. 46.

be as it is. It is a kind of creation account, and it is given in mythical form. In order to explain the existence of the present cosmos Plato had to posit the reality of *three* kinds of being: the transcendent, unchanging world of true being, the unstable world of mere becoming, and a kind of deity called the Demiurge (craftsman). The role of the Demiurge in Plato's thought is limited solely to this act of "creation"; it seems to have been introduced just for this purpose alone. Outside the *Timaeus* the concept is mentioned only twice, and most commentators assume that Plato did not believe in the literal existence of this creator-god.[10] Hence its presence in the *Timaeus* does not alter the basic dualistic form of Plato's cosmology.

The Demiurge is not really a creator, but more of an architect and craftsman. He finds himself confronted on the one hand with the eternal world of ideal being and on the other hand with the world of becoming, which is also eternal. Until the Demiurge takes over, though, the latter world exists only as chaos: unformed matter in unordered motion. It is the Demiurge who brings order out of this chaos and shapes the undifferentiated mass into the present universe. To aid him in this project he uses the world of perfect forms as his blueprint, patterning the objects of this world after them.[11]

Not only is the Demiurge not a true creator; it is generally thought that Plato did not believe that there was an actual

---

10. Renford Bambrough, "Demiurge," *The Encyclopedia of Philosophy*, II:337-8.

11. Frederick Copleston, *A History of Philosophy, Volume I: Greece and Rome, Part I*, new revised ed. (Garden City, New York: Doubleday Image, 1962), pp. 270-78.

point of time in which the chaotic mass became the ordered cosmos. It has always existed as it now does. In Plato's mind the Demiurge, the chaos, and the "creation" itself are just symbols, probably representing the role of Reason in maintaining the orderliness of the universe.[12]

Though this cosmology of Plato may be considered a bit more sophisticated than some of the more primitive myths, it is nonetheless a dualistic world view and partakes of all the shortcomings pertaining thereto.

Gnosticism

Though the examples discussed thus far have been genuine dualisms, they were not especially influential or were not extreme in form. Not until we come to the Gnostics do we find an example of metaphysical dualism both developed to the extreme and presenting itself as a real option in Western (or Near Eastern) thought. Gnosticism is a rather broad category and includes a number of individuals and systems which existed during the first few centuries of the Christian era. During this time it came into conflict with the Christian faith and for a time was a serious challenge to the church. Being highly syncretistic, it adapted easily to Christian terminology and tried to pass itself off as true Christianity. One thing that was constitutive of Gnosticism in all its forms was its radical dualism.

There were two main types of Gnosticism. One was derived from the extreme Iranian dualism which began with two primary principles, Ohrmazd (Ahura Mazda) the good deity and Ahriman (Angra Mainyu) the evil diety. In the

12. *Ibid.*, p. 215; R. Bambrough, "Demiurge," pp. 337-8; and F. M. Cornford, *Plato's Cosmology* (New York: Humanities Press, 1952), pp. 37ff., 176.

Gnostic versions the good deity exists unknown in absolute transcendence as pure Light, while the opposing principle of Darkness and Evil exists independently. The other type of Gnosticism is much the same, except the dark side of the dualism is actually an emanation from the good deity but has become totally alienated from its source.

These different explanations of the original relationship of the two principles make little difference, since their overall dualistic world views remain basically the same. The good deity, the "unknown Father," is infinitely remote and unapproachable except through the hidden knowledge *(gnosis)* provided by the Gnostics. On the opposing side a special personification of evil soon emerges (sometimes called the Demiurge), patterned after the Gnostics' caricature-like perception of the God of the Old Testament. Through a work of creation initiated by the Demiurge, the physical world is finally brought into existence. (In some Gnostic systems the raw material for creation has existed eternally; in some systems influenced by Jewish and Christian teaching the material may actually be created.) Included in this physical creation are the bodies (and souls) of human beings. Enclosed in this outer shell of body-soul, however, is the human spirit, which is a portion of the divine substance that has inadvertently become entrapped in the world. In the Gnostic system the goal is for this inner divine spark to escape from this material prison and return to the realms of light. This is achieved only through the Gnostics' special knowledge.[13]

The heretic Marcion (c. 85-159), called a Gnostic by some but not by others, devised a dualism centering around

13. See Hans Jonas, "Gnosticism," *The Encyclopedia of Philosophy,* III: 336-42. See also Hans Jonas, *The Gnostic Religion* (Boston: Beacon Press, 1958; 2 ed., 1963); and Robert M. Grant, *Gnosticism and Early Christianity,* revised ed. (New York: Harper and Row, 1966).

two gods, the inferior God and Creator of the Old Testament and the true and supreme God manifested in Jesus Christ. The Old Testament God and his creation are not evil; they are just imperfect and oppressive. The good God is absolutely alien to every created thing.[14]

Manichaeism

Special attention must be given to Mani (c. 216-276), the founder of Manichaeism, which R. McL. Wilson calls "one of the most widely influential religions of the ancient world."[15] Mani was such a thorough-going dualist that the terms *Manichaeism* and *metaphysical dualism* are almost synonymous. As Wilson remarks, "The chief characteristic of Mani's system is a consistent dualism which rejects any possibility of tracing the origins of good and evil to one and the same source. Evil stands as a completely independent principle against God."[16]

Mani's doctrine resembled Gnosticism, especially that aspect which had been influenced by Iranian sources. "It is perfectly clear," says Geo Widengren, "that Mani took for his starting-point the ancient Iranian dualism" based on the ultimate antithesis between Ohrmazd the Good and Ahriman the Evil.[17]

Mani's myth of creation begins with two coeternal, independent principles: Light and Darkness, Good and Evil,

14. Hans Jonas, *The Gnostic Religion*, pp. 137ff.

15. R. McL. Wilson, "Mani and Manichaeism," *The Encyclopedia of Philosophy*, V:149.

16. *Ibid.*

17. Geo Widengren, *Mani and Manichaeism*, tr. Charles Kessler (New York: Holt, Rinehart and Winston, 1965), p. 44. See the more complete description of the Iranian myth in chapter three of Widengren's book. See the texts of the Iranian myth in Barbara Sproul, *Primal Myths*, pp. 135-42.

God and Matter. Each is accompanied by five attendants. Here are the opening words:

> Before the existence of heaven and earth and everything in them there were two natures, the one good and the other evil. Both are separate each from the other. The good principle dwells in the place of Light and is called "Father of Greatness." Outside him dwelt his five Sh'kinas: Intelligence, Knowledge, Thought, Deliberation, Resolution. The evil principle is called "King of Darkness," and he dwells in his land of Darkness surrounded by his five Aeons (or, "Worlds"), the Aeons of Smoke, of Fire, of Wind, of Water, and of Darkness. The world of Light borders on that of Darkness without a dividing wall between the two.[18]

Action begins when the Dark forces behold the Light and determine to capture it and absorb it. In defense the Father of Greatness (via the Mother of Life) produces the Primal Man, who, armored with his five Sons of Light, goes forth to meet the enemy and his five attendants, the Sons of Darkness. The Primal Man is defeated, and allows the Dark fiends to devour him and his five sons with the thought of poisoning them. The Primal Man himself is rescued, but part of the Light remains mixed with Darkness.

Now comes the creation of the present cosmos. It is actually created by the good forces of Light as a method of liberating the particles of Light that had become mixed with Darkness. The King of Light orders one of his assistants, the Living Spirit, to kill the five cannibalistic Sons of Darkness and use their body parts to make the universe, with the entrapped particles of Light scattered through the whole. Various astronomical means are devised for extracting the Light. In a

18. Barbara Sproul, *Primal Myths,* pp. 146-7. The next two paragraphs are a summary of the rest of the myth as given by Sproul on pp. 147-51.

last-ditch effort to retain the Light-substance, the King of Darkness creates Adam and Eve, making their bodies from evil matter but pouring into them all the Light particles left at his disposal as their spirits. He then encourages as much reproduction as possible in order to disperse the Light, making it more difficult to rescue.

Mani's intention was to start a new religion. He considered himself to be God's apostle for the last age, the successor of Buddha, Zoroaster, and Jesus. As Wilson remarks, he achieved considerable success. His system, which spread into both the East and the West, was a serious rival to Christianity for a time. Augustine was a follower for a number of years before his commitment to Christianity; some believe that his new and fateful doctrine of original sin had its roots in Manichaean dualism. A number of medieval Christian sects also appear to have been influenced by Mani's teaching, e.g., the Paulicians, the Bogomiles, and the Albigenses.[19]

Medieval Sects

A bit more needs to be said about the dualistic sects of the Middle Ages. Beginning with the Paulicians as early as the fifth century, these sects proliferated until at least the thirteenth century, when the crusades against the Albigenses successfully suppressed them.

According to Philip Schaff, the Paulicians "were a strange mixture of dualism, demiurgism, docetism, mysticism and pseudo-Paulinism, and resemble in many respects the Gnostic system of Marcion." Also, "Dualism was their fundamental principle. The good God created the spiritual world; the bad God or demiurge created the sensual world."

19. R. McL. Wilson, "Mani and Manichaeism," p. 150.

Thus everything material was held in contempt, including church practices involving externals.[20]

Another dualistic group was the Euchite sect of the eleventh century; from them sprang the Bogomiles and the Cathari, which spread into the West as the "new Manichaeans." As Schaff says, "They taught a dualistic antagonism between God and matter."[21] The Cathari themselves were divided into many sects (as many as seventy-two, by one contemporary count). The Albigenses were the Cathari of southern France.[22]

One reason for pointing out the dualistic heresies of these sects is that in some circles they are sometimes counted as heroes for their opposition to the Catholic Church. Some people think it is necessary to identify a "remnant church" in every age so that Christ's promise in Matthew 16:18 will not fail. Others like to locate a "restoration movement" in every period of church history. Thus it is not uncommon to see the Paulicians or the Albigenses cited as the "true remnant church" of their time.[23] Their dualistic theology make them unworthy recipients of this honor, however.

20. Philip Schaff, *History of the Christian Church, Volume IV: Medieval Christianity* (Grand Rapids: Eerdmans, reprint of 1910 ed.), pp. 576-7.

21. *Ibid.*, pp. 578-81.

22. David S. Schaff (completing the work begun by Philip Schaff), *History of the Christian Church, Volume V: The Middle Ages* (Grand Rapids: Eerdmans, reprint of 1907 ed.), pp. 471, 474.

23. E.g., James D. Murch speaks kindly of the Marcionites in *The Free Church* (n.p.: Restoration Press, 1966), p. 38. Alfred T. DeGroot praises the restoration spirit of the Gnostics, Paulicians, and Cathari; and though he notes their dualist tendencies, he does not appreciate the true extent of their heresies. See *The Restoration Principle* (St. Louis: Bethany Press, 1960), pp. 92-99. Alfred Kuen remarks, "Biblical teaching and churches of the apostolic type have not entirely disappeared" in the Middle Ages, though they are often considered heretical. Among other groups Kuen names the Paulicians and the Bogomiles as objects of persecution "because they had committed the crime of wishing to follow the teaching of the apostles as it is transmitted in the New Testament." See *I Will Build My Church*, tr. Ruby Lindblad (Chicago: Moody, 1971), p. 200.

Modern Dualists

Dualism appears occasionally in our modern world. Gilkey notes that it has appeared "in perhaps its most impressive form in the philosophy of Whitehead."[24] Less impressive affirmations of dualism often occur in popular piety, where the implications have probably not been carefully thought out. Here is an example:

> I believe that the Universe always existed. In other words, I believe the Universe was never *created.* It just always was!
>
> I am not talking about the Earth or even the Sun. I am talking about the Universe—the whole ball of wax.
>
> . . . .
>
> If God did not create the Universe, we do not need to ask why He did it, or when, or who created God. Like the Universe, coexistent with it, He always was. The concept that the Universe always existed clears up a lot of philosophical questions that have bothered a lot of people over a long span of time. Think about it.
>
> . . . .
>
> Actually, whether the Universe was created or always existed is not very important either. No one can ever possibly know. . . .[25]

As we have noted, it is common for modernistic theologians to separate the doctrine of creation from the concept of the origin of the universe. E. L. Mascall, for instance, says, "The whole question whether the world had a beginning

---

24. Langdon Gilkey, *Maker of Heaven and Earth* (Garden City, New York: Doubleday Anchor, 1965), p. 46. See also H. P. Owen, *Concepts of Deity* (New York: Herder and Herder, 1971), pp. 76-77.

25. Edward R. Dewey, "Cycles," *Science of Mind* (June 1973), 46:54.

or not is, in the last resort, profoundly unimportant for theology."[26] If this is true, then it follows that it is unimportant whether matter is eternal or not, which is to say that dualism is an acceptable option for the modernistic theologian. Though most may resist this conclusion, some do not. Regin Prenter typically separates the biblical witness to creation from the question of origins, but he goes further by acknowledging a kind of dualism. He sees Genesis I as portraying creation against a dualistic background. "It is God's struggle against death in order that life may be preserved. Creation takes place as God overcomes the powers of chaos, death, and destruction."[27] The biblical world picture, he says, "is essentially dualistic. It sees creation as a ceaseless struggle between God and his enemies."[28]

> . . . Creation as well as redemption is a struggle against the enemies of God. The fear of a metaphysical Manichaeism which operates with the idea of two eternally equal principles —one evil and one good—must not be permitted to minimize this dualistic perspective of the biblical idea of creation. When it is remembered that neither the origin of the world nor the origin of evil can nor need be explained, it also becomes unnecessary for either theology or preaching to choose between a metaphysical monism and a metaphysical dualism. . . .[29]

Thus we see that the dualistic cosmology has been widespread and persistent throughout history and is still present today. It cannot be lightly dismissed as a rival to the Christian doctrine of creation.

---

26. E. L. Mascall, *Christian Theology and Natural Science* (New York: Ronald Press, 1956), p. 155.
27. Regin Prenter, *Creation and Redemption*, tr. Theodor Jensen (Philadelphia: Fortress Press, 1967), p. 194.
28. *Ibid.*, p. 227.
29. *Ibid.*, p. 199.

Implications of Dualism

Dualistic cosmologies are not all the same; some are milder and some are more extreme. All of them, however, have serious anti-Christian implications for a total world view, and the more extreme dualisms lead to a religious parody that is the opposite of Christianity in practically every way. Here we will summarize these implications.

God

The most obvious effect of a dualistic view is its denial of the sovereignty of God. Usually God is equated with the good side of the dualism, but he is still just one of two ultimate realities. The other reality, whatever its nature, coexists with God and thus constitutes a limitation on his power. A limited God is a finite God.[30]

In such a system there can never be a guarantee that the good God will maintain absolute control. The creation itself is often seen as the result of a struggle between God and the powers of Darkness. Redemption is a continuation of that struggle (as Prenter has described it). But who can say that this ends the struggle, that it will not break out again? In principle there can be no absolute conquest of evil, since it is metaphysically based in a reality which has an ultimate and independent ontological status.

In the Christian faith we need to be careful not to think of the relationship between God and Satan in dualistic terms. Satan is an enemy of God, but he is not an eternal, independent entity which has forever coexisted with God. He himself is a creature who depends upon God for his very existence. His opposition to God is an ethical choice, not

30. Langdon Gilkey, *Maker of Heaven and Earth*, pp. 47-48.

a metaphysical necessity. The "struggle" between God and Satan is not a fight between equals or even near-equals. This struggle exists in the first place not because Satan is so strong in relation to God, but in relation to man. It is man that they are fighting for, and the battle must be waged on the level of man. Thus God's conquest of Satan is not an exercise of sheer divine omnipotence, but is the result of redemptive power wielded by God incarnate as the man Jesus Christ. Nevertheless, because God is the Sovereign Creator, we know concerning the creature Satan that "his doom is sure" and that he will not be an eternal threat. This is the assurance which dualism does not permit.

Creation

In most dualisms there is no true concept of creation in the sense of bringing the universe into existence out of nothing. It is usually a case of *constructing* the world out of pre-existing materials, such as eternally-existing matter or the body of a defeated enemy. It is formation, not creation. (In Gnosticism there are some descriptions of creation which appear to be real *ex nihilo* origination of matter. It must be remembered, however, that the syncretistic Gnostics drew many of their concepts from later Judaism and from Christianity itself. The idea of a genuine creation was no doubt one of these borrowed concepts. Unfortunately, their dualistic tendencies required this creation to be the work of the inferior or evil deity.)

Matter

Dualistic theories tend to degrade the material universe, including the physical body of man. Usually matter is considered to be evil, since it is created out of an evil stuff or created by the evil side of the dualism. Augustine cites the Manichaean Faustus as saying, "We believe in two principles; but one we call God, and the other Hyle [matter]. . . . We attribute, as is proper, all the power of evil to Hyle, and all the power of good to God."[31]

Even those dualists who would not label matter as evil per se still look upon it as something less than good, contrary to Genesis 1:31. Philip Schaff notes that while some Gnostics saw matter as intrinsically evil, others agreed more with Plato that matter is just an empty, negative substance.[32] At best it is something to be tolerated and escaped as soon as possible.

When material reality is in itself looked upon as something negative or evil, this has a profound effect upon all religion and morality. Evil thus has a metaphysical basis, rather than an ethical one (as in the case of evil as a free-will choice). Sin is thus blamed upon this finite, mortal, material existence: "I'm only human!"

Man

A metaphysical dualism usually distorts the picture of man's true nature. Authentic human nature *is* a dualism of the physical (body) and the spiritual (soul or spirit), but each aspect is created and is intrinsically good. In a metaphysical dualism the human body is always a negative and usually an evil entity, while the soul or spirit is considered to be divine, a little spark of God that has become trapped

---

31. Augustine, "Reply to Faustus the Manichaean," XXI:1, *The Works of Aurelius Augustine, Volume V,* ed. Marcus Dods, tr. Richard Stothert (Edinburgh: T. & T. Clark, 1877), p. 382.

32. Philip Schaff, *History of the Christian Church, Volume II: Ante-Nicene Christianity* (Grand Rapids: Eerdmans, 1959 reprint of 1910 ed.), p. 454.

in an evil body. Thus man is not just a physical/spiritual being, but a dualism of good and evil, embodying both creator and creature within himself.

Salvation

Since most dualistic systems are religious ones, they include a concept of salvation. It is quite alien to Christianity, however, and usually takes the form of the liberation of the individual spirit (entrapped divinity) from its prison of a material body. The goal is to be able to endure physical existence until release finally comes through special knowledge, the exercise of reason, or death itself. Since the body is negative or evil and not a part of authentic existence, there is no concept of the resurrection of the body. Of course there is no concept of cosmic redemption in the sense of Romans 8:21; there is no longing for new heavens and a new earth.

Christ

Since dualistic systems usually set God in opposition to matter, the concept of incarnation—God becoming flesh (John 1:14)—is wholly foreign to them. Thus when dualism is allowed to invade Christian thinking, as with some Gnostics and the medieval sects, the Christology is severely corrupted. Jesus Christ is still regarded as a kind of Savior, but he is not a true incarnation of God.

The perverted Christology usually takes one of two forms. Often it is docetic. Docetism is the heresy which denies that Jesus had a true human nature. His divine nature (such as it is) is seen as real, but he only *seemed* to have a human body. It was actually a phantom. He received nothing from

Mary. Her body was just used as a receptacle into which the heaven-originated phantom body was placed; she was no more than a tube or conduit through which it passed. Of course there was no real suffering and death, either; nor was there an authentic bodily resurrection. Jesus Christ was never a real human being.

The other kind of Christology favored by dualists is a form of adoptionism. In this view Jesus was a true human being upon whom the heavenly Christ rested for a limited time. Jesus was adopted by God to be a temporary vehicle for his divine presence. This is usually seen as beginning with Jesus' baptism and ending before his suffering and death took place.

Most Gnostics were docetists, though some were adoptionists. Marcion and the Manichaeans were docetists. The Paulicians and Cathari were likewise one or the other, docetists or adoptionists.

We should also note that in systems such as that of the Gnostics, even the divine side of Christ is compromised. The Christ-spirit is not unique but is just one of a whole host of heavenly spirits that have various functions in the struggle against Darkness.

Worship

Because of their low view of matter dualists usually have little use for externals or outward forms of worship. In the Middle Ages this led the dualist sects to reject many of the excesses of the Catholic Church, such as the use of priestly vestments, veneration of relics and images, payment of indulgences, and even the use of altars and crosses. Many later and present-day Protestants have commended these sects for their courage in instituting a "back-to-the-Bible" reformation. They do not deserve this praise, however, because they were actually motivated by their anti-biblical dualistic metaphysics. What is often overlooked is that they usually rejected *all* outward forms of worship, including baptism and the Lord's supper. Concerning the Cathari David Schaff says, "Baptism with water was pronounced a material and corruptible thing, the work of the evil god."[33] Spiritual ceremonies were substituted for physical ones.

The following statement concerning the Paulicians sums up this anti-materialistic view of worship among the dualists:

> They rejected the priesthood, the sacraments, the worship of saints and relics, the sign of the cross (except in cases of serious illness), and all externals in religion. Baptism means only the baptism of the Spirit; the communion with the body and blood of Christ is only a communion with his word and doctrine.[34]

Some might notice the influence of dualistic thinking in the common Protestant view that water baptism (a physical event) can not be the covenanted occasion for the giving and receiving of remission of sins and the indwelling Spirit (a spiritual benefit). Such a view was in fact the result of the influence of Platonic dualism on the thinking of Huldreich Zwingli, from whose mind flowed this "Reformed" view of the sacraments which has practically engulfed the Protestant world.[35] Until Zwingli no one had questioned the propriety of this kind of relation between the physical and

33. David Schaff, *History of the Christian Church,* V:478.

34. Philip Schaff, *History of the Christian Church,* IV:577.

35. See, e.g., Huldreich Zwingli, "Commentary on True and False Religion," *The Latin Works of Huldreich Zwingli,* Volume III, tr. for S. M. Jackson, ed. C. N. Heller (Philadelphia: Heidelberg Press, 1929), pp. 181-183.

the spiritual except the dualist sects, and the extreme form of their dualism kept anyone from accepting their ideas as an authentic alternative Christian view. Zwingli's milder Platonic dualism did not lead him into some of the excesses being described here, but it did cause him to separate baptism in water from baptism in the Spirit, contrary to Ephesians 4:5. Most Protestants have accepted this without questioning its philosophical roots.

Ethics

Finally we must note the implications of dualism for ethics. In general the negative concept of matter, including the physical body, leads to one of two views: antinomianism (libertinism) or asceticism. Concerning the former, some dualists have taken the position that since the material body is not an authentic part of human existence (i.e., not the *real* man), it does not matter what one does with it. Thus they have abandoned themselves to licentiousness and sensuality.

By far the more common view is extreme asceticism, with as much renunciation of material enjoyment as possible. The body is regarded as the seat of evil, and only the most austere regimen can overcome its enticements. Thus most dualists have required a sparse diet, renunciation of property, and celibacy.

Prohibition of sex and even marriage without sex was common among the Gnostics, the Manichaeans, and the Cathari. Among the Cathari,

> The marriage bed was renounced as contrary to God's law, and some went so far as to say openly that the human body was made by the devil. . . . No man or woman living

> in sexual relations could be saved. The opinion prevailed, at least among some Catharan groups, that the eating of the forbidden fruit in Eden meant carnal cohabitation.[36]

"They generally observed an austere code of morals, abstained from marriage, animal food, and intoxicating drinks. A pallid, emaciated face was regarded by the people as a sign of heresy."[37]

MONISTIC THEORIES

We have given considerable attention to dualistic cosmologies and their very serious anti-biblical implications. We now turn to the other alternative to the Christian doctrine of creation, namely, monism. Metaphysical monism is "any theory that tries to reduce all phenomena to a single principle, or to explain them by one principle, or to make statements about reality as a whole."[38] Monism says there is ultimately only one Being or kind of being; all forms of reality are in some sense a part of that being.

Absolute or undifferentiated monism says that only one individual Being actually exists; the existence of a multitude of other individual entities is a false appearance. In Sankaran Hinduism, for example, the human body (like all matter) is an illusion, and the separation of the human soul from the Absolute is also an illusion. The soul (*atman*) *is* the Absolute (*Brahman*). Ordinary monism says only that all existent beings partake of the same *kind* of reality. Only one kind of "stuff" exists, though it may exist in a number of forms and in an infinite number of individual entities. We may call this differentiated monism.

36. David Schaff, *History of the Christian Church*, V:479.
37. Philip Schaff, *History of the Christian Church*, IV:581.
38. Roland Hall, "Monism and Pluralism," p. 363.

Examples of Monism

Basically there are two kind of monism. One says that the only kind of reality which exists is matter; this is *materialism*. The other says that the only true reality is God; this is *pantheism*. Though this distinction is conceptually quite clear, it is not easy to classify certain monistic views as one or the other of these choices. For instance, Max Heinze treats the Pre-Socratics Thales, Anaximander, and Heraclitus as pantheists, though he uses the term "materialistic pantheism."[39] On the other hand, Frederick Copleston calls them materialists, though not in the modern sense of the term; their view was an "abstract materialism."[40]

We will here present some examples of each type of monism, following traditional classifications.

Materialism

Materialism as a world view says that matter is the only thing which exists and that it is self-existing and eternal. God is either omitted altogether or exists as one material entity among others. Usually it is the former.

Whether we call some of the pre-Socratic philosophers pantheists or materialists, the main point is that they were *monists*. They shared the assumption that *everything is one*, that all existing entities are just forms of one basic kind of material. Thales, the "first philosopher" (died c. 545 B.C.), speculated that everything is derived from the single primary

---

39. Max Heinze, "Pantheism," *The New Schaff-Herzog Encyclopedia of Religious Knowledge*, ed. Samuel M. Jackson, et al. (Grand Rapids: Baker, 1964 reprint), VIII:328.

40. Frederick Copleston, *A History of Philosophy, Volume I: Greece and Rome, Part I*, pp. 36-37.

element of *water.* Anaximander agreed that there is but one primary substance, but he said that substance is something different from anything in our experience; it is *indeterminate.* Anaximenes said all is one, and that one is *air.* Heraclitus echoed the theme that all things are one, the essence of all things being *fire.* Parmenides was an undifferentiated monist: the only thing which exists is a single undivided, unchanging, solid, eternal blob of matter; motion, change and space are illusions. Empedocles and Leucippus (the first Atomist) agreed that everything is composed of individual, undivided, unchanging, solid, eternal lumps of matter; but these lumps (atoms) are incredibly small and infinite in number. They move in an infinite void and collide with one another to form observable matter. The post-Socratic philosophers Democritus and Epicurus, and Lucretius the Latin poet, accepted the same view. [41]

Thomas Molnar notes that materialism went into eclipse when Greek speculative philosophy faded, and did not reappear until the twelfth century in Italy. It stayed alive in Renaissance humanism until it was fully revived in the seventeenth century by Gassendi and Hobbes. From that time it has had a steady following.[42]

A thorough-going programmatic materialism was developed in the nineteenth century in Marxism. Karl Marx was greatly influenced by Ludwig Feuerbach, whose fundamental axiom was "Only a sense-perceivable being is a real, true being." Nothing exists outside nature and man.

41. For a good treatment of these early materialists, see Frederick Copleston's *History of Philosophy, Volume I: Greece and Rome.*

42. See Thomas Molnar, *Theists and Atheists: A Typology of Non-Belief* (New York: Mouton Publishers, 1980), chapter two, "Materialism," especially pp. 43ff.

Marx accepted this materialistic world view, but both he and Feuerbach criticized the purely mechanical materialists who gave no distinct ontological place to human thought and consciousness. Marx and his followers argued that chemical and biological processes may give rise to new substances; thus mind, consciousness and even social interaction may originate from inorganic matter, but they are qualitatively distinct from it.[43] This view, combined with Hegel's philosophy of history, became known as dialectical materialism. (It should be noted that despite the qualification just stated, Marxism remains a genuine materialism; physical matter is still the primary principle and the source of all that exists. For Marxism "matter in motion is the ultimate ground of all being and the deepest layer of all existence." Indeed, "matter is primary and eternal, . . . the inner, final cause of everything existing."[44])

In the twentieth century, largely because of the attribution of omnipotence and omniscience to the physical sciences, materialism is widely accepted. As Copleston remarks, "The attempt to give a complete explanation of the world in terms of mechanical materialism has, as we all know, reappeared in a much more thorough form in the modern era under the influence of physical science."[45] Another writer says, "The triumphant progress in the twentieth century of a materialistic biology and biochemistry has almost completely

---

43. Thomas Molnar, *Theists and Atheists*, p. 55; H. B. Action, "Dialectical Materialism," *The Encyclopedia of Philosophy*, II:391.

44. Francis Nigel Lee, *Communist Eschatology* (Nutley, N.J.: Craig Press, 1974), p. 38.

45. Frederick Copleston, *A History of Philosophy, Volume I: Greece and Rome, Part I*, p. 92.

eliminated vitalist notions and supranatural views of life."[46] Molnar refers to James Feibleman's *The New Materialism* to show that the current version of materialism is no different from that of the ancient Atomists. "The facts as stated by Lucretius and Feibleman are the same, only the latter makes use of modern terminology."[47]

As a world view materialism obviously does not have anything resembling a doctrine of creation. There is no Creator; the ultimate stuff of the universe has just always been there. The most a materialist can do is try to explain how the present configuration of matter came about, but his is not a true concept of creation.

Pantheism

Since pantheism by its very name includes a particular concept of God, it would seem to be a more promising world view than materialism. It must be remembered, however, that pantheism is no less a monism than materialism. It asserts that only one kind of reality exists, namely, God (or something roughly equivalent).

Pantheists are of two kinds. Absolute pantheism equates God and the universe: the totality of God is the totality of the universe. We may call this "immanent pantheism," while using the term "transcendent pantheism" for the view which says that the totality of the world is part of God, but God's being extends beyond the world. Nevertheless that which is the world and that which extends beyond it are of the same ultimate essence, the essence of God.

---

46. Keith Campbell, "Materialism," *The Encyclopedia of Philosophy, V:183.*

47. Thomas Molnar, *Theists and Atheists*, p. 33. He refers to James K. Feibleman, *The New Materialism* (The Hague: M. Nijhoff, 1970).

Sometimes the latter type is called panentheism ("all things are in God") to distinguish it from the former type, for which the term *pantheism* is reserved. This may be misleading, however, since both of the above views are monistic, while the more common versions of panentheism today are dualistic, e.g., the process philosophy of Whitehead. I.e., the world exists *in* God, but is not of the same essence as God himself. It may be better to call the monistic views pantheism, and to limit the term *panentheism* to dualistic ones. In any case the following chart shows how the terms are used:

PANTHEISM		*PANENTHEISM*
Immanent		
Transcendent	=	Monistic
		Dualistic

In the Western world the earliest pantheists are usually identified among the Greek philosophers. We have noted how difficult it is to apply such a term to the Pre-Socratics with any degree of precision. Some have called Xenophanes (born c. 570 B.C.) a pantheist because he said, according to Aristotle, that the whole world is God. Others doubt that the title is applicable. Copleston says that Heraclitus, along with Thales and Anaximenes, was a *de facto* materialist;[48] but he also says "his attitude towards God was pantheistic"; "Heraclitus speaks of the One as God."[49] But Copleston later says that it is probably not proper to use the term *pantheism* for any of the Pre-Socratics since their concept of the matter-spirit distinction was quite primitive, and since

48. Frederick Copleston, *A History of Philosophy, Volume I: Greece and Rome, Part I,* p. 36.

49. *Ibid.*, pp. 55, 59-60.

they did not seem to relate in a religious manner to the One. It may be best just to call them monists.[50]

The same applies to some degree to the Stoics,[51] but Copleston avers that they "might with justice be called pantheists."[52] To confuse the issue even more Copleston calls the Stoic doctrine both "a monistic materialism" and "a cosmic pantheism," and Max Heinze just calls it "a mateialistic pantheism"![53] The problem is that the Stoics did indeed speak of God and equate everything with God, but they conceived of God as material being.

According to classical Stoic teaching, the stuff of all things is the Heraclitan fire, which is a divine material substance. It exists in two forms: first, as the pure, primal, active Fire which is God in Himself and which is the active principle that permeates the universe; and second, as the derived, coagulated, passive material of the universe itself. Both of these together are the totality of God. As Copleston says, "All that exists is either the primal Fire—God in Himself—or God in His different states. . . . He is not something entirely different from the stuff of the world, His body, but is a finer stuff."[54]

In his purest essence God exists as the rarefied Fire. The world comes into existence through a process of transformation.

---

50. *Ibid.*, p. 77.

51. Alasdair MacIntyre, "Pantheism," *The Encyclopedia of Philosophy*, VI:31-32. The Stoic school began with Zeno c. 300 B.C. and waned in the late second century A.D.

52. Frederick Copleston, *A History of Philosophy, Volume I: Greece and Rome, Part I*, p. 77.

53. Frederick Copleston, *A History of Philosophy, Volume I: Greece and Rome, Part II*, new revised ed. (Garden City, N.Y.: Doubleday Image, 1962), pp. 132, 232. See also Max Heinze, "Pantheism," p. 328.

54. Frederick Copleston, *A History of Philosophy, Volume I: Greece and Rome, Part II*, pp. 132-133.

> . . . The fiery vapour, of which God consists, is transformed into air and from air is formed water. From part of the water comes earth, while a second part remains water and a third part is transformed into air, which through rarefaction becomes the elementary fire. Thus does the "body" of God come into being.[55]

Ultimately everything will be transformed back into the primal Fire, and another cycle of the eternal process will begin.

Last in the line of Greek pantheists were the Neo-Platonists, the first and most eminent of whom was Plotinus (c. 205-270). Here again the application of the term must be qualified since the exact nature of the relationship between Plotinus' God and the world is not precisely understood.[56]

Plotinus' concept of God is the epitome of absolute simplicity in the technical sense. God is the absolutely transcendent ONE: beyond divisions and distinctions of any kind, beyond rational thought, beyond our highest concepts of being. He is eternal, infinite, and unchanging in every sense of the words, and has absolutely no conscious relations with anything outside himself.

If the One has no conscious relations outside himself, how do we explain the existence of the world? Here Plotinus uses the concept of *emanation*. By a process of emanation, a series of beings come forth out of the One. This coming-forth is a spontaneous, necessary, and eternal process; it is not something willed by the One. Also, Plotinus says that even though all other being in a sense "emanates" from God, still the being of God is left unchanged and undiminished.

---

55. *Ibid.*, p. 133.
56. *Ibid.*, p. 211; Alasdair MacIntyre, "Pantheism," p. 32.

The process of emanation passes through three stages, each characterized by a decreasing excellence. The first being to be produced is the *Nous* (Mind, Thought), which is in itself a concept as high as most peoples' concept of God. From *Nous* proceeds Soul (of which human souls partake), an incorporeal link between the *Nous* and its own emanant production, the material universe. The material world is the lowest level of being. It proceeds ultimately from the One itself via *Nous* and Soul, but it stands at the very opposite end of the continuum from the One. Matter in itself may even be called evil and non-being, though it never really exists totally "in itself," since it is given a particular formal structure by Soul.

The eternal "downward" process of emanation is complemented by an "upward" process of return to the One. This is significant particularly for individual souls, as they must seek to return through Soul and *Nous* to the One. This can be achieved temporarily now through mystical experience and permanently at death when the body no longer is a hindrance.[57]

Some think that even though Plotinus used the concept of emanation, it was only an inadequate metaphor for the real relationship between God and the world. After all, God's essence is not changed or diminished at all by the process, and the lowest level of the hierarchy is actually the very opposite of God. Thus Neo-Platonism may be called pantheism only in a qualified sense, and it may not even be monistic. Copleston says Plotinus was trying to

57. For a fuller explanation of Plotinus' thought on these subjects, see Frederick Copleston, *A History of Philosophy, Volume I: Greece and Rome, Part II*, pp. 208ff.; and A. H. Armstrong, *Plotinus* (New York: Collier Books, 1962), p. 28ff.

present a middle course between creation and complete pantheism, even if we judge such an attempt to be futile.[58] Nevertheless, if Plotinus were trying to give an alternative to creation and emanation, it is significant that he chose the "metaphor" of *emanation* rather than the other, along with the rather specific image of *overflowing.*[59] This means that we are justified in thinking of him as a pantheist more than anything else.

In the Middle Ages and following, some Christian thinkers embraced pantheism, e.g., John Scotus Erigena (c. 810-877) and Jakob Boehme (1575-1624). Apart from a few such cases, most modern Western pantheism has been a form of unbelief, very little different from materialism except in name.[60] Giordano Bruno (1548-1600) was the first prominent representative of this line. He identified God as the totality of all the finite particulars in the universe. "The universe is god and god is the universe."[61] A more famous and influential example is Benedict Spinoza (1632-1677), who said there is only one substance, for which the terms *God* and *Nature* may be used interchangeably. According to Owen, Spinoza is "the purest instance of pantheism" in the Christian era.[62] His system was a true monism in which "finite things exist as modes of one divine substance."[63]

---

58. Frederick Copleston, *A History of Philosophy, Volume I: Greece and Rome, Part II,* pp. 211, 232; see A. H. Armstrong, *Plotinus,* p. 31; Alasdair MacIntyre, "Pantheism," p. 32.

59. A. H. Armstrong, *Plotinus,* p. 51.

60. Thomas Molnar's first chapter in his book *Theists and Atheists: A Typology of Non-Belief* (!) is on pantheism.

61. Thomas Molnar, *Theists and Atheists,* p. 14; Alasdair MacIntyre, "Pantheism," p. 33.

62. H. P. Owen, *Concepts of Deity,* p. 65.

63. James Collins, *God in Modern Philosophy* (Chicago: Henry Regnery, 1959), p. 73.

Since God (or Nature) is eternal, any true concept of creation is excluded, as it must be in any immanent pantheism.

Many later skeptics who rejected Christian faith but were reluctant openly to embrace atheism found an alternative or an inspiration in Spinozan pantheism. MacIntyre names these examples: Johann Goethe (1749-1832), Gotthold Lessing (1729-1781), Friedrich Schleiermacher (1768-1834; "He committed himself to pantheism by asserting that it is the Totality that is divine"), J. G. Fichte (1762-1814), F. W. J. Schelling (1775-1854), and G. W. F. Hegel (1770-1831). MacIntyre says of Hegel, "The Absolute Idea has no existence apart from or over and above its actual and possible manifestations in nature and history. Hence, the divine is the Totality."[64]

A final example of pantheism is Hinduism, whose philosophy of being has permeated much of the East and has made significant inroads into the West in the form of Eastern cults, such as those popularly known as Transcendental Meditation and the Hare Krishna movement. Hinduism is not a completely unified system of belief. Its cosmologies are varied. Besides its pantheistic versions, some see atheistic and even dualistic themes in its scriptures and teachings. It will be noted, however, that the term *dualism* is often used in this context in the sense of differentiated monism as opposed to undifferentiated monism. There is very little true metaphysical dualism in Hinduism.[65]

---

64. Alasdair MacIntyre, "Pantheism," p. 34. Hegel did not like to call his system pantheism. He preferred to speak of the "Absolute Spirit" rather than God. Certainly his Absolute Spirit is *not* God in the Biblical sense, but it is certainly a god in the pantheistic sense. See James Collins, *God in Modern Philosophy*, pp. 235-236.

65. See Ninian Smart, "Indian Philosophy," *The Encyclopedia of Philosophy*, IV:156, "It is convenient to use 'dualism' to mean the doctrine that the self or soul is distinct from, and not identical with, or a mode of, the Divine

(*Continued on page 83.*)

The most influential Hindu viewpoint is the undifferentiated monism of Sankara (c. 788-820), called the Advaita Vedanta. According to Sankara there is only one single undivided reality: the ONE, the Absolute, or *Brahman*. The eternal self or soul (*atman*) within individual persons is actually identical with Brahman. This is not to say that each individual's soul is a *part* of Brahman; rather, each person's soul *is* Brahman in his totality. *Any other impression we may have is an illusion* (*maya*). That there appear to be a number of separate souls (since there are separate persons) is an illusion. All material existence likewise is an illusion—a cosmic illusion shared by all except the enlightened. How did this illusion begin? (This is a way of asking how the universe was "created.") This question can not be answered; "the state of affairs is beginningless."[66]

Though this is the true picture of things, the question about "creation" can be asked on a lower, common-sense level. From the standpoint of the ordinary person, God may be thought of as a personal creator out of whose substance the phenomena of the observable world have evolved (in an eternal process). Those who work on the higher level, however, know that such a creator is himself illusory.[67]

On either level, of course, we have pantheism in the fullest sense of the word.

Being." See also Hajime Nakamura, *Ways of Thinking of Eastern Peoples: India, China, Tibet, Japan*, ed. and tr. Philip Wiener (Honolulu: East-West Center Press, 1964), p. 69. He cites the opinion that "almost all Indian philosophy believes that reality is *ultimately* one and *ultimately* spiritual. Some systems have seemed to espouse dualism or pluralism, but even these have been deeply permeated by a strong monistic character." For an example of dualism, see the discussion of Madhva in Satis Chandra Chatterjee, "Hindu Religious Thought," *The Religion of the Hindus*, ed. Kenneth W. Morgan (New York: Ronald Press, 1953), pp. 224-228

66. Ninian Smart, "Sankara," *The Encyclopedia of Philosophy*, VII:280-281.

67. *Ibid.*, p. 281.

R. C. Zaehner calls Sankara's "absolute non-duality" the culmination of one great stream of Hindu thought, and says it is still the most important philosophy of India.[68] Nakamura states that it has dominated the classical scholarship of India; nearly two-thirds of contemporary Indian pundits belong to this school.[69]

Other strands of Hindu pantheism take the form of differentiated monism. All things are still seen as part of Brahman, but they proceed from him via true emanation and thus have real existence (as opposed to illusory existence). As Zaehner says, "The general teaching of the Upanishads is not that the phenomenal world is unreal . . . : it emanates from the Absolute as sparks are emanated from fire or as a spider's web is woven out of itself by the spider."[70] In the Samkhya school, Brahman is the source of both *purusa* (or *purusha,* conscious spirit) and *prakrti* (or *prakriti,* primal matter). Through an interaction of these two eternally coexisting principles, the natural universe comes into existence as an extension of their being. Since both "prakriti and purusha are parts of the same Supreme Being," this is still a true pantheism.[71]

Most of the Hinduism with which Westerners have contact is definitely pantheistic. This is true of such respected

---

68. R. C. Zaehner, *Hinduism,* 2 ed. (New York: Oxford University Press, 1966), pp. 56, 73.

69. Hajime Nakamura, *Ways of Thinking of Eastern Peoples,* pp. 67-68.

70. R. C. Zaehner, *Hinduism,* p. 55.

71. Radhagovinda Basak, "The Hindu Concept of the Natural World," *The Religion of the Hindus,* ed. Kenneth Morgan (New York: Ronald Press, 1953), p. 86. See also R. C. Zaehner, *Hindu and Muslim Mysticism* (London: University of London Athlone Press, 1960), p. 31. Ninian Smart interprets Samkhya as saying that *prakrti* (primal matter) is the original substance from which both the empirical world and individual soul (*purusa*) evolve. Since the impersonal *prakrti* is the Absolute, Smart describes this as atheism ("Indian Philosophy," p. 156).

Hindu apostles as Radhakrishnan and Ramakrishna; it is true of most of the Eastern cults, as already noted. A very recent example comes from the writing of Bhagwan Shree Rajneesh, who has recently established a controversial outpost in Oregon. Here is his comment on creation:

> To us it seems important to ask about creation. But in existence, nothing is created; it is a continuous and endless beginning. The very concept of creation is childish and irrelevant as far as existence is concerned. The existence has always been: it has never been created and it can never be destroyed. "Creation" means "out of nothing"—and out of nothing, nothing can come. The world, the creation, is in constant change, but nothing can be created or destroyed.
>
> Change is the reality. By "change" I mean that only the form changes, never the substance. The basic remains always the same; only the mode of expression, the form, changes. And this change is continuous, it is eternal.
>
> . . . .
>
> But to the so-called religious mind creation seems significant, because we have conceived of God as the creator, and without creation where will the creator be? God is not the creator; God is existence itself. God is not something separate but the very substance of reality; he is not the creator of reality but the reality itself.
>
> This duality—God and the world, the creator and the created—is due to our dualistic thinking. Our mind goes on creating dualities. But the reality is one; God is not the creator but the creation: the energy, the force, the basic substance of all.
>
> . . . .
>
> The total quantity of existence is always the same. Whether you change A to B or B to C makes no difference to the total; not a single particle can be added to the total and not

a single particle can be subtracted. And this total quantity is God.

The first thing to be understood is that nothing has been created. Existence *is*. Existence exists with no beginning and no end, but with many changes.[72]

Implications of Monism

We have presented a number of major examples of monism as a cosmological view, in both its materialistic and its pantheistic forms. It is no doubt already obvious that all monistic views of the God-world relationship are alien to the biblical view of God as Creator. Anyone who opts for any one of these views by that very choice implicitly accepts a package of beliefs that are opposed to the Christian world view. Here we will summarize some of the main implications of monism.

God

In monistic systems God either is eliminated altogether or is sorely lacking in some of the most important attributes that make God to be God. Regarding the former, it is obvious that all forms of materialistic monism are deliberately atheistic. There is no God-world relationship because there is no God.

What needs to be emphasized is that many of the views that pass as pantheism are for all practical purposes atheism in disguise. What is the difference between the one who says, "The only thing which exists is the universe," and the

72. Bhagwan Shree Rajneesh, *A Rajneesh Reader: The Great Challenge* (New York: Grove Press, 1982), pp. 152-153. See also p. 156: "*Nothing* has been created; everything has always been here." "The total existence is God. You participate in the total."

one who says, "No, the only thing which exists is God; but of course he exists only in the form of the universe"? This applies especially to the view we have called immanent pantheism. H. P. Owen remarks, "If 'God' (*theos*) is identical with the Universe (*to pan*) it is merely another name for the Universe. It is therefore bereft of any distinctive meaning; so that pantheism is equivalent to atheism."[73] Owen says he does not think Spinoza and Hegel fit this category since the God of each transcends the world in some sense.[74] It would seem that Owen is being overly generous, however, since there is no real ontological sense in which God extends beyond the universe for Spinoza (see his famous aphorism, "God, or Nature"—*Deus sive Natura*). The same seems to be true of most modern pantheists, including Hegel. We note again that Molnar treats pantheism as one variety of atheism (along with materialism, humanism, and ultra-supernaturalism).[75] He reminds us of the following pointed statement by Ernest Haeckel in the latter's book, *The Enigma of the Universe*:

> . . . Pantheism is but a polite atheism. . . . Its thesis is the suppression of dualist opposition between god and the world, and the statement that the world exists thanks to itself and its internal force. The pantheist proposition that god and the world are one, is a polite detour signalling to the Lord his dismissal.[76]

Even in those instances where the God of pantheism seems to have a real existence in addition to the universe as such

73. H. P. Owen, *Concepts of Deity*, pp. 69-70.
74. *Ibid.*, p. 75.
75. Thomas Molnar, *Theists and Atheists*, p. 7.
76. *Ibid.*, p. 26.

(as, for instance, in Neo-Platonism and Hinduism), the concept of God is most definitely inferior to the biblical God. Even the so-called highly exalted Absolute of Plotinus lacks the basic quality of *personhood*, which includes the attribute of love. To "elevate" God to the level of abstract, undifferentiated, non-relating transcendence is not a promotion but a demotion.

The fact is that, despite much talk about the "absolutely transcendent One," the main characteristic which the God of pantheism lacks is *transcendence*. This is true because if everything is God, then there is no ultimate ontological distinction between God and anything else which exists, including man. They are all "made of the same stuff," so to speak. Everything is ontologically continuous with God. This must be true even for Neo-Platonism. Even though matter is three steps removed from the One and is "diluted" (or coagulated, as one chooses) to the opposite end of the continuum from the One, there is still a *continuum* of being.

Such is characteristic of monism in general: either there is no God or a low God.

Creation

In a monistic system there can be no such thing as creation, else it would not be a monism. True creation brings into existence a kind of being distinct from the Creator. But of course this does not happen in materialism, since no creator exists. The material universe is eternally existing in itself. Nor does it happen in pantheism, even when the universe is said to be brought into existence with a specific beginning. In pantheism the key words are *transformation* and *emanation*. God or a part of God is transformed into the world, or else in some sense the world emanates or overflows out of the being of God. Thus the world is formed from preexisting material: God himself. This is usually not a conscious or willed decision; it just happens by eternal necessity.

It is just because there is no creation that a monist can not posit a God who is truly transcendent. Only creation guarantees the ontological distinctiveness of God. Barbara Sproul notes how myths with a monistic starting point (a "primordial stew," or Chaos) can never separate the "creator" from his "creation." (She uses these terms, though they do not strictly apply.) She says,

> The creation occurs when part, if not all, of this Chaos coalesces and forms internal divisions, like the internal mass of a cell dividing itself into nucleus and matter. The part that is formed and thereby distinguished from the rest of the unformed mass then acts upon it to produce further distinctions and thereby create the world. Which is the absolute reality here? The Chaos itself? Or the child of Chaos that acts on it? *Both*. They are one. At some point, the myths step back from the mystery and affirm the essential and unbreakable unity of the creator and creation.[77]

Matter

What is the status of matter in a monistic system? Two tendencies prevail whenever creation is rejected. Matter, the physical universe, is either debased or absolutized.

The debasement of matter is seen especially in pantheism, and most prominently in Sankaran Hinduism, where the physical world is only *maya,* an illusion. It is not even real. Molnar says this is true in a sense of every pantheism. If everything is God, then the universe has in a sense disappeared (as Hegel himself suggested). Thus we have *acosmism*

77. Barbara Sproul, *Primal Myths*, p. 10.

to go along with atheism.[78] Even when we are confronted with a theory of emanation or transformation which makes the universe ontologically real, its status is less than good, less than fully authentic. In the case of Neo-Platonism, matter is closer to non-being than to being. Gilkey is correct when he says, "It follows that for pantheism 'creation,' as the origination of concrete particular individuals within space and time, is a 'fall' from the unity and changelessness of the One."[79]

On the other hand, and perhaps paradoxically, monism also tends to absolutize matter. This is true in a sense of pantheism. After all, if God is equivalent to the universe, and the universe is equivalent to God, then there is a "divine significance to Nature and History," as Owen says. He is speaking especially of Spinoza and Hegel, who he says "ascribe an infinite value" to the world.[80] Such an absolutizing of nature appears most obviously in Hinduism's differentiated monism, where every creature is regarded as divine. R. Basak speaks of "the divinity of nature" and "the veneration of the natural world" based on the oneness of the world with the Supreme Being.[81]

Even in materialism matter is absolutized. This is so almost by definition: if matter is the only reality, then it *is* the Absolute. A basic characteristic of deity is usually ascribed to it, namely, eternal self-existence. James Houston notes how many modern materialists (such as some ecologists) both personify and deify nature:

---

78. Thomas Molnar, *Theists and Atheists*, p. 17.
79. Langdon Gilkey, *Maker of Heaven and Earth*, p. 62.
80. H. P. Owen, *Concepts of Deity*, pp. 68-69.
81. R. Basak, "The Hindu Concept of the Natural World," p. 102.

> The Baalism which the prophets condemned is still with us as naturalism. The counter-cultural revolution exhorts us to follow the "new naturalism." Ecologists like Barry Commoner tell us: "Don't mess with Mother Nature." Perhaps more than any other form of secularism, the dominance of nature has tended to eclipse the light of the Creator in the Western world. So one of the most enduring goddesses of the pantheon of Western idols has been "Mother Nature."[82]

This may not be exactly what Owen meant when he said "*all* monists . . . can be called pantheists,"[83] but he is surely not far from the truth. There can be no doubt about this next statement:

> . . . The difference between the various forms of monism are negligible when compared with the difference between all these forms and theism, which rests on the affirmation that all creatures are substantially distinct from the Creator.[84]

Man

Monism produces a similar paradox with regard to the nature of man. This is true whether man is seen as body only or as also having a separable spiritual nature. Both in materialism and in pantheism, man is God. Since pantheism equates everything with God, man himself must be regarded as divine. This applies especially to the soul or inner self, which is usually regarded as being identical with God even if the body is not. In Sankaran Hinduism, for instance, all individual souls are absolutely and numerically the same

---

82. James M. Houston, *I Believe in the Creator* (Grand Rapids: Eerdmans, 1980), p. 30.

83. H. P. Owen, *Concepts of Deity,* p. 68; italics added.

84. *Ibid.*

as Brahman, while the body is just an illusion. In the highest sense of the word, man is God. But this is just as true in materialism, though in a different sense. If anyone believes that matter is all that exists, and that man is the highest form of matter, then man is given the role of God whether this is specifically stated or not. Indeed, this is almost explicit in the philosophy and behavior of modern materialists, to whom individual autonomy is sacred and whose creed is "There is no one over you."

The paradox is that monism often denies the value and authentic existence of *individual* human beings. This is obvious in the dialectical materialism of Marxism, where the welfare of individuals is always subordinated to the Marxist concept of the collective good. The Russian Gulag and the Cambodian Holocaust are examples. But the reality and authenticity of individuals are denied also in pantheism, especially in its transcendent form.[85] The individual self knows its true existence only when it is reunited with the One whence it came; its very existence as a separate entity is part of the "fall" of which Gilkey speaks. "Salvation" consists in reunion with or reabsorption into the One. So said Plotinus and Sankara.

Religion

This leads to a final implication of monism, namely, its effect on religion. Though some pantheists speak of and practice worship, consistent monism actually removes the ground and rationale for worship. Certainly if there is no God, as in materialism, there can be no worship in the true sense of the word. But if man *is* God, as in pantheism, even

85. Langdon Gilkey, *Maker of Heaven and Earth*, pp. 61-62.

though worship may occur, it is inconsistent. Should God worship himself?

Owen remarks that "the religious possibilities of pantheism are strictly limited."[86] Indeed, many of the early pantheists developed no religious associations with their "deity," and the same is true of Spinoza and the post-Spinozan pantheists. Even though they may speak of the Totality as God, religiously it is the same as if there were no God at all. The revealing question is this: what existential difference would it make to a pantheist if there were no "God," or if he suddenly stopped calling reality God and just called it the universe? When the Hindu pantheist Rajneesh is asked the question, "Does God exist?" he does not even answer it because, he says, to most people it is a meaningless question. A question is meaningful only if its answer will change the inquirer in some way. "As I see it," Rajneesh says, "whether God exists or not, people remain the same. They are interested only for the sake of peripheral knowledge. They are not really concerned; the question is not existential."[87] This is exactly what we would expect of a pantheist.

The closest thing to authentic religion within the whole framework of monism is the practice of mysticism. Mysticism basically is seeking after the experience or feeling of oneness with the larger entity of which one is only a part. Thus even a materialist can speak of a mystical experience in the sense of the feeling of oneness with Nature. Classical mysticism occurs most prominently in the Neo-Platonic and Hindu traditions, where the highest religious experiences are achieved in those exercises which produce temporary union with the One (e.g., "transcendental meditation").

---

86. H. P. Owen, *Concepts of Deity*, p. 73.
87. B. S. Rajneesh, *A Rajneesh Reader*, pp. 190-191.

Worship in the sense of praise and prayer to a personal Creator is significantly absent.

In this chapter our goal has been to survey the pagan alternatives to creation and the concept of God as Creator. We have examined the two broad categories of dualism and monism. We can not help but be impressed with the pervasiveness of these viewpoints in world history. We are also struck by the fact of how utterly alien these systems are in relation to biblical teaching. The gods of the dualists and monists alike are indeed idols—empty pretenders to the exalted throne of the God of Israel, the God of our Lord Jesus Christ.

The key element in understanding the difference between the true God and the false ones is the fact of *creation*. We now turn to a consideration of this doctrine as taught in Scripture.

Chapter Three

THE BIBLICAL DOCTRINE OF CREATION

Knowledge of God must begin with the doctrine of creation. As the Catholic theologian Joseph Pohle has said, "Unless we know God as the Creator of all things, we do not know the true God."[1] Indeed, the whole Christian faith rests upon this foundation. The following comments by Langdon Gilkey must be taken seriously:

> . . . The idea that God is the Creator of all things is the indispensable foundation on which the other beliefs of the Christian faith are based. It affirms what the Christian believes about the status of God in the whole realm of reality: He is the Creator of everything else. On this affirmation logically depends all that Christians say about their God, about the world they live in, and about their own history, destiny, and hope.[2]

In the last chapter we saw that the religious and philosophical world in general has rejected the concept of creation. The typical non-Christian opts either for monism or for dualism. In this chapter we will see how the Christian doctrine of creation stands out in unique contrast against this pagan background. First we will discuss the theological concept of creation; then we will present the biblical data about creation.

---

1. Joseph Pohle, *God: The Author of Nature and the Supernatural,* ed. Arthur Preuss (St. Louis: B. Herder, 1912), p. 8.

2. Langdon Gilkey, *Maker of Heaven and Earth* (Garden City, N.Y.: Doubleday Anchor, 1965), p. 4. See also p. 115: "Rather, as the foundation upon which all that is Christianly significant about God is based, the idea of the Creator is an indispensable and primary element in any Christian theology."

THE CONCEPT OF CREATION

The definition of creation has become fairly standardized over the years. The first Vatican Council (1870) defined it in this way:

> This one true God, by his goodness and omnipotent excellence, not to augment or add to his beatitude, but to manifest his perfection by the good things which he imparts to creatures, by entirely free design formed out of nothing from the beginning of time at once both the spiritual creature and the corporeal, that is to say, the angelic and the worldly, and thereafter the human, as if jointly constituted of spirit and body.[3]

The Protestant Louis Berkhof gives a similar definition:

> . . . Creation in the strict sense of the word may be defined as that free act of God whereby He, according to His sovereign will and for His own glory, in the beginning brought forth the whole visible and invisible universe, without the use of preexistent material, and thus gave it an existence, distinct from His own and yet always dependent on Him.[4]

C. C. Crawford sums it up tersely in these words: "By Creation we mean that free act of God by which in the beginning He made, without the use of preexisting materials, the whole visible and invisible universe."[5]

These definitions contain three basic ideas: (1) God created the universe out of nothing; (2) creation was a free act;

---

3. Henricus Denzinger and Adolfus Schönmetzer, eds., *Enchiridion Symbolorum,* 32 ed. (Freiburg: Verlag Herder, 1963), item 1783/3002, p. 587. English translation from Claude Tresmontant, *Christian Metaphysics,* tr. Gerard Slevin (New York: Sheed and Ward, 1965), p. 54.

4. Louis Berkhof, *Systematic Theology* (London: Banner of Truth Trust, 1939), p. 129. Italics omitted.

5. C. C. Crawford, *Survey Course in Christian Doctrine,* Volume I (Joplin, Mo.: College Press, 1962), p. 47.

(3) and creation is inclusive of both the spiritual and the material realms. Each of these points will now be discussed.

Creation from Nothing

Each of the definitions listed above include the idea of creation out of nothing, or creation *ex nihilo*. This is the intent of the expression "without the use of preexisting materials." Thus as a means of bringing something into existence, creation is opposed to both generation and formation. Generation is the process of bringing something into existence out of one's own being, as in pantheistic emanation or human procreation. In this case the preexisting material is the "creator's" own self. Formation is the act of a craftsman who makes an object out of raw material available from some other source, as in the case of Plato's Demiurge or a human sculptor. The Christian doctrine of creation in its primary and most specific sense denies both of these alternatives. The universe—including both its spiritual and its material content—was not generated out of God's own essence, nor was it formed out of a mass of eternally-existing matter. It was created out of nothing.

Sometimes the picture is confused when the word *nothing* (or the Latin *nihil*) is used as a name for something that actually exists, such as especially the preexisting, unformed matter—the primeval Chaos—out of which the dualist's God triumphantly wrests the universe. Some have suggested that the term has been used in this sense by the Greek philosophers[6] and by Gnostics of all ages.[7] According to Hendrikus

---

6. Arnold Ehrhardt, *The Beginning: A Study of the Greek Philosophical Approach to the Concept of Creation* (Manchester: Manchester University Press, 1968), pp. 164ff.

7. Emil Brunner, *The Christian Doctrine of Creation and Redemption: Dogmatics, Volume II*, tr. Olive Wyon (Philadelphia: Westminster, 1952), p. 10.

Berkhof, "Since Heidegger it has again acquired that kind of ontological meaning in our popular-philosophical speech."[8] Karl Barth's doctrine of nothingness (*nihil, das Nichtige*) is an example. According to Barth, when God created the universe he separated the good creation from chaos or nothingness, which was rejected and banished. This very act of rejection imparted to the nothingness an absurd, limbo-like existence of unreal reality and impotent power.[9] The good creation always exists in proximity to this *nihil,* and is menaced and threatened by it:

> . . . There is a whole monstrous kingdom, a deep chaos of nothingness, i.e., of what the Creator has excluded and separated from the sphere of being, of what He did not will and therefore did not create, to which he gave no being, which can exist only as non-being, and which thus forms the menacing frontier of what is according to the will of God. . . .[10]

H. Berkhof notes that Barth's "'Nothing' becomes a nondescript sort of thing in between a *nihil negativum* and a *nihil ontologicum*."[11] His view becomes very difficult to distinguish from dualism.

The concept of an ontological nothing, besides being an apparent contradiction of terms, was never intended to be the meaning of biblical creation *ex nihilo.* In fact, this is the

---

8. Hendrikus Berkhof, *Christian Faith: An Introduction to the Study of the Faith,* tr. Sierd Woudstra (Grand Rapids: Eerdmans, 1979), p. 155.

9. Karl Barth, *Church Dogmatics, Volume III: The Doctrine of Creation, Part I,* tr. J. W. Edwards et al. (Edinburgh: T. & T. Clark, 1958), pp. 101ff., 366.

10. Karl Barth, *Church Dogmatics, Volume III: The Doctrine of Creation, Part 2,* tr. Harold Knight et al. (Edinburgh: T. & T. Clark, 1960), p. 143.

11. Hendrikus Berkhof, *Christian Faith,* pp. 155-156.

very kind of thing that the doctrine is meant to exclude. "Out of nothing" means "not out of anything." It means that before creation there was nothing except God, and after creation there was also the universe which was not God but rather was absolutely distinct from God's own being and existence.

The concept of creation from nothing is typically rejected in pagan philosophy, which rather contends that *ex nihilo, nihil fit*: "from nothing, nothing comes." Parmenides articulated this idea by saying that being can not arise from not-being. Others echoed this opinion, especially Empedocles and the Atomists. Arnold Ehrhardt cites the following fragment attributed to Melissus (fifth century B.C.): "What has been has always been, and will always be. For if it had come into being, before its coming into being it would without fail have been nothing. If therefore it was nothing, it could not in any way have become something out of nothing."[12]

Such objections as this seem to posit, however, a state of nothingness in which absolutely nothing at all—not even God—exists. Out of such absolute nothingness it is impossible for something spontaneously to come into existence. We agree. But this is not the Christian notion of creation *ex nihilo*. We do not begin with absolute nothingness; we begin with the eternal God: "In the beginning God" (Genesis 1:1). Though God uses no preexisting material to make the universe, his own will and power are the cause of its existence. There is no violation of the law of sufficient cause, as if the universe were an effect without a cause.

Creation as Relation or Origination?

It would seem that the doctrine of creation *ex nihilo* would be at least a statement of the fact that the universe

12. Arnold Ehrhardt, *The Beginning*, p. 7.

had a beginning. It would also seem important to affirm that the universe had a beginning, as over against dualistic interpretations of matter as eternal. It is significant, however, that in modern philosophy and theology the doctrine of creation is more and more being separated from the concept of the beginning of the universe. The idea of creation *ex nihilo* is either questioned or reinterpreted to stand for a particular kind of relationship between God and man. The idea of a beginning is dismissed as unimportant.

Typically the idea of creation is interpreted as an affirmation of man's dependence on God. As Ronald Hepburn says, "The Christian doctrine of creation is primarily about the ontological dependence of the world upon God; and it is of only secondary interest whether that world has a literal beginning, a first moment."[13] James Houston says that the church has been misled by too much emphasis on creation *ex nihilo*, a doctrine which he characterizes as speculative and uncertain.[14] Thus we are not surprised when he says, "So creation is not principally an account of origins, but of dependence upon God."[15]

This disavowal of interest in origins is common. J. S. Whale says:

> The Christian doctrine of creation does not arise from our interest in explaining the world or accounting for its "origin" at some approximately datable time in the cosmic past. The doctrine of creation "out of nothing" is not a scientific description of the beginning of the time series. . . .[16]

---

13. Ronald Hepburn, "Creation, Religious Idea of," *The Encyclopedia of Philosophy*, ed. Paul Edwards (New York: Macmillan, 1967), II:252.

14. James Houston, *I Believe in the Creator* (Grand Rapids: Eerdmans, 1980), pp. 51, 272.

15. *Ibid.*, p. 163.

16. J. S. Whale, *Christian Doctrine* (Cambridge: Cambridge University Press, 1941), p. 32.

The Christian physicist C. F. von Weizsäcker says, "I do not know whether the world has had a beginning."[17] E. L. Mascall says,

> . . . The notion of creation is not primarily concerned with a hypothetical act by which God brought the world into existence at some moment in the past, but with the incessant act by which he preserves the world in existence so long as he wills that it shall exist.[18]
>
> . . . Cosmological theories as such are of no ultimate theological importance. Whether matter is continually coming into existence or not, whether the world has an infinite past or had a first moment a finite number of years ago, makes no difference to the question of the ground of the universe's existence.[19]

Mascall states emphatically, "The whole question whether the world had a beginning or not is, in the last resort, profoundly unimportant for theology."[20] Regin Prenter makes the same point: "The biblical witness concerning creation accounts for the origin of the world as little as it does for the origin of evil."[21]

The content of the doctrine of creation is limited solely to the religious relationship between God and man: "*Creatio ex nihilo* means nothing less, but nothing more either, than

---

17. C. F. von Weizsäcker, *The Relevance of Science: Creation and Cosmogony* (London: Collins, 1964), p. 150.

18. E. L. Mascall, *Christian Theology and Natural Science* (New York: Ronald Press, 1956), pp. 132-133.

19. *Ibid.*, pp. 161-162.

20. *Ibid.*, p. 155.

21. Regin Prenter, *Creation and Redemption*, tr. Theodor Jensen (Philadelphia: Fortress Press, 1967), p. 199.

that God is the sole ground of our existence."[22] Emil Brunner says, "The Christian statement on Creation is not a theory of the way in which the world came into being—whether once for all, or in continuous evolution—but it is an 'existential' statement." It is my affirmation of God's lordship over my life. "For the idea of Creation means that I, together with the whole of Nature to which I belong, am absolutely dependent upon God."[23] Gustaf Aulen says the same thing:

> . . . Faith in God as Creator is not a theory about the origin of the world through a "first cause," etc. It has in reality nothing in common with a rational explanation of the universe. It arises out of the confrontation with the life-giving, sovereign God, and the relationship between God and man is determined by this encounter.
>
> . . . .
>
> It is, therefore, of fundamental importance to emphasize that faith's affirmations about creation do not imply a theoretical proposition about the origin of the universe, but rather a religious statement about the nature of the relation between God and man.[24]

Fritz Buri gives what is perhaps the ultimate reinterpretation of creation. It is not a question of creation *ex nihilo* at the beginning of time, he says; rather, the "genuine biblical sense" of creation is "the experience occurring in one's own historicity of the unconditionedness of a creative

---

22. Hendrikus Berkhof, *Christian Faith*, p. 156. He is summarizing Karl Barth's view.

23. Emil Brunner, *The Christian Doctrine of Creation and Redemption*, pp. 35, 9.

24. Gustaf Aulen, *The Faith of the Christian Church*, tr. Eric H. Wahlstrom and G. E. Arden (Philadelphia: Muhlenberg Press, 1948), pp. 181-182.

beginning which creates order in the midst of chaotic relativities."[25]

Even Langdon Gilkey, despite his excellent exposition of the meaning of creation in his book *Maker of Heaven and Earth,* nevertheless rejects creation as an absolute beginning, a first moment in the total universe. Creation, he says, is a myth which refers not to a particular event but to "the relation of all events, and therefore of my own life, to the Source and Ruler of all existence." It can not be a statement of origins and a religiously significant statement at the same time.[26]

There are some legitimate cautions included in the references above. One is that creation is not necessarily an event "in time" as such, because prior to creation there was no such thing as time in any sense familiar to us. Time itself was part of the creation. Thus we are not sure what we mean when we say "prior to creation," since this posits the existence of time before time began. This problem is more semantic than actual, however. It is due to our inability to conceive of or formulate propositions about the eternal "pre-creation" state. This inability does not preclude our saying that the universe had a beginning, however, since this notion necessitates only a concept of the initial moment of existence and the continuing post-creation existtence. We do not have to speculate about the nature of things "before" creation in order to affirm the fact of creation as a beginning point.

Another caution is that we should not *limit* the event of creation to a single beginning point while excluding God's

---

25. Fritz Buri, "How Can We Still Speak Responsibly of God?" *Andover Newton Quarterly* (November 1967), 8:137.

26. Langdon Gilkey, *Maker of Heaven and Earth,* pp. 310-318, 348.

continuing relation to the universe. This is urged against the Deistic concept of a one-time Maker who originates the world then abandons it. This is, of course, a legitimate concern. God's continuing creative preservation of the world in existence is as vital as the initial act of creation. But it is unfair to accuse those who believe in creation as a beginning point of denying the continuing work of God. We reject the implication that one must opt for one or the other; this is a false choice! We may and we do affirm both.

A final caution is that the doctrine of creation as a beginning of the universe should not be interpreted in terms of a single cosmological theory, such as the "big bang" or the "steady state" theory. This is indeed a valid objection and should be heeded by all. It seems to be a main concern of many of the theologians quoted above; they insist that the *way* or *manner* in which the universe came into existence is not relevant. This is true up to a point. However, the concept of the manner of creation is usually confused with the very *fact* of creation. *That* the universe had a beginning is rejected along with any particular theory of *how* it began. But these are not the same thing. One can affirm the former without committing himself to any version of the latter. Indeed, the doctrine of creation *ex nihilo* is above all a statement of the fact that the universe had a beginning. Also, though no one cosmological theory is necessarily required by creation *ex nihilo,* some are specifically excluded. We are referring to all theories which posit the eternality of matter, or even the eternal creation of matter, as in the "steady state" theory. Thus it is wrong to say that creation is compatible with *any* such cosmology. The fact is that the doctrine of creation *ex nihilo* is *not* a statement of the manner of creation, but it does rule out certain theories.

The whole suggestion that creation has to do with relationships and not with origins is a false choice. It is true that the doctrine of creation involves the relationship of dependence; it entails the absolute dependence of man and the universe upon God. But this is not something contrary to or incompatible with creation as the origination of the universe. In fact, just the opposite is the case. It is *just because* creation is the absolute origination of the universe that the universe (including man) is absolutely dependent upon God. The former is what makes the latter true. *Why* is the universe dependent upon God? Because it owes its very origin to him. To try to affirm dependence without origination is to posit an effect without a cause.

Creation ex nihilo in Scripture

Some may feel uncomfortable with the concept of creation from nothing because the term itself is not found in the Bible. The term *ex nihilo* is found first in the Latin version of II Maccabees 7:28, where a mother includes these words in counsel to her son: "I beseech thee, my son, look upon the heaven and the earth, and all that is therein, and consider that God made them of things that were not; and so was mankind made likewise."

Although the Bible does not use this specific terminology, nevertheless the idea of creation *ex nihilo*, including the fact of a beginning point for the universe, is taught in both Testaments. We may begin with the opening verses of the Bible: "In the beginning God created the heavens and the earth. And the earth was formless and void, and darkness was over the surface of the deep; and the Spirit of God was moving over the surface of the waters" (Genesis 1:1-2). The very first sentence—"In the beginning God created the heavens and the earth"—is an affirmation with profound implications. R. F. Weidner cites the following statement to summarize its depth:

> This simple sentence denies *atheism*, for it assumes the Being of God. It denies *polytheism*, and among its various forms, the doctrine of two eternal principles, the one good and the other evil—for it confesses the one eternal Creator. It denies *materialism*, for it asserts the creation of matter. It denies *pantheism*, for it assumes the existence of God before all things, and apart from them. It denies *fatalism*, for it involves the freedom of the Eternal Being.[27]

But does it refer to creation from nothing? Three considerations are relevant. The term "in the beginning" points in this direction. As Pohle notes, it is used without qualification and therefore can only mean "in the beginning of all things," that is, "at a time when nothing yet existed, and from whence all things date their existence."[28] Other references to the concept of beginning will be discussed below.

Genesis 1:1 also uses the Hebrew term *bara'*, translated "created." We must be careful that our claims for this word are not too strong. For example, Leo Scheffczyk says this word "means a work of God altogether *sui generis*, independent of any pre-existent material and realized without effort on the part of him who wills it."[29] This is partly true but partly misleading. Sometimes the word is used for human activity (see Joshua 17:15, 18, where it is used for cutting

---

27. Revere F. Weidner, *Theologia, or The Doctrine of God* (New York: Revell, 1902), p. 80. He quotes from *Murphy* but gives no source.

28. Joseph Pohle, *God*, p. 14.

29. Leo Scheffczyk, *Creation and Providence*, tr. Richard Strachan (New York: Herder and Herder, 1970), p. 6.

down trees). However, in the Hebrew *qal* form, it is used only of divine activity. But even then, it does not necessarily exclude preexisting materials (see Genesis 1:21, 27). Basically the *qal* form of *bara'* refers to a new and extraordinary act, the initiating of something new. As such it is the Hebrew word closest in meaning to creation from nothing. Scheffczyk makes another statement which is essentially correct:

> The term *bara* so forcefully conveys the Creator's independence of any other creative principle that this text (Gen. 1:1) has usually been taken to imply a *creatio ex nihilo*; and though such a concept is not formally expressed here, it is quite consistent with the text . . . .[30]

Thomas E. McComiskey expresses the same thought:

> The limitation of this word to divine activity indicates that the area of meaning delineated by the root falls outside the sphere of human ability. Since the word never occurs with the object of the material, and since the primary emphasis of the word is on the newness of the created object, the word lends itself well to the concept of creation *ex nihilo*, although that concept is not necessarily inherent within the meaning of the word.[31]

Dr. E. J. Young acknowledged this limitation, but he asserted that the use of this term, in view of its pregnant meaning, along with the expression "in the beginning," can only be taken to mean creation *ex nihilo*.[32]

A third consideration from Genesis 1:1 is the reference in the next verse to a "formless and void" earth. Pohle

---

30. *Ibid.*, p. 7.

31. Thomas E. McComiskey, "bārā'," *Theological Wordbook of the Old Testament*, ed. R. Laird Harris et al. (Chicago: Moody Press, 1980), I:127.

32. A judgment expressed in the classroom at Westminster Theological Seminary.

suggests that verse one speaks of the initial act of creation, and verse two speaks of the result, namely, matter in a chaotic, unformed state. Thus if the creation involved the use of preexisting matter, then we are told that God fashioned unformed matter out of unformed matter. But this seems irrational. "Consequently, the original production was strictly a creation out of nothing."[33] This point assumes that Genesis 1:1 chronologically precedes verse two, and is not simply a summary statement of everything that follows up through Genesis 2:4. Even if it is the latter, it is difficult to exclude the notion of an initial creative act preceding the existence of the unformed state in verse 2. Hence the argument has some force.

The conclusion is that creation from nothing is strongly suggested by Genesis 1:1-2.

Three specific passages from the New Testament must now be considered. The first is John 1:3, "All things came into being through Him; and apart from Him nothing came into being that has come into being." That John is consciously adapting the language of Genesis 1:1 is obvious from his use of "in the beginning" (twice: 1:1 and 1:2) and from his reference to creation (1:3). The Greek word translated "come into being" is *ginomai.* This is a quite common word, being used often of events which "happen" or "come to pass." It also is used of people or things in the sense of "become," or, as Thayer's Greek-English lexicon says, "to come into existence, begin to be, receive being." Thus it is a most appropriate word to express the concept of *ex nihilo* creation. That this is the intention here is seen from the similarity with Genesis 1:1; it is also seen from the contrast between the eternal Creator (the Logos) and all created

33. Joseph Pohle, *God*, p. 15.

things in John 1:3. Without *ex nihilo* origination, the things which "came into being" would have been in a real sense just as much "in the beginning" as was the Logos; and the whole point of the passage—the exaltation of the Logos—would be undermined.

A second passage is Hebrews 11:3, "By faith we understand that the worlds were prepared by the word of God, so that what is seen was not made out of things which are visible." The word translated "made" is again the word *ginomai*. Some have taken this passage to be a denial of creation from nothing. The reasoning is this: if the things that are seen were not made out of visible entities, they must have been made out of *invisible* stuff, but stuff nonetheless; hence the world was created out of preexisting material. But this is not the intention of Hebrews 11:3. It says the things we see were not made out of *phainomena*, that is, out of *other* things which are seen or which can put in an appearance. That is, *things were not made out of other things*. Buswell gives this strict translation: "By faith we understand that the cosmic processes were set in order by the word of God, so that not from things which put in an appearance did that which we look upon come into being."[34]

A third passage is Romans 4:17, which describes God as one "who gives life to the dead and calls into being that which does not exist." Here the two greatest works in the repertoire of omnipotence are laid side by side: calling life into existence out of its opposite, and calling being into existence out of *its* opposite, non-being or non-existence itself. There is no more forceful statement of creation from

34. James O. Buswell, Jr., *A Systematic Theology of the Christian Religion* (Grand Rapids: Zondervan, 1962), I:136.

nothing in the Bible, or anywhere. Pohle says that the expression "that which does not exist" must mean absolute nonexistence, "since the divine 'call' signifies an omnipotent *fiat,* in virtue of which Being . . . emerges from the abyss of non-being."[35]

This statement calls attention to another biblical teaching that emphasizes creation from nothing, namely, the concept of creation by God's simple *fiat* or word. This idea appears in all three of the New Testament passages discussed above, though in John 1:3 the agency of the *personal* Word (Logos) is the point. In the other passages the idea is that God has only to speak, and the world appears out of nothing. This same point is made in Psalm 33:6, 9: "By the word of the Lord the heavens were made, and by the breath of His mouth all their host. . . . For He spoke, and it was done; He commanded, and it stood fast."

One final aspect of the biblical teaching about creation from nothing needs to be discussed, namely, its emphasis on the fact of a *beginning.* This is in response to those who say that creation means relation, not origination. This idea just does not seem tenable in view of the many biblical references to the beginning of creation and the foundation of the world. In Job 38:4 God speaks of the act of creation as "laying the foundation of the earth," which certainly represents the beginning point. See also Psalm 102:25, especially as quoted in Hebrews 1:10, "Thou, Lord, in the beginning didst lay the foundation of the earth." Psalm 90:2 uses another image to indicate origination: "Before the mountains were born, or Thou didst give birth to the earth and the world, even from everlasting to everlasting, Thou art God."

35. Joseph Pohle, *God,* p. 16.

In the New Testament the terms *beginning* (*archē*) and *foundation* (*katabolē*) are frequently used in a cosmic sense. The phrase "beginning of creation" (*archē ktiseōs*) occurs, as in Mark 13:19: "For those days will be a time of tribulation such as has not occurred since the beginning of the creation which God created, until now." See also Mark 10:6 and II Peter 3:4. Matthew 24:21 has the parallel expression "beginning of the world" (*archē kosmou*). "Foundation of the world" (*katabolē kosmou*) occurs in Matthew 25:34; Luke 11:50; Hebrews 4:3; 9:26; Revelation 13:8; 17:8. Sometimes we find just "from the foundation" (Matthew 13:35) or "from the beginning" (Matthew 19:4, 8; John 8:44; I John 1:1). And of course we have "in the beginning" in John 1:1.

That the writers are intending to refer to a beginning point is seen from another more specific time indicator, namely, the use of the preposition *before* with these same expressions. In John 17:24 Jesus says to the Father, "Thou didst love Me before the foundation of the world." Ephesians 1:4 says "He chose us in Him before the foundation of the world." According to I Peter 1:20, Christ "was foreknown before the foundation of the world." See also Psalm 90:2, "Before . . . Thou didst give birth to the earth and the world, even from everlasting to everlasting, Thou art God." This clearly refers to a beginning point prior to which (the language is less than appropriate) the universe did not exist and only the eternal God did exist. Proverbs 8:22-31 also contains numerous references to such a beginning point, as Wisdom personified speaks of being the companion of the Lord "at the beginning of His way, before His works of old." Even before the waters and the earth appeared, says Wisdom, I was there. "When He marked out the foundations of the earth; then I was beside Him."

What is clear from this and the other biblical testimony is that creation was an act of origination, an absolute beginning point when God brought into existence without the use of any preexisting materials the whole created universe. This is creation *ex nihilo.*

Creation ex nihilo in Christian Thought

References to creation from nothing are found in post-apostolic writers from the mid-second century onwards. It was a part of the conscious faith of the church from its beginning. The first extant statement is from "The Shepherd of Hermas," who said, "First of all, believe that there is one God who created and finished all things, and made all things out of nothing."[36] Also in the second century Athenagoras argued that God can surely raise the dead since he created our bodies in the first place. "For if, when they did not exist, He made at their first formation the bodies of men, and their original elements, He will, when they are dissolved, in whatever manner that may take place, raise them again with equal ease."[37] At about the same time Theophilus of Antioch wrote, "All things God has made out of things that were not into things that are, in order that through His works his greatness may be known and understood."[38] He ridiculed the opinions of philosophers who say matter is eternal and the world uncreated. Such a view

36. "The Pastor of Hermas," II:1, tr. F. Crombie, *The Ante-Nicene Fathers,* Volume II, ed. Alexander Roberts and James Donaldson (New York: Charles Scribner's Sons, 1913), p. 20.

37. Athenagoras, "On the Resurrection of the Dead," III, tr. B. P. Pratten, *The Ante-Nicene Fathers,* Volume II, p. 150.

38. Theophilus, "To Autolycus," I:4, tr. Marcus Dods, *The Ante-Nicene Fathers,* Volume II, p. 90.

entails a puny idea of God. "But the power of God is manifested in this, that out of things that are not He makes whatever He pleases."[39] God's holy prophets have "taught us with one consent that God made all things out of nothing; for nothing was coeval with God."[40] Near the end of the second century (or the beginning of the third) Tertullian asserted, "There is one only God, and . . . He is none other than the Creator of the world, who produced all things out of nothing through His own Word."[41]

In the third century Origen rejected the idea that matter is uncreated. This is a view, he said, "which we believers can not share, since we believe God to have made the things that are out of the things which are not."[42] The fourth-century writer Lactantius is very explicit: "Let no one inquire of what materials God made these works so great and wonderful: for He made all things out of nothing."[43]

Also in the fourth century Athanasius spoke out strongly for creation *ex nihilo* against those who asserted the eternality of matter.

> . . . But others, including Plato, who is in such repute among the Greeks, argue that God has made the world out of matter

---

39. *Ibid.*, II:4, p. 95.

40. *Ibid.*, II:10, pp. 97-98.

41. Tertullian, "The Prescription Against Heretics," XIII, tr. Peter Holmes, *The Ante-Nicene Fathers*, Volume III, ed. Alexander Roberts and James Donaldson (New York: Charles Scribner's Sons, 1908), p. 249.

42. Origen, "Commentary on John," XVIII, tr. Allan Menzies, *The Ante-Nicene Fathers*, Volume IX, ed. Allan Menzies (New York: Charles Scribner's Sons, 1912), p. 306.

43. Lactantius, "The Divine Institutes," II:9, tr. William Fletcher, *The Ante-Nicene Fathers*, Volume VII, ed. Alexander Roberts and James Donaldson (New York: Charles Scribner's Sons, 1913), p. 53.

> previously existing and without beginning. For God could have made nothing had not the material existed already; just as the wood must exist ready at hand for the carpenter, to enable him to work at all. But in so saying they know not that they are investing God with weakness. For if he is not himself the cause of the material, but makes things only of previously existing material, he proves to be weak, because unable to produce anything he makes without the material . . . . And how could he in that case be called maker and artificer, if he owes his ability to make to some other source—namely, to the material? So that if this be so, God will be on their theory a mechanic only, and not a creator out of nothing; if, that is, he works at existing material, but is not himself the cause of the material. For he could not in any sense be called creator unless he is creator of the material of which the things created have in their turn been made . . . .
>
> Thus do they vainly speculate. But the godly teaching and the faith according to Christ brands their foolish language as godlessness. For it knows that it was not spontaneously, because forethought is not absent; nor of existing matter, because God is not weak; but that out of nothing, and without its having any previous existence, God made the universe to exist through his word . . . .[44]

In his attack on creation *ex nihilo* James Houston gives a very scanty and somewhat confused summary of the early Christian witness to this doctrine, implying that it was tenuously held and that it soon vanished.[45] For this judgment he is heavily dependent upon the likewise scanty and quite biased

---

44. Athanasius, "On the Incarnation of the Word," II & III, tr. Archibald Robertson, *Christology of the Later Fathers*, ed. Edward R. Hardy, "Library of Christian Classics," Volume III (Philadelphia: Westminster, n.d.), pp. 56-57.

45. James Houston, *I Believe in the Creator*, p. 273.

account of Arnold Ehrhardt. In his book *The Beginning* Ehrhardt mentions a few writers from the second and third centuries. He implies that the doctrine was held mainly as a basis for the conviction that the world is a sham and will pass away (an encouragement for martyrs). Referring to the mid-third century he says, "At that time *creatio ex nihilo* vanished from the *regula fidei.*"[46]

Such a representation of early Christian thought is quite inaccurate. The references cited above already show this to be the case. Other citations could be given. Pohle gives a concise survey of the literature, concluding with a quotation from Chrysostom in the late fourth century.[47] A longer survey is given by Tresmontant. He cites specific references up through Basil in the fourth century. Then he summarizes:

> Henceforth this became an accepted teaching in Christian thought, and we find it expressed by Gregory of Nyssa, Epiphanius, Ambrose of Milan, Augustine, Theodoret of Cyrus, and John Damascene. Christian thought has come to realize explicitly a metaphysical distinction between creation and fashioning, between the work of God and the work of man. . . .[48]

The last author named, John Damascene, wrote in the early eighth century. Denzinger's book of official Catholic documents lists four references to creation from nothing prior to Vatican I, namely, from Leo (447), Innocent III (1208), the fourth Lateran Council (1215), and the Florentine Council (1442).[49] The idea that this doctrine faded early

46. Arnold Ehrhardt, *The Beginning,* pp. 167-168.

47. Joseph Pohle, *God,* pp. 17-19.

48. Claude Tresmontant, *The Origins of Christian Philosophy,* tr. Mark Pontifex (New York: Hawthorn Books, 1963), pp. 45-55; quotation from p. 54.

49. Henricus Denzinger, *Enchiridion Symbolorum,* items -/285, 421/790, 428/800, and 706/1333; pp. 101, 256, 259, 338.

is false. It always has been and continues to be at the very core of sound biblical thinking.

The Uniqueness of the Christian Doctrine

We close this section by emphasizing the uniqueness of the biblical witness to creation from nothing. It is of course possible that the human mind can conceive the idea of creation from nothing even without revelation. After all, many of the Greek philosophers considered the idea; but they usually rejected it, since "from nothing, nothing comes." Arnold Ehrhardt says he has found four Greek sources affirming creation from nothing, but these lone suggestions were not taken seriously by their contemporaries. A more typical response was that if the world is created from nothing, then it too is nothing, a sham.[50]

In his book about myths of creation, Charles Long has a whole chapter on myths of "Creation from Nothing," including of course Genesis 1. Some of the language is quite surprising, and may reflect either vestiges of the original knowledge of creation or influence from biblical sources. A closer look shows that most of the myths are not really true *ex nihilo* concepts, though. For instance, the *Rig Veda* hymn seems to be no more than the standard pantheistic emanation from the primordial One.[51] In the Zuni myth the creator forms the universe out of himself.[52] In the Maya

50. Arnold Ehrhardt, *The Beginning*, p. 166.

51. Charles H. Long, *Alpha: The Myths of Creation* (New York: Collier Books, 1969), pp. 173-174; see the translation in Barbara Sproul, ed., *Primal Myths: Creating the World* (San Francisco: Harper and Row, 1979), pp. 183-184. Sproul calls this "one of the most profound and sophisticated of creation myths."

52. Charles Long, *Alpha*, p. 191.

and Maori myths the deity is already surrounded by a womb of dark water when he begins to create.[53]

The point is that a doctrine of pure *ex nihilo* creation is rare indeed. The possible exceptions mentioned here are little-known and non-influential exceptions to the rule, a rule well-stated by Brunner: "No philosophy—save that which begins with revelation and to which usually the very name of philosophy is denied—contains the idea of Creation, in the sense of *creatio ex nihilo*."[54]

A Free Act

The second element included in most definitions of creation is that it is a *free act* of God. This means that God freely chose to create and was not under any constraint or compulsion of any kind. He did not have to create; he did so only because he wanted to.

Free or Necessary?

A number of world views picture the relation between God and the world as a necessary one. This is especially true of many pantheistic views. For example, in Neo-Platonism the procession of the world from the One (via *Nous* and Soul) is necessary and eternal. It is a non-conscious, spontaneous act without any willing or planning or choice.[55]

Even within Christendom popular theology often describes God as *needing* to create for one reason or another. Sometimes God is pictured as being lonely and needing companionship: "I'm lonely! I'll make me a world!" Creation

---

53. *Ibid.*, pp. 174-179.

54. Emil Brunner, *The Christian Doctrine of Creation and Redemption*, p. 12.

55. A. H. Armstrong, *Plotinus* (New York: Collier Books, 1962), pp. 30-31.

is thus the conscious act of a personal God (unlike pantheism), but it is an act necessitated by some imperfection within the divine nature. A more common scenario is to depict God as having to create not from the emptiness of loneliness but from the fullness of love. God is seen as simply bursting with a superabundance of goodness and love, and he just has to create the world as an outlet for this love. For instance, H. Martensen says,

> . . . In a certain sense one may say that God created the world in order to satisfy a want in Himself; but the idea of God's love requires us to understand this want as quite as truly a *superfluity*. For this lack in God is not, as in the God of Pantheism, a blind hunger and thirst after existence, but is identical with the inexhaustible riches of that liberty which can not but will to reveal itself.[56]

Alexander Campbell says that God created from the "necessity" of love, in order to "find a vent for his goodness," a "vent for the communication of blessedness."[57]

An extreme expression of this kind of thinking is found in the writings of C. S. Lovett, who says that God "desperately . . . loves us and needs our love in return." God doesn't have everything he needs. Lovett continues,

> I hope you won't be offended, but here are some things I feel are genuine needs of God:
>
> 1. He needs to be loved for WHO He is.
> 2. He needs attention and praise.
> 3. He needs to be comforted at times.
> 4. He needs affection.

---

56. H. Martensen, *Christian Dogmatics*, tr. William Urwick (Edinburgh: T. & T. Clark, 1898), p. 114.

57. Alexander Campbell, "Theology, Natural and Revealed," *The Millennial Harbinger*, Fourth Series, Volume III (May 1853), pp. 287-288.

5. He needs to feel wanted.
6. He needs to feel included in what we do and not left out.
7. He needs to feel needed.

> We're so conditioned to the fact that God is almighty and all powerful, it is hard for us to think of Him as needing anything. . . . But without any profound reasoning, can you imagine what it would be like to be a God of love with no one to LOVE? That would be horrible. That's why God made us in the first place. As the GREAT LOVER, He needs people to love and to be loved by him in return.[58]

In another place Lovett says, "God was not out of work when He made man. He was lonesome," so He created man "to satisfy His need for company." "God was hungry for fellowship."[59]

Such thinking is false; it is totally unsupported by Scripture. God has no lack or internal pressure that requires him to create. Loneliness and love are not problems for God because God is tri-personal (i.e., trinitarian). We must not think of God as existing even prior to creation as a single, lone person in splendid isolation. The Father, the Son, and the Holy Spirit (as we now know them) existed together in a completely satisfying relationship of mutual love.

Thus the creation was God's free choice, a choice motivated only by desire and not by need. God did not *have* to create, but he *wanted* to create. Thus it was his freely-willed choice to create rather than not to create at all; it was also his freely-willed choice to create this particular

---

58. C. S. Lovett, "Why You Should Minister to the Lord!" *Personal Christianity* (October 1978), 18:3.

59. C. S. Lovett, *Jesus Wants You Well!* (Baldwin Park, Cal.: Personal Christianity, 1973), pp. 58-59.

world rather than some other one. *Whatever* God does he does because he wants to and not because he has to: "Our God is in the heavens; He does whatever He pleases" (Psalm 115:3). He "works all things after the counsel of His will" (Ephesians 1:11). This freedom to choose is specifically applied to creation: "Worthy art Thou, our Lord and our God, to receive glory and honor and power; for Thou didst create all things, and because of Thy will they existed, and were created" (Revelation 4:11).

The Purpose of Creation

Since creation is a free act of God, it is appropriate to ask concerning the *purpose* for which God decided to create. We have said that God was motivated by desire. By this we do not mean that there arose within God some spontaneous emotional longing which could only be filled by creating. This would be no different from creating on account of need. We mean rather that God determined to create; he decided that he wanted to create. It was a freely-arrived-at, conscious decision. The question here has to do with the purpose for which God wanted to create. What did he desire or plan to accomplish by this act?

In general there are two approaches to answering this question. One says that God created for the sake of the creature; the other says that God created for his own sake. Many have opted for the former approach because they are afraid that the latter view speaks of selfishness or of weakness on God's part. It seems egoistic and vain for God to create simply for his own glory; thus (it is said) he must have created only to shower his love and goodness upon his creatures.

Our view is that both of these ends are involved in creation. God created for the sake of his *goodness* and for the sake of his *glory*. We must say, however, that the latter is the primary end while the former is only the secondary end.

It is true that God created to express his goodness and to share his love with creatures made in his own image. This theme has found expression in Christian thought almost from the beginning. In the third century Origen said,

> . . . God, the Creator of all things, is good, and just, and all-powerful. When He in the beginning created those beings which He desired to create, i.e., rational natures, He had no other reason for creating them than on account of Himself, i.e., His own goodness.[60]

Augustine said, "God made what was made not from necessity, nor for the sake of supplying any want, but solely from His own goodness."[61] Also "It is enough for the Christian to believe that the only cause of all created things . . . is the goodness of the Creator, the one true God."[62]

It is generally agreed that the ultimate recipient of God's goodness in creation is the rational creature made in his own image with the ability to receive this goodness and acknowledge God as its source. T. F. Torrance says,

> . . . What we can not understand is that God who has no need of the world should have reason to create such a rational world, yet it is that reason hidden deep in God that

60. Origen, "De Principiis," II.ix.6, tr. Frederick Crombie, *The Ante-Nicene Fathers,* Volume IV, ed. Alexander Roberts and James Donaldson (New York: Charles Scribner's Sons, 1913), pp. 291-292.

61. Augustine, "The City of God," XI:24, tr. Marcus Dods, *Basic Writings of Saint Augustine,* Volume II, ed. Whitney J. Oates (New York: Random House, 1948), p. 166.

62. Augustine, "The Enchiridion," IX, tr. J. F. Shaw, *The Works of Aurelius Augustine,* Volume IX, ed. Marcus Dods (Edinburgh: T. & T. Clark, 1873), p. 181.

> ultimately lies behind all the reasonableness of the created order. In so far as that reason is disclosed in the incarnation, it is to be equated with the sheer mystery of God's love which knows no reason beyond its own ultimateness as the love that God is. That is to say, the reason for the creation is theologically traced back to the free, ungrudging will of God's love to create a reality other than himself which he correlates so closely with himself that it is made to reflect and shadow forth on its contingent level his own inner rationality and order. . . .[63]

Noting that only God is pure *agape* (love), Hugh Silvester says, "Indeed that impossible question 'Why did God create at all?' might conceivably receive an answer in the statement 'God is *agape*.' Loving and creating are both outwardgoing activities." So, says Silvester, God created: "the 'stuff' itself, monomers and polymers, inorganic, vegetation, fishes, birds, mammals, vertebrates and invertebrates, reptiles and insects. . . . But where should He finish? This matter could not be complete until He made a creature that could return His *agape*."[64]

Scripture teaches that God created the physical universe for man's good. After preparing the earth as a home for man, God created man himself (male and female) to subdue it and rule over it (Genesis 1:28-30). Nature was made to serve man. Robert Milligan states this point well:

> God's favor to man is further manifested in the fact, that for his special benefit the whole earth, with all its rich treasures of mineral, vegetable, and animal wealth, was provided.

63. T. F. Torrance, *Divine and Contingent Order* (New York: Oxford University Press, 1981), p. 35.

64. Hugh Silvester, *Arguing with God* (Downers Grove, Ill.: InterVarsity Press, 1971), p. 59.

> For him, all the matter of the Earth was created in the beginning. For him, all the gold, and silver, and copper, and iron, and granite, and marble, and coal, and salt, and other precious minerals and fossils were treasured up . . . . For him, the light and the atmosphere were produced. For him, the world was clothed with grass, and fruits, and flowers. For him, the Sun rose and set in the firmament, and the stars performed their apparent daily and yearly revolutions. For him, the sea and the land were filled with living creatures, and the air was made vocal with the sweet voices of birds. All these things were provided for the good and happiness of man; and then he was himself created to enjoy them. . . .[65]

Speaking of the bounty of this world, Paul says that God "richly supplies us with all things to enjoy" (I Timothy 6:17). James speaks of the good things and perfect gifts which God bestows upon us (James 1:17). See Acts 14:17: God's goodness in nature satisfies our hearts with food and gladness.

The goodness that motivated God to create bestows upon us much more than the treasures of nature. In the ultimate outpouring of goodness God gives us himself in fellowship. This is why he has made creatures in his own image, i.*e*., personal beings who can know him and respond to him in an I-Thou relationship. Thus the blessings of nature are not just for us to enjoy as if this enjoyment were an end in itself. We are to enjoy them specifically as gifts of God's love. That is to say, we are ultimately to *enjoy the Giver himself*. Even apart from or in the absence of things of this world, we are to enjoy God just for himself; we are to rejoice in our knowledge of God and our relationship with Him.

---

65. Robert Milligan, *An Exposition and Defense of the Scheme of Redemption* (St. Louis: Bethany Press, 1962 printing), p. 36. Italics omitted.

> . . . Though the fig tree should not blossom, and there be no fruit on the vines, though the yield of the olive should fail, and the fields produce no food, though the flock should be cut off from the fold, and there be no cattle in the stalls, yet I will exult in the Lord, I will rejoice in the God of my salvation. The Lord God is my strength, and He has made my feet like hinds' feet, and makes me walk on my high places (Habakkuk 3:17-19).

The Psalmist says that his one desire is "all the days of my life, to behold the beauty of the Lord" (Psalm 27:4). "I will go to the altar of God," he says—"to God my exceeding joy" (Psalm 43:4).

For the sake of his goodness, then, God created the world, i.e., in order to bless the hearts of rational creatures with the goodness of his own love. But we disagree with those who say that this was the *only* reason why God created. To this we must add that God created for the sake of his glory, that he might both manifest his glory in creation and be glorified by it. Indeed, this is the *main* purpose of creation.

As we have noted, some think that such a motive is unworthy of God, as if this were pure egoism and vanity. But we must remember that God is *God* and not man. Just because he is *God,* the all-powerful and sovereign source of all that exists, he *deserves* the praise and honor and satisfaction that he receives from finite creatures. In receiving glory and honor from his creatures, he is not usurping a place that is not rightfully his. The very fact of *ex nihilo* creation makes this so. If he were simply one among other beings existing co-eternally, then such a motive might be presumptuous. But not so for the Creator: "Worthy art Thou, our Lord and our God, to receive glory and honor and power; for Thou didst create all things, and because of Thy will they existed and were created" (Revelation 4:11). The Creator owes us nothing; we owe him everything. "For from Him and through Him and to Him are all things. To Him be the glory forever. Amen" (Romans 11:36).

That all of God's acts are ultimately for the sake of his glory is clearly seen in Scripture. In relation to various deeds God says, "I shall be sanctified" (Ezekiel 38:16); "I glorify Myself" (Ezekiel 39:13); "I shall set My glory among the nations" (Ezekiel 39:21); "I have created for My glory" (Isaiah 43:7); I act "for my holy name" (Ezekiel 36:22). "For my own sake, for My own sake, I will act," says the Lord; "For how can My name be profaned? And My glory I will not give to another" (Isaiah 48:11). "I shall magnify Myself, sanctify Myself, and make Myself known in the sight of many nations; and they will know that I am the Lord" (Ezekiel 38:23). We exist "to the praise of His glory" (Ephesians 1:12, 14).

This applies especially to creation. All things are *through* God and *for* God (Hebrews 2:10; see Romans 11:36). As Louis Berkhof says, "the true end of creation" is "not in anything outside of God, but in God Himself, more particularly in the external manifestation of His inherent excellency."[66] Berkhof stresses the idea of manifestation: God created primarily not to receive glory but to manifest or declare his glory. "The heavens are telling of the glory of God; and their expanse is declaring the work of His hands" (Psalm 19:1). Certainly God's glory is displayed in the creation. Even the gifts of nature that bless man's heart are a witness to God (Acts 14:17). This is why we look upon the outpouring of goodness as a secondary purpose of creation; it

66. Louis Berkhof, *Systematic Theology*, p. 136.

serves the greater purpose of manifesting the glory of the Creator.

At this point we may express disagreement with Berkhof over a small point. Berkhof says God's primary end in creation is to manifest his glory and not to receive glory. The latter is a subordinate end.[67] It seems to me, however, that Berkhof is just being overly sensitive to the criticism that the latter purpose as the supreme end of creation would be selfishness on God's part. It seems clear from Scripture that God wants to receive glory from the moral creatures made in his own image, and that this is the primary purpose for creation.

We must remember that whatever God receives from creation, he does not receive it because he needs it but because he has determined to want it. As such God has created just for the joy and satisfaction which he himself receives from the works of his own hands. The world is here not just for man to enjoy, but for the Maker to enjoy as well. Even if there were not moral creatures included in the universe, God would still receive a measure of pleasure from it. At various stages in the process of creation we are told that "God saw that it was good" (Genesis 1:10, 12, 18, 21, 25). In the midst of the great poetic description of creation in Psalm 104, the Psalmist cries out, "Let the glory of the Lord endure forever; let the Lord be glad in His works" (Psalm 104:31). God tends his world as a gardener tends his plot (Job 36-41); he cares about it even when man's destiny is not the issue. He sometimes sends rain just "for His world" (Job 37:13); he determines "to bring rain on a land without people, on a desert without a man in it, to satisfy the

67. *Ibid.*, pp. 136-137.

waste and desolate land, and to make the seeds of grass to sprout" (Job 38:26-27).

Thus it would seem to be too extreme to say, as Pohle does, that "a purely material world without rational denizens would be repugnant."[68] However, it is definitely true that God's highest purpose in creation—to be glorified—is fulfilled in the highest way through the creation of persons in his own image, personal beings who can acknowledge God's glory as manifested in his works and who can praise and adore him on account of it. Without the presence of rational creatures, the universe would be like a book with no reader, a voice with no one to hear, a beautiful house with no inhabitant.[69] Thus says Isaiah 45:18, God "formed the earth and made it, He established it and did not create it a waste place, but formed it to be inhabited." That his highest purpose is to receive glory from these inhabitants is seen in Jesus' command in Matthew 6:33, "But seek first His kingdom and His righteousness; and all these things shall be added to you." God's "kingdom" (*basileia*) in its basic sense is his *kingship*, his dominion, his lordship, his *glory*. Thus Jesus says that our highest goal ("Seek *first*") is to see that God's kingship and glory are exalted in our deeds and words.[70] The things that contribute to our own good ("all these things" —see verses 25-32) are secondary. The same is seen in Paul's exhortation in I Corinthians 10:31, "Whether, then, you eat or drink or whatever you do, do all to the glory of God." The identification of "Love the Lord your God" as

68. Joseph Pohle, *God*, p. 86.

69. *Ibid.*

70. See Jack Cottrell, *His Way*, 2 ed. (Cincinnati: Standard Publishing, 1979), pp. 89ff.

the greatest of all commandments (Matthew 22:36-37) points in the same direction. God's highest purpose of creation is achieved when his rational creatures are seeking above all else to please him. On account of sin, this purpose will be finally achieved only in the *new* creation, when *all* the inhabitants of the new earth by God's grace will be seeking only to glorify him forever.

> For behold, I create new heavens and a new earth; and the former things shall not be remembered or come to mind. But be glad and rejoice forever in what I create; for behold, I create Jerusalem for rejoicing, and her people for gladness. I will also rejoice in Jerusalem, and be glad in My people. . . (Isaiah 65:17-19).

Surely what is achieved in the new creation can be identified as God's main purpose in the original creation. (See II Corinthians 5:5.) As Lightner says, "The biblical testimony seems clear enough. God created all things, including man, to display His glory and that through the manifestation of His glory He might receive praise and honor."[71]

We have seen that the purpose of creation is twofold. God created primarily for the sake of his glory, and secondarily for the sake of his goodness. In this light we can understand why the Westminster catechisms began with the question "What is the chief end of man?" and gave the answer "To glorify God, and to enjoy Him for ever."[72]

Visible and Invisible

The last element appearing in the various definitions of creation is the reference to the "whole visible and invisible

---

71. Robert P. Lightner, *The First Fundamental: God* (Nashville: Thomas Nelson, 1973), p. 41.

72. "The Shorter Catechism," *The School of Faith*, ed. and tr. T. F. Torrance (London: James Clarke & Co., 1959), p. 263. The language of the "Larger Catechism" is just slightly expanded (p. 185).

universe." This is taken from Colossians 1:16, "For in Him all things were created, both in the heavens and on earth, visible and invisible, whether thrones or dominions or rulers or authorities—all things have been created through Him and for Him." The visible universe refers to the physical world of our own existence; the invisible universe refers primarily to the spiritual world of angels. Both were created by God.

The Visible Universe

The entire physical universe, organic and inorganic, came into existence by means of God's *ex nihilo* creation. This does not mean that each individual item in the universe, i.e., each original butterfly, dog, or pine tree, was created out of nothing. It means that every single atom or every individual electron which exists, out of which the larger items are made, has come into existence out of nothing through God's creative act. This is called the *primary creation*. Larger items, from molecules to galaxies, are God's creation in the sense that the very essence of which they are composed was brought into being by God. The configuration and arrangement of matter into the organized universe, as described in Genesis 1, can also be called "the creation" in a broader sense of the term. This is sometimes called *secondary creation*. As we have noted earlier, it is not necessary for the purpose of this book to deal with the question of the six days of Genesis or the question of evolution versus creation (in the secondary sense).

"In the beginning God created the heavens and the earth" (Genesis 1:1). In this verse and in many other places the term *heavens* refers not to heaven as the dwelling-place of God but to "the heavens above" in the sense of the cosmos: the moon, the planets, the stars, the galaxies. It refers to the rest of the universe, as compared with the earth. See Genesis 2:1, 4; Psalms 8:3; 19:1. The whole universe, the whole cosmos is the creation of God. This is a staggering thought, especially when we consider just a few of the facts about the size of the cosmos. For instance, our sun is just one of a total of around 100 billion stars in the Milky Way galaxy. It is estimated that there are nearly 100 billion galaxies within the observable universe. Our galaxy is approximately 100,000 light-years wide (a light year is about 5,865,696,000,000 miles). The average distance between neighboring galaxies is 10 million light-years. The magnitude of the act of creation is simply beyond our comprehension, "for He spoke, and it was done"! (Psalm 33:9).

It is generally thought that God created not only the matter from which physical entities are composed, but also the space-time continuum in which matter exists. This is probably the case, though it is very difficult for our finite minds to conceive of existence apart from time and space. We should also consider the probability that time and space are not characteristics just of the physical universe but of created existence as such, both physical and spiritual. Thus even angels to some degree are subject to limitations of time and space, and human beings will always be time-space creatures just because they will always be *creatures*.

The Invisible Universe

The invisible universe is the world of spiritual realities as distinguished from physical. This includes the souls or spirits of human beings, which are at home within the physical universe but are not made of the physical stuff of the universe. This also includes the whole world of angels, both good and bad. This invisible universe is part of the creation of God.

We must be careful about the use of terms in this connection. We should especially note that the terms *natural* and *supernatural* are not the exact equivalents of *physical* and *spiritual*. The natural universe contains both physical and spiritual realities, the latter being the spiritual natures of human beings. The human spirit is not supernatural. We must also be careful not to use either the term *spiritual* or the term *supernatural* to refer to some supposed sphere or realm where both God and created angelic spirits are equally at home. Sometimes we use the expressions "the spiritual realm" or "the supernatural" in such a manner, as if God and angels exist somehow on the same plane. But this is not the case. When God brought the angels into existence, even if this were before he created the physical universe, he was causing to exist a whole order of being different from himself. Though angels are spirit and God is Spirit, they are not metaphysically equivalent. Angels are *created, finite* spirits, and thus subject to at least some of the limitations of space and time. Thus the creation of the angels required the creation of some kind of "spiritual space," a spiritual realm with no prior existence, inhabited by the angelic hosts and co-existing with physical space. (It may be that the term *heavens* sometimes refers to this spiritual sphere, as in Colossians 1:16.) If this sphere is referred to as *supernatural*, then the exclusive sphere of God's existence should be called the *divine*. Some prefer to reserve the term *supernatural* for God and to call the angelic world *supra-natural*. There is no standard use of these terms, however. The important point is to remember that both the natural world and the sphere of created angelic spirits have been created by God and are distinct from the divine plane of existence.

The rest of this discussion will be devoted to the angelic world. We stress again the fact that all angels are created. This means that they can not properly be worshiped (Revelation 19:10; 22:8-9). It also means that they are not infinite, i.e., they do not have the attributes of omniscience and omnipresence. Though their knowledge and spatial mobility far exceed that of human beings, they do not know everything nor can they be everywhere at the same time. This applies also to the fallen angels, including Satan. It is important to remember this.

We do not have much information about the creation of the angels. Whether they were created at the same time as the physical universe or sometime before is not clear. We know that angels were present and that the angelic fall had already occurred by the time we get to Genesis 3. John 8:44 suggests that this had already occurred even before the creation of the physical universe, since Satan is described as "a murderer from the beginning." We can not be dogmatic about this, however. The number of angels is also uncertain, though it is very large. John says that he saw at one time "thousands upon thousands, and ten thousand times ten thousand" (Revelation 5:11, NIV).

Angels are sometimes referred to as *spirits* (I Kings 22:21; Zechariah 6:5; Luke 8:29; Hebrews 1:14). This means that they are incorporeal; they do not have physical bodies such as human beings have. Whether they have certain shapes or something resembling bodies in their own sphere is not clear. That they are spirits also means that they are moral creatures made in God's image. The fact that they are (or were) capable of sinning means that they are free moral creatures just as man is. See II Peter 2:4.

The word *angel* literally means "messenger." The term can be used in a generic sense for any messenger of any kind. For instance, the word occurs twice in Malachi 3:1. The first time it refers prophetically to John the Baptist; the second time it refers to the Messiah himself. The created spiritual beings we usually call angels were created to serve as God's messengers, doing whatever he commissions and empowers them to do. They simply carry out his will.[73] The variety of their functions probably accounts for the variety of the names applied to angels, such as cherubim, seraphim, principalities, powers, thrones, dominions, and archangels. Some of these names also refer to rank. An archangel is a chief angel; Michael is the only one specifically so named in Scripture (Jude 9).

We know that some angels sinned (II Peter 2:4). This includes Satan, who was probably an archangel on a level with Michael (Jude 9; Revelation 12:7). The angels who sinned with him are probably the demons or evil spirits who are now *his* angels (Matthew 25:41). They are apparently confirmed in their sin and are condemned already (II Peter 2:4; Jude 6), but they are allowed to work in opposition to God's purpose for man up until the last day (Revelation 20:7-10). Of course they work within the sovereign control of God and within the limitation imposed by him.

The angels who did not sin are apparently confirmed in their holiness and will continue to serve God forever and ever.

73. See Louis Berkhof, *Systematic Theology*, pp. 147-148, for a brief description of their duties.

THE BIBLICAL DATA

Thus far in this chapter we have concentrated on the meaning of the concept of creation. We have drawn upon biblical data insofar as it has been necessary to explain the concept. We have not yet, however, gained a sufficient impression of the depth and breadth of the biblical emphasis on creation. Thus in this section our purpose is to draw together the mass of Scripture pertaining to the fact of creation and the description of God as Creator. We will see that the doctrine of creation is not an incidental aspect of God's truth nor a seldom-mentioned fact; it is rather one of the main themes in Scripture.

The Creation

Numerous passages of Scripture affirm the fact of creation. Most of these echo the first verse of the Bible in that they mention the creation both of the heavens above and the earth with its divisions, e.g., the sea, the dry land, the mountains, or vegetation. The following is a medley of references simply stating the fact that God created the universe.

> In the beginning God created the heavens and the earth (Genesis 1:1).
>
> In six days the Lord made the heavens and the earth, the sea and all that is in them (Exodus 20:11).
>
> In six days the Lord made heaven and earth (Exodus 31:17).
>
> O Lord, the God of Israel, who art enthroned above the cherubim, Thou art the God, Thou alone, of all the kingdoms of the earth. Thou hast made heaven and earth (II Kings 19:15; Isaiah 37:16).
>
> For all the gods of the peoples are idols, but the Lord made the heavens (I Chronicles 16:26; Psalm 96:5).

Thou alone art the Lord. Thou hast made the heavens, the heaven of heavens with all their host, the earth and all that is on it, the seas and all that is in them (Nehemiah 9:6).

When I consider Thy heavens, the work of Thy fingers, the moon and the stars, which Thou hast ordained; what is man . . .? (Psalm 8:3-4).

The heavens are Thine, the earth also is Thine; the world and all it contains, Thou hast founded them. The north and the south, Thou hast created them (Psalm 89:11-12).

Thou didst give birth to the earth and the world (Psalm 90:2).

For the Lord is a great God, and a great King above all gods, in whose hand are the depths of the earth; the peaks of the mountains are His also. The sea is His, for it was He who made it; and His hands formed the dry land (Psalm 95:3-5).

Of old Thou didst found the earth; and the heavens are the work of Thy hands (Psalm 102:25, quoted in Hebrews 1:10).

He established the earth upon its foundations, so that it will not totter forever and ever. Thou didst cover it with the deep as with a garment; the waters were standing above the mountains. At Thy rebuke they fled; at the sound of Thy thunder they hurried away. The mountains rose; the valleys sank down to the place which Thou didst establish for them (Psalm 104:5-8).

Lift up your eyes on high and see who has created these stars, the One who leads forth their host by number (Isaiah 40:26).

It is I who made the earth, and created man upon it. I stretched out the heavens with My hands, and I ordained all their host (Isaiah 45:12).

Surely My hand founded the earth, and My right hand spread out the heavens (Isaiah 48:13).

Heaven is My throne, and the earth is My footstool. . . . For My hand made all these things, thus all these things came into being (Isaiah 66:1-2, quoted in Acts 7:49-50).

It is He who made the earth by His power, who established the world by His wisdom; and by His understanding He has stretched out the heavens (Jeremiah 10:12; 51:15).

I have made the earth, the men and the beasts which are on the face of the earth by My great power and My outstretched arm (Jeremiah 27:5).

Ah Lord God! Behold, Thou hast made the heavens and the earth by Thy great power and by Thine outstretched arm! (Jeremiah 32:17).

All things originate from God (I Corinthians 11:12).

By the word of God the heavens existed long ago and the earth was formed out of water and by water (II Peter 3:5).

Worthy art Thou, our Lord and our God, to receive glory and honor and power; for Thou didst create all things, and because of Thy will they existed, and were created (Revelation 4:11).

A number of passages refer specifically to the creation of man. These are listed separately below.

And God created man in His own image, in the image of God He created him; male and female He created them (Genesis 1:27).

In the day when God created man, He made him in the likeness of God. He created them male and female, and named them Man in the day when they were created (Genesis 5:1-2).

And the Lord said to him, "Who has made man's mouth?" (Exodus 4:11).

Ask now concerning the former days which were before you, since the day that God created man on the earth (Deuteronomy 4:32).

> The Spirit of God has made me, and the breath of the Almighty gives me life. . . . I too have been formed out of the clay (Job 33:4, 6).
>
> Yet Thou hast made him a little lower than God (Psalm 8:5).
>
> Know that the Lord Himself is God; it is He who has made us, and not we ourselves (Psalm 100:3).
>
> Thy hands made me and fashioned me (Psalm 119:73).
>
> But now, O Lord, Thou art our Father, we are the clay, and Thou our potter; and all of us are the work of Thy hand (Isaiah 64:8).
>
> Have you not read, that He who created them from the beginning made them male and female (Matthew 19:4)?
>
> But from the beginning of creation, God made them male and female (Mark 10:6).

A few miscellaneous details are given about the creation in addition to the simple fact that it occurred. First, God created by the word of his command. "By the word of the Lord the heavens were made, and by the breath of His mouth all their hosts. . . . For He spoke, and it was done; He commanded, and it stood fast" (Psalm 33:6, 9). All created things should praise God, "for He commanded and they were created" (Psalm 148:5). Creation was "by the Word of God" (Hebrews 11:3; II Peter 3:5). These passages are probably not a reference to the personal Logos, but most likely are speaking of the Creator's commandments of Genesis 1: "Let there be light" (v. 3); "Let there be an expanse in the midst of the waters" (v. 6); "Let the dry land appear" (v. 9); "Let the earth sprout vegetation" (v. 11); and so on. The point is that the omnipotent Creator simply willed these things into existence. (References to the creation as "the work of Thy fingers" or "the works of Thy hands," as in Psalm 8:3, 6, are anthropomorphic or figurative expressions.)

Second, God created by his wisdom. "O Lord, how many are Thy works! In wisdom Thou hast made them all" (Psalm 104:24). "The Lord by wisdom founded the earth; by understanding He established the heavens" (Proverbs 3:19). In Proverbs 8:22-31 a personified Wisdom relates her role in the creation. For instance, "When He established the heavens, I was there, when He inscribed a circle on the face of the deep, when He made firm the skies above, when the springs of the deep became fixed, . . . when He marked out the foundations of the earth; then I was beside Him, as a master workman" (8:27-30). Some have taken the term *wisdom* to be a veiled reference to the Holy Spirit, but there does not seem to be any basis for this. To say that God created by his wisdom is to say that the world is good, and that it is the best world for achieving the purposes which God had for creating in the first place.

Third, creation is the work of the Father, the Son, and the Holy Spirit. The references above to *word* and *wisdom* do not have to be pressed into service to make the point, since it is specifically stated in other places. Genesis 1:2 describes the Spirit as bringing order to the formless mass: "And the Spirit of God was moving over the surface of the waters." The New Testament ascribes creation to the preincarnate Logos: "All things came into being through Him; and apart from Him nothing came into being that has come into being" (John 1:3). "Yet for us there is but one God, the Father, from whom are all things, and we exist for Him; and one Lord, Jesus Christ, through whom are all things, and we exist through Him" (I Corinthians 8:6). Speaking of Christ, Colossians 1:16 says, "For in Him all things were created, both in the heavens and on earth . . .—all things have been created through Him and for Him." Hebrews 1:2 says that God made the world through His Son, and Hebrews 1:10 says that Psalm 102:25 is speaking of the Son: "Thou, Lord, in the beginning didst lay the foundation of the earth, and the heavens are the works of Thy hands." The New Testament emphasizes the role of the pre-incarnate Christ in the work of creation in order to demonstrate his divine nature.

Fourth, creation is a fact which we accept on faith. It was not witnessed by any observer; we do not have an eyewitness account of this event. We know it happened only because the Creator has told us so, and we accept his word on faith. "By faith we understand that the worlds were prepared by the word of God, so that what is seen was not made out of things which are visible" (Hebrews 11:3).

Fifth and last, creation terminology is employed to describe God's work of redemption. God's election and miraculous establishment of Israel as his chosen people are called an act of creation. God is called Israel's Maker and Creator (Isaiah 43:1; 45:11). God refers to his people as the one "whom I have created for My glory, whom I have formed even whom I have made" (Isaiah 43:7; see Isaiah 51:16). The redeemed in Christ are spoken of as the new creation: "If any man is in Christ, he is a new creature" (II Corinthians 5:17). "For we are His workmanship, created in Christ Jesus for good works" (Ephesians 2:10). See Galatians 6:15; Ephesians 4:24; Colossians 3:10. Speaking of redemption in terms taken from the creation itself shows us the stupendous magnitude of the redeeming activity of God.

The Creator

The Bible not only speaks often of the fact of creation; it also speaks of God on numerous occasions in a way that calls attention to his role as Creator. Sometimes the terms *Creator* and *Maker* are used as titles. God is "the Creator" (Romans 1:25), "your Creator" (Ecclesiastes 12:1), "a faithful Creator" (I Peter 4:19), and "the creator of the ends of the earth" (Isaiah 40:28). He is "the builder of all things" (Hebrews 3:4). He is "the Maker of all" (Jeremiah 10:16), "the Maker of all things" (Isaiah 44:24), and "Maker of heaven and earth" (Psalm 115:15). Concerning people, "the Lord is the maker of them all," rich and poor (Proverbs 22:2). He is "my Maker" (Job 32:22; 35:10; 36:3), "our Maker" (Psalm 95:6), "your Maker" (Isaiah 51:13), "his Maker" (Isaiah 17:7; 45:9), and "their Maker" (Isaiah 27:11).

Sometimes when God speaks or is spoken about, the fact that he is the Creator of heaven and earth is interjected in order to emphasize his power or his trustworthiness or his authority. He is God, the One who created all things. The addition of this kind of descriptive clause shows how prominent the concept of creation is in the Bible. So that this may be impressed upon our minds, we present below another medley of Bible references:

> My help comes from the Lord, who made heaven and earth (Psalm 121:2).
>
> Our help is in the name of the Lord, who made heaven and earth (Psalm 124:8).
>
> May the Lord bless you from Zion, He who made heaven and earth (Psalm 134:3).
>
> Give thanks to the Lord of lords . . . , to Him who made the heavens with skill . . . , to Him who spread out the earth above the waters, for His lovingkindness is everlasting (Psalm 136:3-6).
>
> How blessed is he whose help is the God of Jacob, whose hope is in the Lord his God; who made heaven and earth, the sea and all that is in them (Psalm 146:5-6).

Thus says God the Lord, who created the heavens and stretched them out, who spread out the earth and its offering, . . . "I am the Lord" (Isaiah 42:5-6).

For thus says the Lord, who created the heavens (He is the God who formed the earth and made it, He established it and did not create it a waste place, but formed it to be inhabited), "I am the Lord" (Isaiah 45:18).

You have forgotten the Lord your Maker, who stretched out the heavens, and laid the foundations of the earth (Isaiah 51:13).

Thus says the Lord who made the earth, the Lord who formed it to establish it, the Lord is His name, "Call to Me, and I will answer you" (Jeremiah 33:2-3).

For behold, He who forms mountains and creates the wind . . . , the Lord God of hosts is His name (Amos 4:13).

He who made the Pleiades and Orion . . . , the Lord is His name (Amos 5:8).

The One who builds His upper chambers in the heavens, and has founded His vaulted dome over the earth . . . , the Lord is His name (Amos 9:6).

I fear the Lord God of heaven who made the sea and the dry land (Jonah 1:9).

Thus declares the Lord who stretches out the heavens, lays the foundation of the earth, and forms the spirit of man within him . . . (Zechariah 12:1).

They lifted their voices to God with one accord and said, "O Lord, it is Thou who didst make the heaven and the earth and the sea, and all that is in them" (Acts 4:24).

You should turn from these vain things to a living God, who made the heaven and the earth and the sea, and all that is in them (Acts 14:15).

The God who made the world and all things in it, since He is Lord of heaven and earth, does not dwell in temples made with hands (Acts 17:24).

> Abraham . . . believed . . . God, who gives life to the dead and calls into being that which does not exist (Romans 4:16-17).
>
> It was fitting for Him, for whom are all things, and through whom are all things, in bringing many sons to glory, to perfect the author of their salvation through sufferings (Hebrews 2:10).
>
> The angel . . . swore by Him who lives forever and ever, who created heaven and the things in it, and the earth and the things in it, and the sea and the things in it, that there shall be delay no longer (Revelation 10:6).
>
> Worship Him who made the heaven and the earth and sea and springs of waters (Revelation 14:7).

With these references we conclude the chapter on the biblical doctrine of creation. We have discussed the concept and fact of creation as taught in the Bible. We have emphasized the uniqueness of the biblical doctrine as opposed to non-Christian concepts of the God-world relationship. We have stressed the *importance* of this doctrine in relation to the rest of one's beliefs. This is a crucial point, one that can not be pressed too strongly. It may truly be said that the fact of *ex nihilo* creation is the essential starting-point for a valid world view.

In the following chapter we will discuss some of the more direct implications of the doctrine of creation before turning to a consideration of the nature of the Creator himself.

Chapter Four

THE IMPLICATIONS OF CREATION

At the beginning of the last chapter we cited a statement by Langdon Gilkey that is worth repeating at this point:

> . . . The idea that God is the Creator of all things is the indispensable foundation on which the other beliefs of the Christian faith are based. It affirms what the Christian believes about the status of God in the whole realm of reality: He is the Creator of everything else. On this affirmation logically depends all that Christians say about God, about the world they live in, and about their own history, destiny, and hope. . . .[1]

This is not an exaggeration. The implications of creation are indeed mind-boggling.

When we speak of the *implications* of creation, we mean those other elements of our world view which are true because creation is a fact, those elements which would have to be discarded if creation itself were rejected. Many of these are truths we have taken for granted all our lives, even though we may not have noticed that their truth depends on the fact that we live in a God-created world.

The main implications of creation, of course, have to do with God himself; these will be discussed in the next chapters. In this chapter we will deal with the significance of creation for several other major categories, as follows: nature, man, worship, and ethics. We will conclude with a discussion of the primacy of creation in relation to redemption.

CREATION AND NATURE

Our first point is the significance of creation for the nature of the material universe itself, which we will call *nature*.

1. Langdon Gilkey, *Maker of Heaven and Earth* (Garden City, N.Y.: Doubleday Anchor, 1965), p. 4.

How does the fact of creation affect the status of nature? Would we have the same attitude toward nature if we thought it were not the product of God's *ex nihilo* creation?

Matter Is Good

We emphasize first of all that creation ensures the *goodness* of matter, the stuff out of which the universe is made. Matter is good in itself, and it is good in the multitude of its individual embodiments. God's pronouncement at the conclusion of the six days of creation tells us this: "And God saw all that He had made, and behold, it was very good" (Genesis 1:31). I Timothy 4:4 echoes this point: "For everything created by God is good, and nothing is to be rejected, if it is received with gratitude."

Such a view of nature is by no means to be taken for granted. As Hendrikus Berkhof notes, "Outside the Israelite-Christian tradition this vision is found only by way of exception."[2] It is very common to find matter condemned as evil and opposed to God, as in the metaphysical dualisms of Gnosticism and Manichaeism. It is also common to see matter dismissed as unreal, as in the Sankaran Hindu notion of *maya*, or in metaphysical religions such as Christian Science.[3] Sometimes, even when its reality is acknowledged, matter is regarded as negative, dispensable, or degenerate. Examples of this are Plato and Plotinus, though each arrives at his conclusion in a different way.

---

2. Hendrikus Berkhof, *Christian Faith: An Introduction to the Study of the Faith*, tr. Sierd Woudstra (Grand Rapids: Eerdmans, 1979), p. 161.

3. In *Science and Health with Key to the Scriptures*, Mary Baker Eddy says, "God, Spirit, being all, nothing is matter" (p. 113). "The fading forms of matter, the mortal body and material earth, are the fleeting concepts of the human mind" (pp. 263-264). Since Mind and matter are opposites, both cannot be real (p. 270). "Matter is an error" (p. 277). "Matter and death are mortal illusions. Spirit and all things spiritual are the real" (p. 289).

Over against such views the Christian says *No*! Matter is good because it is the creation of the good God. As Gilkey says, "Since all that is comes from God's will as its sole source, nothing in existence can be intrinsically evil."[4] There is nothing evil, for instance, about the human body. When the Bible condemns "the flesh" (e.g., Galatians 5:16-21), it is not talking about the body as such, but about the sinful mentality, the whole person controlled by sin. Bodily appetites, such as for sex or for food, are certainly not evil in themselves. When Paul said, "Everything created by God is good" (I Timothy 4:4), he was condemning those who forbid marriage and the eating of some foods (see I Timothy 6:17; Acts 14:17). Matter itself is not evil, nor is it the source of evil. The source of evil is ethical, not metaphysical. It is not due to some inherent weakness or lack in the creation; it is due rather to the freely-willed decisions of moral beings. Evil enters when the good things of God's creation are used for the wrong ends or are made ends in themselves, as when one's appetites become his god (Philippians 3:19).

Matter is not opposed to God, but is part of God's purpose. It is not something God has to overcome in order to achieve his goal. He made it to glorify himself (Psalm 19:1) and to be the matrix of man's existence. Thus nature serves both God and man. Though the presence of sin has distorted its purpose, God's solution is not to discard or destroy it but to redeem and renew it (Romans 8:18ff.; II Peter 3:10ff.).

From man's perspective matter is not something negative or dispensable, something to be simply tolerated now and escaped later with gratitude. The negative elements of bodily existence, such as suffering and death, are the consequences

---

4. Langdon Gilkey, *Maker of Heaven and Earth*, p. 50.

of sin; they are not inherent in human nature as such. Salvation is not the shedding of the body but the redemption of the body (Romans 8:23).

Though it may seem superfluous to most of us to insist on it, the fact of creation means that matter is real rather than illusory. Matter has an integrity of its own, a genuine status in existence, bestowed upon it by the act of creation. The difference between Creator and creature is not the difference between real and unreal. Both are real.

Matter Is Contingent

Creation tells us that even though matter is real and good, it is not absolute or ultimate; it is not something divine or sacred. The forces of nature are *natural*, not supernatural. No immanent, pantheistic divinity animates the material universe, as in Stoicism. Because it is created, the universe is finite or limited. It is *contingent*. The opposite of contingence is necessity. If something exists necessarily, then it is impossible for it not to exist or for it to exist in any other way. Only God exists in this manner. If something is contingent, however, then it is possible that it might not have existed at all or that it might have existed in an entirely different way. This is true of all created being simply because its existence is the result of God's free decision to create. Matter owes it existence to God; it is completely dependent on God.

The key word is *dependent*: whatever is contingent is dependent on something else. Creation necessarily entails dependence. As Gilkey says, "The fundamental characteristic of creatureliness is its radical dependence."[5] Matter

5. *Ibid.*, p. 56.

depends on the Creator not only for its very origin, but for its continuing existence. The One who gave it being could also consign it back to nothingness if he so desired. Such contingency does not impinge upon the reality of matter; it simply keeps us from regarding it as infinite or absolute.

Nature Is Dependable

Matter is not only dependent; it is dependable. That is to say, material existence is rational and predictable; we can depend upon it to act according to fixed patterns. It is not irrational, capricious, unpredictable or absurd, as if it were the plaything of some whimsical deity. As H. Berkhof says, "It is not a haunted house or a bizarre fairy tale. We can depend on it. We can orient ourselves in it, feel secure in it, and make plans for its and our future."[6]

It is creation that guarantees the dependability of nature. Because the Creator himself is rational and faithful, so is the product of his creation. It has been "given a rationality and reliability in its orderliness which depend on and reflect God's own eternal rationality and reliability."[7] It is orderly and intelligible; it operates according to stable patterns known as natural laws.

Science Is Possible and Legitimate

A final implication for nature is that the fact of creation has made science a possible and valid enterprise. This may come as a surprise to those who tend to think of science as being autonomous or even as being in opposition to biblical

---

6. Hendrikus Berkhof, *Christian Faith*, p. 162.

7. Thomas F. Torrance, *Divine and Contingent Order* (New York: Oxford University Press, 1981), p. viii.

faith. The fact is generally recognized, however, that the development of modern science was made possible when the implications of the doctrine of creation as outlined above finally emerged out of the shadow of certain dominating pagan influences.[8] Though we should be careful not to claim too much, e.g., that science would *never* have been launched apart from biblical presuppositions, nevertheless it is true (as Dillenberger says) that "the flowering of science did occur in the context of Christian history."[9] This was due in large measure to the acceptance of matter as real, contingent, and dependable—the very characteristics guaranteed by the fact of creation.

As long as nature is endowed with an aura of divinity, which can occur in either a pantheistic or dualistic context, there is a reluctance to probe its mysteries or violate the sacred presence with mundane investigations. Nature is too awesome for science to develop. But the doctrine of creation de-mythologizes, de-divinizes, and de-sacralizes nature. Von Weizsäcker puts it this way: "Since God now is so highly exalted above the whole world, everything in the world is of the same nature: it is a creature of God, it is not God. Thus God himself has deprived the world of its divinity."[10] Thus creation brings the world down to an approachable and manageable level. Like man, it is finite and contingent and thus appropriate for scientific investigation.

---

8. See Langdon Gilkey, *Maker of Heaven and Earth*, pp. 123-129.

9. John Dillenberger, *Protestant Thought and Natural Science* (Nashville: Abingdon Press, 1960), p. 16. It is Dillenberger who cautions us not to overstate the case for a necessary connection between Christian thought and science (pp. 16-17).

10. C. F. von Weizsäcker, *The Relevance of Science: Creation and Cosmogony* (London: Collins, 1964), p. 50.

A different kind of barrier to the development of science was the idea that nature is too insignificant to merit investigation. This view prevailed in Platonism, which dominated Western thought for centuries. According to the Platonic dualism, concrete individualities are but mere reflections or shadows of the world of forms. To learn the true nature of physical objects one must concentrate not on them but on the intelligible forms. This is done not through science but through philosophy. "Thus," says Gilkey, "science based on empirical description and analysis was impossible for Greek thought because the data of sensation were essentially irrelevant to the aim of the inquiry, which was to know the intelligible form." Over against this notion, however, stands the idea of created matter, endowed with true reality and integrity in its own right and worthy of direct investigation. Gilkey continues,

> Now the conception which effected this fundamental reinterpretation of the world's order, and so provided those presuppositions of modern science, was the Christian idea of creation. It is no accident that modern science has developed in a culture formed and dominated by this conception, for when nature was thought of as possessing an order stemming from the Creator's will rather than from its own inherent intelligible forms, then modern science became possible. . . .[11]

The concept of the dependability or rationality of nature is the other factor which opened the door to science. T. F. Torrance emphasizes this point in his book *Divine and Contingent Order.* Creation bestows upon nature, he says, both

11. Langdon Gilkey, *Maker of Heaven and Earth,* pp. 129-130.

contingence and contingent order (i.e., rationality), and "there is no doubt . . . that modern empirical science owes its existence to the injection of these notions . . . into the basic stock of ideas in our understanding of nature."

> . . . The general effect of the Judaeo-Christian view of creation was to restore confidence in the rational integrity and authentic reliability of the world of nature . . . . It was only when it was understood to have a distinctive lawfulness of its own that nature was allowed to be really natural and to supply out of its own inner form rational evidence for scientific reasoning.[12]

Creation out of nothing confers upon the universe not only an inherent rationality but also contingence, freedom, and stability—the combination of which "makes scientific exploration of the universe not only possible for us but incumbent upon us."[13] Along the same line von Weizsäcker comments that the concept of the regularity of the laws of nature "could hardly have arisen without the Christian concept of creation. . . . In this sense I called modern science a legacy, I might even have said a child, of Christianity."[14]

These concepts of the reality, contingence, and rationality of nature, all understood from the fact of creation, provided what Robert Blaikie calls the "psychological prerequisite" for the development of science. "In historical fact," he says, "it was only when mediaeval Christendom, deeply influenced by Greek thought-patterns, was released into the freedom of the Hebrew/Christian distinction between Creator and creation, God and nature, that modern science was born."[15]

---

12. T. F. Torrance, *Divine and Contingent Order*, p. viii; see pp. 26-27.
13. *Ibid.*, p. 21.
14. C. F. von Weizsäcker, *The Relevance of Science*, p. 163.
15. Robert J. Blaikie, *"Secular Christianity" and God Who Acts* (Grand Rapids: Eerdmans, 1970), p. 52.

CREATION AND MAN

We turn now to the significance of creation for human existence in particular. We have already touched on this in the previous section with reference to the material aspect of human nature, i.e., the body. What is true of matter in general is true of man's body. Here we will discuss some further implications of the creatureliness of man.

Wholly a Creature

The first point is that man is wholly a creature; every aspect of his being is created by God. This stands in sharp contrast to many pagan anthropologies in which man is a hybrid, partly of the earth and partly divine. This is particularly true of dualistic systems such as Gnosticism, in which the body is considered to be evil and the spirit a partaker of the divine nature. Some pantheistic systems are similar, e.g., Neo-Platonism and Hinduism, in which the spirits of man are literally of the divine essence. In all of these views only the divine spirit in man is the real, authentic person.

Some Christians have uncritically taken the same kind of view of human nature, depicting the spiritual nature of man as actually a part of God and thus uncreated. For example, C. C. Crawford describes man as twofold. The body "was a divine creation; whereas the spirit that was breathed into it was a divine gift." God implanted a spirit in the body when "out of His very own essence He breathed into the hitherto lifeless form all the essential elements of personal life." Thus man is twofold: "he is essentially spirit (self, ego); and spirit dwells in a body of flesh." Genesis 2:7 is interpreted thus by Crawford: "The picture here is that of the Creator stooping down and placing His lips and nostrils to the inanimate form which he had created, and then expelling an infinitesimal portion of His very own essence into it."[16]

Perhaps Crawford was reflecting the language of Alexander Campbell, who describes man thus: "Lord, what is man? Thine own offspring, reared out of the dust of earth, inspired with a portion of thine own spirit, and endowed with an intellectual and a moral, as well as with an animal nature." There is thus "divinity stirring within him."[17]

We must be blunt about this: such ideas are pagan, not Christian. Man in no sense partakes of the ontological essence of God. When II Peter 1:4 says that we "might become partakers of the divine nature," the apostle is talking about our sharing in the communicable attributes of God as creatures made in God's image. That is, we may develop the attributes of a holy character, just as God is holy (I Peter 1:15-16; see Ephesians 4:22-24; Philippians 3:9-10). Man is not divine, but is wholly created; both body and spirit are created being.

To say that man is a creature means two things: he is *finite* but *good*. Like matter in general, the whole of human existence is finite or contingent. We are not self-existent but owe our total existence to the Creator. "Know that the Lord Himself is God; it is He who has made us, and not we ourselves; we are His people and the sheep of His pasture" (Psalm 100:3). This means that we are totally dependent upon God. Such dependence should be acknowledged and confessed, and it should be a major element in our religious consciousness.

---

16. C. C. Crawford, *Survey Course in Christian Doctrine*, Volume I (Joplin, Mo.: College Press, 1962), pp. 142-143.

17. Alexander Campbell, "An Address on Colleges," *The Millennial Harbinger*, Fourth Series, Volume IV (February 1854), pp. 63-64.

To say that we are finite is nothing new to most of us; we are all well aware of the fact that we are limited by space and time. This is of the essence of creaturehood. This applies to the spirit as well as to the body. Since the spirit is created, it too is bound by the limitations of space and time. Thus it is futile for a person to seek for ways in which his spirit might escape from the "prison" of the body, as if being in a body is what limits us. This is not the case. *Being a creature* is what makes us finite, body *and* spirit.

Now this must be emphasized: though we are finite, our created existence is good. This applies to both body and spirit also. Some think that finite existence is evil as such, but this is not so. God made us finite; this is our authentic nature. It is wrong to want to be anything else. Our finitude should not be a source of despair; we should not fret over it but should accept it as the way God made us. (This does not apply to death as a limit on our existence, since human death was not an original part of authentic human existence. It is the result of sin, Romans 5:12; 8:10.) Neither should we use our finitude as an excuse for sin, e.g., "I'm only human!" Nor should we posit too wide a gulf between the body and the spirit, being deceived by the pagan idea that only the spirit is the "real man, the part that counts."[18] The body, too, is part of the "real man"; it is part of our authentic existence as creatures of God. We should also cast aside all concepts of salvation that exclude "the redemption of our body" (Romans 8:23). Bodily creation and bodily resurrection go hand in hand.

That man is a wholly created being also rules out all concepts of salvation that project divinity for man. This applies

18. John W. Casey, "Liberty, Legalism, or License?" *Christian Standard* (April 8, 1967), 102:211-212.

to the Mormon and Armstrong heresy that those with full salvation will be divine in the highest sense of the word, completely equal with Jehovah. It also applies to those who think that once we are saved we will automatically take on some of the attributes that belong exclusively to the infinite Creator, such as omniscience (cf. this false interpretation of "know fully" in I Corinthians 13:12) or eternality (i.e., no longer being bound by time). The finite simply cannot become infinite.

A Creature with Meaning

A second point is that the fact of creation gives meaning and purpose to man's individual existence. In many ways the most important questions man can ask himself are "Who am I?" and "Why am I here?" This point cannot be stressed too strongly: apart from the fact of creation, there are no answers to these questions. But in the light of creation, such questions are meaningful and answerable. This is true because creation itself is a purposeful, deliberate act performed by a personal being with a specific goal in view. The fact of creation thus ensures purpose and meaning for that which is created. God had a purpose for creating, and man is central in that purpose. Thus I can focus each moment of my life around that purpose, and I can direct my life toward fulfilling its God-given goal. I know who I am; my life has identity. I do not have to despair in the throes of Heideggerian "thrownness"; I do not have to take a chance on "creating" my own meaning *ex nihilo*. Gilkey puts it well: "The Christian understanding of creation as an act of a free and loving divine will is the sole basis for our confidence that our finite life has a meaning, a purpose, and a destiny which no immediate misfortune can eradicate."[19]

To understand the meaning of our own existence, then, we must go back to the question of the purpose of creation. Why did God create? We have seen that man was created to receive God's goodness and to give God glory. This twofold purpose is fulfilled only in a relationship of submission and fellowship. In the words of H. Berkhof, "The realization of that purpose begins to happen wherever man no longer seeks only himself, but seeks his purpose in fellowship with and obedience to God."[20]

Gilkey points out that some cultures, notably the Hellenistic and Indian, have virtually equated finiteness and evil. Their view is that it is impossible as such to find meaning in finite existence. But, says Gilkey, the fallacy of this view is exposed by the fact of creation. Though existence *is* finite, it is good and meaningful because it is the deliberate creation of God.[21] Realizing that finite existence is meaningful, we must still remember that the *source* of this meaning lies not within the finite but outside it, in the transcendent God.

In our search for the meaning of life it is important to see that creation gives meaning not just to the cosmos as a whole but to the individual life of *each person* in the cosmos. As we have seen, it is typical of some views, especially the monistic ones, to discount the importance of individual existence, which is ultimately swallowed up and obliterated in union with the One or in advancing the cosmic cause. A good example of this point is the philosophy textbook

---

19. Langdon Gilkey, *Maker of Heaven and Earth*, p. 77.

20. Hendrikus Berkhof, *Christian Faith*, p. 165. See Langdon Gilkey, *Maker of Heaven and Earth*, pp. 275ff.

21. Langdon Gilkey, *Maker of Heaven and Earth*, p. 186.

written by the humanist James Christian, *Philosophy: An Introduction to the Art of Wondering.* His first chapter is entitled "The World-Riddle," which is the "eternal question: What is the meaning of existence?"[22] That this is the underlying theme of the whole book is seen in this statement: "Philosophy's role in our lives—in fact its sole reason for being—is to deal with *meaning,* and it works with questions of meaning at all levels of experience. In its ultimate concerns it deals with the meaning of life."[23] Now, the last chapter of the book is entitled "Meaning/Existence," and we might think that after 560 pages of philosophizing some suitable answer would be forthcoming. Here is his conclusion:

> Each man tries in his personal, and perhaps desperate, way to make this short life/time meaningful. We identify with the things of our universe which are comparatively timeless—with the rock-ribbed mountains, the washing oceans, the stars, with evolution, with life itself—in order to appropriate a little part of their time-spans, their seeming immortality. Or we alleviate nonbeing by losing our selves within great causes and great principles and great people; or by becoming a part of the teleocosmic drama of our society or our religion.
>
> Behind all this is the burden of our consciousness of death. We must attempt to be immortal, to be God, and to ease the dread of non-existence.
>
> But to strive to feel one with the stars—what is this but to die? Stars die. Earth's light will go out; life may dim and vanish, here. No matter: *we are* a part, an ever-so-tiny part,

22. James L. Christian, *Philosophy: An Introduction to the Art of Wondering,* 3 ed. (New York: Holt, Rinehart and Winston, 1981), pp. 2-3. Italics omitted.

23. *Ibid.*, p. 42.

> of the infinite program of the universe. I do not deceive myself into thinking I am buying time by longing for the suns or immersing myself in life. *I am* one with the stars. *I am* one with life. I identify, rightly, with all birth and all death of all time. And when I die, I shall not need to feel as though I never was at all; but rather *that* I was, and that is enough. I was a part of it all. I remain a part of all past and all future. I am a moment within the energy-systems of motion and life and purpose.
>
> Does this ease my loneliness? Yes. . . .[24]

We may note that this statement says that the meaning of life is found in the fact that each individual life is a small part of the cosmic whole. My personal existence means nothing in itself; it is merely one dot in an infinite series of dots. We may also note that this statement actually gives *no answer whatever* to the question of meaning. It is beautifully poetic but existentially empty. The author begins his book by acknowledging the *fact* of existence and asking the *meaning* of existence; in the end he simply says the meaning of existence *is* the fact of existence! When I die, he says, the only thing I need to know is "*that* I was, and that is enough"! This demonstrates very clearly the impotence of materialistic monism to answer the question of meaning. The locus of meaning lies only in the transcendent Creator, and materialism is limited to seeking it in the finite. The search is futile.

Purpose in History

Another significant point about James Christian's pathetic attempt to wring meaning out of uncreated matter is this.

24. *Ibid.*, pp. 559-560.

He says his individual life has meaning because it is a part of the cosmic whole, "an ever-so-tiny part, of the infinite program of the universe." But these are empty and deceptive words, for without a personal Creator there can be no "program" for the universe. Indeed, Mr. Christian does not attempt to identify one. He wants us to find the meaning of our individual lives in the totality of existence, but the totality itself has no meaning!

This is the fallacy in every non-creationist's attempt to find meaning in smaller contexts of existence while ignoring the absurdity of the whole. Gilkey refers to this as the attempt to create a "small garden" of coherence "out of the wasteland of the totality of being."[25] He rightly notes, however, that such efforts are doomed to fail because "small meanings" are dependent on the coherence and meaning of the whole, and the whole has meaning only in reference to its origin in the transcendent Creator. Without creation, all "local meanings" are dissolved in the acid of cosmic purposelessness. As Gilkey puts it,

> Thus the local meanings of life float on the surface of the vast river of historical destiny whose course largely determines their possibility. The question, therefore, of the nature and direction of that river is scarcely an irrelevant one. If there is in the fundamental structure of things a coherence and a purpose that includes within its scope all the forces that determine our life, then there is some security for our small meanings, and we can safely base our life upon them—as the secularist seeks to do. If, however, these local values rest on a blind nature and an undirected history, then this necessary sense of fundamental coherence has no footing—nor does the secularist faith that these small meanings will always "be there" to make life good have any ground.[26]

25. Langdon Gilkey, *Maker of Heaven and Earth*, p. 189.
26. *Ibid.*, pp. 191-192. See also his perceptive statement on p. 195.

But here is the very point of creation: there *is* meaning in the totality of things, since all are a part of the Creator's purpose in the original creation. Not just individual lives, but the whole of cosmic history is bound up in this purpose. History is going somewhere; it has a goal. It was *created* with a goal. The intrusion of sin has altered the manner in which this goal will be reached (i.e., through redemption), but it *will* be reached. We can be sure that the omnipotent Creator is able to bring the universe to its intended end (telos) despite the negative forces that have arisen to challenge him. The biblical theme which embodies the story of how God is carrying out his cosmic purpose is the *Kingdom of God* (with "kingdom" being understood mainly as "kingship" or "lordship"). All of history is moving toward the day when God will establish with finality the universal acknowledgement of his lordship ("to Me every knee will bow, every tongue will swear allegiance"—Isaiah 45:23).[27]

Contrary to James Christian's empty words, the Christian doctrine of creation provides a real "program of the universe." Within this context my individual life has meaning. But when creation is rejected and blind chance is seen as the origin of man and his history, the only consistent philosophy combines the inevitability of cosmic death with meaninglessness and despair. This is well illustrated in the famous admission by Bertrand Russell in his essay, "A Free Man's Worship,"

> . . . That man is the product of causes which had no prevision of the end they were achieving; that his origin, his

---

27. This is not a statement of universal *salvation*. Those who are *forced* to bow only by the circumstances of the parousia and the judgment will be condemned forever.

> growth, his hopes and fears, his loves and his beliefs, are but the outcome of accidental collocations of atoms; that no fire, no heroism, no intensity of thought and feeling, can preserve an individual life beyond the grave; that all the labours of the ages, all the devotion, all the inspiration, all the noonday brightness of human genius, are destined to extinction in the vast death of the solar system, and that the whole temple of Man's achievement must inevitably be buried beneath the debris of a universe in ruins—all these things, if not quite beyond dispute, are yet so nearly certain, that no philosophy which rejects them can hope to stand. Only within the scaffolding of these truths, only on the firm foundation of unyielding despair, can the soul's habitation henceforth be safely built.[28]

The fact of creation banishes such a specter of hopelessness.

CREATION AND WORSHIP

A third point is that the fact of creation is the very foundation for our worship of God. The Bible stresses the fact that creation in itself makes God *worthy* of worship. As Psalm 33:6-9 says,

> By the word of the Lord the heavens were made, and by the breath of His mouth all their host. He gathers the waters of the sea together as a heap; He lays up the deeps in storehouses. Let all the earth fear the Lord; let all the inhabitants of the world stand in awe of Him. For He spoke, and it was done; He commanded, and it stood fast.

---

28. Bertrand Russell, "A Free Man's Worship," *Mysticism and Logic* (Garden City, N.Y.: Doubleday Anchor, n.d.), pp. 45-46.

When we consider the awesomeness of creation from nothing, what other response could we possibly make? "Come, let us worship and bow down; let us kneel before the Lord our Maker" (Psalm 95:6). "Worship Him who made the heaven and the earth and sea and springs of water" (Revelation 14:7). It is the only response congruous with creation. For this reason the attendants before God's throne cast their crowns before him saying, "Worthy art Thou, our Lord and our God, to receive glory and honor and power; for Thou didst create all things" (Revelation 4:11).

The fact of creation also makes God *alone* worthy of worship; it is the basis for our *exclusive* worship of God. Creation divides reality into two qualitatively distinct categories: the Creator and the created. Only the former is worthy of worship; it is folly as well as sin to worship anything in the category of the created. Gilkey says, "In all of creation there is nothing worthy of man's ultimate worship, for there is nothing that is not finite, partial, and transitory. The doctrine of creation is a great bulwark against idolatry."[29] No wonder Paul says anyone is a fool who has "exchanged the truth of God for a lie, and worshiped and served the creature rather than the Creator, who is blessed forever" (Romans 1:22-25).

One aspect of worship that is especially grounded in the fact of creation is stewardship or giving. God's ownership of all things is clearly taught in Scripture: "For every beast of the forest is Mine, the cattle on a thousand hills. I know every bird of the mountains, and everything that moves in the field is Mine" (Psalm 50:10-11). What gives God the right to claim exclusive ownership of all things? The fact

29. Langdon Gilkey, *Maker of Heaven and Earth*, p. 57.

that he is their Creator: "The earth is the Lord's, and all it contains, the world, and those who dwell in it. For He has founded it upon the seas, and established it upon the rivers" (Psalm 24:1-2). "The heavens are Thine, the earth also is Thine; the world and all it contains, Thou has founded them" (Psalm 89:11; see Psalms 95:4-5; 100:3).

This means that all our possessions really belong to God; we have received them from his hand to use them as stewards. "What do you have that you did not receive?" (I Corinthians 4:7). Thus when we give anything to God or to the church or to Christian causes, we are only giving back to God that which is his own. When the Israelites gave for the purpose of building the temple, David offered the following sacrifice of praise, which well defines the whole concept of stewardship:

> Blessed art Thou, O Lord God of Israel our father, forever and ever. Thine, O Lord, is the greatness and the power and the glory and the victory and the majesty, indeed everything that is in the heavens and the earth; Thine is the dominion, O Lord, and Thou dost exalt Thyself as head over all. Both riches and honor come from Thee, and Thou dost rule over all, and in Thy hand is power and might; and it lies in Thy hand to make great, and to strengthen everyone. Now therefore, our God, we thank Thee, and praise Thy glorious name. But who am I and who are my people that we should be able to offer as generously as this? For all things come from Thee, and from Thy hand we have given Thee. For we are sojourners before Thee, and tenants, as all our fathers were; our days on the earth are like a shadow, and there is no hope. O Lord our God, all this abundance that we have provided to build Thee a house for Thy holy name, it is from Thy hand, and all is Thine (I Chronicles 29:10-16).

CREATION AND ETHICS

Another area greatly affected by the doctrine of creation is ethics. The two basic questions in ethics are "What ought I to do?" and "Why ought I to do it?" These are the questions of *norm* and *obligation*. The answers to both questions are found only within the context of creation. Apart from creation there is no such thing as ethical obligation and there are no such things as absolute norms for conduct.

Ethical Obligation

The question of obligation is the question of authority. What gives anyone the right to tell others what to do? If someone says "Do this!" why should we do it? What is the ground of authority? In a world without God as Creator, there is no answer to this kind of question. There is no inherent reason why one person *ought* to do the bidding of another. The most we could have would be a hypothetical obligation, i.e., one which begins with "if." That is, *if* you want to achieve the greatest happiness of the greatest number, then you ought to do this. *If* you want to perpetuate human life, then you ought not to do that. But who says that anyone should want to do either? In the final analysis, without a Creator all ethics becomes an exercise of "might makes right": if you do not want to get hurt, then do as I say. But there is no true authority or oughtness in such a statement; it is just another kind of hypothetical obligation.

True and absolute ethical obligation is grounded in the fact that God is our Creator. When God says, "Listen to My voice" (Jeremiah 11:7), why should we listen? When Jesus says, "Keep My commandments" (John 14:15), why should we? "You should diligently keep the commandments of the Lord your God, and His testimonies and His statutes which He has commanded you" (Deuteronomy 6:17). Who says? Well, *God* says, and he just happens to be the Creator. Being Creator gives God the rights of ownership: "The earth is the Lord's, and all it contains, the world, and those who dwell in it. For He has founded it upon the seas, and established it upon the rivers" (Psalm 24:1-2). God as Creator (and therefore owner) has the absolute right to lay down the rules for his creation. It is not a right based just on his sheer omnipotence; it is a moral right. The result is that we as creatures are under the absolute obligation to do whatever our Creator tells us. There are no "ifs." This obligation is absolute, unchanging and eternal because it is based on a fact that can never be altered, namely, the fact that we are creatures of God. As the Puritan writer Stephen Charnock has said, "By this act of creation, which extended to all things, he became universal Sovereign over all things. . . . His dominion of jurisdiction results from creation." It makes no difference whether we acknowledge it or not; "God hath a natural dominion over us as creatures, before he hath a dominion by consent over us as converts. As soon as ever anything began to be a creature, it was a vassal to God as a lord."[30]

Ethical Norms

The question of ethical norms is similar to that of obligation. Who has the right to formulate the rules of conduct by which everyone should live? Indeed, who has the *ability* to formulate such rules? Who has enough knowledge to know what standards of conduct are best for human society as a whole? The fact is that every human being, since he is

30. Stephen Charnock, *The Existence and Attributes of God* (Grand Rapids: Kregel reprint, 1958), p. 669.

finite, is quite limited by what is sometimes called the "egocentric predicament." This means that everyone is limited by the circumstances of his own existence, i.e., the particular time, space, and perspective from which he views the world. Try as we might, we can never completely transcend ourselves; hence the "predicament." This leads to the idea that everything anyone says is *relative* to his own perception of things, or relative to the culture or point of history in which he lives. In view of the fact that *everyone* is so limited, we are told that there can be no such things as absolute truth or absolute norms of conduct. All ethical rules are relative; situation ethics is the best that we can do.

The fact is that this scenario is correct—*if* it is true that everyone is bound by the egocentric predicament. But here is where creation makes the difference. Since God is the Creator of this space-time world, he stands outside it, he transcends it and thus is not limited by it. God, and God alone, is not bound by an egocentric predicament. He has absolute knowledge of his creation, and absolute wisdom as to its proper ends and the best means of achieving those ends. Thus the norms of conduct which he reveals to us are *absolute*, not relative. He may, of course, deliberately limit certain commandments to particular eras or to specific people; but when he speaks his will in the form of the moral law for all mankind, what he says is absolutely binding.

We must always view God as the ultimate source of our ethical norms. The Bible calls him our Lawgiver: "For the Lord is our judge, the Lord is our lawgiver, the Lord is our king" (Isaiah 33:22). "There is only one Lawgiver and Judge, the One who is able to save and to destroy" (James 4:12). It is important to see, though, that his laws are given to us in his role as Creator. Both ethical norms and ethical obligation are grounded in creation, not in providence or redemption. As soon as man was created, the "work of the Law" was written on his heart (Romans 2:14-15) by virtue of his being made in God's image. The Creator-creature relationship, apart from any other consideration, forms the basic context for the ethical life of man.

The Christological Fallacy

We do not mean to deny the fact that the work of redemption has had a profound effect upon ethics. It has—especially in the area of motivation. But we *do* mean to deny what has become a significant trend in ethical thinking, namely, that Jesus Christ in his role as Redeemer is the true basis for ethical obligation and the primary source of ethical norms. This way of thinking may be called the "Christological fallacy." It is a serious error which must be properly discerned and rejected.

The fallacy sometimes appears in relation to ethical obligation, usually in the form of a confusion between the categories of obligation and motivation. Obligation is the fact that one *ought* to do something; motivation is the reason why he actually *does* it. What actually motivates us to obey God's commandments? Is it just the fact that we ought to? Is it the fear of hell if we do not? Is it the desire to deserve heaven? Is it our grateful love for our gracious Redeemer? It is a fact that the saving grace of God in Jesus Christ provides a new orientation for our motivation to obey. It excludes law-motives such as fear and greed, and it challenges us to obey from a loving heart (John 14:15; Galatians 5:6). But it is also a fact that the work of redemption does not alter one iota the absolute *obligation* to obey, which continues to be based on the fact of creation.

This point seems to be missed, for instance, in Stephen Mott's *Ethics and Social Change*, in which he declares that Christian ethics is grounded in God's acts of grace. How can he say this? Basically because he melds the concepts of obligation and motivation together and discusses them in terms that actually apply only to motivation. Here are some of his comments:

> But why does God have that authority over us? Why do we keep God's commandments? . . . The "why" now does not call for purely rational explanations, rather it asks why in fact you as a person seek to obey this God. It was with this question in mind that Karl Barth stated that God does not have authority over us because of a particular definition of God. We recognize this claim because God is "the God who is gracious to us in Jesus Christ." Barth here has encapsulated a central truth of New Testament theology and ethics. Our obedience to God is inextricably bound up with our reception of divine grace in and following conversion.[31]

Mott's first question, his reference to authority, and his reference to God's claim on us, all have to do with obligation; but Mott equates them all with motivation and transfers them to the sphere of redemption where they do not belong.

Mott dismisses the law and creation as being ineffective for producing right ethical conduct; this is why ethics must now be grounded in redemption. Only the work of God in Christ can move us to right action. "The authority which God's

31. Stephen Charles Mott, *Biblical Ethics and Social Change* (New York: Oxford University Press, 1982), p. 23.

commands have over us, our understanding of their meaning, and even the ability to carry them out, all stem from the reality that it is our salvation in Christ which now defines our basic identity."[32] Again we see the confusion between obligation (authority) and motivation, leading to a dismissal of creation's proper role in ethics.

An even more serious example of the Christological fallacy as it applies to ethical obligation is W. Carl Ketcherside's *The Death of the Custodian*. In this book Ketcherside rightly describes grace as delivering us from law as a means of salvation; but he goes further and declares that grace delivers us from law altogether, even to the point that no commandments actually apply to us now as commandments, i.e., we are not under obligation to *obey* them. The New Testament is a book of suggestions, and the love of God implanted in our hearts motivates us to follow them. Love replaces law. Here are some specific statements:

> Law is always external. It is always imposed from outside. It can never make man good. It can only make him wish he had been good. The coming of Jesus brought an end to law as a basis of anyone's relationship to God. Law, as a written code, was suspended and superseded by grace and truth. We are no longer governed by a written code. We are not under law, but under grace.[33]

"Faith in Jesus lifts us out of the area of written codes and shows us 'the more excellent way,'" namely, love, which is a divine principle infused into our hearts which "spontaneously and automatically responds in harmony with His will."[34] What about the New Testament writings?

32. *Ibid.*, p. 26.

33. W. Carl Ketcherside, *The Death of the Custodian* (Cincinnati: Standard Publishing, 1976), pp. 78-79.

34. *Ibid.*, pp. 89, 85.

> . . . The Scriptures are a collection of "love letters," written in familiar terms. They do not represent the will of God imposed, but the mind of God exposed. They act as guidelines, showing how Christ would react under conditions faced by saints on earth. They are instructional material intended to inform subjects how to prepare for the coming of their King.[35]

Of course a disciple of Jesus *will* keep his commandments, but because of love and not because he feels obligated to do so. "Everyone must make a choice between love of law and the law of love." "If one is obligated by his relationship to Jesus to keep His commandments, even though he is gathered up in love, he still must be under a code of laws."[36]

It is too bad that Ketcherside does not see that there is no incompatibility between absolute *obligation* to obey the Creator's commandments and a *motivation* of love grounded in God's grace. Grace frees us from law (i.e., law-keeping) as a means of salvation, but it does not free us from the obligation to obey God's commandments as an ethical code. The latter in no way impinges upon grace. To say otherwise is to fall prey to the Christological fallacy.

This fallacy also appears in relation to the question of ethical norms. As we have already suggested, God's role as Lawgiver is grounded in the fact of creation. It is as Creator that he declares his will to us. This means that God can reveal his moral law to his creatures at any time through his spokesmen (prophets and apostles), and his creatures can receive it and understand it without reference to redemption or to the Redeemer. Certainly the redemptive work of God is important for ethics, as we have seen. And certainly it is not irrelevant even with regard to ethical norms.

35. *Ibid.*, p. 99.
36. *Ibid.*, p. 132.

To be sure, the life and teachings of the Redeemer add important dimensions to our knowledge of God's will for our lives. The fallacy, however, is to think that somehow all ethical norms must be strained through the sieve of the gospels, as if only the incarnate Logos were a valid source of ethical information. An example of this is Langdon Gilkey. The doctrine of creation, he says, must be seen through the eyes of Christ; and this is "supremely true in ethics." When Christians try to discern the meaning of right behavior, "they must look only to Christ for that meaning. This is ethically what being a Christian is, namely to understand Jesus Christ to be the only clear clue to the Father's will for us." Also, "it is in Jesus Christ that the purpose of God in creation is revealed to us, and so it is in Him alone that we can discover God's will for our attitudes and our behavior."[37]

We should note the use of the expressions "look only to Christ" and "in Him alone." This is saying that Jesus Christ is the final, complete, and exclusive norm for conduct. Such thinking is not uncommon. John Drescher says, "Christ is the full and final message to us of God's will."[38] Myron Augsburger says that Jesus is "God's ultimate revelation," and that God's will for humanity is seen "fully in Jesus Christ."[39] Usually included in this thinking is the idea that Jesus actually came for the purpose of revealing a newer and higher ethic, far beyond anything that the world had known before, even through the Old Testament.

---

37. Langdon Gilkey, *Maker of Heaven and Earth*, pp. 273-275.

38. John Drescher, "Why Christians Shouldn't Carry Swords," *Christianity Today* (November 7, 1980), 24:16-17.

39. Myron S. Augsburger, "A Christian Pacifist Response" and "Christian Pacifism," *War: Four Christian Views*, ed. Robert Clouse (Downers Grove, Ill.: InterVarsity Press, 1981), pp. 59, 86.

The Christological fallacy emerges here to its fullest extent. Underlying it is the erroneous assumption that the main purpose of the incarnation was *revelation,* including the revelation of ethical norms. But this is false. The main purpose of the incarnation was *redemption.* Of course Jesus did give us revelation, including much that is relevant for ethics. But since this was not his main purpose, we should not think of the gospels as a complete and exclusive textbook on ethics. The teachings of the Creator, indeed the teachings of *Jesus* as Creator and Lord, are not limited to the red-letter portions of the gospels. Jesus said that he would give further teachings through his apostles as they were inspired by the Holy Spirit (John 16:12-15). The *whole Bible*, rightly divided and interpreted according to accepted hermeneutical principles, is our textbook on ethics. Only when we see this do we do justice to the lordship of Jesus, who speaks to us not only in his incarnate state but also as the pre-incarnate Logos who created all things (John 1:3) and as the ascended Lord whose chosen messengers speak to us with his own authority (John 16:12-15; I Thessalonians 2:13).[40]

THE PRIMACY OF CREATION

Thus far we have discussed the far-reaching significance of God's work of creation. We have seen how it relates to nature, to man, to worship, and to ethics. The discussion could be extended even further. But the last section has raised a question with which we must now deal, namely, the relation between creation and redemption. The question is, which of these is the primary framework of existence?

---

40. For a fuller discussion of this, see Jack Cottrell, "The Errors of Pacifism," *Christian Standard* (August 8 and 15, 1982), 117:4-6/6-8.

The question may be stated another way: does creation stand in its own right as an independent work of God, or is it subordinate to the purpose of God in redemption?

What we have referred to above as the Christological fallacy with relation to ethics is actually only a small part of a much larger point of view in which redemption is seen as God's primary work, and in which Christ as Redeemer is seen as the basic epistemological touchstone by which every doctrine, including creation, is known and understood. The position taken here is that this view is false and leads to a distortion not only of the doctrine of creation but of the doctrine of redemption as well.

The View That Redemption Is Primary

We must first of all describe and give examples of the view that redemption is the primary work of God and creation secondary. There are actually two aspects of this view, one having to do with the reality of things and the other having to do with how we *know* this reality. The former says that in reality redemption *is* the fundamental work; the latter says that redemption in Christ is the key to knowledge and understanding of all other works of God. Barth uses the terms *ontic* and *noetic* for these two aspects; we find it convenient to use them here also.[41]

Noetic Primacy

What is our sure and certain source of knowledge about God and his works? The original and traditional Christian answer to this question is that the revealed and/or inspired

41. Karl Barth, *Church Dogmatics, Volume III: The Doctrine of Creation, Part 1*, tr. J. W. Edwards et al. (Edinburgh: T. & T. Clark, 1960), p. 28.

words of Scripture are this source. Scripture, said the Reformers, is our "formal principle," namely, the epistemological basis for Christian faith. Many have agreed that the Bible and the Bible alone is our only infallible rule of faith and practice. But much of modern Christendom has abandoned this view of the Bible. This has resulted in the need to find a new "rule of faith," a new norm for doctrinal truth. If the Bible as such can no longer guarantee sure knowledge of God, what can? The new answer is Jesus Christ. The incarnate Christ has been substituted for the Bible as the new "formal principle" of Christianity, as the new "infallible rule of faith and practice."

Many have adopted this view as their basic general principle for all of theology. An early example of this is the book *Prolegomena to Systematic Theology* by E. O. Davies. There may be a number of lesser sources for religious knowledge, says Davies, but there is only "one infallible source" by which all the others are measured.

> The main source of material, then, in Systematic Theology is CHRIST. In constructing our view of God and man, and their mutual relations, we give the foremost place to the teaching of Jesus Christ. And by the teaching of Jesus Christ we mean firstly, and mainly, what He taught during His public ministry in Palestine about nineteen centuries ago.[42]

Among more recent examples, the most prominent is Karl Barth. His view that Jesus Christ is the only Revealed Word of God and the only source of knowledge of God is well known. We quote Herbert Hartwell's summary of Barth's view:

---

42. E. O. Davies, *Prolegomena to Systematic Theology* (London: Hodder and Stoughton, 1909), pp. 207-208.

> Again, the *Church Dogmatics* is wholly christological in the sense that in it, generally speaking, every theological proposition has as its point of departure Jesus Christ, the Son of God and the Son of Man, in the unity of His person and work. This christological concentration of the *Church Dogmatics,* and indeed of Barth's theology as a whole, is "unparalleled in the history of Christian thought."[43]

Closely akin to Barth's view and almost as influential is that of Emil Brunner. Here is Brunner's statement:

> The Christian Faith is simply faith in Jesus Christ. Therefore the whole of Christian theology is simply the explication of faith in Christ. . . . The doctrine of God, of His Nature and of his Will, of the Creation and the Divine government of the world, of man as created in the Image of God and as sinner, of the Old Covenant and the preparation for the New—all these doctrines are elements in the one faith in Jesus Christ. All that has hitherto been presented (in this book) as the content of the Christian Faith has only been possible because all this truth is derived from Jesus Christ alone.[44]

One or two other examples of the conversion of Christ into a general epistemological principle will suffice. In his 1966 Bampton Lectures David Jenkins declared that "Jesus is the key to the understanding of the cosmos." That is, to discover that Jesus is the Christ "is to discover the fact that is determinative of one's understanding of all other facts." This is "the central implication of the recognition of Jesus

---

43. Herbert Hartwell, *The Theology of Karl Barth: An Introduction* (Philadelphia: Westminster Press, 1964), pp. 15-16.

44. Emil Brunner, *The Christian Doctrine of Creation and Redemption: Dogmatics, Volume II,* tr. Olive Wyon (Philadelphia: Westminster Press, 1952), p. 239.

as the Christ."[45] In an article called "Making Jesus Central" Stuart Cook states that "true restoration involves restoring Christ to His rightful centrality." Cook understands this to include epistemological centrality. He says, "Every spiritual concept, practice, or deed must find its essential meaning and value in Jesus Christ—His identity, perfect life, atoning death, triumphant resurrection, and glorified status." In a paragraph headed "Jesus Christ: the test of all true doctrine" he says,

> If Christ is truly to be preached, then every doctrine and ordinance of the faith must be dependent on Him, His nature, character, and deeds, for meaning. It will not do to make Him simply the authority for its force or the origin of its concepts. The "doctrine of Christ" will be that doctrine which centers on Jesus Christ. . . . It must not be on doctrine *as doctrine*, but Christ that we teach.[46]

This general theological principle is of course applied to the doctrine of creation. The view often stated is that the fact and purpose of creation can only be known through Jesus Christ. Barth again is a primary example. Berkouwer sums up Barth's approach thus: "It is not possible to say anything that is meaningful about creation outside of Jesus Christ. Only in *Him* can we understand creation," namely and specifically, in Jesus of Nazareth.[47] In Barth's words, there is a "noetic connexion" between Christ and creation, and that is "the fact that the reality of creation is and can

---

45. David E. Jenkins, *The Glory of Man* (New York: Charles Scribner's Sons, 1967), pp. 35-36.

46. Stuart D. Cook, "Making Christ Central," *Christian Standard* (April 19, 1981), 116:13-14.

47. G. C. Berkouwer, *The Triumph of Grace in the Theology of Karl Barth*, tr. Harry R. Boer (Grand Rapids: Eerdmans, 1956), p. 53.

only be known with clarity and certainty in the Person of Jesus Christ. . . . Jesus Christ is the Word by which the knowledge of creation is mediated to us." We must see that "from every angle Jesus Christ is the key to the secret of creation."[48]

Emil Brunner is quite specific in his choice of Jesus rather than the Bible as his source of knowledge about creation:

> . . . The emphasis on the story of Creation at the beginning of the Bible has constantly led theologians to forsake the rule which they would otherwise follow, namely, that the basis of *all* Christian articles of faith is the Incarnate Word, Jesus Christ. So when we begin to study the subject of Creation in the Bible we ought to start with the first chapter of the Gospel of John, and some other passages of the *New* Testament, and not with the first chapter of Genesis. . . .[49]
>
> . . . It is only from this point of view that we can understand what the world is, as Creation; and this purpose is revealed in Jesus Christ. From Him alone—and not from the Old Testament story of Creation which knows nothing of Christ—can we understand what God's creation of the world really means.[50]

Similarly Gilkey says "it is because of the knowledge of the love of God gained in Jesus Christ that the meaning and purpose of creation are known." Thus, he says, "the doctrine of creation takes its peculiar stamp from the character of Jesus Christ. It is a 'Christological' doctrine through and

48. Karl Barth, *Church Dogmatics*, III/1, p. 28; see pp. 23-24.
49. Emil Brunner, *The Christian Doctrine of Creation and Redemption*, p. 6.
50. *Ibid.*, p. 14.

through, and must always be understood in the closest relation to what we know of God in Christ."[51] Nels Ferre says succinctly, "Crucifixion explains creation."[52]

Ontic Primacy

In the above examples we have seen the alleged "noetic connexion" between Christ and creation as understood by many modern theologians. But this is not the whole picture; indeed, it is only the beginning. The idea is not only that Christ as Redeemer is the sole source of our knowledge of creation, but also that the work of redemption is somehow prior to and inclusive of the work of creation. Creation serves the larger purpose of redemption. As Barth says, "Where there is a genuine noetic connexion, we can always count on the fact that it has an ontic basis. This is the case here."[53] Thus Barth describes Jesus as the beginning and the goal of creation.[54] "Everything is created for Jesus Christ and His death and resurrection." That is, "God created man to lift him in His own Son into fellowship with Himself."[55] "The history of Jesus Christ" is "the end and meaning of creation."[56] This means that from the very beginning God purposed to have fellowship with man *as redeemed* in Jesus Christ. The creation is simply a means toward that end, the first step to accomplishing the basic purpose of redemption. As Hartwell says, "Creation serves the exclusive purpose of setting the stage for the realization of God's covenant of

51. Langdon Gilkey, *Maker of Heaven and Earth*, pp. 269, 273.

52. Nels F. S. Ferre, *Christ and the Christian* (New York: Harper and Brothers, 1958), p. 226.

53. Karl Barth, *Church Dogmatics*, III/1, p. 28.

54. *Ibid.*, p. 232.

55. *Ibid.*, p. 376.

56. *Ibid.*, p. 387.

grace with man in Jesus Christ."[57] If anyone finds this difficult to understand, he must simply realize, as Colin Brown says, that for Barth "there is only one principle underlying God's dealings with men—Jesus Christ." That is, "all God's dealings with men are effected in and through Jesus Christ."[58]

Emil Brunner not unexpectedly says the same thing:

> . . . Jesus Christ, as the personal manifestation of God, is the Goal of the world, for whom, in whom, and through whom the world has been created. It is indeed for this end alone that God has created the world; that in it He should manifest His glory and give Himself to His Creation; this is the meaning of the world, and it is its goal. It is the Logos who was in the beginning, through whom, in whom, and unto whom, all things have been created.[59]

That is, God created the world just so he could manifest himself to it in the person of Jesus Christ. In a similar vein James Houston says that "Jesus Christ Himself is what the creation is all about," and that "one cannot speak of creation without reference to Jesus Christ." To see Christ "is to see the mirror in which God has contemplated the plan of the universe."[60]

---

57. Herbert Hartwell, *The Theology of Karl Barth,* p. 118. See G. C. Berkouwer, *The Triumph of Grace,* p. 53: "In creation we are exclusively concerned with the relationship of creation to Jesus Christ. By Him and with a view to Him and to His grace the world was created." Thus he summarizes Barth.

58. Colin Brown, *Karl Barth and the Christian Message* (London: Tyndale Press, 1967), pp. 116, 134.

59. Emil Brunner, *The Christian Doctrine of Creation and Redemption, p. 14.*

60. James M. Houston, *I Believe in the Creator* (Grand Rapids: Eerdmans, 1980), pp. 135, 142-143.

Another example is Helmut Thielicke's view of Christ's suprahistoricity. Thielicke declares that "the creation of the world itself has christological significance; salvation is projected in it. The love which caused God to give his only begotten Son . . . is already at work in the plan to create the world." God created "with a view to salvation"; there is a "christological background of creation." Thus redemption is not just the correction of the Fall; "it relates to the purpose of the whole project of creation."[61]

Finally we cite a very good recent expression of this viewpoint, that of Hendrikus Berkhof in his book *Christian Faith*. Berkhof understands that this view is in opposition to the traditional one, nevertheless: "Consciously we take our starting-point in the view that creation is the preamble of and pointer to salvation"; thus there is an "introductory relation of creation to salvation."[62] Creation is "the first of the series of God's redemptive deeds." "The world was created in view of Jesus Christ; God would not have created the world if not in connection with his coming and exaltation."[63]

Creation Is Primary

Berkhof notes that this reversal of the traditional viewpoint "has far-reaching consequences for the study of the faith."[64] He could not be more correct; unfortunately these consequences are mostly bad. We will now undertake a

61. Helmut Thielicke, *The Evangelical Faith, Volume Two: The Doctrine of God and of Christ*, tr. and ed. Geoffrey W. Bromiley (Grand Rapids: Eerdmans, 1977), pp. 291-292.

62. Hendrikus Berkhof, *Christian Faith*, pp. 167-168.

63. *Ibid.*, pp. 166-167.

64. *Ibid.*, p. 167.

critique of the view just described and a defense of the concept of the primacy of creation.

We assert first of all that God's original decision to create was independent of and prior to any thought or reference to the need or possibility of redemption. Thus the purpose of creation originally stood alone and was fully realizable without the incarnation, the cross, the resurrection, or Christology as such. Of course, when we use the term *prior to,* we do not mean it in a chronological sense but in a logical sense. It is the assumption of our finite minds that the eternal God in the counsels of eternity did not arrive at this comprehensive plan for the world in chronologically sequential stages. Nevertheless we must assume that there is a relationship of logical dependence among the various elements of the plan, and this is what we mean when we say "prior to."

Why must we say that God's decision to create was prior to the contemplation of redemption? Because if we say with Barth and others that creation serves the purposes of redemption, then we must say that God created the world *so that* he could redeem it. This means that the original creation, by God's design, must have been in *need* of redemption. All the imperfections of sin and human death would have been incorporated into it from the beginning. If someone says no, all of that came from the Fall, then we must say simply that God's original plan must have included the Fall—not just by way of foreknowledge, but by intention. The only way that redemption can be the purpose of creation is if the elements requiring redemption are also included within the purpose. But this seems highly objectionable in itself, as well as being contrary to Scriptural teaching that God is not the author of sin (James 1:13).

Thus God's purpose in creation stands in its own independent integrity. The purpose of bestowing love and receiving glory did not necessarily require redemption for its accomplishment. Everything God desired from his creation could have been achieved by means of creation alone. This does not mean that the original creation was *perfect* in every way. There was still much to be done in terms of "subduing the earth" (Genesis 1:28). But its future was projected in terms of development, not redemption. Even from the beginning it was "very good" (Genesis 1:31). There was nothing in it that required the further step of redemption to make it good or to enable the accomplishment of its purpose.

Why, then, was this purpose not achieved without the need for redemption? Why was redemption *added* to the total plan? Because of the sin factor. This statement must be read very carefully: the need for redemption to be included in the plan arose *only* as the result of God's *foreknowledge* of man's free-will choice of sin. Sin was not part of the original purpose of creation, but free will was. Thus this purpose involved a universe in which sin was a possibility, but not necessarily a reality. Thus in a sense God's purpose to bestow love on and receive glory from free moral creatures involved a risk, but it was a risk he was willing to take.

How can we speak in terms of *risk* for the omniscient God? Does he not foreknow everything? Did he not foreknow from the beginning that his free-will creatures would sin? Yes, but we must remember the point about logical dependence as discussed above. Even in the mind of God some things are "prior to" others in this sense. And that is the case with God's original decision to create free-will creatures and his foreknowledge that they would sin. He had already determined to create them "before" he knew that they would sin. Of course God knew (not *foreknew*) all *possible* futures that could ensue from such a creation even "before" making the final decision to create. But possible futures are not *real* futures, and we cannot say that there was foreknowledge at this point. Foreknowledge has to do with reality, not possibility. Thus God's foreknowledge of what would actually take place in his planned universe was dependent on the irrevocable decision to create this particular world. Stated another way, the decision to create this specific universe had to "precede" God's foreknowledge of what would be *the* future of this universe, including his foreknowledge of the Fall and the need for redemption. But once God had *committed* himself to this decision, even before he actually carried it out in terms of Genesis 1, he *did* foreknow its future, including the entrance of sin. This led to what might be called an adjustment in the total plan, namely the inclusion of the element of redemption through Jesus Christ. Thus redemption is incorporated into the overall plan and enables God to carry out his *original* purpose of creation *in spite of* the intrusion of sin and death.

The following chart shows the logical sequence in the eternal (pre-creation) counsels of God:

1. Decision to create a universe.
    2. Decision to create a universe with free-will creatures.
        3. Knowledge of all possible futures of all possible universes with free-will creatures.
            4. Decision to create this particular universe.
                5. Foreknowledge of the real future of this particular universe.
                    6. Decision to include redemption in the plan.
                        7. Creation.

We must remember that this outline shows only logical dependence; confusion is sure to arise if we allow ourselves to think of it as a time sequence. For instance, we should not think of God as actually changing his plan, or as making one plan and replacing it with another. There was only one plan. Nor should we think of God as first foreknowing a "real" future which never actually comes to pass (one with sin but without redemption), which would be a contradiction; and then later foreknowing the *real* future (the one including redemption).

What does this mean for the overall relationship between creation and redemption? It means that God did not create with the idea that he was just beginning a project that would simply be carried forward another step by the incarnation. He was not just setting the stage for the work of Jesus Christ. The purpose of creation is the primary, original, and independent purpose of God. Creation is thus the over-arching category, the comprehensive framework within which everything else must be fitted, including redemption. Creation does not serve the purposes of redemption, but redemption serves the purposes of creation. Creation is not just a means toward the goal of redemption, but redemption is a means toward the goal of creation. The same is true of Jesus Christ himself: he is not the goal of creation; he is the *means of achieving* that goal.[65]

Here we raise a question: if creation was for the purpose of redemption, how can we escape the conclusion of universal

65. At this point we should note again, as H. Berkhof says, that this view is the one to be found (in various degrees of sophistication) throughout most of the history of Christendom. He points out that there are still strong voices in support of this view in contemporary theology (*Christian Faith*, pp. 167-168). A good representative is the Lutheran theologian Gustaf Wingren in his book *Creation and Law*, tr. Ross Mackenzie (Edinburgh: Oliver and Boyd, 1961).

salvation? If the whole creation is somehow embraced in the more comprehensive purpose of redemption, then must not everyone be saved? If someone says no, hell will still be quite densely populated, then we must say simply that God's original plan must have included hell itself along with its population—and all this within the one over-arching purpose of redemption. Neither of these alternatives is acceptable; neither is biblical.

How, then, are Christ and creation related? Of course, as we have seen, the New Testament emphasizes his role as Creator. "All things came into being through Him; and apart from Him nothing came into being that has come into being" (John 1:3). We have "one Lord, Jesus Christ, through whom are all things, and we exist through Him" (I Corinthians 8:6). "For in Him all things were created . . . all things have been created through Him and for Him" (Colossians 1:16). God "made the world" through him (Hebrews 1:2). There are two things to be emphasized about these passages. First, they refer not to something done by Jesus of Nazareth, but to the work of the pre-incarnate Logos who *became* Jesus of Nazareth. Nevertheless, because of the continuity between the person of the Logos in his pre-existent state and the person of Jesus, it is appropriate to speak of *Christ* as Creator. Second, the references to Christ as Creator are given not to reveal some long-hidden purpose for the creation but simply *to identify Jesus of Nazareth as God.* Who *is* this Jesus? He is the one who created the universe! He is *God,* the very Creator himself! These passages are not saying anything about Jesus which cannot properly be said about God as such. All four passages say that the world was created "through him" (*dia* with the genetive), but Hebrews 2:10 says the same thing of God the Father. What about the supposedly key statement in Colossians 1:16, that all things were created "for him" (*eis auton*)? This is also duplicated in Hebrews 2:10 in the statement that all things are "for" God the Father. Here the construction is *dia* with the accusative, which in the New Testament generally denotes "for the sake of."[66] In other words, all things are created *for God*, and Jesus *is* God. To invert the whole order of creation and redemption on the basis of a phantom Christological point in Colossians 1:16 is totally irresponsible.

What, then, shall we say about Ephesians 1:10, which speaks of "the summing up of all things in Christ, things in the heavens and things upon the earth"? What about Ephesians 3:11, which speaks of "the eternal purpose which He carried out in Christ Jesus our Lord"? This does not reflect on the original purpose of creation itself, but on the *means* by which God determined to carry out his purpose once sin had entered the picture. His purpose is to be accomplished now *through* the redemptive work of Jesus Christ. This shows that we should not (and indeed we do not intend to) take anything away from the glory and majesty of Christ's redemptive work. It is only through him that God's purpose can be carried out! Praise him to the highest heavens! "Worthy is the Lamb that was slain to receive power and riches and wisdom and might and honor and glory and blessing" (Revelation 5:12)! But again let us not invert the proper order: Christ is not the purpose of creation; creation is the purpose of Jesus Christ. He came to redeem it, to put it back on the right track (so to speak) toward its original goal. And he did! This is glory in the highest magnitude, and it is glory enough. Let us not distort the whole

66. Albrecht Oepke, "διά," *Theological Dictionary of the New Testament*, ed. Gerhard Kittel, tr. Geoffrey Bromiley (Grand Rapids: Eerdmans, 1964), II:70.

structure of Christian doctrine in order to divert glory to Christ as Redeemer when he already *has* that glory as the eternal Logos-Creator.

We must now address the issue of whether knowledge of the creation comes only through Jesus Christ. The answer to this is a flat *no*. This is another aspect of the Christological fallacy, the attempt to make Christ an epistemological principle rather than the Redeemer which he came to be. Jesus' primary purpose was redemption, not revelation.[67] He *was* a Revealer, of course, and that in the highest and most glorious way simply because of who he was (Hebrews 1:1-3). But this is not the main reason for which he came. He came to die and rise again in triumph over all his enemies, and ours. Why should the latter be his principal purpose and not the former? Because only Jesus could do the latter, but God has many other ways of revealing to us what he wants us to know. This is what revelation and inspiration are all about. When God wants to reveal anything to us, such as the fact and purpose of creation, he can do so quite adequately through his inspired prophets and apostles. Thus knowledge of God and his works comes to us from God as *God*, not necessarily from God as Redeemer. It is God the Creator who tells us about the creation. Because of the reality of revelation and inspiration, the very words of God are given to us in written form in Scripture. *This* is our source of knowledge about God. The Reformers are still right: the Bible is our "formal principle," our epistemological principle. Jesus Christ is not.

---

67. See the good discussion of the distortion of this fact by modern theologians in Carl Braaten, *New Directions in Theology Today, Volume II: History and Hermeneutics* (Philadelphia: Westminster Press, 1966), pp. 11-16. See also Gustaf Wingren, *Creation and Law*, pp. 11ff.

This means that we do not need Jesus Christ in order to *understand* what creation is all about; rather, we need Jesus in order to be able to fulfill the purpose of creation. In fact, if we did not know about creation, we probably would have a difficult time understanding what *Christ* is all about. Barth's "noetic connexion" should be reversed: we understand Christ only because of the creation. Creation explains crucifixion, to correct Ferre. It is significant that redemption is often spoken of in terms of creation (i.e., God is Israel's Maker; the church is Christ's new creation), but the Bible never calls creation an act of salvation or an act of grace (contrary to the common misuse of such language).

Since the traditional approach to creation and redemption turns out to be right after all, how can we explain the radical change instituted by modern theology? The noetic reversal we can explain by the loss of confidence in the Bible as the inspired and inerrant word of God. As H. Berkhof plainly puts it, "Historical criticism has put an end to this type of thinking."[68] Or as Brunner scoffs, to begin to learn of creation by starting with Genesis is "to fall back into a 'Biblicism' which has already been abandoned in principle."[69] When the Bible was rejected as God's true word, the *incarnate* Word, Jesus Christ, was pressed into service as "the only rule of faith and practice." Of course this explains in a large measure the ontic reversal, too. But another factor has entered here, namely, the theory of evolution. With theologians becoming more and more convinced that the evolutionary model is correct, especially with regard to the origin of man, it simply became convenient to think of the (supposed) original imperfect state (primitive man, sin,

68. Hendrikus Berkhof, *Christian Faith*, p. 167.

59. Emil Brunner, *The Christian Doctrine of Creation and Redemption*, p. 7.

death) as the first step of a planned two-part operation. Creation thus was not "very good" at the beginning but was only "very good" in potential; a later act was required to bring out this potential. Thus the incarnation.[70] Such a view, of course, impinges not only on the integrity of the creation but also on the reality of the fall.

At this point we will attempt to set forth briefly how all of the factors discussed in this section fit together. When we ask the question, "What should be central in our lives?" we should see that this question must be answered in different ways on different levels. I.e., central in what way? If we mean *essentially* central, the answer is that God the Creator is central. That is, we can explain the essence of our existence only in light of the creation, and our primary relationship to God is to God as Creator. The creation-relation is the decisive reference point for the basic facts of our existence. For instance, our *knowledge* of God, as we have seen, comes to us from God the Creator. This applies not only to the written revelation of Scripture, but to the general revelation of God which comes through the witness of creation itself (Psalm 19:1; Romans 1:18ff.). Also, the *will* of God is known to us as the will of God our Creator. Thus ethics is grounded in creation, not redemption (as we have already seen). Also, *sin* against God is sin against God the Creator; this sin-relationship with the Creator is what brings about the need for redemption. These are the points that have caused many theologians, especially those of Lutheran persuasion, to see that *law* (grounded in the creation-relation) must precede *gospel* (grounded in redemption). Also, we should note that since man's essential relation to God is to God as Creator, this is the universal God-man relationship.

70. See Langdon Gilkey, *Maker of Heaven and Earth*, pp. 117ff.

All men are related to God the Creator in that all know him, all know his will, and all have sinned against him. But not all are related to God as Redeemer; this is an acquired relationship.

The question of centrality must also be asked another way. If we mean what is *epistemologically* central, then the answer is that the Bible is central. It is typical today when such a statement is made for some observers to wax hysterical and accuse the speaker of "bibliolatry" or of elevating the Bible above the Lord of the universe himself. This kind of response usually comes, however, from those who do not understand the primary role of epistemology and the difference between form and content. The question of epistemology is basic in any field of inquiry, i.e., how do we get knowledge about our subject matter? But this is only a formal question and is not in competition with the content learned thereby. When we say that the Bible is epistemologically central we mean that it and it alone is our source of knowledge about the One who is central in our lives. This is the meaning of the time-honored slogan, "The Bible and the Bible alone is our only infallible rule of faith and practice." Faith in the Bible as our source of truth about Christ does not contradict our faith in Christ as the source of our salvation.

This leads to a final way in which the question about centrality can be asked, namely, what is *existentially* central in our lives? The Christian must answer that Christ is central when the question is asked this way. This means that our strongest *felt* relationship to God is the relationship we have with Christ our Lord and Savior. He is the One whom we know most about and to whom we feel the closest. As the One who has saved us from our sins, we owe him more than we owe anyone else. He is usually central in our worship. We want our lives to be Christ-centered and Christ-honoring. Our very name is *Christ*ian. In short, all our conscious service to God is in the name of Jesus Christ (Colossians 3:17). This is the way it ought to be. But let us not demote Christ and distort truth by trying to make him an epistemological tool.

In summary we are saying that the Creator is the essential center of our lives; the Bible is the epistemological center; and Jesus Christ is the existential center.

We close this chapter on the implications of creation as we started it, namely, with a quotation from Langdon Gilkey. We remember that Gilkey speaks of creation as a "Christological" doctrine, but nevertheless he has a tremendous grasp of the fundamental importance of creation in relation to all else. We preface the lengthy quotation with this short one: "The doctrine of creation concerns that fundamental relation between God and the world on which depends the other significant ideas that make up the Christian Gospel."[71]

> Among the many activities of God, His creative activity is surely the one most essential for our existence. It is through this activity that we are brought into being, and it is this activity, therefore, that establishes our deepest, because our most essential, relation to God: He is our Creator and thus our Lord. Correspondingly, the doctrine of God as Creator is, perhaps, the most fundamental conception we can have of God. That is, creation is that activity of God by means of which we define what we mean by the word "god." It is quite natural, of course, that Christian devotion and Christian thought should concern themselves most with God's redeeming activity in Jesus Christ, for upon this our knowledge of

71. *Ibid.*, p. 41.

God as Loving Father, and so of our hope for salvation, most directly depends. Nevertheless, the centrality of God's redeeming activity to our life and thought should not blind Christians to the divine work of creation, which, if not so close to our hearts, is just as significant for our existence and just as important if we are to think rightly about God. Through God's redeeming works we know that He is supremely righteous and supremely loving. But when we ask *who* is supremely righteous and loving, the answer comes in terms of God's original activity, creation: the Creator of heaven and earth, the Lord, is He who judges and redeems us. The transcendent "Godness" of God, what gives Him deity and so ultimate significance to our lives, is most directly manifested to us through His creative activity as the transcendent source of all being and of all existence. Without this transcendent aspect of "deity," the judgment and love of God would be ultimately unimportant to us, and the redemption promised by them impossible for God. The idea of creation, therefore, provides the most fundamental, if not the most characteristic, definition of God in the Christian faith. Among all the activities of God, creation is that activity or attribute which sets him apart as "God."[72]

---

72. *Ibid.*, pp. 83-84.

Chapter Five

THE TRANSCENDENCE OF GOD

In the last chapter we discussed some of the major implications of the fact of creation, as we related it to the subjects of nature, man, worship, and ethics. However, as yet we have not discussed the most important implication of all, namely, what does the fact of creation tell us about the nature of God himself? That is the topic for this chapter.

In considering the various attributes of God, we prefer not to select just one of them and speak of it as the "most important" or the "most basic" of all. This is because we do not want to leave the impression that some attributes are *less* important, so that no one will be tempted to draw the erroneous conclusion that God could possibly give up some of these allegedly "lesser" attributes and still be God. Such is not the case. However, if we were ever pressed to point to a specific attribute and label it the most fundamental of all the characteristics of deity, we would have to point to the *transcendence* of God.

The word *transcendence* comes from a Latin term which means "to climb over, to go beyond." Ray Anderson gives the following summary of the word's use:

> From an etymological consideration, "to transcend" originally meant to climb over or across some obstacle. It then came to mean, in a figurative sense, the experience of being overwhelmed or surpassed. Then in a somewhat curious shift of meaning, it came to represent that which could not be crossed over. In being stopped by an object too great to be surmounted, one is said to have come up against something "transcendent," that is, too great to be transcended. The term is now used almost exclusively in

> the sense of going beyond something, or an extension beyond the limits of something. . . .[1]

As one can see, it is a word that describes a relationship between two entities, one of which *transcends* or goes beyond the other. In the context of theology it describes the relation between God and his creation. To say that God is transcendent means that he goes beyond the universe, that he is separate from it, distinct from it in some sense. This is the result of the fact of creation: *because* God is the absolute Creator of the universe, he is transcendent to it. This is the heart of the distinction between Creator and creature; no more basic statement about the nature of God can be made.

In the following pages we will first give a brief historical survey of the problem of transcendence; then we will present the biblical teaching on the subject.

TRANSCENDENCE: EXTREME VIEWS

The main problem, of course, is to determine exactly in what sense God is "separate" from the universe, if at all. In the history of religious thought various solutions to the problem have been proposed. Among those which can safely be labeled erroneous are two views which lie at the extreme ends of the spectrum. One view tends to exaggerate God's transcendence and separate him from the world in too radical a fashion. The other view tends to deny his transcendence altogether. The formulation of these extreme viewpoints seems to have been abetted by two erroneous

1. Ray S. Anderson, *Historical Transcendence and the Reality of God* (Grand Rapids: Eerdmans, 1975), p. 13.

assumptions: (1) that transcendence is a *spatial* concept, i.e., that it implies a spatial separation of God from the world; and (2) that transcendence is the opposite of *immanence,* with immanence referring to God's spatial presence *within* the world. Thus we may refer to the unacceptably extreme views as exaggerated transcendence and exaggerated immanence.

Classical Examples

The classical examples of exaggerated immanence are certain of the pantheistic world views. Not all pantheistic systems fall into this category. For instance, in Neo-Platonism and Hinduism God in his most authentic form is quite distinct from the universe. In other such systems, however, the being of God is totally immersed within the world. An example is classical Stoicism, which viewed all reality as God in his two basic forms, fine and coarse. The finer, spiritual material—the primal Fire—is God in himself; the coarser material—the physical universe—is God's "body." The primal Fire is completely immanent within the universe in the same way that spirit dwells within a body. The Stoics called this Fire the *pneuma* and the *logos*, the active principle imbedded in the world which is the source of all its motion and individual actualization.[2]

The pantheisms of Spinoza and those influenced by him, which for all practical purposes identified God and the universe, are likewise examples of extreme immanence. Mascall quotes the following lines from Pope's *Essay on Man* (I, ix) as descriptive of this view:

---

2. Frederick Copleston, *A History of Philosophy, Volume I: Greece and Rome, Part I,* new revised ed. (Garden City, N.Y.: Doubleday Image, 1962), pp. 132-133.

All are but parts of one stupendous whole,
Whose body Nature is, and God the soul.[3]

At the other end of the spectrum is the concept of exaggerated transcendence. It may be found in some of the classic Greek philosophies. For instance, Aristotle's "Unmoved Mover" is totally separate from the world in being, thought, and action. His relationship with the world is one of passive non-involvement. His only activity is thought, and his only thought is of himself.[4] God's utter transcendence was also emphasized in Neo-Pythagoreanism and Middle Platonism (first century B.C. and after), in Philo, and in Plotinus' Neo-Platonism.[5]

Some of the early church fathers were apparently influenced by this Greek conception, since they interpreted the God of the Bible in terms of exaggerated transcendence. The idea seemed to be that God is too exalted to get involved in *any* interaction with created being; thus he brings forth the Logos from his own essence to act as a Mediator in *all* his relationships with the world, beginning with creation itself. For instance, Justin Martyr describes God as one "who remains ever in the supercelestial places, invisible to all men, holding personal intercourse with none, whom we believe to be Maker and Father of all things."[6] When the

---

3. E. L. Mascall, *He Who Is: A Study in Traditional Theism* (London: Darton, Longman & Todd, Libra edition, 1966), p. 129.

4. Frederick Copleston, *A History of Philosophy, Volume I: Greece and Rome, Part I,* pp. 58-59.

5. *Ibid.*, pp. 191, 198, 203, 209. See Hendrikus Berkhof's comments on this aspect of Greek philosophy in *Christian Faith: An Introduction to the Study of the Faith,* tr. Sierd Woudstra (Grand Rapids: Eerdmans, 1979), pp. 107-109.

6. Justin Martyr, "Dialogue of Justin, Philosopher and Martyr, with Trypho, a Jew," LVI, *The Ante-Nicene Fathers,* Volume I, ed. Alexander Roberts and James Donaldson (New York: Charles Scribner's Sons, 1913), p. 223.

Bible says "The Lord spake to Moses" or "The Lord came down,"

> . . . you must not imagine that the unbegotten God Himself came down or went up from any place. For the ineffable Father and Lord of all neither has come to any place, nor walks, nor sleeps, nor rises up, but remains in His own place, wherever that is, quick to behold and quick to hear, having neither eyes nor ears, but being of indescribable might . . . . How, then, could He talk with any one, or be seen by any one, or appear on the smallest portion of the earth, when the people at Sinai were not able to look even on the glory of Him who was sent from Him . . .? Therefore neither Abraham, nor Isaac, nor Jacob, nor any other man, saw the Father and ineffable Lord of all, and also of Christ, but [saw] Him who was according to His will His Son, being God, and the Angel because He ministered to His will; whom also it pleased Him to be born man by the Virgin; who also was fire when He conversed with Moses from the bush. . . .[7]

Another of the second-century apologists, Athenagoras, says this:

> That we are not atheists, therefore, seeing that we acknowledge one God, uncreated, eternal, invisible, impassible, incomprehensible, illimitable, who is apprehended by the understanding only and the reason, who is encompassed by light, and beauty, and spirit, and power ineffable, by whom the universe has been created through His Logos, and set in order, and is kept in being—I have sufficiently demonstrated. . . .[8]

---

7. *Ibid.*, CXXVII, p. 263.

8. Athenagoras, "A Plan for the Christians," X, tr. B. P. Pratten, *The Ante-Nicene Fathers,* Volume II, ed. Alexander Roberts and James Donaldson (New York: Charles Scribner's Sons, 1913), p. 133. A similar statement is found in the apologist Theophilus' "To Autolycus," XXII, tr. Marcus Dods, *The Ante-Nicene Fathers,* Volume II, p. 103.

Near the end of the second century Clement of Alexandria echoes this view. "The First Cause," he says, "is not then in space, but above both space, and time, and name, and conception."[9] And since "God is far from calling aloud in the unapproachable sanctity, separated as He is from even the archangels," he must speak and relate to the world through the Logos, the First-begotten.[10]

A more recent and more familiar example of extreme transcendence is found in eighteenth-century Deism. According to this view God created the universe as a kind of self-winding perpetual motion machine and then determined not to interfere any further with its natural operations. Thus we may admire the Creator's handiwork; but he remains remote and withdrawn, declining all involvement with the on-going world. One writer says this of Deism:

> . . . God has been thrust into the frigid altitudes of infinite space. There was a limited monarchy in heaven, as well as on earth. Providence was the spectator of the curious machine which it had constructed and set in motion, but the operation of which it was neither able nor willing to control. . . .[11]

Partly because of a misunderstanding of biblical imagery and partly because of naive cosmological views, popular piety has often been guilty of picturing God as being spatially remote—"up yonder," "away beyond the blue," "far beyond the starry skies." Taken literally, such expressions contribute to a sense of separation from God and lead to an unwarranted

---

9. Clement of Alexandria, "The Stromata, or Miscellanies," V.xi, *The Ante-Nicene Fathers*, Volume II, p. 461.

10. *Ibid.*, VI.vii, p. 493.

11. R. H. Tawney, *The Acquisitive Society* (London: G. Bell, 1924), p. 13; cited by E. L. Mascall, *He Who Is*, p. 128.

criticism of the biblical notion of transcendence. Some of this will be apparent in the next section.

The Modern Debate

To understand the contemporary debate over transcendence we need to begin with the religious Liberalism of the early twentieth century. This is the theology rooted in Schleiermacher and Ritschl, and represented on the continent by such men as Adolf Harnack and in America by such theologians as W. N. Clarke, William Adams Brown, Walter Rauschenbusch, and Harry Emerson Fosdick.

Liberalism's doctrine of God was one of extreme immanence. It was heavily influenced by nineteenth-century speculations in the areas of biblical criticism and science, particularly the theory of evolution. The most basic assumption in Liberal thought was the principle of continuity, which is the idea that all of reality is one great related whole. Nature, man, and God are all parts of the same continuum of being, qualitatively alike and differing only in degree. Cauthen calls this the "dominating motif" of Liberalism. He says,

> . . . This theme manifests itself in every area of thought and permeates all liberal theology. There is practically no end to its application. It reduces the distinction between animals and men, men and God, nature and God, reason and revelation, Christ and other men, Christianity and other religions, . . . the natural and supernatural, the human and divine natures of Christ, etc.[12]

Following this principle Liberalism denied that there is any great distinction between God and man, or God and

---

12. Kenneth Cauthen, *The Impact of American Religious Liberalism* (New York: Harper and Row, 1962), p. 9.

the universe in general. It especially rejected any deistic view of God's withdrawal from the world, and it also reacted strongly against fundamental orthodoxy's view of a transcendent God who intervenes with miraculous powers on certain occasions but for all practical purposes is absent most of the time. Liberalism stressed instead the immanence of God. There is only one realm, one process, one world, in which God is present as its soul or Immanent Spirit. As such he permeates the whole; he is present everywhere and at all times as a "permanent, pervasive influence which imparts a divine quality to all of existence."[13] As one representative of this view has put it,

> The traditional conception of God which has come down to us from the Middle Ages through the Latin church is undergoing a profound transformation. The idea that God is transcendent, not only exalted above the world by His moral perfection, but separated from it by the infinite reaches of space, is yielding to the idea of Deity as immanent in His creation. . . .[14]

Another representative of the Liberal mind, Henry Drummond, said it this way:

> . . . If God appears periodically, he disappears periodically. If he comes upon the scene at special crises he is absent from the scene in the intervals. Whether is all-God or occasional-God the nobler theory? Positively, the idea of an immanent God, which is the God of Evolution, is infinitely

---

13. *Ibid.*, p. 10; see pp. 209-212. See also p. 48: "An immanent Spirit, Christlike in nature—this is the heart of the liberal doctrine of God."

14. Alexander V. G. Allen, "The Continuity of Christian Thought," *American Protestant Thought: The Liberal Era*, ed. William R. Hutchison (New York: Harper Torchbook, 1968), p. 57.

> grander than the occasional wonder-worker who is the God of an old theology. . . .[15]

The Liberal theologian William Newton Clarke projected a utopian future if this conception of God could just prevail:

> This thought of the immanence of the transcendent God is a magnificent conception, that is destined powerfully to influence religion, theology, science, and common life. It is at once so vast and so new an idea as scarcely to have begun its work. If our own God thus pervades the universe with his presence, purpose, and action, then indeed "every place is hallowed ground." Nothing is profane, all is sacred. The universe is sanctified by the presence of its God, and we have no right to think of nature or of life without the reverence for which his presence calls. Christian thought will some day more strongly grasp this splendid conception, that the God and Father of Christ, our Father who is in heaven, is present in his whole creation, providing it with power to exist and end to exist for. By this thought worthily grasped all life will be elevated and purified. Religion will be freshly inspired, theology will be transfigured, and science will become a spiritual worship.[16]

The book *The Divinity of Christ* by Disciples theologian Edward Scribner Ames shows how these concepts of continuity and immanence affect one's view of Jesus. In Ames' words, "I do not believe there is a natural and a supernatural order, a human and a divine sphere of being. Life is one: its differences are those of degree." There is "no validity

15. Henry Drummond, *The Ascent of Man*, 7 ed. (New York: James Pott & Co., 1898), p. 334.

16. William Newton Clarke, *An Outline of Christian Theology*, 3 ed. (Edinburgh: T. & T. Clarke, 1899), pp. 158-159. Another good example of this view is Clarke's disciple, William Adams Brown. See the discussion of Brown in Kenneth Cauthen, *The Impact of American Religious Liberalism*, pp. 41ff.

to the old dualism of the natural and supernatural, the human and the divine"; therefore "we are not any longer concerned with the 'divinity' of Christ but rather with his goodness and his worth."[17] We may say that God was in Christ, but not in any special, abnormal way. God is immanent in every person. If his presence is more obvious in Jesus than in most this is because "Jesus Christ is a kind of pledge and promise of what other human beings may accomplish."[18]

Around 1920 when Karl Barth began to lead the Neo-Orthodox revolt against Liberalism, the almost-exclusive immanence of God was one of the main targets of this attack. In Barth's mind this view was devastating to the very deity of God, and it made man self-sufficient. Thus he rejected this major premise of Liberalism and emphasized again the transcendence of God. He described God as *totaliter aliter*—Wholly Other, and stressed the great gulf of "infinite qualitative distinction" between God and man. As Barth put it in the revised edition of his commentary on Romans (1922),

> . . . If I have a system, it is limited to a recognition of what Kierkegaard called the "infinite qualitative distinction" between time and eternity, and to my regarding this as possessing negative as well as positive significance: "God is in heaven, and thou art on earth." The relation between such a God and such a man, and the relation between such a man and such a God, is for me the theme of the Bible and the essence of philosophy. . . .[19]

---

17. Edward Scribner Ames, *The Divinity of Christ* (Chicago: The Bethany Press, n.d.), pp. 27-28, 46.

18. *Ibid.*, p. 34.

19. Karl Barth, *The Epistle to the Romans*, 6 ed., tr. Edwyn C. Hoskyns (New York: Oxford University Press, 1933), p. 10.

At least at this point in his thinking, "this is Barth's starting point. When he says that God is the 'Wholly Other,' he intends the words to be taken with strict literalness. God has nothing in common with man. He is unutterably transcendent."[20]

Barth's rejection of the Liberal doctrine of immanence was a move in the right direction; however, many have felt that he went too far and presented a one-sided view of transcendence. Barth himself later recognized that this was so, a fact that he acknowledged in his monograph on *The Humanity of God.*[21] Despite such attempts at moderation, though, the effects of his original emphasis on an exaggerated transcendence were impossible to expunge from his system, because his whole theological method was determined by it. Especially affected was his view of revelation: God is so qualitatively distinct "that the finite cannot know the infinite, . . . nature and history cannot manifest what is beyond the relative, and . . . human thought cannot comprehend or convey divine revelation."[22] Man's only knowledge of God comes when the eternal touches time in the person of Jesus of Nazareth, the one true Word of God. This means that all theology must be Christocentric in the sense that the incarnate Christ is the "only infallible rule of faith and practice," thus demoting the Bible and distorting the whole body of Christian doctrine. (We discussed this briefly in the last chapter as the "Christological fallacy.")

---

20. H. Maldwyn Hughes, *The Christian Idea of God* (London: Duckworth, 1936), p. 70. See also Heinz Zahrnt, *The Question of God: Protestant Theology in the Twentieth Century*, tr. R. A. Wilson (New York: Harcourt Brace Jovanovich, 1969), pp. 24ff.

21. Karl Barth, *The Humanity of God*, tr. J. N. Thomas and T. Weiser (Richmond: John Knox Press, 1960). See H. Zahrnt, *The Question of God*, pp. 85ff.

22. Carl F. H. Henry, *God, Revelation and Authority, Volume II: God Who Speaks and Shows, Fifteen Theses, Part One* (Waco: Word Books, 1976), p. 53.

Other voices joined with Karl Barth in emphasizing transcendence. One was that of Rudolf Bultmann. As Morris Ashcraft says, "Along with other dialectical theologians he speaks of God as wholly other, and alludes to the sharp line of demarcation between God and man." He shows a "deep reverence for the transcendent God."[23] Though this may be the case, this is not the element of Bultmann's thinking that was noticed. Far more influential was his characterization of biblical cosmology as a three-layered universe and his call for demythologizing the New Testament message. His famous essay on "New Testament and Mythology" begins thus:

> The cosmology of the New Testament is essentially mythical in character. The world is viewed as a three-storied structure, with the earth in the centre, the heaven above, and the underworld beneath. Heaven is the abode of God and of celestial beings—the angels. The underworld is hell, the place of torment. Even the earth is more than the scene of natural, everyday events . . . . It is the scene of the supernatural activity of God and his angels on the one hand, and of Satan and his demons on the other. . . .[24]

All such supernatural intervention, especially the miraculous, is myth, according to Bultmann; and no one really takes it seriously any more. "For all our thinking to-day is shaped irrevocably by modern science." Thus we must demythologize the biblical message by "stripping the Kerygma from its mythical framework."[25] Whether Bultmann would have

23. Morris Ashcraft, *Rudolf Bultmann* (Waco: Word Books, 1972), p. 62.

24. Rudolf Bultmann, "New Testament and Mythology," *Kerygma and Myth: A Theological Debate*, ed. Hans Werner Bartsch, tr. Reginald H. Fuller (New York: Harper Torchbook, 1961), p. 1.

25. *Ibid.*, pp. 3-4.

approved of it or not, this element of his thought actually helped to suppress the concept of transcendence in contemporary theology and helped to keep alive the Liberal doctrine of immanence. It was a stepping-stone to the Neo-Liberal theology of the present as it appears especially in secular theology and political theology.[26]

Other such stepping-stones were Paul Tillich and Dietrich Bonhoeffer. Tillich contributed to the process via his rejection of the "natural-supranatural" dualism—a cosmology which he considered to be as outdated as Bultmann's three-tiered universe. According to Tillich there is no "supranatural divine world alongside the natural human world." Such a view merely posits God as *a* being among other beings and thus brings him down to the level of the finite. But neither can we simply opt for pantheism, which "identifies God with the universe, with its essence or with special powers within it." Over against both of these "dangerous" views Tillich set forth his alternative: God is

> . . . the infinite and unconditional power of being or, in the most radical abstraction, . . . he is being-itself. In this respect God is neither alongside things nor even "above" them; he is nearer to them than they are to themselves. He is their creative ground, here and now, always and everywhere.[27]

Several themes in the later writings of Dietrich Bonhoeffer have been interpreted along these same lines, especially his concept of transcendence as "the 'beyond' in the midst

---

26. Helmut Thielicke says, "In Bultmann's hermeneutics the immanentist presupposition of modern science and history is the decisive theological premise." *The Evangelical Faith, Volume Two: The Doctrine of God and of Christ,* tr. and ed. Geoffrey W. Bromiley (Grand Rapids: Eerdmans, 1977), p. 69.

27. Paul Tillich, *Systematic Theology* (Chicago: University of Chicago Press, 1957), II:5-7.

of life." From a practical viewpoint he rejected the idea that God is to be called on only in emergencies or to fill in the gaps in our knowledge. God is present, he said, not just at the borders but at the very center of life, in the midst of all our activities.[28]

Though some feel it is a misuse of Bonhoeffer to say he advocated a secular theology without a transcendent God,[29] nevertheless he, Bultmann, and Tillich have in fact formed the basis for the secular and political theologies of the present day, which are little more than the old Liberalism in new terminology. The idea of God as a supernatural being who transcends the universe is rejected; God is instead interpreted as a particular dimension within the universe. As Leslie Dewart plainly asserts, God's transcendence is an attribute of his immanence, and he is completely within the world.[30] Thus we have the interesting concept of "immanent transcendence," as Ray Anderson puts it.[31]

The manifesto which launched Neo-Liberalism into the main stream of theological thinking today was John A. T. Robinson's *Honest to God* (1963). Robinson canonized Tillich, Bultmann, and Bonhoeffer. He called for a total rejection of God as a transcendent, supernatural being; God is not "up there" nor "out there," but "down here" as the "ultimate depth of all our being, the creative ground and meaning of all our existence."[32]

---

28. Dietrich Bonhoeffer, *Letters and Papers from Prison,* tr. Reginald H. Fuller (New York: Macmillan, 1962), pp. 164ff., 218-220.

29. See, for instance, Ray Anderson, *Historical Transcendence and the Reality of God,* p. 37.

30. Leslie Dewart, "God and the Supernatural," *Commonweal* (February 10, 1967), 85:527-528.

31. Ray Anderson, *Historical Transcendence and the Reality of God,* p. 25.

32. John A. T. Robinson, *Honest to God* (London: SCM Press, 1963), p. 47.

Exactly how to express the transcendent dimension of this world was the problem with which Robinson was wrestling; indeed, it is one of the major problems for secularized theology today. Many use the model of interpersonal relationships to describe this transcendent dimension, i.e., God transcends us as other persons are transcendent to us. This is precisely where we encounter him in everyday life, namely, in the free and loving interpersonal relationships we have with our neighbors. As Robinson has said, since God is love, we meet him in every human relationship of love and service.[33] Or as Ronald Gregor Smith has put it, we believe that we encounter the transcendent eternal Thou in every I-thou relationship.[34] Jose Miranda agrees that God is known only through one's neighbor, specifically through the neighbor who is in need of love and justice. If we want to discover God, we must seek him "in the implacable moral imperative of justice," for "he is knowable exclusively in the cry of the poor and the weak who seek justice. . . . Transcendence does not mean only an unimaginable and inconceivable God, but a God who is accessible only in the act of justice."[35] (We recognize here, of course, the perspective of liberation theology.)

Another common suggestion is to interpret transcendence in historical terms, especially with reference to the *future*. God is transcendent in the same way the future transcends the present. Indeed, God *is* the transcendent power and potential of the future. Such a view is usually found in the

---

33. *Ibid.*, pp. 52-53, 60, 70.
34. Ronald Gregor Smith, *Secular Christianity* (London: Collins, 1966), p. 123.
35. Jose Miranda, *Marx and the Bible: A Critique of the Philosophy of Oppression*, tr. John Eagleson (Maryknoll, N.Y.: Orbis Books, 1974), pp. 48-49, 60, 64.

context of the theology of hope or in political and liberation theologies. An example is Harvey Cox. The problem, says Cox, is to "maintain an affirmation of transcendence within the context of a culture whose mood is relentlessly immanentist." The only way theology can do this, he asserts, is to "leave behind the God who 'is' and begin its work with the God who 'will be.'" Cox follows the maverick Catholic, Teilhard de Chardin, and the Marxist, Ernst Bloch, in thinking of transcendence as "the pressure exerted by the future on the present." God is indeed outside of history, "in this case not 'above' but *ahead*."[36] Peter Hodgson speaks in similar terms, adopting Pannenberg's suggestion that transcendence is experienced as "the *power of the future*."[37] He continues, in the best rhetoric of liberation theology,

> God transcends us as the future, the end, the "whither" toward which all life is oriented. God's word is the power of the future that calls us forward. Freedom is experienced as the gift of the future, liberating humanity from past burdens and oppressions. To be radically open *for* the future *by the power* of the future is the essence of freedom. Now, Jesus is the agent by whom the power of the future ingresses. . . .[38]

If most of this sounds strange to us, indeed, if it sounds hardly at all like Christianity or even theism, the reason is that Neo-Liberalism has abandoned metaphysical and ontological categories in speaking of God. In traditional Christian terms it would be atheism, pure and simple. (Consider, for instance, Cox's longing for the time "when the corpse

---

36. Harvey Cox, *On Not Leaving It to the Snake* (New York: Macmillan, 1969), pp. 5-11.

37. Peter C. Hodgson, *New Birth of Freedom: A Theology of Bondage and Liberation* (Philadelphia: Fortress Press, 1976), pp. 162, 286.

38. *Ibid.*, p. 307.

of the dead God of metaphysical theism is finally interred."[39]) "God" is just the name given to the most meaningful transcendent dimension of this world. Since the "transcendent" is not sought outside this world as such, it is commonly referred to as this-worldly transcendence, secular transcendence, or even (as we have noted) immanent transcendence. In spite of all the ingenuity brought to bear in this search for an adequate non-ontological way to define transcendence, however, the effort must be declared a failure, futile and forlorn. Attempts to redefine biblical data and biblical terminology apart from metaphysics are either desperate or deceitful, since the results bear practically no resemblance to the original claims of Scripture. Whatever may be the truth and value of the concepts of personal transcendence and historical transcendence, they are meaningful in reference to God only if the God to whom they refer is also ontologically transcendent, i.e., only if God exists as an objective, ontological reality distinct from this world.[40]

TRANSCENDENCE: THE BIBLICAL VIEW

Thus far we have seen that the concept of the transcendence of God has been subjected to a great deal of misinterpretation, and that there is a need for a strong reaffirmation of the biblical concept of transcendence today. In the remainder of this chapter such a reaffirmation will be given.

---

39. Harvey Cox, *On Not Leaving It to the Snake*, pp. 11-12.

40. For further discussion of Neo-Liberal concepts of transcendence, see Jack Cottrell, "The Transcendence of God," *The Seminary Review* (Spring 1968), 14:59-69. See also Ray Anderson, *Historical Transcendence and the Reality of God*, especially chapter 1. Considering the fact that most contemporary views reduce God to a dimension of the cosmos, we are tempted to apply to these views the label of "panencosmism," with apologies to Charles Hartshorne.

God is transcendent in two senses, ontologically and epistemologically. The first refers to the "beyondness" of God's being as compared with all created being; the second refers to the fact that God is "beyond" our knowledge. In this chapter we are dealing only with God's ontological transcendence. We are asking the question of God's essence or being. In human terms, we will attempt to describe the nature of God's essence insofar as Scripture has enlightened us on this subject. We realize that there is a great deal of objection to the very concept of the being of God, especially by those who feel that metaphysical terminology is a relic of the dead past. We believe that such objections ignore the clear teaching of the Bible, however, which tells us much about the nature of God.

The basic biblical statement about the essence of God is John 4:24, "God is spirit." The basic biblical fact undergirding God's transcendence is creation *ex nihilo*. God alone is the uncreated Creator. Putting these concepts together, we conclude that we may describe God's essence as *uncreated spirit.*

God the Uncreated

God is spirit; in the next section we will see more precisely what this means. At this point we would only note that angels also are spirits, and that human beings are partly spirit (we will limit our remarks to the latter). Though this does not mean that we are of the *same* essence, it does mean that in a real sense we are *like* God (Genesis 1:26). Thus whatever meaning we finally give to the concept of transcendence, it cannot mean that God is "wholly other" in an absolute sense. Man has been created in God's image and likeness; this likeness has its ontological roots in man's nature as spirit. We must not speak of a continuity of being between man and God in a Neo-Platonic sense; nor do we need to posit an *analogy* of being in a Roman Catholic sense. But Brunner is correct when he says that we cannot discard the "analogy of being" concept together (contra Barth), because Genesis 1:26 tells us that there is a genuine likeness between God and man.[41]

The Creator/creature Distinction

God is spirit, true; but he is *uncreated* spirit. This is the most decisive and determinative thing we can say about God. The fact that God is uncreated makes him qualitatively different from all created reality, both spiritual and material. This is what we mean when we speak of the transcendence of God. It does not mean that God is separated from us by "the infinite reaches of space"; it means that his essence is altogether different from the essence of creatures. As Gilkey puts it,

> The first meaning of divine transcendence is that God "transcends" other beings in the mode of His existence. As traditional theology has put it: God "exists" in a different way than do other things; He *is* differently, He possesses a different mode or kind of being. . . .[42]

"That is to say, the substantive existence of God is distinct from that of the world."[43] If creatures had come into existence by some process of emanation, that is, if their being were

---

41. Emil Brunner, *The Christian Doctrine of God: Dogmatics, Volume I*, tr. Olive Wyon (Philadelphia: Westminster Press, 1950), pp. 175-176.

42. Langdon Gilkey, *Maker of Heaven and Earth* (Garden City, N.Y.: Doubleday Anchor, 1965), p. 86.

43. *Ibid.*, p. 94.

some kind of extrusion from God's own being, then we could not speak of transcendence. But this is not the case. All things, including angelic and human spirits, have been created out of nothing. Only God is uncreated and infinite; all else is created and finite. There is an ontological gulf between God and his creatures. This is the point of transcendence; this is his "beyondness" or "otherness." (Remember: man is not now and never will be divine.)

The Bible speaks of this ontological gulf when it says that God "alone possesses immortality" (I Timothy 6:16); that is, only God the uncreated one is by nature eternal and imperishable. Romans 1:23 condemns the foolishness of idolaters who forsake the *incorruptible* God in order to devote themselves to *corruptible* things, including man and all kinds of animal life. Verse 25 makes the distinction very clear: "For they exchanged the truth of God for a lie, and worshiped and served the creature rather than the Creator, who is blessed forever. Amen."

The characterization here of God as *Creator* and all else as *creature* is significant, for it pinpoints the fact of *ex nihilo* creation as the basis of God's transcendence. Apart from creation, God would not be transcendent; he would then be "just another being," or *a* being among other beings. But creation excludes this way of looking at God. It puts God in a totally unique category. Brunner says,

> . . . Only He who, in the strict sense of the word, is the Lord of the world, the Creator, can be "Wholly Other." Only the Creator Lord, by His very nature, is different from all other existence, in such a radical and absolute manner as indeed only Creator and creature can be different. The Creator has no trace of "the world" or of "the creaturely" in Himself,

> and conversely, the creature as such has no trace of "non-creatureliness," of "divinity" . . . .[44]
>
> As the One who alone is Creator, God stands "over against" His creation, because it does not participate in His Being as Creator—the "Wholly Other." The fact that God is the Wholly Other refers to that which distinguishes Him as Creator from the creature. . . .[45]

"This ontological distinction between God and His creatures is the result of God's creative act"; it is "one of the basic meanings of creation."[46]

Even if we are reluctant to say that the transcendence of the Creator is the most fundamental of his attributes, we can freely say that the *recognition* of God's transcendence is fundamental to our whole concept of and relationship to him. In Gilkey's words, "He is our Creator and thus our Lord. Correspondingly, the doctrine of God as Creator is, perhaps, the most fundamental conception we can have of God. That is, creation is that activity of God by means of which we define what we mean by the word 'God.'" This "transcendent 'Godness' of God" is "what gives Him deity and so ultimate significance to our lives."[47]

The Holiness of God

The basic biblical term for the transcendence of God is *holiness*. In Scripture God is characteristically described

---

44. Emil Brunner, *The Christian Doctrine of God*, pp. 158-159. Unfortunately this statement by Brunner is true only if we understand *ex nihilo* creation as the *origination* of the created world—a meaning which Brunner himself rejects.

45. *Ibid.*, p. 176.

46. Langdon Gilkey, *Maker of Heaven and Earth*, p. 95.

47. *Ibid.*, pp. 83-84.

as "the Holy One" (Hosea 11:9, 12), "the Holy One of Israel" (Psalm 71:22; Jeremiah 51:5; throughout Isaiah), the "holy God" (Isaiah 5:16), and the one whose name is holy (Psalms 30:4; 97:12; 103:1; Matthew 6:9). "Holy is He" (Psalm 99:3, 5); "holy is the Lord our God" (Psalm 99:9). "Holy, Holy, Holy is the Lord of hosts" (Isaiah 6:3; see Revelation 4:8). The etymology of the biblical terms (the adjectives *qādōsh* and *hagios* and their cognates) is somewhat uncertain. Some trace the Hebrew term to a root meaning "to cut, to separate"; but others disagree with this connection. One writer says, "The basic idea is not that of separation . . . , but the positive thought of encounter which inevitably demands certain modes of response."[48] This remark seems to be off target, though, as those who argue that the word means "separate" make a much better case.[49] To say that God is holy means that he is separate and distinct from all else; to say that something in the created world is holy means that it has been separated from the common and ordinary, and devoted to the service of God.

When applied to God the term *holy* has two basic connotations, the ontological and the ethical. In the ethical sense God is holy in that he is separate from man as *sinner*; he is totally righteous and pure and upright in character. This connotation seems to be intended in such passages as Isaiah 30:11; 17:7; Joshua 24:19-20; I Peter 1:15-16. This

---

48. Horst Seebass, "Holy, Consecrate, Sanctify, Saints, Devout," *The New International Dictionary of New Testament Theology*, ed. Colin Brown (Grand Rapids: Zondervan, 1976), II:224.

49. Norman Snaith, *The Distinctive Ideas of the Old Testament* (New York: Schocken Books, 1964), pp. 21ff.; Herman Bavinck, *The Doctrine of God*, tr. William Hendriksen (Grand Rapids: Eerdmans, 1951), pp. 210ff.; Emil Brunner, *The Christian Doctrine of God*, pp. 157ff.

is the sense in which we can be holy as God is holy. But in the more basic sense of the term God is holy in that he is separate from man as *creature*: he is different from man in the very essence of his being; he is transcendent.

That the word has such a non-ethical connotation is seen in its application not just to God and man but also to objects and other non-personal entities. For instance, there can be holy ground (Exodus 3:5), made no longer the same ordinary ground by the very proximity of God's presence. The temple was holy (Psalm 65:4), that is, set apart from all other structures in dedication to special service to God. Within the temple were the holy place and the holy of holies (Hebrews 9:2-3), the latter containing the holy ark of the covenant (II Chronicles 35:3). The sabbath day was holy (Exodus 20:8), being set apart from other days for special remembrance of God. Other items described as holy include anointing oil (Exodus 30:25), censers (Numbers 16:37), bread (I Samuel 21:4), and articles of silver and gold (Joshua 6:19). As Bavinck says, such items are called holy because they are "separated from their ordinary sphere, and placed in a peculiar relation to God and his service."[50] Even the designation of Israel as a "holy nation" (Exodus 19:6) emphasizes the fact that God separated this people from all others to fulfil a special purpose for him.

Thus when the Bible says that God is *holy*, it means above all else that he is "wholly other," that he is transcendent, that he is separate from the world of creatures in his infinite and uncreated majesty. Brunner rightly remarks,

> . . . Holiness is the Nature of God, that which distinguishes Him from everything else, the Transcendence of God in His

50. Herman Bavinck, *The Doctrine of God*, p. 211.

> very Nature, as the "Wholly Other." Hence Holiness is not a quality which God possesses in common with other beings; on the contrary, it is that which distinguishes Him clearly and absolutely from everything else. To be holy is the distinguishing mark peculiar to God alone: it is that which sets the Being of God apart from all other forms of being.[51]

Holiness in the sense of transcendent majesty is clearly seen in the worshipful cry of the seraphim in Isaiah 6:3, "Holy, Holy, Holy, is the Lord of hosts, the whole earth is full of his glory." This is the song that continues around the throne of God without ceasing: "Holy, Holy, Holy, is the Lord God, the Almighty, who was and who is and who is to come" (Revelation 4:8). Moses declared, "Who is like Thee among the gods, O Lord? Who is like Thee, majestic in holiness, awesome in praises, working wonders?" (Exodus 15:11). The Lord himself declares, "They will sanctify my name; indeed, they will sanctify the Holy One of Jacob, and will stand in awe of the God of Israel" (Isaiah 29:23). The redeemed will stand before God and sing, "Who will not fear, O Lord, and glorify Thy name? For Thou alone art holy; for all the nations will come and worship before Thee, for Thy righteous acts have been revealed" (Revelation 15:4).

The equivalence of holiness and transcendence means, as Bavinck says, that "holiness is synonymous with divinity."[52] The *Holy One* of Israel is simply a way of saying the *God* of Israel. There is no one else in the category of uncreated

---

51. Emil Brunner, *The Christian Doctrine of God,* p. 158.

52. Herman Bavinck, *The Doctrine of God,* p. 213. See Gustaf Aulen, *The Faith of the Christian Church,* 4 ed., tr. Eric H. Wahlstrom and G. E. Arden (Philadelphia: Muhlenberg Press, 1948), p. 120: "The expression, the Holy One, is synonymous with God."

divinity, thus "there is no one holy like the Lord, indeed, there is no one besides Thee" (I Samuel 2:2). "For thou alone art holy" (Revelation 15:4). "I am God and not man," says the Lord—"the Holy One in your midst" (Hosea 11:9). When God judges the doubters and the scoffers, he says, it will be for the sake of his holy name, so that people will know that he alone is God. " 'And I will vindicate the holiness of My great name which has been profaned among the nations . . . . Then the nations will know that I am the Lord,' declares the Lord God, 'when I prove Myself holy among you in their sight' " (Ezekiel 36:23). " 'And My holy name I shall make known in the midst of My people Israel; and I shall not let My holy name be profaned any more. And the nations will know that I am the Lord, the Holy One in Israel' " (Ezekiel 39:7).

Thus Snaith says that *holiness* "is the most intimately divine word of all. It has to do . . . with the very Nature of Deity."[53] Holiness may be paraphrased as "the Divine nature, as it is peculiar to God alone."[54] "That God is called the Holy One implies primarily that there is a definite line of demarcation between the divine and the merely human, and that God is God and man is man."[55] The following statement by Gilkey sums it up:

> . . . Holiness, therefore, points to the unconditioned, the transcendent element of deity which absolutely distinguishes God from all creatures; holiness is the "Godness" of God. Thus holiness and the divine transcendence are ideas very closely associated in theology: so far as God transcends His creation, so far is He holy.[56]

---

53. Norman Snaith, *The Distinctive Ideas of the Old Testament*, p. 21.
54. Emil Brunner, *The Christian Doctrine of God*, p. 159.
55. Gustaf Aulen, *The Faith of the Christian Church*, pp. 120-121.
56. Langdon Gilkey, *Maker of Heaven and Earth*, p. 98.

The Exalted One

Another biblical theme that emphasizes transcendence is the *exaltation* of God. God is described as the exalted one, high and lifted up, far above earth and heaven. The language of exaltation raises the question of God's relation to the universe. If the transcendence of God does not imply a *spatial* separation from the world, exactly what is meant when spatial concepts are used? If this kind of imagery is imprecise and inadequate, then how *should* we describe God in his relation to the cosmos?

The language of height dominates the biblical picture of God. God is described as dwelling in the highest heavens. He is called "God on high" (or God of height; Micah 6:6). Isaiah said, "I saw the Lord sitting on a throne, lofty and exalted" (Isaiah 6:1); he is "the high and exalted One" (Isaiah 57:15). "The Lord is exalted, for He dwells on high" (Isaiah 33:5). Moses said, "I will sing to the Lord, for He is highly exalted" (Exodus 15:1). The Lord is called the "Highest One" (Daniel 7:18, 22, 25, 27), the "Most High" (Numbers 24:16; Deuteronomy 32:8; Luke 1:32, 35; Acts 7:48; and elsewhere), and the "Most High God" (Daniel 5:18, 21; Mark 5:7; Acts 16:17). His dwelling place is said to be "in heaven" (I Kings 8:30ff.; Psalms 2:4; 115:3; 123:1; Matthew 6:9). "I dwell on a high and holy place," says the Lord (Isaiah 57:15). He is "in the highest" (Luke 2:14). "The Lord's throne is in heaven" (Psalm 11:4).

How shall we understand this language? Some have taken it to be indicative of a primitive and erroneous world view, the "three-layered" universe ridiculed by Bultmann and so many others. According to this interpretation the Bible's writers actually conceived of the world as having three layers or levels, much like a two-story house with a basement. Man lives on the first floor; Satan and his demons live in the basement; God and his angels live upstairs. Thus the universe is in neat layers that are spatially separate. References to God living "up there" in heaven supposedly support this view, e.g., "We lift up our heart and hands toward God in heaven. . . . The Lord looks down and sees from heaven" (Lamentations 3:41, 50). Also noted are statements such as "The Lord came down on Mount Sinai" (Exodus 19:20), and references to Jesus' ascension (Acts 1:9-11). Other references are said to mention the three stories specifically: "You shall not make for yourself an idol, or any likeness of what is in heaven above or on the earth beneath or in the water under the earth" (Exodus 20:4). Also, "At the name of Jesus every knee should bow, of those who are in heaven, and on earth, and under the earth" (Philippians 2:10). We have already noted how Bultmann labels this as myth and rejects it outright. Indeed, so do many others. How do you tell anyone who lives in the post-Copernican era that God lives "up there" in heaven? Everyone knows that "up" is relative to the rotation of the earth and the earth's own movement on its axis and around the sun, not to mention the sun's own rotation in the galaxy and the galaxy's rush through space. As far as we know, the universe either extends infinitely or extends to its limits with nothing beyond it. So what sense does it make to talk about looking "up" toward God, where he dwells in the heavens?

We do not deny that spatial language is being used in describing God's relation to the universe. God "comes down," "looks down," and "sits in the heavens." The claims that the Bible portrays a three-decker universe are greatly exaggerated, however. Sometimes the reference is simply to the atmosphere, the surface of the earth, and the oceans—the habitats of birds, animals, and fish (see Exodus 20:4; Deuteronomy 4:17-18; 5:8). Created spirits do not live on the earth so are thought of as being above it (e.g., Ephesians 2:2); the dead are buried in the ground so are phenomenologically thought of as "under the earth." (See Philippians 2:10.) Jesus' ascension was not a rocket-trip to outer space; he simply rose above the earth to a waiting cloud (not a moisture cloud, but the cloud of God's presence—Exodus 40:34ff.; Matthew 17:5; Acts 1:9) and disappeared. The so-called stumbling block of a three-story universe is a red herring.[57]

But what about the quite unambiguous statements that locate God up above, in the heavens? The answer is that such statements are quite natural but are not intended to be taken literally. They are natural for two reasons. First, it is almost impossible to think of God without thinking of him as being "somewhere," even if we know he is not localized in any one space. So it is natural to think of him as dwelling in a particular place. Second, because of our tendency to associate height with the good end of every spectrum, it is more than natural to think of God as being located "above," in the highest possible height. The spatial language bears the connotation of *value*, *rank*, or *esteem*. From our perspective, the heavens above are the highest "space" we can imagine; thus God is pictured as being in heaven or in the heavens or above the heavens. The use of the word *heavens* in the physical sense of the highest reaches of the universe has resulted in the use of the same word to

57. John W. Duddington, "The Red Herring of a Three-Story Universe," *Christianity Today* (November 5, 1971), 16:13.

describe the presence of God, "wherever" that may be. To say that God is in heaven is to use the language of exaltation; it ascribes to him the highest honor and glory we can imagine. When LaPlace smirked that he had swept the heavens with his telescope but had not found God anywhere, and when the first cosmonauts crowed that they had not seen God from their puny perch, they were simply missing the whole point. The language is not intended to be spatial; God was never to be considered as "up there" in a literal sense.

That this is so seems clear from a number of Bible passages. Isaiah 66:1-2 (quoted in Acts 7:48-50) has these words of the Lord: "Heaven is My throne, and the earth is My footstool. Where then is a house you could build for Me? And where is a place that I may rest? For My hand made all these things, thus all these things came into being." This is the language of transcendence: the Creator of the universe cannot be located in *any* finite place within it, above or below. He is everywhere. Thus Acts 17:24 says, "The God who made the world and all things in it, since He is Lord of heaven and earth, does not dwell in temples made with hands." Still, verse 27 notes that "He is not far from each one of us." I Kings 8:27 offers a similar judgment: "But will God indeed dwell on the earth? Behold, heaven and the highest heaven cannot contain Thee, how much less this house which I have built!" In this same prayer Solomon refers several times to God "in heaven Thy dwelling place" (verse 30), but verse 27 shows that he does not think of this in terms of physical space. Also, the language of exaltation is pressed to its limit when the psalmist says, "Be exalted above the heavens, O God" (Psalm 57:5, 11). I.e., God is even *higher* than the heavens. See Psalm 113:4-5, "The

Lord is high above all nations; His glory is above the heavens. Who is like the Lord our God, who is enthroned on high?" (See also Psalm 148:13.) Finally we would note Nehemiah 9:13, "Then Thou didst come down on Mount Sinai, and didst speak with them from heaven." God "came down," but he still spoke "from heaven"! Surely this shows that the Bible writers were not projecting God into a heaven of spatial remoteness. These remarks by Snaith are appropriate:

> . . . The God of the Hebrews was essentially active in the world which He had made. . . . He was never thought of by the Hebrews as apart from the world, away in splendid isolation. . . . God was from the beginning transcendent in that He was different from man, but He was by no means transcendent in that He was remote from man. . . . Transcendence does not mean remoteness. It means otherness. . . .[58]

How, then, should we think of God as related to the universe or to space as such? If transcendence is not spatial, what is it? The word is certainly inadequate, but it may be more appropriate to think of it as *dimensional*. We hasten to say that we do not mean this in the same sense as those who say that "God" is just one dimension of this world, after the fashion of the secular theologies. We mean it in the sense that God is a different dimension entirely. (We deliberately say that God *is* a different dimension, and not that he is *in* a different dimension.)[59] Those who need help in understanding this concept should read Edwin Abbott's tantalizing fantasy called *Flatland*.[60] In this delightful tale Abbott

58. Norman Snaith, *The Distinctive Ideas of the Old Testament*, p. 47.

59. We realize that this is one of the views rejected by John A. T. Robinson in *Honest to God*, and by others such as Jerry Gill in "Transcendence: An Incarnational Model," *Encounter* (Winter 1978), 39:39-44. What Gill calls the "realm model" is close to the view taken here; he takes a dimensional view in the sense of this-worldly transcendence.

60. Edwin A. Abbott, *Flatland: A Romance of Many Dimensions*, 5 ed. (New York: Barnes and Noble, 1963).

tells (in first person) the story of an inhabitant of Flatland, a realm with only *two* dimensions. (He even speculates about a realm with only one dimension, a line.) Since Flatlanders experience only what we would call length and width on a flat plane, they have no conception whatever of what we call height, or a third dimension. Even when a spherical being visits Flatland, its inhabitants still cannot conceptualize "space" until the sphere lifts the narrator of the story "up." When the narrator returns to tell his neighbors that there is another dimension—a genuine "up there"—they imprison him as a dangerous kook.

In a similar way we are suggesting that there is a divine dimension which is impossible for us to conceptualize, which is not located "in" three-dimensional space, but which is "adjacent" to it at every point. Thus heaven is not spatial or in space as such, but God is still not far from each one of us, as Acts 17:27 says. In fact, as we will suggest in the next section, there are actually three separate dimensions or realms (not to be confused with the fanciful three-decker universe, or with the three dimensions of space itself). These are the material dimension, the world of space; the spiritual dimension, the realm of created spirits; and the divine dimension, which transcends both the others as the exclusive and unapproachable realm of the infinite, uncreated God—"who alone possesses immortality and dwells in unapproachable light; whom no man has seen or can see" (I Timothy 6:16).

God Is Spirit

We have said that the essence of God may be thought of as uncreated spirit. To this point we have been concentrating on the transcendent element, God's uncreatedness. Now we will give more attention to that which enables us to say that we are like God, namely, God's spirituality. In a sense all of the things that can be said about God as spirit can also be said about human beings as spiritual creatures. It is not God's spirituality that makes him transcendent; it is the fact that he is *uncreated* spirit. So since God is spirit, he is like angels and human spirits in that he is immaterial and personal, for instance. But since he is uncreated, these attributes apply to God in an infinite way and with implications we can only begin to understand. Nevertheless Jesus' description of God as spirit (John 4:24) gives us real insight into the essence of God, and we need not be reluctant to consider what it means. That is the purpose of this section.

The Negative Meaning of God's Spirituality

To say that God is spirit has both negative and positive content. That is, it says something about what God is and what he is not. On the negative side, "God is spirit" means that he is *not* a material or corporeal being; and it means that he is *not* visible to created beings unless he manifests himself to them in special ways. God is *immaterial,* and God is *invisible*.

That spiritual essence is immaterial or non-material is probably the most obvious thing we can say about it. That a spirit (an angel, a human spirit) has real essence is not to be doubted, i.e., it is "made out of" something. Also, that it may have a specific form or shape natural to its own essence is likely. But the point is that spiritual beings are not "made out of" material stuff; they are not formed of atoms and molecules and the elements of this world. Jesus made this point when he appeared to his disciples after the resurrection, and "they were startled and frightened and thought that they were seeing a spirit." But Jesus calmed them and said, "See My hands and My feet, that it is I Myself; touch Me and see, for a spirit does not have flesh and bones as you see that I have." Then he ate some fish to emphasize his point (Luke 24:36-43).

Since God is spirit, he also is non-material; his essence is entirely different from the physical. (We should remember, too, that the spiritual essence of God is also different from the essence of angels and human spirits in that the latter are created while God is not.) Thus since God is spirit, Jesus' statement that "a spirit does not have flesh and bones" applies to him. An obvious application of this is that we should not think of God as being localized in any physically-bounded space, whether in the heavens above or on the earth. The immediate purpose of Jesus' remark that "God is spirit" was to make this very point. The Samaritan woman to whom Jesus was talking referred to the rival claims of the Samaritans and the Jews: "Our fathers worshiped in this mountain; and you people say that in Jerusalem is the place where men ought to worship" (John 4:20). The unspoken question is on which mountain does God *really* live? When Jesus answered, he implied that she did not understand the true nature of God ("You worship that which you do not know"—verse 22). One does not have to go to any particular mountain to worship God, as if God's presence were localized there, as if God had a physical body that could only be in one place at a time. This is not the case, for "God is spirit"!

That God's spirituality means non-materiality is also seen in the contrast God draws between himself as a protector and any merely human helpers. "Now the Egyptians are men, and not God, and their horses are flesh and not spirit" (Isaiah

31:3). Even the strongest material elements have their limits, but God is not material and is not bound by the strength limitations of material being.

Because of the built-in limitations of matter, God warns us and even commands us not ever to put him into the same category with physical creatures, or into the same category with false gods conceived of in material forms. We must remember that our God is spirit; he is not restricted by the natural limitations of material being. This is one of the main points of the second commandment, "You shall not make for yourself an idol, or any likeness of what is in heaven above or on the earth beneath or in the water under the earth" (Exodus 20:4). This is not just a prohibition against idolatry, which is the point of the first commandment. Here God is forbidding his people to make any image which in their minds might capture the essence even of the true God. This cannot be done, says the Lord; don't even try it! In the second giving of the commandments recorded in the book of Deuteronomy, Moses reminds the Israelites that when God originally spoke to them, "the Lord spoke to you from the midst of the fire; you heard the sound of words, but you saw no form—only a voice" (Deuteronomy 4:12).

> . . . So watch yourselves carefully, since you did not see any form on the day the Lord spoke to you at Horeb from the midst of the fire, lest you act corruptly and make a graven image for yourselves in the form of any figure, the likeness of male or female, the likeness of any animal that is on the earth, the likeness of any winged bird that flies in the sky, the likeness of anything that creeps on the ground, the likeness of any fish that is in the water below the earth (Deuteronomy 4:15-18).

Since God is spirit and not matter, we must reject every view of God that sees him as having a material body. This includes especially the Mormon teaching about God. The Mormon theologian James Talmage explains this view. Both the Father and the Son, he says, "are in form and stature perfect men; each of them possesses a tangible body, infinitely pure and perfect and attended by transcendent glory, nevertheless a body of flesh and bones." The Holy Spirit is different, he "is not tabernacled in a body of flesh and bones, but is a personage of spirit."

> . . . Admitting the personality of God, we are compelled to accept the fact of His materiality; indeed, an "immaterial being," under which meaningless name some have sought to designate the condition of God, cannot exist, for the very expression is a contradiction in terms. If God possesses a form, that form is of necessity of definite proportions and therefore of limited extension in space.

"We affirm," he continues, "that to deny the materiality of God's person is to deny God; for a thing without parts has no whole, and an immaterial body cannot exist."[61] Apparently in the Mormon mind all essence is *material* essence; thus if God has any essence at all he must be material. But this is a quite limited conception of the possibilities and of the reality of existing being, and it is contrary to Scripture.

How then do we explain the various biblical passages which do indeed describe God *as if* he exists in a physical body that moves from place to place? Specific bodily parts are often attributed to God. Here are some examples:

God's face: Exodus 33:20, 23; Deuteronomy 31:17-18; Psalms 11:7; 27:8; 30:7; 34:16; Isaiah 59:2; Jeremiah 33:5; I Peter 3:12.

61. James E. Talmage, *A Study of the Articles of Faith*, 13 ed. (Salt Lake City: The Church of Jesus Christ of Latter-Day Saints, 1924), pp. 42-43, 48.

God's eyes: Psalms 11:4; 34:15; Isaiah 1:15; Jeremiah 5:3; 16:17; Amos 9:4, 8; Habakkuk 1:13; Zechariah 4:10; I Peter 3:12.
God's ears: Psalms 17:6; 34:15; James 5:4; I Peter 3:12.
God's mouth: Numbers 12:8; Psalm 18:8.
God's nostrils: Psalm 18:8, 15.
God's arm: Psalm 98:1; Isaiah 30:30; 40:10; 50:2; 51:5, 9; 52:10; 53:1; Luke 1:51.
God's hand: Exodus 13:3; 15:17; 24:11; 33:22; Psalms 20:6; 74:11; Isaiah 31:3; 62:8; Amos 9:2; Matthew 26:64; Luke 1:66; I Peter 5:6.
God's feet: Exodus 24:10; Psalm 18:9.

In addition to these specific references to bodily parts, God is also represented as performing bodily movements or assuming bodily postures. He sits on a throne (Psalm 2:4; Matthew 23:22; Revelation 4:2) with Jesus at his right hand (Acts 7:55-56). He looks down from heaven (Psalms 14:2; 33:13; 102:19), and he hides his eyes (Isaiah 1:15). He comes down from heaven (Exodus 19:11ff.; Micah 1:3), and he walks with his people (Genesis 3:8; Deuteronomy 23:14).[62]

How do we explain these, if God does not actually have a material body? Several points must be made. First, there were times when God manifested himself to his people in human form for purposes of communication. As such he took on a body with bodily parts, and he went through bodily motions. But this does not necessarily mean that this is his true form and essence, any more than his manifesting himself as a pillar of fire means that God is literally like fire (see Exodus 13:21-22). Second, we should not confuse

62. See the more complete listing in Herman Bavinck, *The Doctrine of God*, pp. 86-88.

references to the glorified *human* body of Jesus with a description of his *divine* nature. For instance, Romans 8:29; I Corinthians 15:49; Philippians 3:21; and I John 3:2 are *not* talking about God's spiritual nature but about Jesus' glorified human body, the very same kind of body we will have after the resurrection. One cannot imply from these references that God as such has a body. Third, the references to bodily parts are quite obviously figurative expressions which are intended to emphasize the reality of specific actions and attitudes of God. When these actions and attitudes are described in these terms, they are made concrete in our minds. Thus the reference to bodily parts emphasizes the actions, not the nature of God per se. For instance, God's *face* signifies his presence and his favor; his *eyes* and *ears* signify his knowledge; his *nostrils* signify his anger; his *arm* signifies his power; his *hand* signifies his action and his power. God is even pictured as having *wings* as a symbol of his power to protect (Psalm 17:8).

This way of speaking is often called anthropomorphic, and it is considered to be an expression of God's condescending goodness that he would describe himself for us in human terms so that we might better understand what he is telling us. (*Anthropomorphic* means "in human form.") Such an interpretation is by no means far-fetched, and the fact that language about the human form should be used in reference to God is by no means unworthy of God. If God can assume human form in manifesting himself to man, and if the Logos can actually *become* a human being, then anthropomorphic language is only natural. After all, within the realm of our experience, humanity is the highest form with which God might compare himself. Though he sometimes compares himself with animals and things in order to make specific points,[63] "it is obviously better," as W. H. G. Thomas has said, "to use anthropomorphic expressions than zoo-morphic or cosmo-morphic."[64] In fact, there is no better way for God to keep before us the fact that he is *spirit*, since spiritual being involves preeminently the qualities of life and personhood (as we will see in the next section), and human beings are our primary examples of living, personal being. William Cosser reminds us how important it is to remember that God is the *living* God as opposed to lifeless idols. That is why we *can* speak figuratively of him as a living man, but it also shows the appropriateness of such speech: "It is also through speaking of Him as a human being that one never forgets that He is alive! That is the justification for anthropomorphism."[65]

The other negative aspect of God's spirituality is that he is invisible. He is the one "who alone possesses immortality and dwells in unapproachable light; whom no man has seen or can see" (I Timothy 6:16). He is described as "the King eternal, immortal, invisible, the only God" (I Timothy 1:17); he is "the invisible God" (Colossians 1:15). Romans 1:20 speaks of "His invisible attributes." No man *has* seen God (John 1:18; 5:37; I John 4:12); no man *can* see God (Exodus 33:20; I Timothy 6:16). See also Deuteronomy 4:12-19. The teaching that God is invisible is based not only on the fact that he is spirit; it is also the result of the fact that he is the uncreated, transcendent God. As spirit he is invisible to our mortal eyes; but even spiritual "eyes" do not look upon his pure essence.

---

63. See *ibid.*, p. 88.

64. W. H. Griffith Thomas, *The Principles of Theology*, p. 15; cited by Lewis Sperry Chafer, *Systematic Theology* (Dallas: Dallas Seminary Press, 1947), I:182.

65. William Cosser, *Preaching the Old Testament* (London: Epworth Press, 1966), p. 71.

This may be explained further by reference to the three dimensions of existence mentioned above, namely, the divine, the spiritual, and the material. God is naturally invisible within the material dimension just because he is spirit. But what about those occasions when God himself is said to have appeared to human beings? This has definitely happened in the past. We may think of God's walking in the Garden of Eden (Genesis 3:8). The description of the incident in Genesis 3 leads us to believe that this was not the first time that God had come to walk and talk with Adam and Eve. They must have seen him and talked with him. We may also remember how God appeared to Abraham, as recorded in Genesis 18:1, "Now the Lord appeared to him by the oaks of Mamre." Numerous appearances of "the Angel of the Lord" are probably appearances of God himself, perhaps the Logos.[66] When Jacob wrestled with the Angel of God (Genesis 32:24-32; Hosea 12:4), he declared, "I have seen God face to face, yet my life has been preserved" (Genesis 32:30). Gideon's reaction was similar (Judges 6:22), as was that of Samson's parents: "So Manoah said to his wife, 'We shall surely die, for we have seen God' " (Judges 13:22). In one sense these people did see God, but not in his true spiritual essence. On these and other occasions God took upon himself a human form for the purpose of manifesting himself to various persons. Such manifestations are called *theophanies,* or appearances of God. The bodies in which he appeared were real human bodies, probably created *ex nihilo* for the short duration of the theophany and then dissolved back into nothingness. In this way the Lord, who is invisible to our eyes as spirit, could be seen

---

66. See James A. Borland, *Christ in the Old Testament* (Chicago: Moody Press, 1978).

temporarily in a concrete form. (Because it was not his true essence, those who saw him did not die as they expected.)

Just as God is naturally invisible to the material realm because he is spirit, so also is he naturally invisible to the spiritual realm because he is uncreated and transcendent. The divine dimension is not the same as the spiritual dimension. God is not naturally visible even to angels. Thus *even the appearance of God before the angels in heaven is a theophany.* Unquestionably the angels are constantly in the presence of God; Jesus said the "angels in heaven continually behold the face of My Father who is in heaven" (Matthew 18:10). Job 1 pictures the angels in council before the Lord. Isaiah 6:1ff. pictures seraphim constantly attending him. Daniel describes the "Ancient of Days" seated in heaven: "His vesture was like white snow, and the hair of His head like pure wool. His throne was ablaze with flames, its wheels were a burning fire. A river of fire was flowing and coming out from before Him; thousands upon thousands were attending Him, and myriads upon myriads were standing before Him" (Daniel 7:9-10). Revelation 4 and 5 likewise describe God as seated on a throne, surrounded by worshiping angels. But I do not believe that these are references to the divine dimension itself, nor are they descriptions of the actual invisible and uncreated essence of God. The spiritual dimension—including the angels and including the "heaven" that is the location of God's throne—is a creation of God no less than the material dimension (Colossians 1:16). When God created the angelic beings to attend and serve him, he made himself known to them in a kind of permanent theophany. Thus when we think of God as seated on his heavenly throne, this is just as much a theophany as his walking with Adam and Eve in the Garden of Eden. In one case God takes on material form to be seen in the material realm; in the other case God takes on spiritual "form" to be seen in the spiritual realm. He is naturally invisible to both.

This helps us to understand the biblical references to occasions when men have seen or will see God in his heavenly form. In Exodus 24 Moses, Aaron, Nadab, Abihu, and seventy Israelite elders ate a covenant feast in the very presence of God. "And they saw the God of Israel; and under His feet there appeared to be a pavement of sapphire, as clear as the sky itself. Yet He did not stretch out His hand against the nobles of the sons of Israel; and they beheld God, and they ate and drank" (Exodus 24:10-11). These men saw God, but not in his pure divine essence. This was much more than a material theophany, but it was not more than the spiritual theophany in which God is manifest before the angels at all times. By miraculous power, if he so desires, God can open the eyes of mortal man and permit him to see into the spiritual dimension even during this life. (See II Kings 6:17; Isaiah 6:1; Revelation 4:2.) After death and for eternity the redeemed will enjoy the same kind of permanent theophany which the angels are even now privileged to behold. "For the Lord is righteous; He loves righteousness; the upright will behold His face" (Psalm 11:7). "Blessed are the pure in heart, for they shall see God" (Matthew 5:8). "And they shall see His face, and His name shall be on their foreheads" (Revelation 22:4; see Revelation 14:1 to show that this refers to the Father). But even this is not a viewing of the unapproachable divine essence "whom no man has seen or can see" (I Timothy 6:16). When John 1:18 says that "no man has seen God at any time," that is true; men have seen and will see only material and spiritual theophanies of God.

This also helps us to understand the very difficult passage in Exodus 33:18—34:8, where Moses requested to see God. "Then Moses said, 'I pray Thee, show me Thy glory!'" (Exodus 33:18). Now, we know that Moses had already seen God, even in the form of the heavenly presence (Exodus 24:1-11). This may have happened more than once for Moses, since God says of him, "With him I speak mouth to mouth, even openly, and not in dark sayings, and he beholds the form of the Lord" (Numbers 12:8). So what could be the point of Moses' request? Obviously he is asking to see God not just in a theophany, not even the glorious spiritual theophany of heaven itself. He is asking to see the very divine essence of God in his pure glory. This is why God says it is impossible: "You cannot see My face, for no man can see Me and live!" (Exodus 33:20). In this case "face" means "presence": you cannot see the divine presence itself. But, says the Lord, I will place you in a crevice in the rock and cover it with my hand, then I will allow my glory to pass by the crevice, then I will take away my hand—"and you shall see My back, but My face shall not be seen" (Exodus 33:21-23). It is generally agreed that "My back" refers not to a bodily part but to the after-effects or the residue or the wake left by the passing-by of God's unapproachable glory. This is as close as any creature has come to seeing the actual being of God, but even this was not a direct viewing.

Our point has been that the description of God as *spirit* includes the fact that he is immaterial and the fact that he is invisible to mortal eyes. We have noted in this connection that God's invisibility is the result not only of his spirituality but also of his uncreated transcendence.

The Positive Meaning of God's Spirituality

That God is spirit has two positive elements, the first of which is that God is the *living* God. Spirit is associated with life. Even the biblical words for spirit can also mean "breath," i.e., the breath of life. In the New Testament God the Spirit is described as the Spirit of Life who gives life. See Romans 8:2, 6, 11; II Corinthians 3:6; John 6:63. Thus God is very often described in Scripture as the "Living God" (e.g., Isaiah 37:4; Hebrews 3:12). "The Lord lives" (Psalm 18:46)! This will be discussed more fully in another chapter.

The other positive aspect of God's spirituality is the fact that he is *personal*. (We do not say that "God is *a* person," since we believe that our trinitarian God is three persons.) This is probably the most significant thing we can say about the essence of spirit: spiritual beings are persons. Angelic spirits are persons; this includes even the fallen angels. Human spirits are persons. Thiessen correctly remarks, "The very idea of *spirit* implies personality."[67] There is no such thing as an impersonal spirit; it is a contradiction of terms. Thus to think of God as impersonal or as anything less than personal is a denial of Jesus' affirmation that God is spirit. He may be much *more* than what we know as personal being, but he is certainly not less.

The spiritual (i.e., personal) beings with whom we are best acquainted are human beings. As we seek to understand what it means to say that God is personal, it is natural that we should analyze the meaning of human personhood. Some caution against using human personhood as a model for God, however, on the ground that the gulf between God and man is too great. God always transcends such words. We must not create an idea of God in the form of man.[68] This caution needs to be heard, but it must not be

67. Henry Clarence Thiessen, *Introductory Lectures in Systematic Theology* (Grand Rapids: Eerdmans, 1949), p. 121.

68. Helmut Thielicke, *The Evangelical Faith, Volume Two*, p. 103.

pressed absolutely. We must not forget that man is created in God's image, and that man's spiritual nature is what bears this image. Thus God and man are most alike in this very matter of personhood. It is by no means out of line to point out the similarities between human personhood and the personal nature of God as revealed in Scripture. In his brief explanation of the true God to the Athenians, the Apostle Paul reminded them that even pagan poets have recognized that "we also are His offspring." He then concludes, "Being then the offspring of God, we ought not to think that the Divine Nature is like gold or silver or stone, an image formed by the art and thought of man" (Acts 17:28-29). Here Paul is not only stating that God is *not* like lifeless, impersonal material such as silver or stone; he is also affirming that God *is* like his offspring. This is the force of the word *then* or *therefore* in verse 29. I.e., we who are God's very offspring ought to know that our own Father cannot be like manmade material idols. So in our understanding of God's nature as personal, even though our authoritative source of data is the Bible, we may see how this compares with human personhood for purposes of understanding.

At least four elements are characteristic of personhood, in particular the personhood of God. The first is *rational consciousness*, or what we think of as mental activity. This is part of the essence of man's personal nature. Sometimes a human being is defined as "a rational being" or "a thinking being." Though this is not adequate as a complete definition, it is a true description. The same is true for God. He is a thinking being; he has the intellectual attributes of knowledge, wisdom, and understanding. We have no reason to object to the concept of God as infinite Mind, as long as one does not limit God to this alone.

The second element of personhood is *self-consciousness*, or an awareness of self as individual consciousness. Nonpersonal living creatures may have consciousness, as in the case of animals; but there is reason to doubt that animals have an awareness of themselves in an introspective way. Human beings, on the other hand, not only are conscious of what is around them but also may focus their attention upon themselves. That is, they are able to step outside themselves (in a sense) and direct their thoughts back upon themselves as individuals. A person thus can be both thinking subject and analyzed object at the same time.

This is true of God as a person. He has self-consciousness. He can say "I am." In fact, this awareness of himself in terms of an individual center of consciousness seems to be at the very center of God's nature. When Moses asked God for his name, because the Israelites would want to know, God said, "I AM WHO I AM": and he continued, "Thus you shall say to the sons of Israel, 'I AM' has sent me to you'" (Exodus 3:14). This episode also reveals another activity indicative of self-consciousness, i.e., self-naming. Names distinguish individual entities from one another. We may give names to animals or impersonal objects; names themselves do not signify personhood or self-consciousness. But when one gives oneself a name, this indicates self-awareness or consciousness of oneself as an individual. God not only gives himself a name, but he gives himself the name which is the ultimate in self-consciousness. "I AM."[69]

A third element of personhood is *self-determination*. In a human being this would be called the will, or the freedom of the will. It is the freedom to choose and to act as one

69. See *ibid.*, p. 107ff.

chooses. To say that God is personal thus means that what God does is freely chosen by him; he does not act out of a necessity imposed from outside himself. Creation itself is the prime example of God's personhood. Creation from nothing requires a free choice, which is the conscious decision of a personal being. Without a personal God there can be no true creation.

The final element of personhood is *relationships with other persons*. As Thielicke says, "By nature person always includes relation to a Thou, to another personal being."[70] A person is not only a subject who is conscious of himself and of impersonal objects: he is also a subject who is conscious of other subjects, other persons, and who enters into relationships with these persons. It is, as it were, a relational word. For instance, when God is described as love (I John 4:8), which is interpersonal relationship, he is being described as a person. When we are told that our primary responsibility is to love God (Matthew 22:37), we are being told to relate to God in a personal way. Since interpersonal relationships are implemented and carried on by communication, it is indicative of God's personhood that he *speaks*, and that our communion with him is in the form of words (e.g., Scripture, meditation, praise, prayer) rather than the contemplation of an idol or mindless mysticism.

God is spirit. That is, God is personal. He has rational consciousness, self-consciousness, self-determination, and relationships with other persons. This is the way God is portrayed from the beginning of the Bible to its end. Based on Scripture alone, no one would ever think of doubting God's personhood. He is all we think of as personal and no

70. *Ibid.*, p. 104.

doubt much more. Only when autonomous and abstract philosophical ideas of God begin to replace Scripture does one begin to question his personal nature.

Two final remarks must be made relating to the personhood of God. Christian tradition has been accustomed to defining the Trinity as "one God in three Persons." It refers to God as having one essence but as existing as three persons. This whole concept will be examined later. We note at this point, however, that if the above description of personhood is correct, then it would apply to each of the three persons who share Godhood. Each would enjoy rational consciousness, self-consciousness, self-determination, and relationships with other persons. From the present vantage point it would seem that this is the case. For example, the Father is conscious of himself as an individual person as distinct from the Son; the Son freely chooses to perform a certain work (i.e., incarnation and redemption) as distinct from the work of the Holy Spirit; and the Father, Son, and Holy Spirit relate to one another in an interpersonal way.

The other remark concerns the question of whether it is appropriate to refer to God exclusively or even at all in the masculine gender. This question usually arises today from within the cultural phenomenon known as "women's liberation" or the feminist movement. It is pointed out that in many cultures the deity is female. It is also pointed out that the biblical God is transcendent, and that this no doubt means that God transcends all gender distinction. If there is "neither male nor female" within the church (Galatians 3:28), surely there is neither male nor female in God. We say two things in response. First, if one is inclined to make every attempt to avoid genderial exclusivism, may that person be very careful not to demote God into the impersonal category of "it." Our language easily accommodates both the impersonal "it" and the personal "he" or "she," but anything other than these is either artificial or awkward. It is inconsistent with God's personhood to use "it" terminology; and the usually awkward efforts to avoid "he" and "she" tend to detract from the dignity and majesty of God. Second, the biblical witness supports the exclusive reference to God in terms of the personal "he." Attempts to justify referring to God in the female gender are an affront to Scripture, which refers to God in masculine terms (especially the adjectives and pronouns) throughout. We are not saying that God is a man rather than a woman, and there is surely truth to the assertion that God transcends genderial distinctions. What we are saying is that God is a person, so it is appropriate and expedient to refer to him in personal terms. And since God himself has seen fit to use masculine personal terminology in speaking of himself in Scripture, there is absolutely no basis for altering this way of speaking.

The importance of thinking of God in personal terms is summed up in the following statement by Robert Lightner:

> Belief in the personal God of the Bible provides both assurance and comfort for the child of God. Since God is a being who possesses the elements of personality in perfection, He is one with whom the believer can have fellowship. Because He is a person, He knows and understands our deepest longings. As the song writer has so aptly expressed it, we can walk and talk with him in sweet fellowship and prayer. Life would most certainly be hopeless and futile without the intimacy of our God, made possible through the Lord Jesus Christ His Son.[71]

---

71. Robert P. Lightner, *The First Fundamental: God* (Nashville: Thomas Nelson, 1973), p. 68.

In this chapter we have attempted to discuss the essential being of God as transcendent Creator. This has been set forth as the primary implication of creation with reference to the nature of God himself. Because God is the uncreated Creator and all else has been brought into existence by God out of nothing, God is transcendent. This is not a reference to spatial remoteness, but to ontological otherness; God's being is qualitatively different from the creature's. Since God is spirit, though, there is a point of similarity between God and those creatures who are also spirit, namely, angels and men. Since angelic and human spirits are created, they are still qualitatively different from God; but since they are *spirit*, they bear a likeness to God. Spiritual existence, including God's own being, is characterized as immaterial and invisible as well as living and personal.

In the next chapter we will talk about the specific way in which God as uncreated Spirit differs from all created being, even created spirit. Thus it will be a continuation of the subject of transcendence in that it will set forth that characteristic of God which sets him apart and which inheres in his uncreated essence, namely, his infinity.

Chapter Six

THE INFINITY OF GOD

In the last chapter we discussed God's transcendence, the fact that the Creator is qualitatively distinct from his creation in the very essence of his being. He is different from creatures in the mode of his existence, in the very way in which he exists. If there is one word that describes God's unique manner of existing, it is the word *infinite*. The uncreated, transcendent God is infinite in his being.

To say that God is infinite means that he is non-finite, unlimited, unbounded. This is not to be taken in a physical or mathematical sense, as if God were infinitely large or as if he extended infinitely into space. Nor does it refer to a merely quantitative distinction between God and his creatures, as if God and man have the same attributes except God has them to an infinite degree. An example of this would be that God and man have the same kind of knowledge, only man's is limited while God's is unlimited. To an extent this is true, but it is not the whole point or even the main point of infinity. To say that God is infinite means that he is not limited by anything outside himself; he is not subject to the built-in limitations of created being. Finite beings, for instance, are by nature subject to certain restrictions of time and space; the infinite God is not. Also, finite beings are capable of error; they are susceptible to imperfection and inconsistency. The infinite God, however, is not limited by such possibilities.

It should be noted that the infinity of God is not something that can be taken for granted, as if everyone agrees that the concept of God naturally includes this attribute. Many philosophers have deliberately set forth the view that God is finite. H. P. Owen mentions four examples. The first is Plato, who described God as a Demiurge or craftsman who constructed the world out of pre-existing matter after the pattern of the eternal forms. The second example is Aristotle, whose "Unmoved Mover" exists in eternal self-contemplation while passively influencing a world he did not create. The third example is John Stuart Mill, who argued that God as a Cosmic Designer took pre-existing matter and formed as good a universe as his limited power would allow; but unfortunately the product contains many flaws. Owen's last example is Alfred North Whitehead, whose finite God is in the process of maturing and developing along with the world and as influenced by the world.[1]

One thing that will be noticed in all these examples is that God is pictured as existing alongside the eternally pre-existing matter of the universe; he is not the absolute Creator of all things. In a situation such as this it is impossible for God to be anything but finite. The eternally co-existing matter is a factor which can never be under God's complete control and will always limit him to some extent. Only a Creator-God can truly be infinite. Only a God who has brought everything else into existence out of nothing can be free from the limitations inherent in that creation. This is the case with the God of the Bible, the God of Israel and of our Lord Jesus Christ. Because he is the Creator, he is infinite. His creation poses no threat to him, and he is not subject to the limiting factors built into the world, such as space and time. He transcends all the limitations characteristic of creatures. It is no wonder, then, that the concept of an infinite God is far from universal, since the necessary concept of creation *ex nihilo* is practically non-existent outside the sphere of biblical influence. As Owen remarks, "It is very hard to find a clear and consistent parallel to the Christian idea of God as one who creates the world *ex nihilo*,

1. H. P. Owen, *Concepts of Deity* (New York: Herder and Herder, 1971), pp. 49ff. See also H. Orton Wiley, *Christian Theology* (Kansas City, Mo.: Beacon Hill Press, 1940), I:281ff.

or to the Christian idea of him as one who is both infinite and fully personal."[2]

The relation between creation and God's infinity involves what may at first seem like a paradox. On the one hand creation is a necessary condition of God's unlimitedness; but on the other hand, by choosing to create, God imposed some definite limitations upon himself. When God created the world he gave it real existence apart from himself and endowed it with what Brunner calls a "relative independence."[3] This applies particularly to the created spirits who were endowed with free will. When God created angels and men with the ability to choose between good and evil and thus in a real sense to choose their own destinies, he limited the extent of his own involvement in the history of his own world. He committed himself to respect the integrity of man's free will choices, and thereby placed himself in the position of sometimes having to react to the actions of man, and of sometimes having to permit things to happen that he does not specifically desire. As Thiessen remarks, "That is why He did not keep sin out of the universe by a display of His power; that is also why He does not save anyone by force."[4]

Though this may seem like a denial of the infinity of God, in reality it is not, because the limitations placed upon God by creation are *self*-limitations. God is not limited by nature but by choice. He did not have to create at all, nor did the creation have to include free-will beings. (Creation is a *free act.*) Since it is a matter of God's own choice, and since

---

2. H. P. Owen, *Concepts of Deity,* p. 2.

3. Emil Brunner, *The Christian Doctrine of God: Dogmatics, Volume I,* tr. Olive Wyon (Philadelphia: Westminster Press, 1950), p. 251.

4. Henry C. Thiessen, *Introductory Lectures in Systematic Theology* (Grand Rapids: Eerdmans, 1949), p. 126.

there are no limitations imposed on God from without, the fact of creation does not in any way contradict the essential infinity of God; it is in no way an infringement upon his complete sovereignty over what he has made. Self-limitation is consistent with infinity; indeed, the fact that God is free to limit himself as he chooses is the supreme indication of his infinity. Brunner's complete statement on this matter is a good summary of the point we have been making:

> . . . God *limits Himself* by creating something which is not Himself, something "over against" Himself, which he endows with a relative independence. Thus it is God Himself who creates this limitation—hence He is also free to remove it. He creates it, He limits Himself, in order that a creature may have room alongside of Himself, in whom and to whom He can reveal and impart Himself. . . .[5]

Some find the concept of a finite God to be comforting. For instance, it helps them to explain the existence of what they consider to be flaws in the creation. After all, how could we expect a perfect world from an imperfect God? But there are others of us who consider the loss of the infinity of God too heavy a price to pay for this intellectual solace. How far can we trust a finite God for salvation? How can we consider him to be a worthy object of worship? The fact is that we do not have to pay this price, for the infinity of God is a biblical fact. This is the point of this chapter.

As an attribute of God infinity is not like most of the other attributes. It might be called a qualifying attribute, since it qualifies all the others. For instance, God is holy; and his moral holiness is infinite in that it is not limited by any kind of moral defect, weakness, or sin. God is love, and his love

5. Emil Brunner, *The Christian Doctrine of God*, p. 251.

is infinite in that it is not limited by such things as conflict of interest, ignorance of our need, or inability to come to our aid. In this chapter we will be considering those attributes of God which are most clearly demonstrated in his work of creation, and we will see how they are the most obvious ways in which God is infinite. We will see that God is unlimited in his existence, unlimited with regard to time, unlimited with regard to space, unlimited in his knowledge, and unlimited in his power.

UNLIMITED IN HIS EXISTENCE

The first aspect of God's infinity is that he is unlimited in his very existence. This, says Owen, is "the primary and all-determinative sign of God's infinity," and is "the primary point of difference between him and his finite creatures."[6] The word that is often used to describe this characteristic of God is *aseity*. This comes from the Latin expression *a se*, which means "from himself" or "of himself." It literally means that God derives his existence from himself and not from any outside source. A more understandable English term is *self-existence*. God owes his existence to himself; he is the cause of his own existence. Some do not like any of these terms because they seem to leave open the possibility that God was indeed "caused" in some sense, albeit self-caused, or because they do not state precisely enough the main point, which is that God's being is *uncaused*. As Buswell says, "The assertion intended is simply that God's being is uncaused. God is; God always has been; God always will be. His being is not from anything. His being is a brute fact." By the term *brute fact* he means "a fact not causally grounded

6. H. P. Owen, *Concepts of Deity*, p. 13.

upon the abstract laws of logic, and not causally determined by any other fact."[7] God's being is not derived from anything and is not dependent upon anything; he just *exists,* period. Other terms that imply this truth are *self-sufficiency, immortality, indestructibility,* and *independence.* Bavinck prefers the last term; he says that *aseity* has too narrow a connotation. It "merely expresses the fact that God is self-sufficient in his *existence*; but 'independence' has a broader connotation, and indicates that God is self-sufficient in *everything.*"[8] We may note, though, that the latter is true only because the former is true.

With all the above qualifications in mind, we may continue to speak of God's self-existence.

The fact that God is self-existent stands in sharp contrast with all created being, which by virtue of the very fact of creation owes its existence to something outside itself, namely, the Creator. Every bit of being in the whole created universe, material and spiritual, is caused by something else. It is derived and therefore dependent. It depends on God for its origin and for its continuation; without God's sustaining power it would revert to nothingness. This is the essence of finiteness; it is the most basic form of limitation. Assuming that the term is applicable to existence and not just to propositions, we may say that all created being is *contingent.* This means basically that it is possible for it *not* to be; it is possible that it might not have been at all. Since creation was a free act, this applies to the whole of existence outside of God himself.

---

7. James Oliver Buswell, Jr., *A Systematic Theology of the Christian Religion* (Grand Rapids: Zondervan, 1962), I:41.

8. Herman Bavinck, *The Doctrine of God,* tr. William Hendriksen (Grand Rapids: Eerdmans, 1951), p. 144.

Thus we see again how the fact of creation sets God apart from all else. Only the uncreated God is self-existent; and as Bavinck says, this "clearly indicates the unbridgeable chasm existing between the Creator and the creature."[9] Since God has no origin, he is dependent on nothing for his origin nor for his continuing existence. As opposed to the contingent existence of creatures, we may say that God's existence is *necessary*. He exists necessarily; it is impossible for him not to exist. It is his very essence to exist; existence is part of the definition of God, if it is possible to define God at all. Of course, we do not know this about God *a priori*; we know it only because God has revealed himself to us as the self-existent God. This means that God's existence is not a logical necessity, as claimed by the ontological argument; it is rather an ontological necessity.[10]

That God is self-existent means, of course, that it is impossible for him to cease to exist. Thus we consider Thomas Altizer's contention that God literally committed suicide to be ludicrous if not blasphemous. Whether he believes that it really happened or not, this is the basic message of Altizer's "death of God" manifesto entitled *The Gospel of Christian Atheism*. In this book he sets forth the thesis that God became literally and completely incarnate in Jesus of Nazareth, so that when Jesus died, God literally and purposely died. Since the resurrection never actually happened, God stayed dead. He thus annihilated himself; he committed suicide. It is a real event that actually happened, Altizer says.[11] It would be difficult to find a more ridiculous

9. *Ibid.*, p. 145.

10. See H. P. Owen, *Concepts of Deity*, p. 15.

11. Thomas J. J. Altizer, *The Gospel of Christian Atheism* (Philadelphia: Westminster Press, 1966), pp. 44, 83, 86-87, 102ff.

parody of the gospel than this, or a more ridiculous proposal than that the self-existent God could perish.

The biblical teaching concerning God's independence or self-existence is quite clear. It begins with God's self-revealed name in Exodus 3:14. When Moses asked God for his name, "God said to Moses, 'I AM WHO I AM'; and He said, 'Thus you shall say to the sons of Israel, "I AM has sent me to you."'" In this self-description God tells us the most basic fact about himself, that he is the one who IS. The verb "to be" serves quite appropriately as his name. It is generally thought that the name Jehovah or Yahweh is derived from this same Hebrew verb. If this is the case (and we cannot be positive), then every time we see, read, or speak this name for God, we are calling him "He Who Is."[12] In the New Testament three passages in particular convey the thought of God's self-existence. In Romans 1:23 God is described as "incorruptible," and in I Timothy 6:16 we read that he "alone possesses immortality." John 5:26 says simply that he "has life in Himself."

The fact of God's complete self-sufficiency is also emphasized in Scripture. Certainly the one who created the world, says Paul, could not possibly need it for his own sustenance. "The God who made the world and all things in it, since He is Lord of heaven and earth, does not dwell in temples made with hands; neither is He served by human hands, as though He needed anything, since He Himself gives to all life and breath and all things" (Acts 17:24-25). "Or who has first given to Him that it might be paid back to Him again?" (Romans 11:35). God does not need anyone to give him anything, since it already belongs to him. As God declared

12. This was Thomas Aquinas' conclusion. See E. L. Mascall, *He Who Is: A Study in Traditional Theism* (London: Darton, Longman and Todd, Libra edition, 1966), pp. 13, 210ff.

to Job, "Who has given to Me that I should repay him? Whatever is under the whole heaven is Mine" (Job 41:11). God does not need anyone to teach him anything, either: "For who has known the mind of the Lord, or who became His counselor?" (Romans 11:34; see I Corinthians 2:16). Neither does God have to ask permission of anyone before he does anything: "Who gave Him authority over the earth? And who has laid on Him the whole world?" (Job 34:13). No one dares to challenge him: "Will the faultfinder contend with the almighty?" (Job 40:2). "Who has appointed Him His way, and who has said, 'Thou hast done wrong'?" (Job 36:23). If God determines to do something, no one is able to stay his hand: "And I am God. Even from eternity I am He; and there is none who can deliver out of My hand; I act and who can reverse it?" (Isaiah 43:12-13).

The critical importance of God's self-existence and self-sufficiency is seen especially in this last passage, which emphasizes the *freedom* of God. Because God is not limited by any power or being outside of his control, he is free to carry out his purposes without fail. Those who trust in him do not trust in vain, and those who foolishly attempt to oppose him will be crushed. This point is well expressed in the following statement by Gilkey:

> . . . If God depends upon some other principle of equal stature to create the world, if He is finite, then again He is not "free." As finite, His acts are continually conditioned by this other principle, perhaps of chaos, of matter, or of creativity. If He be finite, moreover, He is inescapably governed by the structure of being of which He is merely a part and an illustration. He is like the gods of Greece, who were under the ultimate rule of Fate, or like Whitehead's God who is "in the grip of the ultimate metaphysical ground."

> The will of such a God is not the sovereign principle of existence but only one conditioned voice in a chorus that transcends Him. Such a restricted being is not "God," the object of our ultimate concern and trust, the free Creator, Ruler, and Redeemer of whom the Bible speaks. The unconditioned character of God, and His consequent freedom and sovereignty over all things, are essential to the biblical idea of God. . . .[13]

They are especially essential to ensure his freedom to accomplish his purpose of salvation, and to provide a basis for our complete trust and dependence upon him. And since the fact of creation is the ultimate ground of God's self-existence and freedom, we see that only God the Creator can also be God the Redeemer.

UNLIMITED WITH REGARD TO TIME

A second aspect of God's infinity, his unlimitedness, is that he is unlimited with regard to time. That is, he is *eternal*. As early as Genesis 21:33 he is called "the Everlasting God." Deuteronomy 33:27 says, "The eternal God is a dwelling place, and underneath are the everlasting arms." Isaiah 40:28 gives similar comfort: "The Everlasting God, the Lord, the creator of the ends of the earth does not become weary or tired." He is "the eternal God" (Romans 16:26), the eternal and immortal King (I Timothy 1:17) whose power and divine nature are eternal (Romans 1:20). Time is usually considered to be a part of created reality; and since God transcends his creation, he thus transcends its time limitations. This is true in two ways. God is eternal

---

13. Langdon Gilkey, *Maker of Heaven and Earth* (Garden City, N.Y.: Doubleday Anchor, 1965), p. 110.

in both a quantitative sense and in a qualitative sense. Each of these will now be discussed.

Without Beginning or End

Usually when we think of eternity we think of unending time, that is, time which extends without limits in both directions, past and future. This is sometimes called the linear view of time. God is eternal in this sense. He has existed from eternity past and will continue to exist into the eternal future. He is without beginning and without end. This is simply a consequence of his self-existence. Since God is the great "I AM," since it is his very nature to exist, he has always existed.

Sometimes we are cautioned not to press this concept literally, since it involves a notion of time that is applicable only to the creation. Time in the sense of duration—the sequence of before, now, and after; the sequence of past, present, and future—seems to have been a part of the original creation and thus would have begun only at that point. To project the same kind of sequential duration backwards into the pre-creation eternity may not be appropriate. Whether this is true or not, the fact is that the Bible *does* portray God's eternity in these terms, that is, as an endless quantitative duration. Perhaps it is an example of anthropomorphic language; perhaps this is the only way our time-bound, finite minds can come close to grasping the reality of God's eternity. So at least from our perspective, it is appropriate to think of God as existing eternally, without beginning and without end. That God is eternal means *more* than this, as we shall see in the next section; but it does not exclude his eternal duration.

In fact, the biblical teaching about God's eternity almost always refers to his originless, unending duration. He is the one who has existed from "of old" (Psalm 55:19), "from everlasting" (Psalm 93:2; Habakkuk 1:12), "from eternity" (Isaiah 43:13). He is "the Ancient of Days" (Daniel 7:9, 13, 22). He is also the one who "lives forever" (Isaiah 57:15; Daniel 12:7), who "abides forever" (Psalms 9:7; 102:12), who is "on high forever" (Psalm 92:8). God's own oath is "as I live forever" (Deuteronomy 32:40). In some contexts the words translated "eternal" and "forever" do not mean a literal eternity but have a more limited scope. When used of God, however, they *do* mean unending eternity, as shown by the intensive use of the terms and by the use of other similar expressions. God is not just "forever"; he is "God, our God forever and ever" (Psalm 48:14). "The Lord is King forever and ever" (Psalm 10:16; see Psalm 45:6). In the book of Revelation he is worshiped as the one "who lives forever and ever" (Revelation 4:9-10; 10:6; 15:7). He is from "everlasting to everlasting" (Psalm 41:13). "Before the mountains were born, or Thou didst give birth to the earth and the world, even from everlasting to everlasting, Thou art God" (Psalm 90:2). "Of old Thou didst found the earth; and the heavens are the work of Thy hands. Even they will perish, but Thou dost endure; and all of them will wear out like a garment . . . . But thou art the same, and Thy years will not come to an end" (Psalm 102:25-27; see Hebrews 1:10-12). Jude 25 puts it very succinctly: "To the only God our Savior, through Jesus Christ our Lord, be glory, majesty, dominion and authority, before all time and now and forever. Amen." God is "the one who is and who was and who is to come" (Revelation 1:4, 8; 4:8). God declares, "I am the first and I am the last, and there is no God besides Me" (Isaiah 44:6; see Isaiah 48:12). He says, "I am the Alpha and the Omega, the beginning and the end" (Revelation 21:6; see Revelation 1:8). He is incorruptible (Romans 1:23) and immortal (I Timothy 6:16).

It is in the light of God's eternal duration that we are to understand these passages: "For a thousand years in Thy sight are like yesterday when it passes by, or as a watch in the night" (Psalm 90:4); "with the Lord one day is as a thousand years, and a thousand years as one day" (II Peter 3:8). To one who is eternal, one finite period of time is no more significant than any other finite period of time. What is actually a long period to us is no more than a short one to God. A thousand years is really quite short when compared with eternity.

There are two ways in which God's quantitative eternity transcends the creature's temporal existence. First, only God has existed from eternity past. By virtue of creation, everything else had a beginning, including angels and the spirits of human beings. The idea that the spirits or souls of men have always existed is contrary to creation and has its origin in paganism, not in the Bible. It is God's will that human spirits (and angels) shall continue to exist forever into the future, but this by no means implies that they have always existed. Second, only God is immortal by nature; only God will exist forever because it is impossible for him not to exist. With human beings immortality is a gift; we are not inherently immortal. We will exist forever because God wills us to, not because we have to.

Outside the Flow of Time

God is eternal not only in the quantitative sense described above; he is also eternal in a qualitative sense in that he exists outside the flow of created time and is not bound by its limitations. Because he is the Creator, he transcends all the limiting aspects of the created world, including time. Creaturely time involves the *objective duration* of reality in which there is the sequence of past, present, and future as measured by change and motion. The critical moment in time is always the present; and the present is constantly and relentlessly moving along like a sliding marker, like the bow of a ship cutting through the water. To change the form of the illustration, it is like one great cosmic hoop through which the whole universe from galaxies to electrons is jumping at approximately the same time.[14] All other time is relative to the moment of passing through the hoop (the present), which is the only moment which really "exists." Thus the present is the moment of experience, the arena of action and motion. It is an objective reality shared by the whole of creation, both the spiritual and the material spheres.

Because the creation includes spiritual or self-conscious beings, creaturely time also involves the *subjective awareness* of the sequence of past, present, and future. Subjects as well as objects move along the flow of time, sharing a common present. The present moment for rocks and stars is also the present moment for men and angels. The difference is that the latter—we—are *conscious* of the moment of experience and action; we are conscious of being in the present. We are also conscious of the fact that there are a past and a future, though these are not a part of our immediate consciousness. We can think about the past and think about the future, but we are conscious only of the

14. We say "approximately" in order to make some allowance for the Einsteinian reconstruction of the concept of time, in which there is not necessarily a single universal moment.

present; i.e., consciousness is limited to the moment of passing through the hoop of the present. Thus the whole of creation, spiritual and material, endures along the flowing moment of the present (or passes through the stationary moment of the present); and this moment of the present is the fixed point of experience and consciousness for the creature. This is one reason why we speak of the creature as finite, namely, because he is limited to a single point of consciousness by the nature of created time. He cannot extricate himself from the flow, nor should he want to do so. To be so limited is not a curse; it is part of the good creation and part of the very meaning of creaturehood.[15]

To say that God is not limited by time means that he stands outside its flow, that his experience and his consciousness are not restricted to a single present moment as distinguished from past and future. He stands in a sense above time, so that his consciousness embraces the whole of time in a single act of knowing. His knowledge of the past and the future is as real and infallible as his knowledge of the present. This divine transcendence of time is mostly incomprehensible to us, though several illustrations have been suggested. If we may refer again to Abbott's *Flatland*, we might say that God from the divine dimension can see the scope of time just as a three-dimensional sphere floating above the two-dimensional "Flatland" can see its reality in a way totally impossible to those restricted to the plane itself. We may also use the illustration of a reel of film. When a film is run through a projector, we see the frames one by one. In a sense this is the way we see events in time as such—one frame at a time. But God from his eternal vantage point

15. See Emil Brunner, *The Christian Doctrine of God*, p. 267.

can see the whole reel of time in a single moment, as if it were all present to him at once. The following illustration is similar:

> A visit to the Cyclorama in Atlanta, Georgia, has presented a different concept of the relation of time and eternity. In the Cyclorama one stands on a raised platform in a circular room where the civil war Battle of Atlanta is depicted in a truly remarkable combination of statue and painting artwork. The three dimensional characters and equipment blend imperceptibly into the painting on the walls giving a true sense of continuity. The battle is seen to progress from one side, along a railway, under the viewers platform off into the city on the other side. Along, and on either side of the track are scenes of the progressing battle with the same soldiers, now winning, now losing, now dying on the battlefield. As one stands on the viewers platform he can see the beginning, progression and end of the battle. There is a sense of eternal presence in that scene.[16]

Emil Brunner has stated this point very well:

> . . . As for the Creator, the limitations and laws of the created world do not limit Him, because it is He who posits them and creates them, so also for Him the barriers of the temporal —the separation into past, present, and future—do not exist. God includes and comprehends Time within His Presence; He does not eliminate it, but He fulfills it. God's Being is not timeless; but it is full of time, fulfilling time; all that is temporal is present in Him in the same way, or, to put it more correctly: He is present in the Temporal as a whole as He wills. . . .[17]

---

16. "Eternity—A Different Concept," *The Cable* (October 1979), 5:2.
17. Emil Brunner, *The Christian Doctrine of God*, p. 270.

The basic biblical teaching concerning God's transcendence of the flow of time is found in his great series of challenges to all false gods and idols in Isaiah 40-48. God's claim to be the one true God is based here on his exclusive ability to know the whole scope of history at once, to see it from beginning to end at one and the same moment. God challenges the false gods to recite past history and to foretell the future. They cannot, but he can, because he is God; and his transcendence of time proves it. Isaiah 41:21-26 declares the impotence of anyone besides the true God to break out of the limits of time:

> "Present your case," the Lord says. "Bring forward your strong arguments," the King of Jacob says. Let them bring forth and declare to us what is going to take place; as for the former events, declare what they were, that we may consider them, and know their outcome; or announce to us what is coming. Declare the things that are going to come afterward, that we may know that you are gods . . . . Who has declared this from the beginning, that we might know? Or from former times, that we may say, "He is right!"? Surely there was no one who declared, surely there was no one who proclaimed, surely there was no one who heard your words.

The Lord declares his sovereignty over time in Isaiah 42:8-9, "I am the Lord, that is My name; I will not give My glory to another, nor My praise to graven images. Behold, the former things have come to pass, now I declare new things; before they spring forth I proclaim them to you." The challenge is renewed in Isaiah 44:6-8,

> Thus says the Lord, the King of Israel and his Redeemer, the Lord of hosts: "I am the first and I am the last, and there

> is no God besides Me. And who is like Me? Let him proclaim and declare it; yes, let him recount it to Me in order, from the time that I established the ancient nation. And let them declare to them the things that are coming and the events that are going to take place. Do not tremble and do not be afraid; have I not long since announced it to you and declared it? And you are My witnesses. Is there any God besides Me, or is there any other Rock? I know of none."

Because he stands above time and can see it all from beginning to end, God is able to "plan ahead," as it were. That is, he can project his own purposes into the fabric of the future, announce his plans, and then carry them out as announced. Only the true God can do this!

> Remember the former things long past, for I am God, and there is no other; I am God, and there is no one like Me, declaring the end from the beginning and from ancient times things which have not been done, saying, "My purpose will be established, and I will accomplish all My good pleasure"; calling a bird of prey from the east, the man of My purpose from a far country. Truly I have spoken; truly I will bring it to pass. I have planned it, surely I will do it (Isaiah 46:9-11).

The Lord uses his transcendence of time to formulate predictive prophecies so that no one can deny his claims to be God.

> . . . I declared the former things long ago and they went forth from My mouth, and I proclaimed them. Suddenly I acted, and they came to pass. Because I know that you are obstinate, and your neck is an iron sinew, and your forehead bronze, therefore I declared them to you long ago, before they took place I proclaimed them to you, lest you should say, "My idol has done them, and my graven image and my molten image have commanded them." You have heard; look at all this. And you, will you not declare it? I

> proclaim to you new things from this time, even hidden things which you have not known. They are created now and not long ago; and before today you have not heard them, lest you should say, "Behold, I knew them" (Isaiah 48:3-7).

Sometimes the notion of God's eternity seems to be defined in an extreme fashion as complete timelessness or simultaneity. In other words, with God there is no succession of moments or even consciousness of succession of moments. God's being and God's knowledge are characterized as one eternal NOW, or a single, simultaneous present. There is no such thing as before or after, past or future with God. Louis Berkhof comes close to this extreme when he says that God's eternity "may be defined as that perfection of God whereby He is elevated above all temporal limits and all succession of moments, and possesses the whole of His existence in one indivisible present."[18] Some have carried this to the extent that they see time and eternity as being logically contradictory and ontologically exclusive. This was Kierkegaard's approach, and that is why he regarded the incarnation—God entering time—as the absolute paradox.

What shall we say of this concept of eternity as absolute timelessness? Let us assume for the moment that it may be applicable to God in his self-contained, non-relational existence apart from the creation. But with respect to his relationship to creatures, can we really say that sequence or succession of moments is meaningless and totally nonexistent for God? Because he stands outside the flow of time, does this mean that he has no consciousness of the

18. Louis Berkhof, *Systematic Theology* (London: Banner of Truth Trust, 1939), p. 60. Italics omitted.

passage of time within the creation? In my judgment such conclusions are extreme; they do not necessarily follow from the fact of God's eternity.

We must remember that the fact of creation means that this created universe is real and not illusory. There is a genuine integrity to created time. The succession of moments is not an illusion. History is real. There is an authentic *now*. Everything we read in the Bible leads us to understand that God really and truly interacts with and acts within the universe, and this interaction always takes place at the only point where the universe temporarily "exists," at the only point where action is really possible: the *now*. Thus the eternal God experiences the ever-progressing, ever-changing moment of the present, working within the flow of time itself. He addresses the now in the speech of revelation; he alters the now in his miraculous deeds; he inhabits the now in the incarnate Logos. The work of providence is a continuous interaction with creation; the work of redemption has required the active presence of God in history on countless occasions. In all of this interaction God respects the reality of history and the integrity of the flow of time, i.e., the integrity of the now. He does not violate the succession of moments which he himself set in motion at the time of creation. Thus we cannot say that the whole of history literally *exists* simultaneously in a single moment, an eternal now for God. God cannot act in the world's past, present, and future simultaneously; he relates only to the creaturely now. In other words, God cannot act along the whole continuum of time at will, for the whole continuum as such does not exist simultaneously; only the present "exists." When God acts, he acts in the present. Once the present has become the past, it is unalterable. God can no more change the past nor interact with the past than we can without violating the integrity he bestowed on it at the beginning. Likewise he must wait for the future to become the present before entering into it, though he may have planned and prophesied a particular action long in advance.

There is no contradiction or paradox in this, because time and eternity are not mutually exclusive in a Kierkegaardian sense. Neither is God absolutely timeless in a Platonic sense, as Plato described his world of forms or ideas. On the contrary, it is precisely because God is eternal, existing outside the flow of time and unbounded by its limitations, that he is free to act within it or upon it as he chooses, while always remaining transcendent to it. As Pieper says, "God enters into space and time and still always remains above space and time."[19]

We have said that God experiences the succession of moments in his created universe: he acts in the now; his actions in the past are unalterable; he waits for the future to arrive. How, then, does he transcend time? What has become of his infinity? Two things must be said. One, God remains infinite; his infinity is what gives him the freedom to act within time if he so chooses. This is just one of the limitations he imposed on himself by freely creating this particular kind of world. Second, though God's actions are fed into the flow of time only at the moment of the creature's now, which means that God *experiences* the succession of moments, still his *knowledge* or consciousness is not limited to that now. Because God is eternal, he *knows* the whole scope of time in a single act of knowledge; his consciousness embraces our past, present, and future as if it

19. Francis Pieper, *Christian Dogmatics* (St. Louis: Concordia, 1950), I:442.

were a single moment. That is, past, present, and future do not exist for God as far as his knowledge is concerned, but they do exist as far as his actions in relation to the world are concerned. This simultaneous knowledge constitutes God's transcendence and freedom with regard to time. To be truly *bound* by time is to have consciousness only of the present, as is the case with creatures.

We should also point out that although God knows the whole continuum of history in a single act, he is at the same time conscious of which part of the continuum is the now and which parts are the past and the future.

This part of the discussion is well summed up in the following statement by H. Orton Wiley:

> . . . We must then hold fast the truth that as in self-consciousness, the self transcends the flow of time and yet recognizes this flow, so God also as the Eternal transcends time, but as the God of His creatures He works out His purposes for them under the law of time which He has Himself created. There is succession in the order of things as they exist; there can be no succession in God's knowledge of them. In dealing with His creatures, therefore, God recognizes them as past, present and future in this succession of existence; or as one theologian has so aptly stated it, God knows the past as past, the present as present and the future as future.[20]

The eternity of God as it relates to his creation is really all that we know about his eternity. It is quite common to say that God in his own self-contained existence as such is

20. H. Orton Wiley, *Christian Theology*, I:339. See also the discussion of Charles Hodge's view in James Oliver Buswell, Jr., *A Systematic Theology of the Christian Religion*, I:44-46. Buswell cites a comment by A. E. Taylor: "If God does not know the difference between yesterday and tomorrow, He does not know as much as I do."

totally without a succession of moments; his existence is truly one eternal NOW. Wiley himself says, "He stands superior to time, free from the temporal distinctions of past and future, and in whose life there can be no succession."[21] Morton Smith says, "Eternity is to be distinguished from time in not involving a succession of moments. The name "I AM" has a bearing on this. God eternally is. His being, knowledge, and will are eternally present; there is no history with God."[22] On the other hand, the Bible does use terms suggesting duration in relation to God's being, such as Jude's reference to "before all time and now and forever" (Jude 25). And if God's actions in relation to his creatures are sequential, how can we say that God as such transcends all succession? Are these actions not real to God? Is the incarnation not an event of the *past,* even in God's experience? Must we not affirm that the Judgment Day has not happened yet, *not even for God*? This possible reality of the already and the not yet would not be a limitation for God since his knowledge includes the whole in one perfect act of cognition. But if God's actions (and not only his knowledge) occur in one simultaneous present, then all the actions that God performs occur all at once, and they are all eternal (i.e., they are never not occurring). It would mean that God never really does anything for the first time, and never ceases to do anything that he does. Whether such thoughts are just the vain speculations of the finite trying to embrace the infinite, or whether they suggest the possibility that God's pure eternity does not necessarily exclude succession within his own being, we will not venture to decide.

21. H. Orton Wiley, *Christian Theology,* I:335.

22. Morton H. Smith, "God, The Attributes of," *Encyclopedia of Christianity,* Volume IV, ed. Philip Hughes (Marshallton, Del.: The National Foundation for Christian Education, 1972), p. 370.

One final point must be made here. Only the Creator is transcendent; only the Creator stands above the flow of time and is not bound by its limitations. Since time is a characteristic of creation, all creatures at all times are restricted by it. Angels are not eternal in either a quantitative or qualitative sense. The same is true of human beings. When we die we do not "enter eternity" and exist above time as God does. We are now and always will be—even in heaven—creatures whose consciousness embraces only the now. Temporality is due to the creation, not to the Fall.

UNLIMITED WITH REGARD TO SPACE

A third aspect of God's infinity is that he is unlimited by space. Space, like time, is a product of creation. Created beings are spatial beings. Both the material and the spiritual dimensions are spatial, though not necessarily in the same way. Though spiritual "space" is not like material space, each dimension has spatial limitations. Space of some sort is characteristic of creatures. The material universe is three-dimensional space; this is the only kind of space with which we are truly familiar. We exist in bodies that are spatial and thus limited by the boundaries of space. These limitations include the following: a material body can exist in only one space at a time; only one material body can occupy its space at one time; to get from one space to another a material body must pass through the intervening space. Fully spiritual beings such as angels and demons do not literally occupy our space as we do and are not subject to all the limitations of three-dimensional space as we are; but they are nevertheless created beings and have their own spatial limitations. They occupy their own space—the spiritual dimension—with whatever limits that exist there. And when they interact with material space, they are not totally outside its limits either. For instance, a spiritual creature can be in only one space at one time. Neither angels nor demons are omnipresent. Satan himself cannot be everywhere at once; his demons are his angels or messengers which represent him around the world.

God the uncreated Creator is not a spatial being; he is unlimited by space. He transcends all spatial limitations; he is infinite. A traditional word for this attribute of God is *immensity*. In popular jargon this word means very large in size; thus if we use it we must be careful to exclude such a connotation as this.[23] It does not mean that God is infinitely large, so as to fill all of space physically even to infinity, and in such a way that part of God is in one part of space while another part of God is in another part of space. This is a totally false concept of God, and it is not the concept intended in the use of the term *immensity*. The word itself literally means unmeasurable, and in reference to God it means that he is unmeasurable not because he is too large but because as a non-spatial being the whole concept of measuring just does not apply to him. God is not the kind of being who is subject to measurement. He is qualitatively different from space. Thus we do not ask how tall he is or how much he weighs or anything else of this kind. The term simply means that God is not limited by space. Space is not a limiting factor for God. All the characteristics of space as we know it—extension, location, distance—do not apply to him.

The Bible makes this point on a number of occasions, especially in relation to worship and places of worship. We

23. J. O. Buswell, Jr., suggests that we avoid the word altogether in reference to God because of its spatial connotations. See *A Systematic Theology of the Christian Religion*, I:38.

should never think that worship can take place at only certain physical locations, because God is not spatially *confined* to just one location. We should never think that a house of worship is sufficient to contain the infinite God. Solomon knew this when he dedicated the new temple: "But will God indeed dwell on the earth? Behold, heaven and the highest heaven cannot contain Thee, how much less this house which I have built!" (I Kings 8:27; see II Chronicles 6:18). The same point is made in Acts 7:48-50 (quoting from Isaiah 66:1-2):

> . . . However, the Most High does not dwell in houses made by human hands; as the prophet says: "Heaven is My throne, and earth is the footstool of My feet; what kind of house will you build for Me?" says the Lord; "or what place is there for My repose? Was it not My hand which made all these things?"

Acts 17:24 is similar: "The God who made the world and all things in it, since He is Lord of heaven and earth, does not dwell in temples made with hands." Jesus' statement that "God is spirit" was made in reply to the comment of the Samaritan woman concerning the proper place of worship: "Our fathers worshiped in this mountain; and you people say that in Jerusalem is the place where men ought to worship" (John 4:20). When Jesus replied that "you worship that which you do not know" (verse 22), he was suggesting that the whole concept of a God physically located in one place or restricted in movement from space to space is false. "God is spirit; and those who worship Him must worship in spirit and truth" (verse 24). This can be done on your mountain or in Jerusalem or in both places at once. God is not limited by space.

This points to the most obvious result of God's immensity, namely, his *omnipresence*. Because God is not limited by space, he is universally present to all of space at all times. He is everywhere-present. We should guard against false physical images again, and not think of God as physically diffused through the infinite reaches of space, so that every part of space has at least a little particle of God. This is not the idea. To understand God's omnipresence we should think in terms of the divine dimension and its relation to the material dimension. The divine dimension does not simply physically surround the space-time universe, nor is it invisibly present within it. Rather, the divine dimension intersects every point of space; it interfaces with the material dimension everywhere. The illustration of *Flatland* may be useful again at this point. The inhabitants of the two-dimensional realm of Flatland were conscious *only* of their existence on a plane surface; to them the whole universe existed in only two directions comparable to east-west and north-south on the surface of a map, i.e., length and width. That there might be another totally different segment of reality existing in another direction (i.e., height) could never have occurred to them. And yet, from our perspective, we know that the third dimension of height interfaces with a flat plane at every point on its surface. This is not a totally adequate illustration, but it may help us to see how the transcendent and unlimited God is present in his whole being at every point of our space. This is not the same as saying that God is present *in* all space. He is present *to* all of space, or perhaps we should say that all space is immediately present to him and before him. As Buswell puts it, "I find it helpful to express the omnipresence of God by the thought that everything in the entire universe is immediately in His presence."[24]

24. *Ibid.*

This would be true of both the spiritual and the material realms. God is not located in any one space, such as on a particular mountain, on a certain cloud, or even on a specific heavenly throne. He may make his presence known in the form of a theophany which is localized, but such a visible appearance does not limit God to that one space. God could make himself known in a million simultaneous theophanies and still be fully present to all the rest of creation at the same time. He could do this not just because he is spirit, but because he is God the uncreated Spirit.

Psalm 139:7-10 is a clear statement of the omnipresence of God. Here the psalmist says,

> Where can I go from Thy Spirit? Or where can I flee from Thy presence? If I ascend to heaven, Thou art there; if I make my bed in Sheol, behold Thou art there. If I take the wings of the dawn, if I dwell in the remotest part of the sea, even there Thy hand will lead me, and Thy right hand will lay hold of me.

This shows the futility of Jonah's flight: "But Jonah rose up to flee to Tarshish from the presence of the Lord" (Jonah 1:3; see verse 10). We need not bother trying to go somewhere away from the presence of the Lord; such a place does not exist. "'Am I a God who is near,' declares the Lord, 'and not a God far off? Can a man hide himself in hiding places, so I do not see him?' declares the Lord. 'Do I not fill the heavens and the earth?' declares the Lord" (Jeremiah 23:23-24). No matter where a person might be located, whether in the remotest spot on earth or in a distant galaxy, God is still both very near and also far off. The "far off" is emphasized so that no one may think of escaping God's presence; the "near" is emphasized so that all may know that God may be found if sought. Indeed, God is as near as the nearest point of space, for every point in space is a contact point between us and God. Paul says of all men "that they should seek God, if perhaps they might grope for Him and find Him, though He is not far from each one of us; for in Him we live and move and exist" (Acts 17:27-28).

Before leaving the subject of God's omnipresence, we should note that the Bible speaks of different kinds of divine presence, and it uses the concept of the presence of God in different ways. Up to now we have been discussing what might be called the universal ontological presence of God, his natural omnipresence based on the fact of creation. But sometimes God becomes present in a different way. In addition to being present *to* all of space equally, he actually enters space at specific points and becomes present *in* it for special purposes. Since these purposes most often have to do with redemption, Langdon Gilkey speaks of this type of presence as God's "unique revelatory and saving appearances."[25] We may call it his selective redemptive presence, as distinct from his universal ontological presence. This would include every instance of theophany, in which God becomes locally present to his people. There are many Old Testament examples of this type of presence. For instance, in Exodus 19 we read about God's coming down "on Mount Sinai in the sight of all the people" (verse 11).

> . . . So it came about on the third day, when it was morning, that there were thunder and lightning flashes and a thick cloud upon the mountain and a very loud trumpet sound, so that all the people who were in the camp trembled. . . . Now Mount Sinai was all in smoke because the Lord descended upon it in fire; and its smoke ascended like the

25. Langdon Gilkey, *Maker of Heaven and Earth*, p. 114.

> smoke of a furnace, and the whole mountain quaked violently . . . . And the Lord came down on Mount Sinai, to the top of the mountain. . . . (verses 16-20)

Later God showed himself in a more exclusive spiritual theophany to a few selected leaders of Israel (Exodus 24:1-11). The pillar of cloud bearing the glory of God often appeared before the Israelites (Exodus 33:9; 40:34; I Kings 8:10ff.). In the New Testament the most intensive form of God's selective redemptive presence appears, the incarnation itself (John 1:14); thus Jesus is appropriately called Immanuel, "God with us" (Matthew 1:23). Another example is the inbreaking of the Holy Spirit on Pentecost (Acts 2:1-4), as well as the Spirit's indwelling in the body of every Christian (I Corinthians 6:19).

In addition to these two kinds of presence, the Bible also uses the language of God's presence (or absence) in a figurative sense to represent either (1) his attitude of favor or disfavor, or (2) his availability for aid. Regarding the first of these, being in God's favor is often spoken of as being *near* to God or being in his presence, while being in God's disfavor is represented by the withdrawal of God's presence or by the concept of distance from God. In such cases God's presence or absence is not a metaphysical fact but an ethical reality. The limiting factor is sin, not space. God withdraws from those who oppose him and whose hearts are "far away" from him (Mark 7:6), but he is near to those who sincerely seek him. This is summed up in II Chronicles 15:2, "The Lord is with you when you are with Him. And if you seek Him, He will let you find Him; but if you forsake Him, He will forsake you."

In reference to distance as a symbol of disfavor, we see in Genesis 4:16 that "Cain went out from the presence of the Lord." Also, "The Lord is far from the wicked" (Proverbs 15:29); thus the repentant David prayed, "Do not cast me away from Thy presence" (Psalm 51:11). Because of his anger against Jerusalem and Judah, he did "cast them out from His presence" (Jeremiah 52:3). And because they seek him in the wrong spirit, "they will not find Him; He has withdrawn from them" (Hosea 5:6; see verse 15). This spiritual distance is sometimes described as God's hiding his face from the wicked: "Then My anger will be kindled against them in that day, and I will forsake them and hide My face from them, and they shall be consumed" (Deuteronomy 31:17; see verse 18 and 32:20). "But your iniquities have made a separation between you and your God, and your sins have hid His face from you, so that He does not hear" (Isaiah 59:2). See Isaiah 64:7; Jeremiah 33:5; Ezekiel 39:23-24, 29. The ultimate withdrawal is Hell: "And these will pay the penalty of eternal destruction, away from the presence of the Lord and from the glory of His power" (II Thess. 1:9).

On the other hand, those who find favor with God are said to be in his presence. "The eyes of the Lord are toward the righteous, and His ears are open to their cry. . . . The Lord is near to the brokenhearted, and saves those who are crushed in spirit" (Psalm 34:15, 18). "The Lord is near to all who call upon Him, to all who call upon Him in truth" (Psalm 145:18). Those who repent may once again find God's favor: " 'Return to Me,' declares the Lord of hosts, 'that I may return to you' " (Zechariah 1:3; see Malachi 3:7). He will return and dwell with the penitent: "For thus says the high and exalted One who lives forever, whose name is Holy, 'I dwell on a high and holy place, and also with the contrite and lowly of spirit' " (Isaiah 57:15). "The Lord has taken away His judgments against you, He has cleared away your enemies. The King of Israel, the Lord, is in your midst" (Zephaniah 3:15; see verse 17). In the New Testament era the Gentiles, previously "far off" (Acts 2:39), are now "brought near by the blood of Christ" (Ephesians 2:13). Only Christ breaks through the sin barrier and gives us access to God's presence (Ephesians 2:18; 3:12). The principle remains the same: "Draw near to God and He will draw near to you" (James 4:8). Those who draw near are glad; "they delight in the nearness of God" (Isaiah 58:2). To the faithful God is faithful: "Thou dost set me in Thy presence forever" (Psalm 41:12).

In all of these cases both of favor and disfavor, God's ontological presence, his omnipresence, is constant and does not change. But depending on our own attitude toward him, his presence takes on different meanings for us. To those who arouse his anger, his presence is as barren as his absence; to those who seek him aright, his presence becomes a fountain of blessing. Brunner speaks of this latter presence as *intensive* and not just extensive.[26]

The language of God's presence is also used figuratively to represent God's availability to help in time of need, and his intention to act in a certain way at a specific place. Psalm 42:5 shows this clearly: "Why are you in despair, O my soul? And why have you become disturbed within me? Hope in God, for I shall again praise Him for the help of His presence." When he is in need of help the psalmist prays, "O Lord, do not be far from me" (Psalms 35:22; 71:12). When God wants to assure his people that he will be ready to help them, he declares to them, "I am with you. . . . My Spirit

26. Emil Brunner, *The Christian Doctrine of God*, p. 258.

is abiding in your midst" (Haggai 1:13; 2:4-5). The ultimate assurance is Immanuel, "God with us" (Matthew 1:23). Immanuel himself has promised, "Lo, I am with you always, even to the end of the age" (Matthew 28:20). God's promise to dwell among his people is his promise to strengthen and to bless (Numbers 35:34; I Cor. 3:16; Ephesians 2:22). That the Father forsook Jesus (Matthew 27:46) means that he could not aid him or deliver him from the cross.

Special use of the language of presence in the sense of God's availability to his people is related to worship. Sometimes when we gather to worship or go to God in prayer we say, "We come into your presence." This does not mean that we were not already in God's presence; it means that we are acknowledging his presence and especially his openness and availability to us. It is not inappropriate to speak in these terms: "My soul thirsts for God, for the living God; when shall I come and appear before God?" (Psalm 42:2). Those who seek the Lord in false worship do not find his presence (Hosea 5:6), but those who worship in spirit and in truth can find his presence anywhere (John 4:20-24). Jesus promised, "Where two or three have gathered together in My name, there I am in their midst" (Matthew 18:20). Through Jesus the High Priest we can always "draw near" to the throne of grace (Hebrews 4:16; 10:22).

Our main point in this section is that the infinite God is not limited by space and thus is omnipresent. As we have seen, though, his omnipresence is no blessing for those who oppose him; but it is a great source of blessing and comfort to those whose heart is right before him.

UNLIMITED IN HIS KNOWLEDGE

The next aspect of God's infinity is his unlimited knowledge. "The Lord is a God of knowledge" (I Samuel 2:3) is true without limits. The fact that he is unlimited with regard to space and time could lead to no other conclusion. The God who transcends time knows the whole of history in a single glance; the God who transcends space has every speck of spatial existence constantly before his consciousness. The result is that God is omniscient, he knows everything.

The Omniscience of God

The Bible tells us in no uncertain terms that God knows everything there is to know. His knowledge is total and perfect; he "knows all things" (I John 3:20). "Great is our Lord, and abundant in strength; His understanding is infinite" (Psalm 147:5). "And there is no creature hidden from His sight, but all things are open and laid bare to the eyes of Him with whom we have to do" (Hebrews 4:13). "Oh, the depth of the riches both of the wisdom and knowledge of God! How unsearchable are His judgments and unfathomable His ways! For who has known the mind of the Lord, or who became His counselor?" (Romans 11:33-34).

This last passage points to a fact that we might expect, namely, that the nature of God's knowledge and the manner of his knowing far transcend the limitations of human cognition. We would not expect the infinite God to have to be taught; we would not expect him to have to acquire his knowledge through any process of learning. "'For My thoughts are not your thoughts, neither are your ways My ways,' declares the Lord. 'For as the heavens are higher than the earth, so are My ways higher than your ways, and My thoughts than your thoughts'" (Isaiah 55:8-9). The following statement by Owen sums up this point:

> So far as the manner of God's knowledge is concerned, it excels human knowledge in being wholly intuitive. Our knowledge, although it contains intuitive elements, is largely discursive. It is acquired and confirmed by comparing, classifying, abstracting and drawing inferences from sense-data. God has no need of these piece-meal processes; he knows all things by a direct intellectual intuition. . . .[27]

One other point is that God not only knows all things but is always conscious of all that he knows. A finite mind actually knows a great deal more than it is conscious of at any one time; most things we know are stored away in our "memory banks," so to speak. Insofar as we are able, we will them to our consciousness when we need to think about them. God's knowledge, on the other hand, is a constant and complete consciousness of all things.[28]

The Bible gives us further detail concerning the scope of God's knowledge, as it speaks of specific things which he knows. Putting everything into two general categories we may say that God has perfect knowledge of himself and of everything outside of himself. Concerning the former, we are told that God knows himself to his very depths. "For the Spirit searches all things, even the depths of God. For who among men knows the thoughts of a man except the

27. H. P. Owen, *Concepts of Deity*, p. 30.

28. This distinction may help to explain how the divine Christ could say that he did not know the time of his second coming even though the Father does (Matthew 24:36). Perhaps one of the results of the incarnation was that the *consciousness* of Jesus was limited as that of any human being, in that he only thought about one thing at a time. Yet because he was God, he still had *all* knowledge at his command and could will it into his consciousness whenever necessary. One thing that he did not will into his consciousness, by design, was the time of his second coming.

spirit of the man, which is in him? Even so the thoughts of God no one knows except the Spirit of God" (I Cor. 2:10-11). Concerning things outside himself, we read that "He counts the number of the stars; He gives names to all of them" (Psalm 147:4). On the earth itself he knows such details as the number of hairs on every head (Matthew 10:30), and he keeps track of every bird (Matthew 10:29).

Certainly for our purposes the most important knowledge in the mind of God is his knowledge of ourselves, of the whole human race, of all our needs and deeds. We are told that "the eyes of the Lord . . . range to and fro throughout the earth" (Zechariah 4:10). "His eyes are upon the ways of a man, and He sees all his steps" (Job 34:21). "The Lord looks from heaven; He sees all the sons of men; from His dwelling place He looks out on all the inhabitants of the earth" (Psalm 33:13-14). "The eyes of the Lord are in every place, watching the evil and the good" (Proverbs 15:13). "He understands all their works" (Psalm 33:15), both bad and good. "O God, it is Thou who dost know my folly, and my wrongs are not hidden from Thee" (Psalm 69:5). Alms given, prayers made, and fasting done in secret are still seen by God; "and your Father who sees in secret will repay you" (Matthew 6:4, 6, 18). God's complete knowledge of our works will make the final judgment valid, because God's "eyes are open to all the ways of the sons of men, giving to every one according to his ways and according to the fruit of his deeds" (Jeremiah 32:19). "Because God will bring every act to judgment, everything which is hidden, whether it is good or evil" (Ecclesiastes 12:14).

The psalmist David reflects on God's total knowledge of his life in Psalm 139:

> O Lord, Thou hast searched me and known me. Thou dost know when I sit down and when I rise up; Thou dost understand my thought from afar. Thou dost scrutinize my path and my lying down, and art intimately acquainted with all my ways. Even before there is a word on my tongue, behold, O Lord, Thou dost know it all. Thou hast enclosed me behind and before, and laid Thy hand upon me. Such knowledge is too wonderful for me; it is too high, I cannot attain to it (139:1-6).

In verses 7-10 David concludes from God's omnipresence that no matter where he is, God will know him. Nor can he presume to think that the darkness will hide him from God's eyes: "If I say, 'Surely the darkness will overwhelm me, and the light around me will be night,' even the darkness is not dark to Thee, and the night is as bright as the day. Darkness and light are alike to Thee" (139:11-12). And then in a most touching and significant reflection, David declares that God knew all about him, present and future, while he was still being formed in his mother's womb:

> For Thou didst form my inward parts; Thou didst weave me in my mother's womb. I will give thanks to Thee, for I am fearfully and wonderfully made; wonderful are Thy works, and my soul knows it very well. My frame was not hidden from Thee, when I was made in secret, and skillfully wrought in the depths of the earth. Thine eyes have seen my unformed substance; and in Thy book they were all written, the days that were ordained for me, when as yet there was not one of them (139:13-16).

No wonder David follows this with a word of praise: "How precious also are Thy thoughts to me, O God! How vast is the sum of them! If I should count them, they would outnumber the sand" (139:17-18).

Probably that which magnifies the omniscience of God most in our minds is the fact that God knows the deepest contents of our hearts. John reminds us that "God is greater than our heart, and knows all things" (I John 3:20). Many passages tell us that God knows the heart; see I Kings 8:39; Acts 15:8; Luke 16:15. (This is said of Jesus, too; see Matthew 9:4; John 2:25.) The Lord declares, "I, the Lord, search the heart, I test the mind, even to give to each man according to his ways" (Jeremiah 17:10). As Proverbs 15:11 says, "Sheol and Abaddon lie open before the Lord, how much more the hearts of men!" "The Lord weighs the hearts" (Proverbs 21:2); he understands our thoughts (Psalm 139:2); he "weighs the motives" (Proverbs 16:2); he knows all our desires (Psalm 38:9). God is not limited as man is; God can see both the outside and the inside of our lives. "For God sees not as man sees, for man looks at the outward appearance, but the Lord looks at the heart" (I Samuel 16:7). Thus God knows the heart of the hypocrite and pays no attention to his false worship and vain cries: "There they cry out, but He does not answer because of the pride of evil men. Surely God will not listen to an empty cry, nor will the Almighty regard it" (Job 35:12-13). But on the other hand, because he can judge the heart, "The Lord knows those who are His" (II Timothy 2:19).[29]

Before we can say that God knows *all* things, there is one other category that must be brought within the scope of his knowledge, namely, the future. This will be dealt with in the next section.

---

29. This is why we speak of the "invisible church." Only the Lord who knows the hearts knows who is truly his and who is not. Thus the true borders or boundaries of the church are invisible to man and visible only to God.

The Foreknowledge of God

Does God know the future? Does he have knowledge even of contingent events, primarily human free-will choices, before they actually take place? Does God have genuine foreknowledge? Such questions have been the subject of considerable discussion, and a number of differing answers have been given. Some have concluded that contingent events by their very nature cannot be known in advance, not even by God. Others have taken the position that God *could* know future contingent events, but he chooses not to do so in an act of self-limitation.[30] Those who hold views such as these are usually concerned with preserving the integrity of man's free will. It is thought by many that if God truly knows in advance what our future choices will be, then his foreknowledge renders our choices certain and thus not really free. Another view seeks a compromise between true foreknowledge and no foreknowledge; it posits a kind of conditional foreknowledge of God. According to this view God does not truly foreknow future contingent events, but he *does* know all *possible* free choices with their conditions and consequences. Thus he is not surprised by any actuality, and he has already made plans in advance as to what he will do if Mr. X chooses Y instead of Z, and so on.[31] But this is not really foreknowledge, since true foreknowledge has to do with realities and not possibilities.

All of the views mentioned above must be rejected, since all of them deny that God truly foreknows human free-will

30. See H. O. Wiley, *Christian Theology,* I:358-359.

31. See Herman Bavinck, *The Doctrine of God,* pp. 190-191; E. L. Mascall, *He Who Is,* pp. 119ff.

choices, whereas the Bible plainly declares that he does. As we have already seen in reference to God's eternity, the fact that God transcends the flow of time means that he sees the past, present, and future in one unified act of knowledge; all is present to him in a kind of eternal NOW. God himself says that the very mark of deity is the ability to declare what is going to take place, to announce what is coming (Isaiah 41:21-23). Though no one else has done this, he himself has accomplished it. "I am God, and there is no one like Me, declaring the end from the beginning and from ancient times things which have not been done" (Isaiah 46:9-10).

> . . . And who is like Me? Let him proclaim and declare it; yes, let him recount it to Me in order, from the time that I established the ancient nation. And let them declare to them the things that are coming and the events that are going to take place. Do not tremble and do not be afraid; have I not long since announced it to you and declared it? . . . (Isaiah 44:7-8).
>
> Gather yourselves and come; draw near together, you fugitives of the nations; they have no knowledge, who carry about their wooden idol, and pray to a god who cannot save. Declare and set forth your case; indeed, let them consult together. Who has announced this from of old? Who has long since declared it? Is it not I, the Lord? . . . (Isaiah 45:20-21).

See also Isaiah 42:8-9; 48:3-7. In all of these passages God asserts his exclusive possession of knowledge of the future.

It should not have to be pointed out that the whole possibility of predictive prophecy depends largely upon God's genuine foreknowledge. The mark of a true prophet, says the Lord, is if the thing he predicts comes true (Deuteronomy 18:20-22). After Daniel interpreted Nebuchadnezzar's dream about the statue, he said, "The great God has made known to the king what will take place in the future" (Daniel 2:45). Just before Moses died God told him about the future apostasy of the Israelites (Deuteronomy 31:16-21). It should be pointed out that in these and other cases God is not just declaring what he himself plans to do in the future, but he is also foretelling what human beings will be doing of their own free will.

God also declares the reality of his foreknowledge in connection with the predestination of individuals to salvation. "For whom He foreknew, He also predestined" (Romans 8:29). The saints are chosen, says Peter, "according to the foreknowledge of God the Father" (I Peter 1:2). The death of Jesus involved a similar combination of foreknowledge and predestination, as he was "delivered up by the predetermined plan and foreknowledge of God" (Acts 2:23). That is, because God foreknew certain free-will choices of men like Judas and Pilate, he could arrange in advance the certain death of Christ on Calvary.

There are other specific references to foreknowledge. God foreknew his people Israel (Romans 11:2), and he foresaw the justification of the Gentiles as well (Galatians 3:8). In Psalm 139:4 David mentions how God knows his words before he (David) even speaks them; in verse 16 he says that God knew all the days of his (David's) life before they had even begun. The fact that names have been written in the Lamb's Book of Life from the foundation of the world is a clear indication of God's foreknowledge (Revelation 13:8; 17:8).

Thus we conclude that God truly foreknows the future, even the contingent free-will choices of human beings. How, then, shall we explain this foreknowledge? How is it possible for God to foreknow contingent events? There are two major answers to this question. One is that God foreknows all that is going to happen, including human decisions and actions, because he is the one who has predetermined and decreed that they shall occur in the first place. God's eternal decree is like a pre-established blueprint for universal history; everything that happens happens because it was included in the decree. Certainly God knows what is in his own pre-ordained plan; his absolute predestination of all things is the basis of the foreknowledge. This is the view usually found in Calvinistic theology, having been stated in no uncertain terms by John Calvin himself.[32] The Puritan writer Stephen Charnock says,

> It is not from the infiniteness of his own nature, simply considered, that God knows things to be future; for as things are not future because God is infinite . . . , so neither is anything known to be future only because God is infinite, but because God hath decreed it; his declaration of things to come is founded upon his appointment of things to come. . . . God knows his own decree, and therefore all things which he hath decreed to exist in time, not the minutest part of the world, could have existed without his will, not an action can be done without his will. . . .[33]

Contemporary Calvinists agree. L. S. Chafer says, "What God foreknows is certain, not because he foreknows it, but

---

32. God "foresees future events only by reason of the fact that he decreed that they take place." John Calvin, *Institutes of the Christian Religion*, III.xxiii.6, ed. John T. McNeill, tr. Ford L. Battles (Philadelphia: Westminster Press, 1960), II:954.

33. Stephen Charnock, *The Existence and Attributes of God* (Grand Rapids: Kregel reprint, 1958), p. 205.

because of the fact that He has decreed it."[34] Morton Smith says that God's knowledge is eternal because he has always known everything he was going to do in creation and in history. "Furthermore, this knowledge does not depend on any foresight, but is according to His own sovereign good pleasure. We know things only because they exist, but for God they come to exist if He has known them first."[35]

Louis Berkhof says,

> . . . We are up against a problem here, which we cannot fully solve, though it is possible to make an approach to a solution. God has decreed all things, and has decreed them with their causes and conditions in the exact order in which they come to pass; and His foreknowledge of future things and also of contingent events rests on His decree. This solves the problem as far as the foreknowledge of God is concerned.[36]

This explanation of the foreknowledge of God must be rejected primarily because the concept of an absolutely predetermining eternal decree is not a biblical doctrine and thus cannot be the basis of God's knowledge of the future. (This will be discussed later.) Also it should be noted that such a view solves the problem only by eliminating human free will, despite protestations to the contrary. Anything that is predetermined to the minutest degree cannot be considered contingent. We should also note that this view actually places a limitation on the power and sovereignty of God insofar as it is stated that God *cannot* know truly free choices ahead of time, or that he can know them only

---

34. Lewis Sperry Chafer, *Systematic Theology* (Dallas: Dallas Seminary Press, 1947), I:196.
35. Morton H. Smith, "God, The Attributes of," p. 372.
36. Louis Berkhof, *Systematic Theology*, pp. 67-68.

if he predetermines them. An example of this is Louis Berkhof himself, who says, "Actions that are in no way determined by God, directly or indirectly, but are wholly dependent on the arbitrary will of man, can hardly be the object of divine foreknowledge."[37]

We conclude that the only view that preserves both the integrity of God's foreknowledge and the integrity of human free will is the view that God foreknows future contingent choices simply because he is the transcendent God who stands above time and knows all things in an eternal now. Contrary to Charnock, it *is* from the infiniteness of his own nature that God knows the future. As Brunner puts it, "The Divine Knowledge is not bound to Time and Space, to perception and inference, as ours is. All stands in eternal presence before the eyes of God." He continues,

> As we know the *present* not only as something that is necessary, but also as something that is accidental, contingent, so also God knows the *future* as something contingent. The future stands equally directly before Him as the present stands before us. God knows that which takes place in freedom in the future as something which happens in freedom. This kind of knowing is beyond our powers of imagination, and it is unintelligible . . . .[38]

Francis Pieper agrees that Scripture teaches both infallible foreknowledge and human freedom, though this appears to be a contradiction that may never be resolved in this life.[39]

Several objections have been raised against this explanation of foreknowledge. One is that if God's knowledge is

37. *Ibid.*, p. 68.
38. Emil Brunner, *The Christian Doctrine of God*, p. 262.
39. Francis Pieper, *Christian Dogmatics*, I:450-451.

in the form of an eternal now, then it is not really *fore*-knowledge to him, since nothing is really *future* to the eternal God.[40] In response we note that this is mainly a semantic problem, but we should remember that the Bible does use before-and-after terminology in reference to God and his works. Perhaps this is just an accommodation to our perspective. But we should also remember that God's relationship to the created universe does involve succession of moments and even the consciousness of the sequence of past, present and future. The universe which God created is real, and its history is real; they are not just ideas in the mind of God. It is part of the self-limitation of the Creator that his own knowledge of his creation is in a sense derived from the creation. Even though his knowledge is eternally the same, we may say that his knowledge of the contingent events of his creation is logically dependent on their actual occurrence. At least in this sense it is real *fore*-knowledge.

This leads to a second objection. Calvinists in particular usually reject the whole idea that God's knowledge (or anything about God) could in any way be dependent on anything outside himself. This is seen as a compromise of his absolute sovereignty. This is one reason why the eternal decree is made the basis of foreknowledge; it removes the possibility of God's deriving his knowledge from the historical events themselves. Thus a foreknowledge based simply on God's infinite awareness of the future is not acceptable to those who take the Calvinistic viewpoint. As Louis Berkhof says, "It is objectionable, because it makes the divine knowledge dependent on the choices of man."[41] Or as Bavinck says, "The medium whereby God knows all things is not

40. Herman Bavinck, *The Doctrine of God*, p. 189. See H. O. Wiley, *Christian Theology*, I:356.

41. Louis Berkhof, *Systematic Theology*, p. 68.

the universe but the decree."[42] In response we freely affirm that this concept of foreknowledge—indeed, this whole concept of the Creator and his creation—means that God's knowledge and even his actions to some extent are conditioned by what takes place in the creation. There is no other way to look at it if there is genuine free will within the creation. Unless we believe that God predetermined Adam's sin (and some do), then we must believe that the whole history of redemption from Genesis 3 onward is God's response or reaction to a free-will choice of the creature. Unless we believe that God from the beginning planned and determined that there should be a hell with eternal inhabitants (and some do), then we must believe that hell is God's reaction to free-will choices of his creatures. To say that some of God's decisions are thus conditioned by something outside himself does not compromise his sovereignty, because God freely chose to create such a world, thereby imposing such limitations upon himself. The nature of God is compromised much more severely by arbitrarily maintaining that God in no way reacts to anything outside himself; it makes God ultimately responsible for sin and all its consequences. Likewise the integrity of the created world is compromised. Thus we conclude that there is absolutely no problem with saying that the divine foreknowledge is conditioned in a sense by the reality of the future-happening events themselves.[44] We must remember, though, that God does not have to wait for the events to happen before he knows them. God knows the

42. Herman Bavinck, *The Doctrine of God*, p. 192.

43. For a fuller discussion of this point see Jack Cottrell, "Conditional Election," *Grace Unlimited*, ed. Clark Pinnock (Minneapolis: Bethany Fellowship, 1975), pp. 63-65.

44. See H. O. Wiley, *Christian Theology*, I:357.

events before they actually occur by virtue of his transcendence of time. Thus his knowledge is still eternal, immediate, and complete.

This leads to a final objection, this time from the other side of the theological spectrum. Those who deny true foreknowledge often object that if God actually knows what is going to happen before it happens, then it is *certain* to happen; thus the freedom and the contingency of the future are destroyed. As L. H. DeWolf words it, "If God knows now every choice any man will ever make, then every choice is already determined and freedom is an illusion."[45] But such an objection misses the point of real foreknowledge. God foreknows the free choices of man as real choices, not simply as possibilities which his own recognition nails down as certain. Their certainty is not settled by God's foreknowledge; rather, God's foreknowledge is settled by the reality of the events themselves. The fact that God sees them "ahead of time" from his perspective of eternity does mean that there is no question that they are going to happen as God sees them, but they are going to happen because of the genuine free choices of those involved. God's seeing them does not *make* them happen. Let us consider this analogy. While watching a documentary of a recent historical event, I may say at one point in the film, "I know exactly what these people are going to do next. There is no question about it. They are going to do such and such." And then

45. L. Harold DeWolf, *A Theology of the Living Church* (New York: Harper and Brothers, 1953), p. 109. See also Axel D. Steuer, "The Supposed Incoherence of the Concept of God," *Is God GOD?* ed. Axel D. Steuer and James E. McClendon, Jr. (Nashville: Abingdon, 1981), p. 101: "I would suggest that omniscience does not entail foreknowledge of the free choices of other persons, because such foreknowledge would be logically incompatible with the claim that those choices are in fact free."

on the film the events take place just as I have described them. Did my "foreknowledge" of these events in any way affect the freedom of those involved? No, because I have seen the film before, and that is why I "foreknow" what is going to happen. My certainty as to what would happen has in no way affected the reality of the events; their occurrence is independent of my knowledge of them. Or more accurately, my certainty is dependent upon their reality. Now, this is something like the way God's foreknowledge works, except he sees the reality of the events *before* they happen instead of afterwards. But his foreknowledge no more affects the contingency of the events than does my after-the-fact knowledge of a past event. Thomas Aquinas gave this example:

> . . . At the height of eternity God regards all things from above the movement of time. Events that come to be in time are already present to him. When I see Socrates sitting down, my knowledge is certain and infallible, but it imposes no necessity on Socrates to sit. And so God, in looking at things which to us are past, present, or future, infallibly and certainly knows them as present realities, yet without imposing on them the necessity of existing.[46]

Exactly how it is possible for God to see the future in this way is something that finite creatures will probably never understand.

It should not be necessary to point out that foreknowledge is the exclusive prerogative of the one who transcends time, and that no creature—man, angel, or demon—possesses this attribute of divinity. (See Isaiah 40-48 again.) When either men or angels foresee the future, it is because God

---

46. Thomas Aquinas, as cited by H. P. Owen, *Concepts of Deity*, p. 32.

has so instructed them. Sometimes human beings within the framework of the occult claim the power to know the future, e.g., Edgar Cayce and Jeane Dixon. Sometimes their "prophecies" seem to be fairly accurate. How can we explain this? We should note first of all that if anything genuinely supernatural is happening, it is probably the result of demonic spirits who are working through such individuals. If this is the case, it raises the question as to whether demons have the power to know the future. The answer is still a resounding *no*. Any apparently successful predictions can be explained in one of several ways. First, demons do have a much greater knowledge of the past and present than we do; hence on this basis it is possible for them to make projections about the future that are likely to be much more accurate than human predictions. But even this knowledge is fallible. So even though some of their projections may be accurate, more often than not they are in error, as the track record of any so-called prophet will show upon examination. Second, demons know what they themselves plan to do in the future; so they may announce ahead of time that something will happen then proceed to cause it to happen. Such is not genuine foreknowledge, of course. Third, it is possible that at times God may permit demons or even men to glimpse the future for his own sovereign purposes. Deuteronomy 13:1ff. suggests that sometimes a false prophet may prophesy accurately, but only by God's help, "for the Lord your God is testing you to find out if you love the Lord your God with all your heart and with all your soul." In short, as Pieper says, "Foreknowledge is the exclusive property of the divine Majesty," and any creature who claims to have such power is guilty of "a blasphemous encroachment upon God's prerogative."[47]

47. Francis Pieper, *Christian Dogmatics*, I:452.

Implications of Omniscience

Finally we must inquire into the implications of the divine omniscience. How does the understanding that God knows everything about us affect our own lives and attitudes? What are the practical consequences of God's transcendence of time and space, with the effect that every single aspect of our lives is constantly before him? Basically there are two implications, two consequences—one negative and one positive. First, the omniscience of God is a threat and a warning to the wicked; second, it is a promise and a blessing to the righteous.

God's omniscience is surely a threat to the wicked. The basic warning is this: we cannot hide from God; we cannot hide our wickedness from him. God knows all our works and all our thoughts and will bring them all into judgment. The wicked man likes to pretend that God does not see him: "He says to himself, 'God has forgotten; He has hidden His face; He will never see it' " (Psalm 10:11). "And they say, 'How does God know? And is there knowledge with the Most High?' " (Psalm 73:11). "And you felt secure in your wickedness and said, 'No one sees me' " (Isaiah 47:10). But "woe to those who deeply hide their plans from the Lord, and whose deeds are done in a dark place, and they say, 'Who sees us?' or 'Who knows us?' " (Isaiah 29:15). For God *does* know! "His eyes behold, His eyelids test the sons of men" (Psalm 11:4). "His eyes are upon the ways of man, and He sees all his steps. There is no darkness or deep shadow where the workers of iniquity may hide themselves" (Job 34:21-22). The Lord declares, "My eyes are on all their ways; they are not hidden from My face, nor is their iniquity concealed from My eyes" (Jeremiah 16:17). God's omnipresence ensures his omniscience, to the sorrow of the wicked: "'Am I a God who is near,' declares the Lord, 'and not a God far off? Can a man hide himself in hiding places, so I do not see him?' declares the Lord. 'Do I not fill the heavens and the earth?'" (Jeremiah 23:23-24). Hebrews 4:13 underscores the impossibility of escape: "And there is no creature hidden from His sight, but all things are open and laid bare to the eyes of Him with whom we have to do." The last part of this verse is more accurately translated (as in the NIV) "before the eyes of him to whom we must give account." Thus once again we see that omniscience is God's guarantee that the judgment will take account of our every deed and thought. So, "do not be deceived, God is not mocked; for whatever a man sows, this he will also reap" (Galatians 6:7).

On the positive side, God's omniscience is surely a blessing to the righteous. We are assured of his constant vigilance on our behalf: "For the eyes of the Lord move to and fro throughout the earth that He may strongly support those whose heart is completely His" (II Chronicles 16:9). He is always near to hear us when we pray or cry out to him: "The Lord is far from the wicked, but He hears the prayer of the righteous" (Proverbs 15:29). "The Lord is near to all who call upon Him, to all who call upon Him in truth" (Psalm 145:18). What a blessing it is to know that we are not in the predicament of Baal's prophets, who kept crying out in vain with no one to hear them. Elijah mocked them with these words: "Call out with a loud voice, for he is a god; either he is occupied or gone aside, or is on a journey, or perhaps he is asleep and needs to be awakened" (I Kings 18:27). But this is not the case with our God. Our needs and our troubles do not go unnoticed. When the children of Israel suffered in Egypt, "their cry for help because of their bondage rose up to God. . . . And God saw the sons of Israel, and God took notice of them" (Exodus 2:23, 25). "And the Lord said, 'I have surely seen the affliction of My people who are in Egypt, and have given heed to their cry because of their taskmasters, for I am aware of their sufferings'" (Exodus 3:7; see verse 9). Psalm 34:15 assures us, "The eyes of the Lord are toward the righteous, and His ears are open to their cry." David took comfort in this: "Lord, all my desire is before Thee; and my sighing is not hidden from Thee" (Psalm 38:9). Our heavenly Father knows what we need (Matthew 6:32), and we know that he will supply our needs: "Behold, the eye of the Lord is on those who fear Him, on those who hope for His lovingkindness, to deliver their soul from death, and to keep them alive in famine" (Psalm 33:18-19). Knowing that we are thus known by the all-seeing God gives us a tremendous sense of comfort and trust, and a blessed freedom from anxiety: "Our soul waits for the Lord; He is our help and our shield. For our heart rejoices in Him, because we trust in His holy name. Let Thy lovingkindness, O Lord, be upon us, according as we have hoped in Thee" (Psalm 33:20-22).

In this section we have seen that God's nature as the infinite Creator gives him unlimited knowledge. He knows all things; he is omniscient. This includes a true knowledge of truly contingent future events. An awareness of God's all-inclusive knowledge will cause us either to fear or to trust, depending on our heart's relationship with him.

UNLIMITED IN HIS POWER

The final aspect of God's infinite nature that is displayed most prominently in the mighty act of *ex nihilo* creation is his power. The kind of power required for the creation can only be an unlimited power; thus we say that God is all-powerful or *omnipotent*. The power of God is a constantly-recurring theme in Scripture. "Be Thou exalted, O Lord, in Thy strength; we will sing and praise Thy power" (Psalm 21:13). "Behold, God is exalted in His power" (Job 36:22); "power belongs to God" (Psalm 62:11). "Great is our Lord, and abundant in strength" (Psalm 147:5); "more than the sounds of many waters, than the mighty breakers of the sea, the Lord on high is mighty" (Psalm 93:4).

Some of the more common names for God are associated with the idea of power and strength. The names *El* and *Elohim* cannot be traced with certainty to a definite root, but the most common opinions connect them with words meaning "to be strong, to be powerful." These names are thus equivalent to Mighty One, Leader, or Governor. Morton Smith says,

> . . . Regardless of which of the suggestions is adopted, all carry with them the idea of the overwhelming majesty of God. It is of interest to observe that these are not terms that suggest identification of God with any part of creation. Rather, the thought is of the Mighty One who is behind creation, a Power which man cannot master. . . .[48]

One of the more common names for God in the Old Testament is *El Shaddai* (sometimes just *Shaddai*), which is usually translated "God Almighty" (or "the Almighty"). The occurrences of this title are much more numerous than could be listed here. They begin as early as Genesis 17:1, "The Lord appeared to Abram and said to him, 'I am God

48. Morton H. Smith, "God, The Names of," *Encyclopedia of Christianity*, Volume IV, p. 357.

Almighty.'" The word *Shaddai* probably comes from a root meaning "to overpower or to destroy." Thus when it is combined with *El,* the concept of power is multiplied. Morton Smith says that it must mean "the God who is all-powerful."[49] Bavinck says, "Wherever the name occurs the idea of power and invincible strength is in the foreground. . . . Hence, this name makes God known to us as the One who possesses all power, and is able to overcome all opposition and to make everything subservient to his will."[50] The Septuagint translates *El Shaddai* with the Greek word *pantokratōr,* "Almighty," which occurs in the New Testament in II Cor. 6:18 and in Revelation 1:8; 11:17; 15:3; 16:7, 14; 19:6, 15; 21:22. That God is consistently called "the Almighty" from the beginning to the end of the Bible shows how prominent is his attribute of omnipotence.

H. P. Owen points out that "to call God 'omnipotent' can mean either (a) that he is ruler over all things, or (b) that he can do all things." Owen correctly observes that "both meanings are entailed by the idea of his infinity."[51] In this section we will mainly be concerned with the latter aspect of omnipotence, since other aspects will be discussed later.

Another kind of distinction within the power of God is that between his absolute power (*potentia absoluta*) and his ordained power (*potentia ordinata*). Interestingly enough, these two terms are used in two entirely different ways by various theologians. One approach to this terminology is represented by Charles Hodge. God's absolute power, Hodge says, is the power by which he works directly, without any

49. *Ibid.*, p. 361.
50. Herman Bavinck, *The Doctrine of God,* pp. 101-102.
51. H. P. Owen, *Concepts of Deity,* p. 33.

intervening or secondary causes. This would include the direct exercise of power in such works as creation, miracles, and inspiration. God's ordained power, on the other hand, is the power exercised through secondary causes, as in the case of providence.[52] The other understanding of these terms is the more usual one and will be followed here. According to this understanding the absolute power of God is the unlimited reservoir of power by which he is able to do anything he could ever want to do, even if he does not choose to do it. The ordained power of God is the actual exercise of his power by which he brings about the things he has actually chosen to do.[53]

God's Absolute Power

The omnipotence of God is understood first of all as his absolute power by which he is able to do anything he so desires. There are no limits on his power in the sense that whatever he wants to do, he can do it. It is necessary to emphasize this point in relation to the present creation. If God did not have the absolute power to do as he pleases, someone might say that he has already wanted to do some things that he has not been able to do. In fact, this kind of thinking is not at all uncommon in relation to the problem of evil. Some observers say that an all-good God surely would have created a world without evil and suffering if he had been able to do so; but much evil and suffering are in the world; therefore God must not have been able to

---

52. Charles Hodge, *Systematic Theology* (Grand Rapids: Eerdmans reprint, n.d.), I:410. Other examples are Francis Pieper, *Christian Dogmatics*, I:459; and H. O. Wiley, *Christian Theology*, I:352-353.

53. For an example of this use see Louis Berkhof, *Systematic Theology*, p. 80.

create such a world even though he wanted to. Thus he does not have absolute power; he is not omnipotent.[54]

The concept of absolute power has also been challenged from within the context of twentieth-century theology, especially by those whose theological method has been determined by the Christological fallacy as discussed in a previous chapter. Those who make Christ the epistemological touchstone for understanding every doctrine, including the creation, tend to put less emphasis on the power of God. Hendrikus Berkhof rightly gives credit to Karl Barth for this theological revision, since he is the one who gave "a christological foundation and content to each of the attributes" of God.[55] Berkhof himself follows this method, acknowledging his debt to Barth.[56] He then deals with omnipotence as follows:

> . . . The general and popular idea is that in the biblical witness concerning God the emphasis is on God's omnipotence. But that is a great mistake. On the contrary, the first impression one gets from the biblical account of revelation is that of God's impotence, of how man has taken the initiative away from him, of what we shall call here his "defenselessness." . . .[57]

This defenselessness is seen most obviously in the Christ and reaches its nadir on the cross. But Berkhof also sees it as the prominent element in the creation itself, as he puts the main emphasis on God's self-limitation and surrender of power in the creating of free-will beings who can oppose

---

54. Examples of this view are Plato, David Hume, and Edgar S. Brightman. See the discussion in Howard S. Redmond, *The Omnipotence of God* (Philadelphia: Westminster Press, 1964), pp. 43-46, 56-58, 73-75.

55. Hendrikus Berkhof, *Christian Faith: An Introduction to the Study of the Faith*, tr. Sierd Woudstra (Grand Rapids: Eerdmans, 1979), p. 117.

56. *Ibid.*, p. 133.

57. *Ibid.*, p. 134.

and resist him. This is the point of God's "superior power"; this is the "defenselessness of God's omnipotence."[58]

A similar view is found in Emil Brunner's discussion of "God, the Almighty." Brunner rejects the concept of absolute power; i.e., he denies omnipotence in the sense that God is able to do anything he likes. The whole idea of "being able," he says, is entirely absent from the Bible and comes from philosophical speculation.[59] Brunner also emphasizes creation as a self-limitation of God, and prefers to speak of God's power only in the sense of his ordained power, the power he actually exercises over the world. And this power, he says, is almost always mentioned only in connection with revelation and redemption, its primary example being the cross.[60]

> . . . God shows His Omnipotence in highest sovereignty where the impotence of the Crucified, the defeat of the Son of God, must accomplish the work of revelation and reconciliation. Yes, here in particular the specific nature of the true Omnipotence in the Biblical sense, in contrast to all rational ideas of omnipotence, becomes plain. . . .[61]

In the final analysis the omnipotence of the Almighty God is the power of love to win the hearts of his free creatures.[62]

These denials and modifications of the absolute power of God have one thing in common: they all deal inadequately with the concept of God's self-limitation in the creation of free-will beings. Those who deny omnipotence because they think it is incompatible with the presence of evil in the world

58. *Ibid.*, pp. 134-139.
59. Emil Brunner, *The Christian Doctrine of God*, p. 248.
60. *Ibid.*, pp. 249-253.
61. *Ibid.*, p. 253.
62. *Ibid.*, p. 254.

are not giving enough attention to this self-limiting; those who use the impotence of the cross as the model of divine power give too much attention to it. We will deal with the former problem in the next volume. Regarding the latter problem, the difficulty is not so much in what is affirmed as in what is denied. Certainly the incarnation involves self-imposed weakness; and by all means there is divine power in the gospel, the drawing power of love. But to emphasize this *instead of* the absolute power of the Creator is to set up a false choice. It is not either/or; it is both/and. The divine omnipotence cannot be reduced to *nothing but* the "superior power of defenselessness." It is much more than this.

When we read the Bible without the distorting Christological lenses, we see the absolute power of God taught quite clearly in both Testaments. The title of God Almighty (*El Shaddai* and *Pantokratōr*) surely includes this concept. H. Berkhof recognizes this when he says (erroneously), "In the Bible the term 'almighty' occurs only a few times and then in eschatological contexts. For the present we cannot use it."[63] This is manifestly false. In the Old Testament *El Shaddai* occurs six times in the Pentateuch and once in Ezekiel (Genesis 17:1; 28:3; 35:11; 43:14; 48:3; Exodus 6:3; Ezekiel 10:5). The name *Shaddai* (Almighty) by itself occurs approximately thirty-six times.[64] Even if Berkhof were limiting his remarks to *Pantokratōr,* it is used nine times in the New Testament, once in II Corinthians 6:18, which is hardly an eschatological context: " 'And I will be a Father to you, and you shall be sons and daughters to Me,' says

63. Hendrikus Berkhof, *Christian Faith,* p. 139.

64. Morton H. Smith, "God, The Names of," p. 361.

the Lord Almighty." In addition to the uniform use of this name, the Bible specifically declares that God has absolute power. Jesus said on one occasion, "With God all things are possible" (Matthew 19:26; see Mark 10:27). When Mary asked the angel how the virgin conception of Jesus could possibly occur, she was told, "For nothing will be impossible with God" (Luke 1:37). A similar comment quieted Sarah's doubts when the birth of Isaac was announced: "Is anything too difficult for the Lord?" (Genesis 18:14). Jeremiah 32:27 asks similarly, "Behold, I am the Lord, the God of all flesh; is anything too difficult for Me?" When the wandering Israelites asked for meat to eat, God promised them a whole month's supply. Moses got a bit nervous at this promise and wondered how enough meat would be found to feed 600,000 people for a month. "And the Lord said to Moses, 'Is the Lord's power limited? Now you shall see whether My word will come true for you or not' " (Numbers 11:23). Then he sent them hordes of quail. Also, after God had thoroughly chastened Job, "then Job answered the Lord, and said, 'I know that Thou canst do all things, and that no purpose of Thine can be thwarted' " (Job 42:1-2). The psalmist declares, "Our God is in the heavens; He does whatever He pleases" (Psalm 115:3; see Psalm 135:6). A final passage shows that the concept of absolute omnipotence is grounded in the fact of creation: "Ah Lord God! Behold, Thou hast made the heavens and the earth by Thy great power and by Thine outstretched arm! Nothing is too difficult for Thee!" (Jeremiah 32:17). Thus the absolute power of the Creator is a well-attested fact of Scripture.

Of course there are some things which the Bible itself says that God *cannot do*; and these are sometimes thought to be a contradiction of omnipotence. For instance, God "cannot lie" (Titus 1:2; see I Samuel 15:29; Hebrews 6:18). "God cannot be tempted by evil" (James 1:13). The Lord will not "change his mind" (I Samuel 15:29). Is God's "inability" to do these things an expression of weakness on his part? Hardly! In fact, the opposite is true. If he *could* do these things, it would be an expression of weakness. These are negative acts, not positive ones; to do them would imply a lack of strength. That he cannot do them is not a limitation but rather an affirmation of his power.

Another approach to these "cannots" is that they are contrary to the very nature of God, and obviously omnipotence does not include the requirement that God must be able to contradict his own nature. God could not sin or annihilate himself, for these are impossibilities by the very nature of things, or more specifically, by the very nature of God. Thus we may say with Thiessen that omnipotence means "that God can do everything that is in harmony with His perfections."[65] Perhaps an even better way to say it is that God can do everything he pleases to do, as Psalm 115:3 sums it up; or that he can do whatever he wants to do without being thwarted, as Job 42:2 says. Thus we must believe that God made exactly the kind of world which he wanted to make; he did not want to create something which he was unable to bring into existence.

It is quite common for the skeptical among us to challenge the omnipotence of God by thinking up what seem to be impossible tasks for him to tackle. This is one of Brunner's complaints about the whole concept of absolute power. Just because it is a speculative and not a biblical concept

65. Henry C. Thiessen, *Introductory Lectures in Systematic Theology*, p. 126.

(he says), it gives rise to "all those theoretical, curious, fanciful questions" about whether God is able to do this or that.[66] E.g., could God make the past not to have existed? Could God make a square circle? Could God make 2 and 3 equal 7? Could God make a rock so big that he couldn't move it? Such pseudo-problems as these are likewise outside the realm of possibility because they are contrary to the very nature of God, namely, contrary to his nature as a rational God. Because of who God is—indeed, just because he exists at all—there are certain laws of logic that cannot be violated. The very fact of God's existence establishes the law of non-contradiction (a point that Francis Schaeffer makes very well in *The God Who Is There*); for just as God cannot exist and not-exist at the same time, neither can anything else both be and not-be at the same time. Questions such as the above violate this principle of logic; they are logical contradictions and thus are contrary to God's own nature.[67] Mascall recalls the dictum of Thomas Aquinas in reference to this point: "It is better to say that such things cannot be done, than that God cannot do them."[68] Or as Buswell puts it, "He can do with power anything that power can do."[69]

One other point should be noted again before we leave the question of God's absolute power, and that is the fact of the limitations which God has imposed on himself as the

66. Emil Brunner, *The Christian Doctrine of God*, p. 249.

67. Regarding the question whether God could create a rock so big he could not move it, the contradiction is revealed when we understand that creation itself is the ultimate moving of anything. Thus if God creates a rock, he has already moved it. The question thus asks whether God can move a rock which he cannot move, which is a contradiction.

68. Thomas Aquinas, *Summa Theologica*, I.xxv.3c, cited by E. L. Mascall, *He Who Is*, p. 121.

69. J. O. Buswell, Jr., *A Systematic Theology of the Christian Religion*, I:63.

result of his decision to create this particular world. Since these are *self*-limitations they are not violations of his omnipotence, since in imposing them God has done exactly what he wanted to do without his purposes being thwarted. But now that the limitations have been imposed (e.g., the world has its own reality; human beings have free will), God cannot do certain things without violating the commitments he made in the very act of creation. Thus it is still a matter of God's being true to his own nature. If we say that God cannot determine man's free will choices, we are basically saying that he cannot go against himself, since it was his own free choice to give man freedom in the first place.

God's Ordained Power

In a way Brunner is right. There is not a lot of practical value in arguing over what God *could* do if he *would*.[70] But the Bible does teach the fact of God's absolute power, and there are a few questions that can be dealt with only by virtue of its reality. Of much more practical use, though, is the fact of God's ordained power, namely, the power displayed in the things which he actually *has* done. Truly, the works which God Almighty has already performed are more than enough to establish the majesty of his omnipotence. Most of these will be discussed later; here we will focus just on the almighty power exercised in the mighty deed of creation.

We have pointed out the statement in Jeremiah 32:17, "Behold, Thou hast made the heavens and the earth by Thy great power and by Thine outstretched arm!" Romans 1:20 mentions the fact that certain invisible attributes of

70. Emil Brunner, *The Christian Doctrine of God*, p. 252.

God can be perceived through what has been made, particularly his *eternal power.* The thought of power naturally goes with the idea of creation. Certainly when we think back on the nature of creation from nothing, we must agree that nothing else could ever be a comparable demonstration of sheer power (with the possible exception of resurrection from the dead).

In addition to the bare fact of creation from nothing, the omnipotence of God is magnified even more when we consider the size and nature of the universe so created. Its size is so vast that we cannot even comprehend it. We may remember some data cited earlier: our galaxy of about 100 billion stars is about 100,000 light-years in width, and there are probably close to 100 billion galaxies in the observable universe. Many of these galaxies are visible only through a 200-inch telescope whose lens took ten months to cool and eleven years to polish. Yet God spoke the whole universe into existence with a word! The amount of matter originated in that creative moment could not even be imagined. According to one calculation, our own sun loses nearly five million tons of its matter per second; yet at this rate it will still last for many billions of years!

Perhaps an even more impressive credential of omnipotence—if that were possible—is the nature of the created product, especially its beauty and intricate detail. The microcosm of the atom—the basic building block of the galaxies—demonstrates the miracle of omnipotence under complete control. Our minds cannot appreciate the minuteness of a single atom, nor the wonder of its construction. Electrons (the satellite particles) move around the atom's nucleus at the speed of one quadrillion times per second. By virtue of its satellite-nucleus pattern, an atom is mostly empty space.

The actual material in it (if we can call it that) amounts to only one trillionth of its volume. And by using this one basic construction unit, God has made a universe whose diversity and beauty stagger the senses. On our own earth we can go from mountains of solid granite to the delicate radiance of a butterfly wing. According to a long-forgotten source, a very patient man once counted the tiny "feathers" on one butterfly's wings; the number was 794,544.

Such considerations as these could be multiplied indefinitely, but it would be like trying to add to infinity. For indeed the infinite power of God is already firmly established in reality and in our minds. It is a fact that fills us with awe. Our God is omnipotent!

It is easy for those of us reared within the sphere of biblical influence to take for granted this awesome power of God, because we have become accustomed to thinking about the world as created. We should remember, though, the uniqueness of the biblical teaching about creation, and thus the uniqueness of belief in an omnipotent God. As Buswell points out,

> There is no other religion or philosophy in all the history of human culture which teaches the omnipotence of God. This must be understood in the light of the fact that there is no other monotheism, and no other doctrine of creation from nothing, than that found in the Judeo-Christian tradition or derived from it. . . .[71]

As we close this chapter we may say that this applies to the whole concept of infinity, since the understanding that God is infinite is likewise grounded in the fact of creation.

---

71. J. O. Buswell, Jr., *A Systematic Theology of the Christian Religion*, I:62.

Because God is the uncreated Creator, he is not bound by the limitations of created being. He exists in a totally different way. He is unlimited in his very existence; it is his very nature to exist, and he cannot not exist. He is also unlimited with regard to space and time; he exists outside their limitations. His knowledge is likewise unlimited, as is his power. Such is the nature of the one who is the Maker of heaven and earth.

Chapter Seven

OUR KNOWLEDGE OF GOD

> . . . God as the object of human knowledge, who can fathom that? How can man know God, the Infinite and Incomprehensible, who can be measured by neither time nor eternity, in whose presence the angels cover their faces with their wings, who lives in unapproachable light, and whom no man has seen or can see? How can such an One be known by man, whose breath is in his nostrils, and who is less than nothing and less than vanity? How should he know God whose best knowledge is a thing of shreds and patches? . . . What does he know of things in their origin, essence, and purpose? Is he not ringed round with mystery on every hand? Is he not always standing on the boundaries of the unknown? And is it to be supposed then that such a man, poor, weak, erring, and benighted, should know God, the high, holy, alone-wise, and almighty God?[1]

There is definitely a certain presumptuousness about the very possibility that finite man could know the infinite God. This is especially true in view of what we have already seen about the transcendence and infinity of the Creator. That God's being and his mode of existence are qualitatively different from anything in the realm of creation, that he exists as the divine dimension impenetrable by either men or angels, that he is ontologically transcendent to his creation—these facts immediately raise the question of whether it is even possible to know such a God. In other words, does the ontological transcendence of God entail his epistemological transcendence? Is God beyond our knowledge as well as beyond our being?

1. Herman Bavinck, *Our Reasonable Faith*, tr. Henry Zylstra (Grand Rapids: Eerdmans, 1956), p. 28.

This kind of question must be answered very carefully, since it is possible to go to extremes in either direction. Some have assumed that we can know everything about God; others have assumed that we can never know anything about him. Both views are wrong. The infinite God does transcend our knowledge, but this does not mean that he is unknowable or that we can have no knowledge of him at all. We *do* have knowledge of God, but his transcendence qualifies this in two ways. First, we do know God, but only because he has chosen to make himself known to us. We did not discover God; he revealed himself to us. Second, even though we know something of God through his revelation, we do not know everything about him. Transcendence does not rule out all knowledge, but it does preclude complete knowledge of God.

Thus the subject to be covered in this chapter is the knowledge that we have of God. We shall begin with a look at the biblical teaching about God's epistemological transcendence, i.e., his hiddenness and incomprehensibility. Then we shall see what the Bible says about divine revelation as the means by which the hidden God makes himself, his mind, and his will partially known to us.

EPISTEMOLOGICAL TRANSCENDENCE

When we say that God transcends our knowledge we are saying two things, as already noted. We are saying first that God is hidden from us, that we would not know him unless he took the initiative and revealed himself to us. Also, we are saying that he is incomprehensible, that we could not comprehend the fullness of his being even if his revelation were multiplied a thousandfold beyond what we now have.

The Hiddenness of God

That the transcendent God is hidden from the eyes and minds of his creatures is a recurring theme in Christian thought. Martin Luther is well known for his frequent references to God as *Deus absconditus,* the hidden God.[2] Not surprisingly, Karl Barth treats this subject in a lengthy section of his *Church Dogmatics.*[3] Generally speaking those who base their concept of the hiddenness of God primarily on the biblical doctrine of transcendence usually teach that this hiddenness is breached to some degree by God's self-revelation. Hence God is not absolutely hidden or unknowable. However, since the days of Immanuel Kant the concept of hiddenness has been based on an epistemological theory that arbitrarily excludes the possibility of knowledge of God. Not only is God completely hidden from our minds; he is also prevented from making himself known to us through revelation. The epistemological barrier cannot be penetrated from either side. Thus God's hiddenness is absolute; God is not just unknown but unknowable. This is a pervasive theme in contemporary philosophical theology. God is incognito; he is unfathomable. He is "the absent God whose presence is his absence." He is ambiguous and anonymous. The latter term is suggested by Thomas Altizer, who once told us that God is dead. Now he is saying that perhaps he just became anonymous with a "total anonymity of nothingness,

---

2. See Paul Althaus, *The Theology of Martin Luther,* tr. Robert C. Schultz (Philadelphia: Fortress Press, 1966), pp. 20ff., 274ff. See also John Dillenberger, *God Hidden and Revealed* (Philadelphia: Muhlenberg Press, 1953), throughout; and Hendrikus Berkhof, *Christian Faith: An Introduction to the Study of the Faith,* tr. Sierd Woudstra (Grand Rapids: Eerdmans, 1979), p. 55.

3. Karl Barth, *Church Dogmatics, Volume II: The Doctrine of God, Part 1,* tr. T. H. L. Parker et al. (Edinburgh: T. & T. Clark, 1957), pp. 179-204.

a plentitude of nothingness wherein the apparent absence of God is at bottom the fullness of God's presence."[4]

The Bible itself justifies our speaking of God as being hidden from us. Zophar the Naamathite expresses our sense of futility in trying to find the infinite God: "Can you discover the depths of God? Can you discover the limits of the Almighty? It is high as the heavens, what can you do? Deeper than Sheol, what can you know?" (Job 11:7-8). We should be careful not to exaggerate this point by assuming that God's hiddenness is due totally to his divine transcendence. It is due in part just to the fact that God is personal, having thoughts and plans that remain secreted in his own heart until he tells us about them. This much is true of persons in general, as Paul notes in I Corinthians 2:11, "For who among men knows the thoughts of a man except the spirit of the man, which is in him?" Only the individual knows for sure what he is hiding in the depth of his own heart. The same is true of God, as Paul adds: "Even so the thoughts of God no one knows except the Spirit of God." If God wants to reveal his thoughts, he can do so, just as we can open our hearts to those around us. If he wants to conceal his thoughts from some or from all temporarily, he may simply speak selectively or keep silent temporarily; we can do the same. This surely applies to many of the things labeled as "mysteries," things hidden for a time but eventually made known. For instance, Paul glories in the fact that God revealed to him a mystery previously unknown, namely,

4. Thomas J. J. Altizer, "The Anonymity of God," *Is God GOD?* ed. Axel Steuer and James W. McClendon, Jr. (Nashville: Abingdon, 1981), p. 26. He adds, "The theologian cannot say that God is literally anonymous, for this would be to say nothing at all" (p. 30). If he knows what he is talking about, he has not made it clear in this article.

that the Gentiles were to be included in the people of God along with the Jews (see Ephesians 3:1-10). In a sense the whole gospel of Christ is a mystery, "hidden from the past ages and generations" but now "manifested to his saints" (Colossians 1:26; see 1:27—2:3). The blessings of salvation through Christ were planned by "God's wisdom in a mystery, the hidden wisdom, which God predestined before the ages to our glory." Certainly no one could have read God's mind to discern his plans: "Things which eye has not seen and ear has not heard, and which have not entered the heart of man, all that God has prepared for those who love Him." But, says Paul, "to us God revealed them through the Spirit; for the Spirit searches all things, even the depths of God" (I Corinthians 2:7-10). Perhaps Jesus is speaking of the same kind of things when he says, "I praise Thee, O Father, Lord of heaven and earth, that Thou didst hide these things from the wise and intelligent and didst reveal them to babes" (Matthew 11:25).

In one sense, then, the hiddenness of God corresponds to the private thoughts and plans that nestle in the heart of any person. But it does not end there. Not only the thoughts and intents of his heart but also the very being of God dwells in the unapproachable radiance of transcendent glory. He is hidden from us not just as another person but as the infinite God. " 'For My thoughts are not your thoughts, neither are your ways My ways,' declares the Lord. 'For as the heavens are higher than the earth, so are My ways higher than your ways, and My thoughts than your thoughts' " (Isaiah 55:8-9). The mythical Flatland again offers an analogy. Just as the Flatlanders are totally oblivious to the existence and nature of the spatial dimension, so are we creatures unable to penetrate the divine dimension. We may recall the infinite invisibility of God, who "dwells in unapproachable light; whom no man has seen or can see" (I Timothy 6:16). "The Almighty—we cannot find Him; He is exalted in power" (Job 37:23). "Truly, Thou art a God who hides Himself, O God of Israel, Savior!" (Isaiah 45:15). "The secret things belong to the Lord our God" (Deut. 29:29). "No one knows the Son, except the Father; nor does anyone know the Father, except the Son" (Matthew 11:27).

Though the hiddenness of God is a biblical fact, it must not be construed in the absolute sense of unknowability. That God *can* be known is also taught in Scripture. As Isaiah prophesies, "For the earth will be full of the knowledge of the Lord as the waters cover the sea" (Isaiah 11:9). God declares that those under the new covenant "shall all know Me, from the least of them to the greatest" (Jeremiah 31:34).[5] Indeed, we *must* know God in order to be saved: "And this is eternal life, that they may know Thee, the only true God, and Jesus Christ whom Thou hast sent" (John 17:3). Thus that God is hidden means not that he is unknowable but that he is *unknown* until he reveals himself to us. The following statements are typical: "We can know nothing about Him unless He tells us."[6] "Had God insisted on remaining incommunicado we would know nothing whatever about him. . . . The very nature of divine reality and truth are such that, apart from divine initiative and disclosure,

5. Those under the New Covenant will not have to be taught to know the Lord, unlike those who lived under the Old Covenant. The difference is this: the Israelites came under the Old Covenant by *physical* birth and thus had to be taught to know the Lord; membership in the New Covenant, however, is by conscious choice and the new birth. Thus anyone who comes under the New Covenant already knows the Lord as a precondition.

6. J. I. Packer, *Knowing God* (Downers Grove: InterVarsity Press, 1973), p. 99.

they remain intrinsically hidden."[7] The fact is, though, that God *has* told us; he has *not* remained incommunicado; he *has* taken the initiative and disclosed his reality and truth to us in divine revelation. "The secret things belong to the Lord our God," it is true; "but things revealed belong to us and to our sons forever" (Deut. 29:29). "No one knows the Son, except the Father; nor does anyone know the Father, except the Son, *and anyone to whom the Son wills to reveal Him*" (Matthew 11:27). Through revelation the unknown but knowable God becomes known.

Thus God's hiddenness is a fact; but it is not the last word, simply because he does not choose to remain hidden.

The Incomprehensibility of God

Revelation gives us genuine knowledge of God, but this is not and can never be a full and complete knowledge. Because of his transcendence God will remain forever beyond the comprehension of our finite minds. This incomprehensibility of God is sometimes expressed thus: *finitum non capax infiniti,* "The finite cannot contain or grasp the infinite." God's thoughts and ways are different from ours; they are higher than our thoughts and ways as much as the heavens are higher than the earth (Isaiah 55:8-9). "Behold, God is exalted, and we do not know Him; the number of His years is unsearchable" (Job 36:26). He is "doing great things which we cannot comprehend" (Job 37:5). In this context the great and incomprehensible works of God are the ordinary phenomena of nature:

---

7. Carl F. H. Henry, *God, Revelation and Authority, Volume II: God Who Speaks and Shows, Fifteen Theses, Part One* (Waco: Word Books, 1976), pp. 18-19.

> Listen to this, O Job, stand and consider the wonders of God. Do you know how God establishes them, and makes the lightning of His cloud to shine? Do you know about the layers of the thick clouds, the wonders of one perfect in knowledge, you whose garments are hot, when the land is still because of the south wind? Can you, with Him, spread out the skies, strong as a molten mirror? Teach us what we shall say to Him; we cannot arrange our case because of darkness. . . . (Job 37:14-19)

The text is not asking whether we know the scientific explanations of lightning, clouds, and wind; it is asking if we can understand how God put such a system together in the first place, and how he continues to sustain it. Ecclesiastes 11:5 suggests the answer: "Just as you do not know the path of the wind and how bones are formed in the womb of the pregnant woman, so you do not know the activity of God who makes all things." Our only response can be, "Around God is awesome majesty. The Almighty—we cannot find Him; He is exalted in power" (Job 37:22-23).

Two other texts teach God's incomprehensibility. Isaiah 40:28 asks, "Do you not know? Have you not heard? The Everlasting God, the Lord, the creator of the ends of the earth does not become weary or tired. His understanding is inscrutable." Then Paul declares in the great shout of praise in Romans 11:33-34, "Oh, the depth of the riches both of the wisdom and knowledge of God! How unsearchable are His judgments and unfathomable His ways! For who has known the mind of the Lord, or who became His counselor?"

Again we must remind ourselves that God is not *completely* incomprehensible; he is not unknowable, as if nothing we think or say about God corresponds to his reality. The point is rather that our understanding is incomplete.

On the other hand, we must continue to remind ourselves that this incomplete or partial knowledge of God is *true* knowledge. Some tend to think that unless we have total knowledge, then none of our knowledge is genuine. This is not the case. Carl Henry says it well:

> The fact that we now know only "in part" . . . does not destroy the validity and trustworthiness of that portion of knowledge we have through divine disclosure. That God does not reveal himself to man exhaustively does not mean that he does not reveal himself truly. To say that man cannot fathom fully all the depths of God's being is not to assert divine unknowability.[8]

Our knowledge of God is true and adequate, though it is partial and inexhaustive. Incomprehensibility does not mean that we cannot know anything about God; it just means that we cannot know *everything*.

That God's transcendence makes him incomprehensible to us means that he will always be to an extent shrouded in mystery. There is much that even revelation cannot contain, since revelation must of necessity be given to us in the forms of this world. As Henry says, "Yahweh's voluntary self-disclosure does not wholly cancel his incomprehensibility nor eliminate all mystery."[9] Since this is due to his ontological transcendence, it can never be otherwise. The inviolable distinction between Creator and creature decrees it. God will always be *Deus absconditus*. In fact, this is one of the main lessons we learn about God through his revelation. Hendrikus Berkhof puts it this way:

> When God in his revelation emerges from his hiddenness, he does not by that act cease to be the hidden God; rather, that hiddenness is now fully disclosed. What we

8. *Ibid.*, p. 54.
9. *Ibid.*, p. 47.

> could before at best only surmise, now becomes a clear certainty: how immensely exalted and hidden God is, how unspeakably and surprisingly marvelous his gracious condescension . . . . This does not make the initiate feel proud; rather, each step makes him smaller and humbler. God would not be God if it were otherwise. The more we come to know him, the less we are able to comprehend him with our intellect.[10]

Brunner agrees: "The better we know God, the more we know and feel that His Mystery is unfathomable." Indeed, "we do not fully realize how unknowable, how mysterious God is until we meet Him in His revelation."[11]

This means that we must guard against thinking that the future Revelation of Jesus Christ at his second coming will bring with it some kind of complete knowledge or direct vision of God. This kind of thinking is quite common, even among those who stress the transcendence and hiddenness of God. For instance, Hendrikus Berkhof says, "The direct vision of God is indeed a biblical theme, but then a promise to be fulfilled at the end of time."[12] There will be a "full revelation in the eschaton," he says.[13] Brunner says, "It is also for that complete revelation at the end of the age that the Church waits, in whom the 'faithful' will see God

---

10. Hendrikus Berkhof, *Christian Faith,* pp. 53-54.

11. Emil Brunner, *The Christian Doctrine of God: Dogmatics, Volume I,* tr. Olive Wyon (Philadelphia: Westminster Press, 1950), pp. 117-118. The word *unknowable* is probably too strong.

12. Hendrikus Berkhof, *Christian Faith,* p. 52.

13. *Ibid.,* p. 68. See also pp. 101, 534. On page 534 he says, "In eternal life, God will be fully present and knowable in the reality he has made. In contrast to this present existence of hearing and believing, we may then speak of 'seeing God,' and our drive for ever more knowledge and greater love will have been satisfied."

'face to face.'"[14] Carl Henry speaks of the "present incompleteness of man's revelationally given knowledge."[15] "Not until God's final unveiling at the end of the age," he says, "will we see 'face to face.'"[16] Such statements as these seem inconsistent with these same theologians' strong commitment to the hiddenness and incomprehensibility of God, and they certainly contradict the Creator/creature distinction. At the second coming God will become no less God than he is now, and we will become no more divine. At the most we will see God in the spiritual theophany already viewed by some men (cf. Exodus 24:1ff.) and constantly seen by the angels. But this will still be a theophany and not a direct viewing of the divine essence. Even the saved will not become infinite; our knowledge will be relatively greater than it is now, but it will still be finite and unable to grasp the fullness of the infinite God.

This inconsistent affirmation of a "full knowledge" of the incomprehensible God at the second coming seems to be based on some very questionable exegesis. The "revelation" at the end of time will be a revelation of Jesus Christ (I Peter 1:13) in his glorified human existence. I John 3:2 says that "when He appears, we shall be like Him, because we shall see Him just as He is." This is a reference once again to the incarnate glorified Christ (see verse 5), not to the unincarnate Father. Nevertheless both Henry and Hendrikus Berkhof cite this verse in support of the idea of "full knowledge."[17]

---

14. Emil Brunner, *The Christian Doctrine of God*, p. 21.
15. Carl F. H. Henry, *God, Revelation and Authority, Volume II*, p. 55.
16. *Ibid.*, p. 47.
17. *Ibid.*, p. 47; Hendrikus Berkhof, *Christian Faith*, p. 102.

The "proof text" most often misused in this connection is I Corinthians 13:12, which says, "For now we see in a mirror dimly, but then face to face; now I know in part, but then I shall know fully just as I also have been fully known." Henry cites this verse in support of a "face to face" encounter at the "final unveiling." He even quotes the New English Bible paraphrase, "My knowledge now is partial; then it will be whole, like God's knowledge of me."[18] Brunner makes a similar appeal to I Corinthians 13:12 in support of a future complete, "face-to-face" revelation,[19] as does H. Berkhof. The latter speaks of our present forms of revelation as provisional; "we see in a mirror and thus do not see God face to face."[20] Nevertheless "he is on the way with us to a much more direct and fuller encounter, in which the sun of his presence will break through the thick fogs of the present and we shall see him 'face to face.'" We are accustomed, says Berkhof, "to speak of 'seeing God' 'face to face'. . . . Then our thirst for full knowledge will be forever and fully satisfied."[21]

A complete exegesis of I Corinthians 13:12 is not appropriate here, but we may offer a few concise comments on the text that will show the fallacy of misusing it to support any concept of an eschatological "direct vision" of God. First, even if the "face to face" concept is eschatological at all, it would be referring either to the glorified human

18. Carl F. H. Henry, *God, Revelation and Authority, Volume II*, p. 47.

19. Emil Brunner, *The Christian Doctrine of God*, pp. 20-21.

20. Hendrikus Berkhof, *Christian Faith*, p. 105.

21. *Ibid.*, pp. 100-101. In the last paragraph on page 101 Berkhof seems to realize that such an idea is not consistent with our creatureliness. He does not back down from the concept of "full knowledge," however; he only posits the possibility that it might be achieved gradually instead of all at once. I Corinthians 13:12 is specifically mentioned on page 102.

nature of Jesus Christ or to the spiritual theophany of the Father, not to the bare essence of God. Second, there is no indication in the text as to who or what will be seen "face to face." It does not say "him," "Christ," or "God." Third, it is extremely unlikely that this refers to the time of the second coming at all. The transition from seeing in a mirror dimly to seeing "face to face" takes place while *hope* still remains (verse 13), which indicates that Paul is not thinking of the eschaton at all. Fourth, the "face-to-face" seeing and the dim, riddle-like seeing are simply referring to two kinds of mirror: a poor one which gives only a partial reflection of one's own face, and a high-quality one which allows one to see his own face with clarity. The contrast, as in Numbers 12:8, is between two forms of *revelation*: indirect and incomplete versus direct and clear.[22] Fifth, the "partial" knowledge (verses 9, 12) is not our general finite knowledge but the special miraculous spiritual gift of knowledge comparable with speaking in tongues; see I Corinthians 12:8; 13:1-2, 8. Such "partial" knowledge, Paul says, is to be replaced by something "complete" (*teleion,* verse 10), something which must appear while we are still in the age of hope (verse 12). Sixth, the word *epiginōskō,* translated "know fully" in verse 12, does not necessarily carry the connotation of full and complete knowledge and is used interchangeably with *ginōskō.* See the parallel passages Matthew 11:27 and Luke 10:22, for instance. The translation "know *fully*" is an interpretation. Seventh, the "face-to-face" kind of knowledge is most likely a reference to the

22. See the instructive article on αἴνιγμα by Gerhard Kittel in *Theological Dictionary of the New Testament,* ed. Gerhard Kittel, tr. Geoffrey Bromiley (Grand Rapids: Eerdmans, 1964), I:178-180.

completed New Testament Scriptures, the "complete thing" which was to replace the "partial" tongues, prophecies, and miraculous knowledge needed in the early church.[23]

We are not denying, of course, that there lies ahead a time when we shall see the exalted Christ face to face and shall even look on the face of God in his spiritual theophany; we are simply suggesting that I Corinthians 13 refers to something entirely different. Even if this passage did refer to our final vision of God, it would not support the concept of a direct vision or of full and complete knowledge. Even in eternity the infinite God will transcend both our being and our knowledge. His pure essence will still be hidden; he will still be incomprehensible to our still-finite minds. Surely our knowledge of God will increase, and many of God's mysteries will be cleared up (Revelation 10:7); but God will still be God.

GENERAL REVELATION

That God "did not leave Himself without witness" (Acts 14:17) is true in more than one sense. The transcendent Creator does not remain hidden from his creatures but chooses to reveal himself, his mind, and his will to us. This revelation is our sole source of knowledge of God. We ourselves cannot penetrate the divine dimension and formulate an independent body of knowledge of the Creator, but He can and does cross the boundary from his side and makes himself known to us. Thus the essence of revelation, as Carl Henry says, "is that God steps out of his hiddenness to disclose what would otherwise remain secret and

---

23. See the more detailed comments on this passage in Knofel Staton, *Spiritual Gifts for Christians Today* (Joplin, Mo.: College Press, 1973), chapters 3 and 4.

unknown." He adds, "Revelation is God's unmasking of himself, his voluntary act of disclosure. It comes from eternity, from beyond an absolute boundary that separates man from God."[24]

The concept of revelation is a pervasive theme in the Bible. Basic biblical terms are the Hebrew *gālah*, meaning "to remove, to expose, to uncover"; and the Greek *apokalyptō*, meaning "to uncover, to unveil, to bring to light." An example of the use of *gālah* is Amos 3:7, "Surely the Lord God does nothing unless He reveals His secret counsel to His servants the prophets." *Apokalyptō* is used in I Corinthians 2:10, "For to us God revealed them through the Spirit; for the Spirit searches all things, even the depths of God." There are other terms that specifically mean "to reveal," and a large number of terms that refer to the general concept of God's making himself known to man. Bernard Ramm lists a total of twenty-three verbs and twenty-seven nouns in the New Testament alone which convey the idea of revelation.[25]

Some have said that hiddenness is the distinguishing characteristic of the biblical God. Influenced mainly by Kantian epistemology, Altizer says,

> . . . Unknowability, in this sense, is the primary attribute of God and the primary attribute for faith. Hence Kierkegaard could insist that it is precisely the unknowability or mystery of God that most fundamentally distinguishes faith from paganism, and this Kierkegaardian thesis has been echoed widely in our own century. Here mystery or unknowability is the primary identity of God for us . . . .[26]

---

24. Carl F. H. Henry, *God, Revelation and Authority, Volume II*, pp. 17, 20-21.

25. Bernard Ramm, *Special Revelation and the Word of God* (Grand Rapids: Eerdmans, 1961), pp. 162-163.

26. Thomas Altizer, "The Anonymity of God," p. 21.

Brunner says similarly, "It is precisely this fact which distinguishes the God of the biblical revelation from the gods and divinities of paganism."[27] Their point is that since pagan gods are not transcendent, they are not hidden but are in principle fully knowable by human cognitive powers. There is some truth to this point, but nevertheless hiddenness is not the *most* distinctive characteristic of the God of the Bible. *Revelation is,* at least in this context. The true God is not just the God who is hidden in unfathomable mystery; he is the God "who speaks and shows," as the title of Carl Henry's *opus magnum* says. The characteristic of false gods is that "they have mouths, but they cannot speak" (Psalm 115:5). That is, the craftsman may construct an idol with a mouth, but to no avail; it will forever be mute. Thus Carl Henry rightly makes this point about the significance of revelation:

> The great watershed between the biblical and nonbiblical religions is the self-revealing God who, in contrast with the static gods of other religions, speaks and acts intelligibly. Judeo-Christian religion worships the God who takes the initiative—who plans, creates, judges, reveals and redeems —not some divinity, perhaps ultimately unknowable, that man is left to discern by his own ingenuity.[28]

Most students of Scripture agree that there are two basic kinds of revelation, namely, that which is given in and through the creation in general and that which is given by more specific means such as theophanies and words. These are usually called general revelation and special revelation, and each is a significant source of knowledge of God.

---

27. Emil Brunner, *The Christian Doctrine of God*, p. 117.
28. Carl F. H. Henry, *God, Revelation and Authority, Volume II*, p. 62.

The Fact of General Revelation

General revelation is that revelation which can be traced back to the very act of creation itself. It is God's disclosure of himself and his will by means of the created universe, by means of the things which he has created. It is called *general* revelation for at least two reasons. One, it is by nature available to all mankind in general; it is generally available without the requirement of any special means or actions. Every nation and every individual of mature and normal intelligence has immediate access to this revelation. Two, it is the source of only a general knowledge of God. More specific details concerning his will and intentions for mankind must be disclosed in other ways.

Very few have doubted the reality of this kind of revelation. The notable exception is Karl Barth, whose Christocentrism led him to deny any form of revelation except Jesus Christ himself. Thus he denied that there is a true revelation of God in nature. He conceded that "there is somewhere and somehow for man in the cosmos as such," apart from the revelation in Christ, "a knowability of God which has to be taken into consideration."[29] But the cosmos itself is mute, he says; it only reflects or echoes the true revelation in Christ alone. Thus only those who know the latter can see anything of God in the creation.[30]

---

29. Karl Barth, *Church Dogmatics*, II/1, p. 102.

30. *Ibid.*, pp. 111-112, 119ff. See the discussion of Barth's view in G. C. Berkouwer, *General Revelation* (Grand Rapids: Eerdmans, 1955), chapter II. As Berkouwer says, "An objective knowability of God through the created reality which . . . already bears the traces of its Creator, is rejected by Barth" (p. 30). See also Bruce Demarest, *General Revelation: Historical Views and Contemporary Issues* (Grand Rapids: Zondervan, 1982), chapter VII.

Others who do not deny that God makes himself known to man through the creation nevertheless qualify the concept somewhat. Hendrikus Berkhof, for instance, affirms that God is to some extent knowable in his works of creation; but he questions the terminology of "general" and "special," and he says that even the term "revelation" is too strong for what actually happens. The light that comes from creation is quite dim, indirect, and diffuse; and it does not necessarily result in a true encounter with God. Since he has accepted the encounter concept of revelation, he insists that revelation by definition must include not only the giving of knowledge by God but also the believing reception of it by the individual. Where there is no such response, there is no revelation. Thus every instance of revelation is "special," and "general revelation" is a contradiction in terms.[31]

Another kind of qualification of general revelation is found especially in some Reformed circles. It is the idea that revelation is truly given in a general way through the creation, but because of sin's consequences this creation-knowledge is not actually perceived by the sinner. Examples of this view are G. C. Berkouwer and Cornelius Van Til. Berkouwer, for example, though he does not deny the reality of the revelation itself, says that "no true knowledge of the revelation of God in the works of his hands is obtainable without faith in Christ," and "the revelation of God in the works of his hands can be known only by the illumination of Scripture."[32]

All of these denials and qualifications seem to be contradicted by Scripture. Biblical teaching tells us that there *is*

31. Hendrikus Berkhof, *Christian Faith*, pp. 74-75; see pp. 45-50.

32. G. C. Berkouwer, *General Revelation*, p. 285. See the discussion of Berkouwer and Van Til in Bruce Demarest, *General Revelation*, chapter VIII.

a true revelation of God to be found in that which he has created. It also affirms that there is a genuine knowledge of God received by man through this means. But Scripture does say that this knowledge is usually distorted and rejected by sinful man, so that its results and consequences are quite limited.

General Revelation in Nature

That a general knowledge of God is revealed in a general way to all mankind in general is a fact well attested in Scripture. This knowledge comes both from created nature external to man and from within man's own nature as created by God. Regarding the former the classic passage in the Old Testament is Psalm 19:1-6, which says:

> The heavens are telling of the glory of God; and their expanse is declaring the work of His hands. Day to day pours forth speech, and night to night reveals knowledge. There is no speech, nor are there words; their voice is not heard. Their line has gone out through all the earth, and their utterances to the end of the world. In them He has placed a tent for the sun, which is as a bridegroom coming out of his chamber; it rejoices as a strong man to run his course. Its rising is from one end of the heavens, and its circuit to the other end of them; and there is nothing hidden from its heat.

This Psalm makes it clear that the created universe, especially the "starry heavens above," reveals to us the glory of its Creator. The testimony is abundant: the "speech" and "knowledge" are actually poured forth (verse 2). It is not a literal speech in the form of human language (verse 3), but the message is heard nonetheless. And it is heard by all men in general throughout all the earth (verse 4). A prominent example of this silent but salient testimony is the sun, which traverses the full orb of the earth and is visible to all (verses 4-6). The magnificent phenomenon of the sun witnesses to the glory of its Creator whether one observes it in pure primitive enjoyment and appreciation or whether it is contemplated by methods of sophisticated science. Indeed, the more data we become aware of, the more glorious does the Creator appear to our minds. For instance, current science tells us the following facts. Our sun is 864,950 miles in diameter, or about 110 times that of the earth. Its surface area is 12,000 times that of the earth. Its volume is 335 quadrillion cubic miles (1,306,000 times the earth's). Its mass is over two billion billion billion (or two octillion) tons. Its average surface temperature is around 10,000 degrees Fahrenheit, while the temperature in the interior is as much as 27,000,000 degrees. The pressure at the center is a billion pounds per square inch. It produces energy at the rate of 380 million billion billion (or 380 septillion) watts constantly. A single solar flare—a leaping tongue of fiery hydrogen sometimes reaching hundreds of thousands of miles above the sun's surface—could provide electrical power for the whole world for as much as 100,000,000 years. The earth receives only about a two-billionth of the sun's total energy output, or about 4,000,000 horsepower per square mile of surface. And every inch and every ounce and every degree and every watt of this relatively small star (!) proclaim its Maker's praise. Truly, "the heavens are telling of the glory of God."

Other so-called "nature psalms" (e.g., 29, 104, 147, 148) emphasize the presence and activity of God in his physical creation, as do the concluding chapters of Job (37-41). These passages are not as specific in their assertion (as in Psalm

19) that God's glory is revealed in nature, but the implication is clear. As Demarest says, "The magnificent nature poems that constitute the record portray a universe pulsating with the life of God," a "world luminous with God."[33] Isaiah 40:26 can thus expectantly and confidently invite us, "Lift up your eyes on high and see who has created these stars, the One who leads forth their host by number, He calls them all by name; because of the greatness of His might and the strength of His power not one of them is missing."

The New Testament presents the same teaching about general revelation but even more clearly. When Paul and Barnabas healed a lame man at Lystra and were mistakenly identified as pagan gods incarnate, they appealed immediately to the people's awareness of the transcendent Creator, the "living God, who made the heaven and the earth and the sea, and all that is in them." At least they *should* have been aware of him, because "He did not leave Himself without witness, in that He did good and gave you rains from heaven and fruitful seasons, satisfying your hearts with food and gladness" (Acts 14:15-17). Every rain, every harvest, and every meal is a testimony to the goodness of the Creator. Paul approached the Athenians with a similar though not as precise reference to the presence and sovereignty of "the God who made the world and all things in it." Even a pagan poet, says Paul, can recognize that we are "the offspring of God," i.e., that we are but creatures of the divine Creator (Acts 17:23-29).

The most specific reference to general revelation is in Romans 1:18ff., where Paul is speaking of those who (unlike

---

33. Bruce Demarest, *General Revelation*, p. 235.

the Jews, for instance) do not have the benefit and blessing of God's special revelation. He says,

> For the wrath of God is revealed from heaven against all ungodliness and unrighteousness of men, who suppress the truth in unrighteousness, because that which is known about God is evident within them; for God made it evident to them. For since the creation of the world His invisible attributes, His eternal power and divine nature, have been clearly seen, being understood through what has been made, so that they are without excuse. For even though they knew God, they did not honor Him as God, or give thanks; but they became futile in their speculations, and their foolish heart was darkened. Professing to be wise, they became fools, and exchanged the glory of the incorruptible God for an image in the form of corruptible man and of birds and four-footed animals and crawling creatures. . . . For they exchanged the truth of God for a lie, and worshiped and served the creature rather than the Creator, who is blessed forever. Amen.

Truth and knowledge about God are available to the whole ungodly race, says Paul, "for God made it evident to them" (*phaneroō*, to manifest or reveal; verse 19). How long has it been available? Ever since the creation of the world. And in what way is it made available? It is "understood through what has been made" (verse 20).

Given the fact of creation it is virtually impossible that it could be any other way. When we discussed the fact of God's hiddenness, we pointed out that it is common to say, "We can know nothing about God unless he chooses to tell us." Another statement by Carl Henry expresses this conviction well: "Apart from divine initiative man could not perceive even God's existence, let alone his perfections and purposes; God's very reality would remain wholly problematical had he not chosen to disclose himself."[34] But let us ask ourselves whether it is possible that God might have created a world which bore no trace or indication of its Creator. Does not the creation of necessity bear witness to its Maker? Are not creation and general revelation inseparable? Consider this statement by Brunner:

> . . . But even apart from explicit Biblical evidence, the Christian Idea of the Creator should itself force us to admit the reality of a revelation in Creation; for what sort of Creator would not imprint the mark of His Spirit upon His Creation?[35]

As Bavinck says, "The entire universe is a creation and *therefore* a revelation of God."[36] H. R. Mackintosh states that it would be incredible to think "that man can know God without His will to be known."[37] This is true, but the fact is that in his very decision to create, God willed to make himself known. The creation is *ipso facto* his revelation; every atom bears his signature. Henry states that God's decree to create the universe already anticipated special revelation in that he made beings with the capacity for speech and communication.[38] All we are saying is that the same decree made *general* revelation a foregone conclusion.

We should not be surprised, then, that even a pagan such as Aristotle could make the following statement: "Though God is invisible to every mortal creature, He is visible from

34. Carl F. H. Henry, *God, Revelation and Authority, Volume II,* p. 18.

35. Emil Brunner, *The Christian Doctrine of God,* p. 133.

36. Herman Bavinck, *The Doctrine of God,* tr. William Hendriksen (Grand Rapids: Eerdmans, 1951), p. 42. Italics added.

37. H. R. Mackintosh, *The Christian Apprehension of God* (New York: Harper and Brothers, 1929), p. 70.

38. Carl F. H. Henry, *God, Revelation and Authority, Volume II,* p. 30.

His very work." The pagan Cicero says virtually the same things: "You do not see God, and yet you learn to know God from His works."[39] Honest observation of the creation can lead to no other conclusion, as Paul affirms in Romans 1:20.

General Revelation Within Human Nature

In addition to the revelation from creation around us there is also an element of general revelation in the heart of every man. It is present there by virtue of the creation in that man is created in the image of God. I believe that those are wrong who picture man as a *tabula rasa* or blank tablet, with no innate impressions whatsoever. I also would urge great caution in the delineation of the nature and extent of such revelation, since it is quite common to see this carried to an extreme. We must be sure not to go further than the word of Scripture allows. We must also be careful not to misuse certain biblical statements and to find more in them than was intended. For instance, in my judgment the assertion in Romans 1:19 that "that which is known about God is evident *en autois*" is incorrectly translated "within them" and should rather be translated "among them." The emphasis in this context is on the external not the internal revelation. Another passage so misused, I believe, is John 1:9, which says concerning the Logos, "There was the true light which, coming into the world, enlightens every man." (See also verse 4: "In Him was life; and the life was the light of men.") Some follow the translation here that the Logos "enlightens every man coming into the world" (NASB footnote) and thus conclude that the Logos-Creator is the

39. Cited by Francis Pieper, *Christian Dogmatics* (St. Louis: Concordia, 1950), I:371-372.

epistemological presupposition of every human being. So say Ronald Nash[40] and Carl Henry.[41] Henry in particular cites this passage as teaching general revelation. It is better argued, however, that the "light" provided by the Logos in this context refers to the special revelation that resulted from his incarnation (see verse 18). By coming into the world he brought light for every man, though all do not respond to it. Verse 5 places the shining of the light in the context of the incarnation: "The light shines in the darkness; and the darkness did not comprehend it." Verse 7 says that John the Baptist bore witness to the light (i.e., as incarnate in Christ), so that all men might believe through him. The "all" in verse 7 corresponds to the "every man" in verse 9. That is, the light which makes faith possible is made available to all through the incarnation of the Logos. The passage does not seem to say more than this; to link it with the concept of general revelation leaves the door open for all kinds of excesses and speculations as to the nature and content of innate knowledge.

Whether based on questionable exegesis or on speculative phenomenological analysis of religious experience, the concept of an "intuitional knowledge of God" is a venerable tradition. John Calvin's famed *sensus divinitatis* has established the pattern for many followers of Scripture:

> There is within the human mind, and indeed by natural instinct, an awareness of divinity. This we take to be beyond

40. Ronald Nash, *The Word of God and the Mind of Man* (Grand Rapids: Zondervan, 1982), p. 67.

41. Carl F. H. Henry, *God, Revelation and Authority, Volume II*, pp. 84-85; Carl F. H. Henry, *God, Revelation and Authority, Volume III: God Who Speaks and Shows, Fifteen Theses, Part Two* (Waco: Word Books, 1979), pp. 205, 209, 344.

> controversy. To prevent anyone from taking refuge in the pretense of ignorance, God himself has implanted in all men a certain understanding of his divine majesty. . . .[42]

Bruce Demarest has espoused this concept and states it in quite extravagant language: "Man, created in the image of God and universally illumined by the Logos, effably intuits the reality of God as a first truth."[43] "Our thesis is that the human mind intuitively grasps the existence of a Power, a Perfection, and a Personality who is primal, uncaused, and infinite."[44] Besides his appeal to both Romans 1:19 and John 1:9, Demarest draws some *non sequitur* conclusions from Genesis 1 and Acts 17:28 which do not warrant comment. He also appeals to Romans 1:32 and Romans 2:14-15. As we will see below, these passages do suggest an inward general revelation, but not necessarily of the extent that Demarest wants to find in them.

A classical representative of the intuitive theory from the standpoint of the analysis of religious experience is Friedrich Schleiermacher, who said that the whole religious enterprise begins with an inherent "feeling of absolute dependence."[45] In the early part of this century Rudolf Otto propounded his "idea of the holy," saying first of all that Schleiermacher did not go deeply enough into the

---

42. John Calvin, *Institutes of the Christian Religion*, I.iii.1, ed. John T. McNeill, tr. Ford Lewis Battles (Philadelphia: Westminster Press, 1960), I:43. See the discussion of this element of Calvin's thought in Edward A. Dowey, Jr., *The Knowledge of God in Calvin's Theology* (New York: Columbia University Press, 1952), pp. 50ff.

43. Bruce Demarest, *General Revelation*, p. 228.

44. *Ibid.*, p. 229.

45. Friedrich Schleiermacher, *The Christian Faith*, English translation edited by H. R. Mackintosh and J. S. Stewart (New York: Harper Torchbook edition, 1963), I:12ff.

religious psyche. This feeling of dependence, which he called the "creature-feeling," presupposes the consciousness of something upon which one depends. It is actually the "effect of another feeling element, which casts it like a shadow, but which in itself indubitably has immediate and primary reference to an object outside the self." This object he labeled "the numinous," which is equivalent to God.[46] This consciousness of "the numinous" or "the holy" is an *a priori* factor "universally and necessarily latent in the human spirit," an "*a priori* category of the mind" which may be called general revelation.[47] W. R. Matthews expounds an intuitional view of God based on the work of Schleiermacher and Otto.[48]

It seems to me that the religious psychology approach to general revelation is inappropriate. It is extremely precarious because of the inherent ambiguity of subjective religious experience. Hence our only basis for conclusions concerning innate general revelation must be the Bible. Here we do find some indication of inborn awareness of truth from God, especially as it relates to morality. As noted above, in Romans 1:18ff. the Apostle Paul is discussing the sinfulness of the Gentiles, or those who have access only to general revelation. Here he mentions only the knowledge of God available through the external creation. In the second chapter of Romans Paul begins to stress the sinfulness of the Jews as well, or those who have access to special revelation also. His point is that both Jew and Gentile stand in

46. Rudolf Otto, *The Idea of the Holy*, revised ed., tr. John W. Harvey (New York: Oxford University Press, 1926), pp. 10-11.

47. *Ibid.*, pp. 144, 179.

48. W. R. Matthews, *God in Christian Experience* (New York: Harper and Brothers, 1930). "The foundation of the theories of Schleiermacher and Otto appears to be sound," he says (p. 8).

the same relation to God: each has broken the law available to him and each stands condemned by law. If one wonders how the Gentiles could be counted as lawbreakers since they were not given a specially-revealed law, the Apostle explains in Romans 2:14-15 that knowledge of the law and of sin are part of man's nature as man:

> . . . For when Gentiles who do not have the Law do instinctively the things of the Law, these, not having the Law, are a law to themselves, in that they show the work of the Law written in their hearts, their conscience bearing witness, and their thoughts alternately accusing or else defending them.

This passage teaches us two things about general revelation. First, it teaches an inborn knowledge of God's law. When Paul says that the Gentiles "do not have the Law," he is referring to a specially-revealed law such as the Jews had. Though Gentiles do not have law in this form, they still have law; it is "written in their hearts." Specifically it is the *work* of the law that is written in their hearts. That is, a heathen will not wake up one morning and suddenly find himself reciting the ten commandments, but nevertheless God made us so that his law has an effect (work) upon our hearts. There are certain things that are instinctively recognized as right and wrong. We are not talking here about detailed religious and civil laws, but about what is called the basic moral law. When Paul says that such things are done "instinctively" (literally "by nature") and that they are "written in the heart," he can only be talking about something that can be explained only by the fact that we have been created in the image of God. We may say that there is a universal sense of basic decency and responsibility, something which C. S. Lewis diplomatically labels the *Tao* and which he says is discoverable in every culture and religion in every age and place.[49]

The second thing which this passage teaches is that in addition to the innate consciousness of law, each person has a conscience which reacts to that law. The conscience itself is not to be equated with that law or law-sense. Knowing *what* is right or wrong is not the function of the conscience; the conscience cannot tell us that a particular act is right or wrong. Thus the admonition to "always let your conscience be your guide" is extremely bad advice, since the conscience in itself is not a source of knowledge. It *needs* a guide, that is, it can operate only when a law-code of some kind is already present. In this sense it is something like a computer; it can function only when it is programmed from the outside. Paul's point in Romans 2:15 is that this programming was done via creation; the law by which the conscience is supposed to function is written in the heart. The specific function of the conscience is simply that of a moral alarm system. In addition to *knowing* that a particular course of action is wrong, because of our conscience we cannot desire or pursue that course of action without a magnification of the sense of wrongness in our hearts or without a sense of guilt. The conscience will fail to function properly (a) when the law-code that guides it has been distorted or corrupted or (b) when the individual has become insensitive to it.

The discussion of Romans 2:14-15 leads to the question of an innate sense of God himself. Does this passage teach an intuitional knowledge of God? Let us note carefully that this is not specifically mentioned in the passage. Only the

---

49. C. S. Lewis, *The Abolition of Man* (New York: Macmillan, 1947), pp. 29ff., 93ff.

moral sense and the conscience are mentioned. But do not these things implicitly require a knowledge of God? Whence the moral sense? And to what avail is the sense of guilt if it is not understood as a guilt *before God*?

Before trying to answer these questions we should examine what Paul says at the end of Romans 1. When the Gentiles (those without special revelation) repudiate the true knowledge of God that comes through creation, they fall into all sorts of sins including homosexual acts, greed, malice, envy, murder, deceit, gossip, slander, pride, disobedience to parents, and strife. They become "without understanding, untrustworthy, unloving, unmerciful." Then Paul declares, "And, although they know the ordinance of God, that those who practice such things are worthy of death, they not only do the same, but also give hearty approval to those who practice them." This statement suggests two things. One, it seems to fill out the content of the law written in the heart as mentioned in Romans 2:15. The Gentiles, says Paul, know that these things are wrong, "that those who practice such things are worthy of death." How do they know? It is written in their hearts. Two, this statement seems to relate the effect of conscience to a sense of guilt specifically before God. "They know the ordinance *of God*," Paul says; they know that God has ordained that those who do such things are worthy of death. In this sense the conscience "hails men anticipatively before God's judgment bar," as Carl Henry pointedly states.[50]

But the question remains, is the knowledge of God himself something given inwardly or derived from external nature? Let us note again that Paul does not specifically

50. Carl F. H. Henry, *God, Revelation and Authority, Volume II*, p. 130.

affirm an innate sense of God. In fact we can now say that there is *no* clear and compelling statement to this effect anywhere in Scripture; thus the affirmation of an intuitional knowledge of God seems to be going beyond what is warranted by biblical teaching. Besides being unwarranted, it is also unnecessary, since all that could be gained by asserting an intuitional knowledge is already in hand via the knowledge of God that comes from external creation. A knowledge from within would not add anything to the knowledge from without. The latter is perfectly adequate to give conscience its desired effect. The same person who has the awareness of the laws of basic decency written on his heart has a knowledge of the source of those laws via "what has been made." The sense of guilt and responsibility generated inwardly by the conscience must instinctively be related to the Creator and Lord whose reality and presence are infallibly impressed upon the consciousness by nature's witness.

Thus we conclude that God the Creator has provided a general revelation of himself and his will by the creation itself. "All nature sings" of the glory and power of God, and the creature made in God's image has the basic ingredients of morality implanted within his heart.

Knowledge Received Through General Revelation

The next question has to do with the result of general revelation. Exactly what knowledge is actually received by man through these general means? Two issues are at stake here. One is the question whether any knowledge *at all* is received; the other is whether any *saving* knowledge is received.

The Fact of Creation Knowledge

Regarding the former question, we have seen that some deny the very existence of general revelation as such; thus they would naturally deny that knowledge is received thereby. But we have seen that the Bible clearly teaches the reality of general revelation. We have also noted that some grant the reality of the revelation but deny that any real knowledge is gained from it by sinful man. The key word here is *sinful* man. It is not denied that man before the Fall had genuine knowledge through the creation; the contention is that the Fall has so affected man's mind that he cannot or will not receive what knowledge is available to him in this way. Fortunately it is not necessary to discuss the whole issue of the Fall and its consequences in order to show that this is an untenable view. We shall see from the clear teaching of Scripture that man the sinner has true knowledge of God from the creation alone.

The key passage again is Romans 1:18ff. Verse 20 does not simply say that God's eternal power and divine nature are *revealed* through creation; it says they are actually seen and *understood*. The word translated as "understood" is *noeō*, which means "to perceive with the mind, to have understanding, to think upon." Thus the truth about God actually registers in the minds of all men. Verse 21 also says specifically that they "knew God." In addition to these specific statements, the nature of the Gentiles' response to this general revelation also shows that it is truly received and understood. Verse 18 says that they *suppress* the truth in unrighteousness, and verse 25 says that they *exchange* the truth of God for a lie. This terminology shows that they are clearly in possession of the truth at one point but rebelliously reject it in one way or another. Also, verse 20 says that because they do have a true knowledge of God but do not honor him aright, *they are without excuse.* This is explained further in verse 21, "For even though they knew God, they did not honor Him as God, or give thanks." The knowledge of God through creation carries with it the correlative sense of responsibility to make two simple responses: to honor or worship God as God and to thank him for creature-blessings. When the Gentiles do not do this, they are without excuse. It would not be possible for them to be considered inexcusable unless they have true knowledge.

Hendrikus Berkhof's contention that the term *revelation* should not be used in this context because a true encounter with God does not take place simply shows the arbitrariness of this typically modern definition of revelation. Berkhof complains that the effect of this so-called "revelation" is only negative; "it lures men to idolatry and serves only to make them 'without excuse'; thus revelation in the sense of an encounter does not take place."[51] Does this mean that it is not revelation? No. In the first place revelation is revelation whether it is perceived by man as such or not, contrary to Berkhof's statement that "revelation is not even revelation if it is not perceived and acknowledged as such from the other side."[52] Even if every man should blind his eyes to the glory of God in nature, it would still be perceived by the angels. Also, even if it were true that revelation must be "perceived and acknowledged" by man to be revelation, it is arbitrary to assume that this acknowledgement must always be positive. As we have seen, Romans 1:18ff. shows that the Gentiles do truly "perceive and acknowledge" this revelation; there *is* an encounter, even though it is a negative

51. Hendrikus Berkhof, *Christian Faith,* p. 76.
52. *Ibid.*, p. 57.

one. That the term *revelation* is appropriate for such a negative encounter is shown in II Thessalonians 1:7.

We may ask at this point concerning the content of the knowledge received through general revelation. Romans 1:19 speaks of "that which is known about God," while verse 25 speaks of the "truth of God" (see verse 18). What is this truth? First of all, the very reality or existence of God, since God "did not leave Himself without witness" (Acts 14:17). The heavens declare the glory *of God* (Psalm 19:1); his own "divine nature" is clearly seen (Romans 1:20). Thus the existence of God is known, even though he is invisible (Romans 1:20). Also known is the fact that the invisible God is the Creator as distinct from his creatures (Romans 1:25). Revealed as well are his glory (Psalm 19:1; Romans 1:23) and his power (Romans 1:20). His eternity and immortality are also known (Romans 1:20, 23). His goodness is seen from his works (Acts 14:17). Also understood is our duty as creatures to worship and serve the Creator and to give him thanks (Romans 1:21, 25; Acts 14:17). The general revelation also includes the basic moral law (Romans 1:26-31; 2:14-15), and the knowledge that one ought to do right (Romans 2:15). Finally it includes the knowledge that God is a righteous judge (Romans 1:32). Most of these items are summed up in the term "divine nature" (theiotēs) in Romans 1:20. This term refers to "the sum of the invisible perfections that characterize the reality of God."[53] It means "that which shows God to be God, and gives Him the right to worship."[54]

---

53. Bruce Demarest, *General Revelation*, p. 239.

54. Hermann Kleinknecht, "θειότης," *Theological Dictionary of the New Testament*, ed. Gerhard Kittel, tr. Geoffrey Bromiley (Grand Rapids: Eerdmans, 1965), III:123.

If one asks by what means a man or woman is able to receive such an impressive body of knowledge, the answer is that it is possible because the creation clearly reveals it and because the human recipient has been made in the image of God with the capacity to receive it and know it. This knowledge is not the product of human reason in the sense that it is a body of conclusions derived from a series of premises. Thus it is not dependent on an individual's powers of reasoning or his philosophical ability. The knowledge is actually revealed in creation in a non-verbal form, and we perceive it by immediate and involuntary inference. All we have to do is verbalize it; but it makes an impression on the heart even if it is not verbalized.

The Limitation of Creation Knowledge

The second question to be discussed here is whether any *saving* knowledge is received through general revelation. This is not necessarily the same question as to whether any heathen will be saved. An affirmative answer to the latter question is quite common. Huldreich Zwingli is well known for his view that a whole host of pagan philosophers will surely grace the halls of heaven, including Socrates, Aristides, Camillus, and the Catos. His reasoning is this: "There has not lived a single good man, there has not been a single pious heart or believing soul from the beginning of the world to the end, which you will not see there in the presence of God."[55] The second Vatican Council speaks in a similar fashion:

---

55. Huldreich Zwingli, "An Exposition of the Faith," *Zwingli and Bullinger*, tr. G. W. Bromiley (Philadelphia: Westminster Press, 1953), pp. 275-276.

> . . . Those who, through no fault of their own, do not know the Gospel of Christ or his Church, but who nevertheless seek God with a sincere heart, and, moved by grace, try in their actions to do his will as they know it through the dictates of their conscience—those too may achieve eternal salvation. Nor shall divine providence deny the assistance necessary for salvation to those who, without any fault of theirs, have not arrived at an explicit knowledge of God, and who, not without grace, strive to lead a good life. . . .[56]

This is also a very common assumption in popular piety. One often hears, "Surely God will not condemn a person for not believing in Jesus when that person has never even *heard* about Jesus. Therefore the heathen are saved."

Whether "the heathen" or even *some* heathen are saved is not the main question we are addressing here. Our question is whether general revelation contains any knowledge that can lead to salvation. Can a person be saved through what he knows about God from general revelation alone? Even if we assume for the moment that some or all heathen will be saved, is this *because of* what they know through the creation, or is it *in spite of* it?

In his systematic theology called *The Word of Truth* Dale Moody argues that general revelation is sufficient for salvation. He notes that some say general revelation "has only a negative function that leaves a man without excuse." He rejects this idea, though: "But what kind of God is he who gives man enough knowledge to damn him but not enough

---

56. "Dogmatic Constitution on the Church," paragraph 16, *Documents of Vatican II*, ed. Austin P. Flannery (Grand Rapids: Eerdmans, 1975), pp. 367-368. The text as given in the Eerdmans edition actually says, "those too many achieve salvation." Since this is an obvious error we have changed *many* to *may* in our quotation.

to save him?"[57] Moody cites Romans 2:14-16 and concludes, "The witness of conscience, when followed, may lead to acquittal at the final judgment."[58] If one objects that only Christ can save, Moody replies that revelation from the pre-existent and even post-existent Son of God is possible apart from the historical Jesus. "Could not the pre-existent one make himself known to people before Abraham and to those today who never heard of Abraham, much less Jesus?"[59] Those who have only the "starlight of general revelation" will not be judged as if they had the Light of the World and then rejected it. "Guilt before God is gauged by the light people have, and those who follow the light they have will surely be accepted by God."[60] Acts 17:27 shows that it is possible for a heathen to find God, and verse 30 says there is "a time of ignorance that is excusable."[61] In short Moody is saying that although the light of general revelation is much dimmer than that of special revelation, there is enough to light the pathway to heaven.

Our own opinion is that Moody is quite wrong, and that the Bible nowhere teaches that a person can be saved from sin and condemnation through his response to the light of creation alone. General revelation simply does not give us any knowledge of redemption or of the Redeemer. At times it seems that Moody and others, in their zeal to argue against the extreme position of Karl Barth, do not keep two questions separate in their minds, namely, (1) Is there such a

---

57. Dale Moody, *The Word of Truth: A Summary of Christian Doctrine Based on Biblical Revelation* (Grand Rapids: Eerdmans, 1981), p. 59.

58. *Ibid.*

59. *Ibid.*, p. 61.

60. *Ibid.*, pp. 61-62.

61. *Ibid.*, p. 64.

thing as general revelation? and (2) Can one be *saved* through general revelation? To answer the former question in the affirmative does not necessarily entail an affirmative answer for the latter. All knowledge of God is not saving knowledge. Thus in Acts 17:27, where some heathen are described as seeking God "if perhaps they might grope for Him and find Him," we cannot assume that the *finding* in this case means anything more than *knowing.* There is no indication that it has anything to do with salvation. The same is true of any supposed pre- or post-incarnation revelation by the Logos. The scope of the works of the Logos extend far beyond salvation alone. In other words if someone is going to connect salvation with general revelation, he must be able to appeal to something more specific than the *fact* of general revelation alone.

Well, then, what about the specific "witness of conscience," as it is called? Moody and others seem to assume that the limited knowledge the heathen have of God's law will serve to save them if they follow it. They point to Paul's statement in Romans 2:15 that the conscience will either "accuse or excuse," and they conclude that some will thus be excused by their conscience in the day of judgment. With regard to this specific statement of Paul it must be pointed out that he is saying that the conscience will either accuse or excuse *with regard to particular acts,* not with regard to a person's whole life. It will accuse him if he violates a specific law, and it will excuse him if he conforms to it. The conscience works like this every day; that is its function. It is not designed to be the deciding factor on the judgment day. It is a mistake to connect this statement in verse 15 (which is part of a parenthesis) to the reference to the judgment in verse 16. Verse 16 relates to the action in verses 12-13. But is it not true, as Moody says, that guilt is gauged by the light people have, and that those who follow it will be accepted by God? Yes indeed, but the key words are "those who follow" and "when followed." And the main point of the Apostle Paul in this section of Romans is that *no one follows the light or law that he has,* whether it be dim or bright! The Jews have law, but they have broken it. The Gentiles have law in a different form, but they also have violated it. *If* a person did indeed follow what law he had, if he were a "doer of the law," then he would indeed be justified on the basis of that law. But this is just the point that Paul is making: law absolutely cannot justify anyone, because *no one* has lived by the law that he has. Sincerity is not enough to save, and partial obedience is not enough to save. Only a complete obedience would save, and such does not exist. This is why the gospel of Jesus Christ is so essential, because it offers salvation on a completely different basis from obedience to law. It is ironic that Moody or anyone should take these statements by Paul, which are so integral to his overall presentation of the exclusiveness of salvation through the gospel of grace, and try to make them say just the *opposite* of what Paul is saying by them.

Well, then, if we cannot say that the heathen are saved through knowledge, can we say that they are saved through ignorance? Moody appeals to Paul's statement in Acts 17:30: "Therefore having overlooked the times of ignorance, God is now declaring to men that all everywhere should repent." Thus, says Moody, there is a "time of ignorance that is excusable," and many people are still living in it because they have not yet heard the gospel.[62] This is similar to the

---

62. *Ibid.*

common idea that God will surely not condemn someone for not obeying the gospel if he has never heard the gospel. The implication is that his ignorance will be his excuse. Let us note first that this is not what Paul is saying in Acts 17:30. He does not say that God has overlooked men's ignorance, but the *times* of their ignorance. The word *hypereidon* occurs only here in the New Testament. It means "to overlook, to take no notice of, to despise, to disdain." To say that God overlooked the times of ignorance means that in the times before the gospel God was making no attempt to carry out a worldwide preaching and repentance campaign. He was overlooking that era, or passing it by as it were. But now by his grace, through the preaching of the gospel, he is calling on all men to repent. The implication is that in the "time of ignorance" men were condemned rather than excused, and it was not God's purpose to do anything about it. But now through the missionary activity of the church God is giving to all the opportunity to be saved. Let us then note that in Romans 1:20 Paul says that rather than being *excused* because of ignorance, the heathen are "*without* excuse." Does this mean, then, that they are condemned on account of their ignorance? Not at all. This would be very unjust. True, they do not know the gospel; but they are not condemned for not knowing the gospel. Why then are they condemned? Because they *do* know general revelation and have not lived up to it! They *do* know God, and they *do* know that they should honor him as God and give him thanks; but they do not do this. This is why they are condemned—not because of what they are ignorant of but because of what they know. That they have not heard the gospel is beside the point. When a person is condemned for his abuse of general revelation, the condemnation is just (Romans 1:32).

This brings us finally to Moody's question, what kind of God would give man enough knowledge to damn him but not enough to save him? This question assumes that general revelation should have or is somehow intended to have something to do with salvation, and it suggests that if it cannot redeem then somehow God has failed or been unjust. But herein lies the basic fallacy, the basic error of this whole way of thinking, namely, the notion that general revelation is a work of God the Redeemer. The fact is that it is not. *General revelation grows solely out of the work of creation.* It is a revelation of God as Creator, not God as Redeemer. It speaks to man as creature, not to man as sinner. This is how it was intended to function from the beginning, and this is how it still functions. From the beginning man has been able to respond either positively or negatively to this revelation. By responding positively man is able to avoid condemnation. By responding negatively man comes under God's just condemnation. The fact is that mankind uniformly responds negatively and thus all are "without excuse." Does this mean, then, that general revelation has only a negative function—that it only damns and does not save? No. To put the question in this way is to renew the fallacy that such revelation is not a function of creation but somehow has an intended purpose for a post-Fall world. The point is that general revelation was not intended either to save (positive) or to condemn (negative). It was intended only for the positive purpose of declaring the glory of the Creator and giving general guidance to the creature. There is absolutely no excuse for the 1901 American Standard Version translation of Romans 1:20, "that they may be without excuse," as if the very *purpose* of the general revelation were to leave the sinner with no excuse. No. The "being without excuse" is the *result* but not the purpose of general revelation. But just as it is not designed to damn, neither is it designed to save. It reveals God only as Creator, not as Redeemer. It has no redemptive content. It gives us no information about the great and distinctive doctrines of Christianity such as the Trinity, the incarnation, the virgin birth, the person of Christ, the atonement, the resurrection, the person and work of the Holy Spirit, conversion, baptism, justification by faith, sanctification, and the second coming. But this is not a shortcoming of general revelation. It does not give us this information because it was never intended to do so; its purpose is fulfilled quite well without it.

We conclude, then, that general revelation as a function of creation gives an abundance of knowledge about the Creator and his expectations with regard to his creatures. We note sadly that none of us has lived up to these expectations. Every individual has broken the law that he knows; even those under general revelation alone are lawbreakers and are thus condemned. Does this mean that the heathen are lost? Yes, that seems to be the very point Paul is making in Romans 1:18ff. And general revelation cannot provide enough knowledge to save them. Does this mean, then, that God *is* the kind of God that would give men enough knowledge to damn him but not enough to save him? OF COURSE NOT. This suggestion (by Moody) totally ignores the fact of *special* revelation. Just *because* the general revelation cannot function redemptively, God has gone "above and beyond the call of duty" to accomplish redemption through Jesus Christ and to provide us with a whole body of knowledge about that redemption through special revelation.[63]

---

63. The question whether God would give man enough knowledge to damn him but not enough to save him is born more from feeling than from reason.
(Continued on page 348.)

Man's Rejection and Distortion of General Revelation

The final thing to note about general revelation is that although it provides knowledge about the Creator, rebellious man alters and distorts this knowledge and even rejects it and replaces it with lies of his own making. We are not talking here about a simple sin against what one knows to be the truth; we are talking about an alteration of the truth itself—a willing, knowing, sinful alteration of the truth. When Paul talks about the Gentiles in Ephesians 4:18 he says that they are "darkened in their understanding, excluded from the life of God, because of the ignorance that is in them, because of the hardness of their heart." There *is* an ignorance, even of the truth available via the creation; but it is a *willful* ignorance and thus one for which the rebel is responsible. There is not only an ignorance, says Paul, but also a hardness of heart that helps to create the ignorance. Romans 1:18 makes this very clear. He says, "For the wrath of God is revealed from heaven against all ungodliness and unrighteousness of men, who suppress the truth in unrighteousness." Because of unrighteousness men suppress the truth about God, and because they suppress it God's wrath is against them. Romans 1:21-25 shows how men have created their own false philosophies and false religions even in the face of revealed truth. They reject the simple service of the Creator and proceed to build speculative, "sophisticated"

63. (Continued from page 347.)
In a sense the creation knowledge is enough to "save" if one will only live by it. Thus one could answer, "Of course not, but general revelation itself can do either one." The fact that it cannot save a man once he has sinned against it is not a charge against the revelation or against the Creator; it is the fault of the sinner alone.

philosophical systems: "They became futile in their speculations, and their foolish heart was darkened. Professing to be wise, they became fools." By suppressing and distorting their knowledge of the true God they are able to create gods of their own which are patterned after animals or after man himself. Thus have arisen all sorts of false religious systems.

Some contend that the effects of sin upon the mind of man are so severe that any response to general revelation on the part of sinful man would be impossible. For instance, Berkouwer's and Van Til's position that man can have no true knowledge of God through creation is based on their understanding of total depravity and its effects. Also, Karl Barth's rejection of general revelation as such is accompanied by his conviction that sin has completely obliterated the image of God in man, thus destroying any possible point of contact between the Creator and his creatures. This is a view that he and Emil Brunner have debated rather heatedly.[64] Our own view is that those are wrong who say that men *cannot help* distorting the truth of general revelation; Paul's language suggests that it is a willful act. Indeed, it is difficult to see how they can be "without excuse" unless it were possible for the truth to be known and retained. Sinful man deliberately suppresses the truth in order to follow his own will and to hide from the one against whom he rebels. H. Berkhof is right in a sense when he says that God's hiddenness has now become a double hiddenness.[65] But the second

---

64. See the volume entitled *Natural Theology*, tr. Peter Fraenkel (London: Geoffrey Bles, 1946). It includes Emil Brunner's "Nature and Grace" and Karl Barth's reply, "No!" Both were originally published in 1934. See the discussion of their views in Bruce Demarest, *General Revelation*, chapter VII; and in John Baillie, *Our Knowledge of God* (London: Oxford University Press, 1939), pp. 17-34.

65. Hendrikus Berkhof, *Christian Faith*, p. 54.

hiding is not of God's doing but man's. God the Creator is by nature hidden behind his transcendence, but now sinful man hides behind his own falsehoods while convincing himself that they are true.

However, we must agree that sin has had *some* effect upon man's ability to handle general revelation and therefore upon the epistemological effectiveness of the general revelation itself. One does not have to espouse an extreme view such as inherited total depravity or the complete destruction of the image of God in order to say that sin has a deteriorating effect upon the mind and will of man. An individual's own sins create within him a vicious circle of sin/weakness/more sin/more weakness. Paul says that we are dead in *our own* trespasses and sins (Ephesians 2:1). We must say that sin *does* damage (but not destroy) the image of God in the sinner, because personal redemption includes the process of the *renewing* of that image (Eph. 4:22-24; Col. 3:9-10). Part of that renewal is a renewal unto "true knowledge," as Colossians 3:10 says. The sinner's heart willfully suppresses and distorts the truth of general revelation; but once it has been suppressed and distorted, it becomes virtually unattainable without further help. This applies both to the truth about God revealed from without and to the truth about morality revealed from within.

Thus a redemptive special revelation is necessitated not only by man's sin and the need for redemption, but also by this denial and distortion of the general revelation. In other words, there is an epistemological need for more and clearer special revelation as well as a redemptive one. Man not only needs knowledge of God as Redeemer; he also needs undistorted and straightforward knowledge of God as Creator. Apart from the special revelation sinful man may draw many conclusions about God, about service to God, and about morality; and some of them may be correct. But only through God's corrective and clarifying special revelation can we be *sure* that such conclusions are correct, complete, and consequential. Now that sin has entered the picture, the following statements by Carl Henry apply specifically to special revelation: "Apart from God's self-unveiling any affirmations about the Divine would be nothing more than speculation. . . . The only confident basis for God-talk is God's revelation of himself."[66]

This is why many if not most Protestants have been very skeptical of if not actually hostile toward what is called "natural theology." Natural theology is the attempt to set forth a reliable doctrine of God by means of the natural powers of reason alone, based solely on general revelation. Primary examples are medieval Catholicism and Enlightenment rationalism. Karl Barth's attack on general revelation was aimed mainly at this kind of natural theology. In fact, Emil Brunner hints that Barth actually confused these two concepts and that this confusion was a principal cause of the debate between him and Barth on this subject. At the same time Brunner confesses that his own loose use of language contributed to the confusion.[67] Brunner's point is, quite correctly, that one can accept the reality of general revelation while rejecting the validity of natural theology. As Brunner notes, Romans 1:18ff. makes it clear that human beings even as sinners cannot help but have thoughts about God derived from the revelation in creation. But it also

66. Carl F. H. Henry, *God, Revelation and Authority, Volume II*, p. 18.
67. Emil Brunner, *The Christian Doctrine of God*, p. 132.

shows that man's distorted vision results in a misunderstanding and alteration of the nature and meaning of this revelation.[68]

The insufficiency of general revelation for man in his present state also affects our attitude toward the non-biblical religions. We have not said that sinful man can discern no truth at all from the inward and outward general revelation. We have actually affirmed the opposite. This is why we are not surprised to find a great deal of truth in the great religions of the world. They may include some perceptive insights into the divine nature, and they may even prescribe a way of life that does great justice to Romans 2:14-15. However, we must not hesitate to condemn all non-Christian religions as part of the broad road that leads to destruction. Their truth is inevitably mixed with falsehood, as Paul indicates (Romans 1:21-25). And even if it were not, their lack of a message of redemption would still render them futile. Through the general revelation alone they can know God only as the Creator who is Lord and Lawgiver; they cannot know him as Redeemer. This is why the Bible may cite an occasional comment from a pagan as being true (e.g., Acts 17:28), but at the same time it utterly condemns all religions outside the circle of special revelation.[69]

In conclusion to this section on general revelation we would note the inscription on the Athenian altar, "To an Unknown God" (Acts 17:23). Quite correctly it did not say "To an Unknowable God," since the true God *can* be known.

---

68. *Ibid.*, p. 134.

69. Thus we would agree in principle with Karl Barth's rejection of all extra-biblical religions (or even "religion" itself as opposed to true Christianity) as forms of unbelief. See *Church Dogmatics, Volume I: The Doctrine of the Word of God, Part 2*, tr. G. T. Thomson and Harold Knight (Edinburgh: T. & T. Clark, 1956), pp. 297ff.

But sadly enough the true God is *unknown* to those who rely on general revelation alone. This is why we rejoice that God has also given us special revelation.

SPECIAL REVELATION

We commented earlier on Psalm 19:1-6, that great Old Testament witness to general revelation. We may note here without comment that the last half of this Psalm praises God for his specially revealed word in Scripture. It says in part,

> The law of the Lord is perfect, restoring the soul; the testimony of the Lord is sure, making wise the simple. The precepts of the Lord are right, rejoicing the heart; the commandment of the Lord is pure, enlightening the eyes. The fear of the Lord is clean, enduring forever; the judgments of the Lord are true; they are righteous altogether. They are more desirable than gold, yes, than much gold; sweeter also than honey and the drippings of the honeycomb. Moreover, by them Thy servant is warned; in keeping them there is great reward. . . . (verses 7-11)

Thus within this one Psalm our only two sources of knowledge of God are set forth, namely, general and special revelation. Without question the latter is the more significant of the two, especially now that we are sinners.

The difference between these two kinds of revelation is evident from their names. General revelation is that which is immediately available to all men in general and which gives us a general knowledge of God. Special revelation, on the other hand, is revelation given to a specific individual or group of individuals at a specific place and a specific time, and which may include knowledge that is much more specific and detailed than could be given via general revelation. It is particular, not universal. This particularity is mentioned in Psalm 147:19-20, "He declares His words to Jacob, His statutes and His ordinances to Israel. He has not dealt thus with any nation; and as for His ordinances, they have not known them. Praise the Lord!" That is, the Law of Moses was given to Israel and not to Babylon or any North American Indian group. The more specific nature of its content is suggested in Amos 4:13, "For behold, He who forms mountains and creates the wind and declares to man what are His thoughts, . . . the Lord God of hosts is His name." Through special revelation God can declare his thoughts and plans as well as general truths about himself.

In order to explain how God the Creator makes himself known to us through special revelation, we shall discuss the subject under two main headings, namely, its form and its content.

The Form of Special Revelation

Though we are dealing with special revelation as a single category, we recognize that it has come to us "in many portions and in many ways," as Hebrews 1:1 says. Here we will present only a brief survey of the various forms it has taken, while commenting in detail only on those problem areas that relate to our knowledge of God as Creator.

The Mighty Acts of God

The three main forms of special revelation are the mighty acts of God, the spoken words of God, and the visible presence of God. The first of these is a rather broad and nebulous category which serves to include those forms which do not properly belong to the other two. It embraces all those occasions in which God miraculously intervenes in history in order to work a specific work or accomplish a specific purpose. Sometimes this intervention is only in the mind of an individual, while most of the time it is an action performed on the objective stage of history.

Sometimes God reveals himself by acting upon the mind of a person in order to produce a dream or a vision which does not in itself contain any word revelation. The events acted out before the mind's eye may be real or they may be symbolic; in any case the sole purpose is to reveal something to the recipient of the dream or vision. Such dreams may be given to pagans in order that a man of God may interpret them. Examples are the dreams given to Pharaoh (Genesis 41:1-7) and interpreted by Joseph (Genesis 41:25-36), and the dream of Nebuchadnezzar interpreted by Daniel (Daniel 2:26-45). At other times God's prophets were shown visions which served as object lessons, such as the locust swarm and the plumb line shown to Amos (Amos 7:1, 7). Possibly the bulk of the great scenes shown to the Apostle John recorded in the book of Revelation came to him in this way (cf., e.g., the opening of the seals in chapter six).

More often, however, when we refer to the "mighty acts of God," we are thinking of the actual deeds and accomplishments of God performed before the eyes of many observers in open history. Some of these may be small and have a very limited purpose, e.g., the urim and thummim (Exodus 28:30; Numbers 27:21) and the guiding of lots (Acts 1:26). Sometimes the revelation is in the form of a non-verbal theophany, as the pillars of cloud and fire (Exodus 13:21-22). More often the revelation comes through a mighty and marvelous miracle which displays the power of God before all who witness it or hear of it. Primary examples are the ten judgments (plagues) on the false gods of Egypt and their worshipers, and the opening of the Red Sea for the deliverance of the people of Israel (Exodus 7-14). Other examples would be the fall of Jericho's walls (Joshua 6), the consumption of Elijah's sacrifice by fire from heaven (I Kings 18), and the healing of the lame man by Peter and John in Acts 3.

A point that needs to be emphasized very strongly is that although all such acts of God in history serve to reveal His nature or his will to some extent, revelation is not the primary purpose of most of them. Some of the lesser ones may be viewed as primarily revelatory, such as the guiding of lots and the guidance by the pillar of fire. But the primary purpose of most of the great miracles of God can be called revelation only in a very special sense. The main purpose of a miracle is evidential, that is, it serves as proof or as a sign that the message of the miracle-worker is an authentic message from God. It is a sign that bears witness to something beyond itself. As Paul says, "The signs of a true apostle were performed among you with all perseverance, by signs and wonders and miracles" (II Cor. 12:12). Hebrews 2:4 adds, "God also bearing witness with them, both by signs and wonders and by various miracles and by gifts of the Holy Spirit." In other words the mighty miraculous acts of God are revelatory only in the secondary sense that they are *pointers* to the more specific word revelation which they are designed to confirm. And we may add finally that some of the mightiest acts of all were performed not for the purpose of revelation but for the sake of *redemption*. These include especially the miracles connected with the Exodus and the mighty works of Jesus in the cross and resurrection.

Our conclusion is that the "mighty acts of God" are the least effective form of special revelation and are designed primarily for this purpose only when a very simple message is to be communicated. In most cases the acts of God are not intended primarily for revelation but are meant to accompany or be accompanied by the more specific form of revelation through words. I.e., miracles in general are intended to accompany word revelation in order to confirm it, and the mighty redemptive acts must be accompanied by word revelation in order to explain them. This conclusion is quite traditional, but it stands in direct opposition to the modern theological trend of locating *all* revelation in God's mighty acts. As John Baillie explains,

> No affirmation runs more broadly throughout recent writing on our subject than that . . . all revelation is given, not in the form of directly communicated knowledge, but through events occurring in the historical experience of mankind, events which are apprehended by faith as the "mighty acts" of God, and which therefore engender in the mind of man such reflective knowledge of God as it is given him to possess. . . .[70]

In our judgment this affirmation is drastically wrong and contradicts everything the Bible itself says about revelation.

---

70. John Baillie, *The Idea of Revelation in Recent Thought* (New York: Columbia University Press, 1956), p. 62. See G. Ernest Wright, *God Who Acts* (London: SCM Press, 1952), p. 12; "The title for the book presented something of a problem because of the danger of misunderstanding what was meant. 'God Who Acts' was chosen to point up the contrast with the more customary expression, 'God Who Speaks'. Christian Theology has tended to think of the Bible chiefly as 'the Word of God', though in point of fact a more accurate title would be 'the Acts of God'." See James Barr's penetrating critique of the neo-Protestant idea that the Bible itself portrays revelation as acts of God and not words in "Revelation Through History in the Old Testament and in Modern Theology," *Interpretation* (April 1963), 17:193-205, reprinted in *New Theology No. 1,* ed. Martin E. Marty and Dean Peerman (New York: Macmillan, 1964), pp. 60-74.

The Spoken Words of God

This leads to a consideration of the next form of special revelation, namely, the spoken words of God. The Creator is a God who speaks as well as acts, and he speaks verbally in human language. "He declares his words to Jacob, His statutes and His ordinances to Israel" (Psalm 147:19). His words may come to man in a number of ways. Many times God has spoken orally and audibly from heaven. The revelation of the Ten Commandments in the hearing of the whole nation of Israel is an example (Exodus 19-20). When Moses recounted this event before the entrance into Canaan, he reminded them that "the Lord spoke to you from the midst of the fire; you heard the sound of words, but you saw no form—only a voice. So He declared to you His covenant which He commanded you to perform, that is, the ten commandments" (Deut. 4:12-13). Then Moses comments, "Has anything been done like this great thing, or has anything been heard like it? Has any people heard the voice of God speaking from the midst of the fire, as you have heard it, and survived?" (Deut. 4:32-33). Also, audible communication was God's ordinary way of speaking to Moses (i.e., in his own speech): "Thus the Lord used to speak to Moses face to face, just as a man speaks to his friend" (Exodus 33:11). Sometimes the voice came from the pillar of cloud, as when God spoke directly to Moses, Aaron, and Miriam (Numbers 12:4-9). Also we are told that at the baptism of Jesus God spoke directly from heaven saying, "This is My beloved Son, in whom I am well-pleased" (Matthew 3:17). Sometimes the Lord himself does not speak audibly but uses a messenger or spokesman to speak his words for him. This can happen even against a person's will if God simply takes over his vocal apparatus, as in the case of Balaam (Numbers 23-24). Or it may happen with a willing prophet, as with David: "The Spirit of the Lord spoke by me, and His word was on my tongue" (II Samuel 23:2). Or the spokesman may be an angel, as in the case of Gabriel's messages to Zacharias and to Mary (Luke 1).

Verbal revelation may be given in other forms. Instead of being delivered audibly the words may be written. This happened when God himself wrote the ten commandments on two tablets of stone and gave them to Moses (Deut. 5:22). This would also be the case when a prophecy is written entirely through the inspiration of the Spirit, as in the case of Isaiah 53, for example. Verbal revelation may also be given wholly within the mind, as in the case of a dream or vision in which God delivers a message to the recipient (see Numbers 12:8). This may have been the way God called Samuel (I Samuel 3:1-14), and it was the way the angel spoke to Joseph (Matthew 1:20-23; 2:13).

No phenomenon is more widely and firmly attested in Scripture than the reality of verbal revelation from God to man. The words spoken by or from God may be in the form of a promise, a warning, a commandment, or a proposition. The propositional revelation is a communication of truth from the mind of God to the mind of man.

At the same time nothing is more characteristic of modern theology than the *denial* of verbal revelation from God to man. It is typical of our anti-intellectual age to question the revelance of words in general, as Carl Henry points out;[71] but surely there is no more far-reaching expression of this

71. Carl F. H. Henry, *God, Revelation and Authority, Volume I: God Who Speaks and Shows, Preliminary Considerations* (Waco: Word Books, 1976), pp. 24ff.

trend than the rejection of revelation in the form of words. Leon Morris gives the following summary of this viewpoint:

> . . . Traditionally Christians have seen the revelation in the very words of the Bible, but in recent times many scholars have attacked the whole idea of verbal or propositional revelation. They prefer to think that God reveals himself in the mighty deeds that are recorded in the Bible, while regarding the words in which these deeds are recorded as not of primary importance. They see the writers of the books of the Bible as seized by the conviction that God has acted and as being anxious accordingly to record what God has done. But the revelation is in the deeds themselves and not in the record. For example, it would be said that God revealed himself in whatever events underlay the Exodus story but that the words in which the events are enshrined are not specially important. In fact many scholars hold that the actual events were very different from those we think happened if we take the relevant accounts as straightforward narrative. That God acted is not doubted. That the words in which God's acts are recorded form part of the revelation is not only doubted but rejected.[72]

If God does not give us revelation in the form of words, then just what is revealed? The answer is that God reveals *himself,* but he does *not* reveal propositional or cognitive truth; he does not reveal information or truths about himself or about anything else. As John Hick says, "According to this nonpropositional view, the content of revelation is not a body of truths about God, but God himself coming within the orbit of man's experience by acting in human history." We must understand that "theological propositions, as such, are not revealed, but represent human attempts to

72. Leon Morris, *I Believe in Revelation* (Grand Rapids: Eerdmans, 1976), pp. 43-44.

understand the significance of revelatory events."[73] As H. Berkhof puts it, "One no longer speaks of revealed truths, but of the God who reveals himself, and preferably of God's 'self-revelation.' "[74]

The classical explanation of this position in recent times is John Baillie's book, *The Idea of Revelation in Recent Thought.* In his second chapter he explains revelation as "the divine self-disclosure," or a disclosure *of* a subject or person *to* another person. "In the last resort it is not information about God that is revealed, but very God Himself incarnate in Jesus Christ our Lord." Revelation is the *action* of God in which he unveils his hiddenness and discloses himself.[75] Baillie cites the often-quoted pronouncements of William Temple, "What is offered to man's apprehension in any specific revelation is not truth concerning God but the living God Himself." And, "There is no such thing as revealed truth. There are truths of revelation; but they are not themselves directly revealed."[76] Baillie adds his own aphorism: "God does not give us information by communication; He gives us Himself in communion."[77] This means two things. One, "what is fundamentally revealed is God Himself, not propositions about God." And two, "God

---

73. John Hick, *Philosophy of Religion*, 2 ed. (Englewood Cliffs, N.J.: Prentice-Hall, 1973), p. 60.

74. Hendrikus Berkhof, *Christian Faith*, p. 72.

75. John Baillie, *The Idea of Revelation*, p. 28.

76. *Ibid.*, p. 33. He is citing William Temple, *Nature, Man and God* (London: Macmillan and Co., 1934), pp. 317, 322. Temple's complete statement on page 317 (not page 316 as Baillie has it) is as follows: "From all this it follows that there is no such thing as revealed truth. There are truths of revelation, that is to say, propositions which express the results of correct thinking concerning revelation; but they are not themselves directly revealed." Both this and the other quotation from Temple are in italics in the original.

77. John Baillie, *The Idea of Revelation*, p. 47.

reveals Himself *in action*" and not words. God has indeed spoken, but he has "spoken through events."[78]

One other point needs to be noted. In the modern way of thinking the self-disclosure of God in an event of history is not truly revelation *until* that event has been *perceived* as an act of God and acknowledged as such by an observer. Until this happens it is just a bare event; but when an individual perceives God in it, it becomes an *encounter* event. Then it is truly revelation. Some believe it takes a special act of God to enable the observer to recognize God in an event. Baillie says, "The illumination of the receiving mind is a necessary condition of the divine self-disclosure."[79] We may recall H. Berkhof's words, that "revelation is not even revelation if it is not perceived and acknowledged as such from the other side," and we may note that he adds that "we need the illumination of our mind to be able to perceive the supernatural in the natural."[80] Emil Brunner has said the same thing, that revelation is not complete until it is received by some individual through the inner testimony of the Holy Spirit.[81] This combination of the objective self-revealing of God in the person of Jesus Christ and the subjective personal encounter through the Spirit yields revelation.[82]

The problem here of course is not necessarily with what is affirmed but with what is denied. Though we do not accept the need for subjective illumination in order to perceive God's working in history, we are certainly comfortable with

78. *Ibid.*, pp. 49-51.

79. *Ibid.*, p. 64.

80. Hendrikus Berkhof, *Christian Faith*, p. 57.

81. Emil Brunner, *The Christian Doctrine of God*, pp. 19-20.

82. *Ibid.*, pp. 26, 29.

the idea that God reveals himself, or that revelation is a self-revelation of God. But this kind of language is often a veiled denial of *word* revelation, and this is what disturbs us very much. The fact is that revelation as event-encounter has *replaced* the idea of word revelation for much of modern theology. If we inquire into the reasoning behind this denial of the latter, we usually find an answer that brings us back to one of the main themes of the doctrine of God as Creator, namely, the divine transcendence. Surely we cannot think (we are told) that the puny categories of man's finite mind are sufficient to enclose the infinite God. Surely we cannot believe that our faltering, imperfect human language is a fit vehicle for truth about the perfect God. Surely we cannot suppose that *anything* that partakes of the relativity of this world can contain the thoughts of the Absolute. Even if God wanted to address us in our own language, he could not do so; for by the time his infinite and absolute thoughts were squeezed into our finite and relative structures, they would be utterly and completely changed. Their original identity would be totally lost. The barrier of transcendence just cannot be bridged. As Ronald Nash sums up this point,

> . . . Today, the reason most often given for God's inability to speak is His transcendence. This radical otherness of God means, among other things, that the human mind is incapable of comprehending the divine mind. Once this point is granted, it follows that the word of God can never be the communication of truth; divine revelation can never contain a cognitive content that can be apprehended by the human mind. This network of ideas accounts for what is perhaps the central phalanx in the contemporary assault on the knowability of God. It can be summed up in the statement that *no revelation is propositional.*[83]

83. Ronald Nash, *The Word of God and the Mind of Man*, p. 36.

> . . . Because God is totally transcendent, because He is unlike anything else in human experience, human language is an unfit instrument to capture ideas or express truths about God. Nor are human rational faculties adequate for knowledge about the transcendent. Cognitive knowledge about God is an impossible dream. . . . The implication is that God could not communicate genuine information about Himself even if He wanted to.[84]

How do we respond to this line of reasoning? Of course we do not deny the transcendence of God; it is the main corollary of the fact of creation. But we do reject the particular understanding of transcendence presupposed in the denial of word revelation. It is not the biblical idea of transcendence, but a philosophical one derived mainly from the thought of David Hume and Immanuel Kant, as Ronald Nash shows.[85] Also, we would say that rather than being a barrier to word communication, the transcendence of God is the very thing that makes it possible. Because he is transcendent, God is omnipotent and omniscient. With such a God, all things are possible. Surely the accomplishment of a valid verbal communication with man is a small task for him. By his infinite power he laid the groundwork for such communication in the very beginning when he created man in his own image. Thus there is enough similarity between the mind of man and the mind of God to make a verbal exchange meaningful, even though the former is finite and the latter infinite. Also we must remember that it is God who initiates the exchange; it is the all-wise God who speaks across the barrier of transcendence. Even though the language of revelation is human language, it is not the result

84. *Ibid.*, p. 47.
85. *Ibid.*, chapters 1 and 2.

of finite man's feeble groping for God. It comes from the infinite, omniscient God who *knows how* to cross the Creator/creature gap with meaningful communication. It is not the *fact* that the revelation comes in admittedly human language; it is rather the *source* of this language that is determinative. Can human language express divine truth? Yes—when it comes from the transcendent God himself. Just because *we* grope and fumble for the proper words to express what we may know only hazily is no reason why God should be tongue-tied and unable to express—even in human language—what *he* knows *perfectly.* Thus we agree wholeheartedly with Nash: "There is nothing in the nature of the divine transcendence that precludes the possibility of our knowing the mind of God."[86]

Before leaving this section on revelation as spoken words of God, we must ask one other question, namely, are the words of the Bible a revelation from God? For those who deny that revelation comes in the form of words, the answer of course must be no, not in any true sense of the word. If revelation is given only in the form of God's actions, especially in the person of Jesus Christ, then at best the Bible is a *record* of these actions, or a witness and pointer to these actions, or a record of the reflections of those who first encountered God through these actions. The Bible may be all of these things, and as such it may even be the occasion for our *own* encounter with God (i.e., our own experience of revelation); but it can never be in itself a literal revelation.

John Hick makes this point quite clearly. He notes that when revelation is understood as propositional, the Bible is usually called the Word of God or even the words of God. But according to the nonpropositional view, only Jesus Christ should properly be called *the* Word of God. "The

86. *Ibid.*, p. 14.

Bible is not itself the Word of God but is rather the primary and indispensable witness to the Word." Though it is a thoroughly human book, it happens to be the only set of documents we have which contains the records of those men who witnessed the great historical events in which God was perceived to be acting.[87] H. Berkhof is a good example of this view. He says,

> . . . Scripture cannot be identified with revelation. It is the human reaction to it. Here we meet revelation indirectly, in the mirror of the human witness. And when this witness is itself the product of a history of interpretation, we have to speak of a double indirectness.[88]

The Bible is still important, though, since "nowhere else but in Scripture does the word of the primary witnesses to revelation come to us." These recorded words of those who had a first-hand encounter with God serve to "mediate an encounter with God" for us, too.[89] We should note well the words of Carl Henry: "The emphasis on Scripture as witness to revelation—or more ambiguously as 'revelation in the form of witness'—is a neo-Protestant formula for denying that Scripture has revelational status."[90]

In the final analysis, then, when word revelation is denied the Bible loses its final and absolute authority. The final authority is in the non-cognitive revelational event; any verbal response to that event, including the Bible, is at least one step removed from revelation and thus one step removed from final authority. The biblical writers experienced revelation when they encountered the revelation events; but

87. John Hick, *Philosophy of Religion*, pp. 64-65.

88. Hendrikus Berkhof, *Christian Faith*, p. 87.

89. *Ibid.*, pp. 87-88.

90. Carl F. H. Henry, *God, Revelation and Authority, Volume II*, p. 88.

their experience was just that—an experience. The revelation was in the experience, not in the verbal formulations that came after the experience. Their verbal formulations (i.e., Scripture) are important in that they are the reflections of the first generation of those who experience revelation. But this is the point: *they are only the first.* Through their testimony *we too* are enabled to have a genuine encounter with the revelation event; i.e., we too can experience revelation. Through the illumination of the Holy Spirit, revelation as the combination of event and encounter *still continues today*; and the biblical records are not qualitatively different from our own reflections on their and our encounters. Thus the Bible is completely relativized and brought down to the level of our own preaching and theologizing. As H. Berkhof affirms, the continuing interpretive transmission of the biblical witness is "one continuous revelational event."[91] Emil Brunner has said the same thing. The witnessing work of the Spirit that produces a revelation encounter, he says, "is never ended, never finished." Since the very same Spirit who witnessed to the Apostles witnesses to us, "there is no difference between the Apostles and the members of the Christian Church." Thus the Spirit "retains the right to teach mankind more and more clearly, never, however, establishing once for all a definitive doctrine."[92] Thus we should never expect nor seek unity of doctrine.[93]

It is important to see that this whole way of speaking is predicated ultimately on the assumption that there is no such thing as word revelation. In our judgment this assumption along with all its consequences outlined above is totally

---

91. Hendrikus Berkhof, *Christian Faith*, p. 91.

92. Emil Brunner, *The Christian Doctrine of God*, pp. 31-32.

93. Emil Brunner, *Revelation and Reason*, tr. Olive Wyon (Philadelphia: Westminster Press, 1946), p. 201.

foreign to both the phenomena and the claims of the Bible. The Bible *does* depict revelation as coming to us in the form of words, and the Bible also presents itself as at least containing such word revelation and as in a sense *being* word revelation. We cannot go into the technical distinction between revelation and inspiration here; but we may note that when this distinction is observed, all of the biblical writings are not strictly revelation though all are inspired and therefore approved by God. On the other hand it is possible to regard inspiration itself as a special mode of revelation (though not in the sense of dictation necessarily); thus Paul can say that all Scripture is "God-breathed" (II Timothy 3:16). Since this is the case, i.e., since every word is at least supervised and approved by God, we can speak of the whole Bible as revelation from God or as the very words of God. The biblical writings are, as Paul says of the Old Testament (Romans 3:2), the "oracles of God," the very spoken words of God. Thus they bear the divine authority of God himself.

The Visible Presence of God

The third form in which God gives special revelation is through his own visible presence. This form usually embodies one or both of the above (divine acts and/or divine words) as done or spoken by God himself as visibly present. Certain Old Testament theophanies fall into this category. The spiritual theophany in Exodus 24:10 probably did not involve accompanying words or deeds, but it was nevertheless a revelation of God in his visible presence. The Lord's appearance to Abraham in Genesis 18 included word revelation, as did his communion with Adam and Eve implied in Genesis 3. The "Angel of the Lord" appearances usually involved word communication and sometimes marvelous deeds (see Judges 6:21; 13:19-20).

Theophanies such as these appear to be a kind of prelude to what is usually regarded as the highest form of revelation, the visible presence of God in the person of Jesus Christ. Jesus as the Incarnate Logos is the climactic and clearest revelation of God. The very heart of God is revealed by his personal presence—his character, his attitudes, his priorities, his spirit. Since Jesus is God in the flesh, his acts are the acts of God and his words are the words of God. Thus he reveals God in the other two forms while adding the third form of personal, visible presence. Kenneth Kantzer describes this aspect of the work of Jesus in this way:

> The consummating mode of revelation in all Scripture, which serves to tie all other modes together, is the person of Jesus Christ. Jesus Christ differs from other modes in that He is not so much a mode of the divine communication as He is the divine being Himself, communicating to man directly in and through His incarnation in the human race. Jesus Christ combines both the act of revelation and the word of revelation. He is God acting; and when He speaks, He is in turn, God speaking with divine authority and divine infallibility.[94]

The biblical teaching concerning Jesus' prophetic role as Revealer is abundant. It is best summed up in Hebrews 1:1-3, which emphasizes the appropriateness of the Son as the supreme revelation of the Father:

---

94. Kenneth Kantzer, "The Communication of Revelation," *The Bible: The Living Word of Revelation*, ed. Merrill C. Tenney (Grand Rapids: Zondervan, 1968), p. 76.

> God, after He spoke long ago to the fathers in the prophets in many portions and in many ways, in these last days has spoken to us in His Son, whom He appointed heir of all things, through whom also He made the world. And He is the radiance of His glory and the exact representation of His nature . . . .

A major biblical image for knowledge is *light*, and this image is often applied to Jesus. II Corinthians 4:6 says, "For God, who said, 'Light shall shine out of darkness,' is the One who has shone in our hearts to give the light of the knowledge of the glory of God in the face of Christ." The Logos, says John 1:9, "was the true light which, coming into the world, enlightens every man"; for "in Him was life; and the life was the light of men" (John 1:4). When the prophet Simeon held the infant Christ, he described him as "a light of revelation to the Gentiles" (Luke 2:32). In describing himself Jesus said, "I am the light of the world; he who follows Me shall not walk in the darkness, but shall have the light of life" (John 8:12). He said, "I have come as light into the world" (John 12:46).

His own deity makes Jesus uniquely qualified to reveal the nature and mind of God. "No man has seen God at any time; the only begotten God, who is in the bosom of the Father, He has explained Him" (John 1:18). Jesus Christ as the incarnate Logos explains one aspect of his mission: "All things have been handed over to Me by My Father; and no one knows the Son, except the Father; nor does anyone know the Father, except the Son, and anyone to whom the Son wills to reveal Him" (Matthew 11:27). When Philip said, "Lord, show us the Father," Jesus replied, "Have I been so long with you, and yet you have not come to know Me, Philip? He who has seen Me has seen the

Father" (John 14:8-9). Jesus tells us that his very words are a revelation from the Father: "For I did not speak on My own initiative, but the Father Himself who sent Me has given Me commandment, what to say, and what to speak. . . . Therefore the things I speak, I speak just as the Father has told Me" (John 12:49-50; see 14:24). His prophetic purpose is summed up in his testimony before Pilate: "For this I have been born, and for this I have come into the world, to bear witness to the truth" (John 18:37).

While there is general agreement that the visible presence of God in Jesus Christ is the supreme form of revelation, there is significant disagreement as to the relation between Christ as revelation and other forms of revelation. The extreme position on this subject is espoused by Karl Barth, who declared that Jesus Christ is not just the supreme revelation but is the *only* revelation of God. We may refer to other things as revelation, but that could be true only in a relative and therefore a less than real sense. "Revelation as such is not relative. Revelation in fact does not differ from the Person of Jesus Christ." He alone is the absolute revelation which is the only true revelation.[95] "God's revelation is Jesus Christ, God's Son."[96] "God's revelation is the event of Jesus Christ."[97] The only possible way for God to reveal himself is by becoming flesh, by becoming a human being. Thus only the incarnation of the Logos can possibly be revelation. "To be revelation it had to be an incarnation."[98] What about the Bible? "We distinguish the Bible as such

95. Karl Barth, *Church Dogmatics, Volume I: The Doctrine of the Word of God, Part 1*, tr. G. T. Thomson (Edinburg: T. & T. Clark, 1936), p. 134.

96. *Ibid.*, p. 155.

97. Karl Barth, *Church Dogmatics*, I/2, p. 49.

98. *Ibid.*, p. 43.

from revelation."[99] The Old Testament era is the time of the *expectation* of the revelation; hence "the Old Testament is the witness to the genuine expectation of revelation."[100] The New Testament era is the time of the *recollection* of the revelation; the New Testament is the witness to this recollection.[101] John Baillie sums up Barth's position thus:

> . . . He stands, as did Ritschl and Herrmann in previous generations, in the tradition of that Lutheran christocentrism which made Christ the Mediator no less of knowledge than of salvation; the christocentrism which denies that except in His Incarnation in Jesus of Nazareth God has ever spoken to man at all; the christocentrism which seizes eagerly on the New Testament declaration that 'neither knoweth any man the Father, save the Son, and he to whomsoever the Son will reveal him,' and understands that to mean that not merely God's fatherliness but His very reality was made known to men through Jesus alone. Except through revelation, he teaches, there is no knowledge of God, and there is no revelation except in Christ . . . .[102]

A position similar to this but not quite so extreme is the idea that Jesus Christ is not the only revelation, but he is the *normative* revelation. Hendrikus Berkhof takes this view. "The Bible," he says, "contains statements to the effect that there is revelation from God also outside of Israel and Christ."[103] Thus he denies the Barthian extreme. Nevertheless Berkhof says that "Jesus Christ is the central revelation," and that "this even must be the starting-point and guide for our thinking about revelation in general."[104] The

99. *Ibid.*, p. 463.
100. *Ibid.*, p. 70.
101. *Ibid.*, pp. 101ff.
102. John Baillie, *Our Knowledge of God*, pp. 17-18.
103. Hendrikus Berkhof, *Christian Faith*, p. 47.
104. *Ibid.*, pp. 47, 50.

key statement is that "*the divine revelation in Christ is indeed normative, but not exclusive.*" There are other truths, but "all such truths are fragmentary and broken unless they have become integrated in him as the center."[105]

Emil Brunner's view is similar to H. Berkhof's. He begins with a description of Old Testament revelation, which came in a variety of forms including speech. Indeed, word revelation through the prophets was the "decisive and standard" form of Old Testament revelation. However, this form of revelation was only temporary; it was preparatory and provisional. It was an inferior mode which prepared the way for that which is now the only real revelation, the person of Jesus Christ.[106] Jesus as the new form of revelation is not a word as such, nor is he speech in the form of a group of sentences. He is "God Himself present, acting in His own Person," and not just words about him. Henceforth we must speak of the Old Testament revelation as being "merely" words or "only" words. Now we have the real revelation himself, and "its form is no longer this merely provisional, indirect form—a 'pointer' to something beyond." It is "He Himself, not His speech," that is the revelation.[107]

> . . . The spoken word is now no longer the revelation itself, or to put it more exactly, it is no longer directly "revelation," but only indirectly. The spoken word is an indirect revelation when it bears witness to the real revelation: Jesus Christ, the personal self-manifestation of God, Emmanuel. The spoken word, the "word" in the actual sense of speech, "saying something in words," has thus been relegated to a secondary position. . . .[108]

---

105. *Ibid.*, p. 48.
106. Emil Brunner, *The Christian Doctrine of God*, pp. 16, 22-23.
107. *Ibid.*, pp. 23-24.
108. *Ibid.*, p. 25.

Christ as the true revelation "takes the place of the spoken word." Anything in the form of human speech can now be called revelation only indirectly, only insofar as it witnesses to Him. "This truth," says Brunner, "is of decisive importance for theology; only by its means will it be possible to repair the damage inflicted on Western theology" by those who want to consider the very words of Scripture as somehow revealed. Those who do this are abandoning the newer and higher form of revelation and are trying to resurrect the displaced and inferior Old Testament revelational form, namely, "that the Divine revelation is a spoken Word of God, and even a doctrine."[109] The only legitimate Christian doctrine is that which is based on revelation (i.e., on Jesus Christ); Christ is thus the criterion and norm for doctrine. The Bible has a relative authority in that it is the primary witness to the one revelation in Jesus Christ, "but it is in no way the *norm* of our knowledge and our doctrine."[110]

Sometimes even in conservative circles we encounter the idea that the revelation given through the incarnate Christ has a higher authority than any other revelation. In chapter three above we discussed examples of this as related to ethics. We saw that there is a tendency to take the words of Jesus as recorded in the gospels as being uniquely normative for Christian conduct. (After all, they *are* in red letters, are they not?) This kind of thinking is abetted by such incautious language as Wiley's statement, spoken of Christ, that "He alone is the true Revealer."[111]

109. *Ibid.*, pp. 27-28.

110. *Ibid.*, pp. 43-49.

111. H. Orton Wiley, *Christian Theology* (Kansas City, Mo.: Beacon Hill Press, 1940), I:139.

We find it necessary to reject these views, Barthian or otherwise, as distortions of the role of Jesus Christ as a revelation of God. This is all a part of the same general problem discussed earlier as the Christological fallacy, i.e., the erroneous hermeneutical method which gives redemption and God's redemptive purposes primacy over creation, and which therefore makes redemptive categories determinative for all other doctrine. And since the incarnate Christ is associated with redemption, Christological categories are thus made to be the source and standard of all knowledge of God. The following statement by Karl Barth will remind us of this point:

> . . . A church dogmatics must, of course, be christologically determined as a whole and in all its parts, as surely as the revealed Word of God, attested by Holy Scripture and proclaimed by the Church, is its one and only criterion, and as surely as this revealed Word is identical with Jesus Christ. . . .[112]

But now we see this Christological fallacy carried a step further, in that the primary category in Christology is *revelation*. That is, Jesus Christ is interpreted *primarily* as a Revealer of God. The need for redemption is cast in noetic terms: man lacks true knowledge of God, or he lacks the knowledge that will persuade him to repent. Redemption itself is thus accomplished *by means of* revelation; thus the main purpose for which Christ came is to reveal the true nature of God, the knowledge of which results in our salvation. In fact, Karl Barth goes so far as to equate reconciliation (his word for the redemptive work of Christ) with revelation. "Revelation . . . does not differ from the Person

---

112. Karl Barth, *Church Dogmatics*, I/2, p. 123.

of Jesus Christ, and again does not differ from the reconciliation that took place in Him."[113] Also,

> . . . The work of the Son or Word is the presence and manifestation of God which, in view of the fact that it is a miraculous event amid human darkness and despite this darkness, we can only designate revelation. The word reconciliation is another word for the same thing. So far as God's revelation as such achieves, what only God can achieve, namely, the restoration of man's communion with God, destroyed, nay annihilated by us, so far as, in the fact of revelation, God's enemies are already his friends, revelation itself is reconciliation. . . .[114]

What is the result of this kind of thinking? When priority is given to redemptive categories and when redemption is seen basically as achieved through revelation, Jesus Christ as the *one essential revelation* is given epistemological priority over all other forms of revelation, if these are allowed at all. But when this happens, all other forms of revelation, including the teachings of the apostles and prophets, are at best demoted to a secondary level. As Brunner so well exemplifies this point, "The word of Scripture is not the final court of appeal, since Jesus Christ Himself alone is this ultimate authority."[115] This demotion of Scripture is done in part in order to preserve the *uniqueness* of Christ. Certainly Christ is unique, and his work is unique. But where

---

113. Karl Barth, *Church Dogmatics*, I/1, p. 134.

114. *Ibid.*, p. 468. Carl Braaten has rightly called attention to this primacy of the noetic in much of modern theology in *New Directions in Theology Today, Volume II: History and Hermeneutics* (Philadelphia: Westminster Press, 1966), pp. 11ff.

115. Emil Brunner, *The Christian Doctrine of God*, p. 47.

his work is seen (rightly) to be primarily the accomplishment of redemption and not revelation, his uniqueness can be preserved without doing violence to the other forms of revelation. But if Christ's unique work consists primarily in revealing the heart of the Father, then his revelation must be set on a level of higher authority than any other, which necessarily requires the abandonment of Scripture as "the only rule of faith and practice."

We reject this whole approach to revelation on two grounds. First, revelation as such is not *primarily* a category of redemption but of creation. Revelation was originally and properly the work of God as Creator: "For behold, He who forms mountains and creates the wind and declares to man what are His thoughts, . . . the Lord God of hosts is His name" (Amos 4:13). And this should be particularly noted: this point applies to *special* revelation as well as to general revelation. This fact is not always observed as it should be. Sometimes general revelation is seen as a function of nature, while special revelation is seen as a work of grace (a redemptive category). Louis Berkhof asserts, "General revelation is rooted in creation" and "is addressed to man as man," while "special revelation is rooted in the redemptive plan of God" and is addressed to man as sinner.[116] Clark Pinnock says,

> . . . While Scripture undoubtedly alludes to a general revelation of God in the created order, its predominant emphasis is upon special revelation. Remedial redemptive revelation enjoys centrality in the Bible. It is soteric, restorative and therapeutic. The invisible, hidden and transcendent God, whom no man has seen nor can see, has planted His Word

116. Louis Berkhof, *Systematic Theology* (London: Banner of Truth Trust, 1939), p. 37.

in the human situation that sinners might be brought nigh unto God. . . .[117]

Now we would certainly agree that the special revelation as we have it in the form of Scripture is soteric or remedial in its intent. This form of special revelation has been directed to sinners and adapted to sinners; it gives us "the wisdom that leads to salvation" (II Timothy 3:15). But this is not the original purpose of special revelation; it is not exclusively a redemptive work. The fact is that there was special revelation given to man before the Fall and before the need for redemption ever arose. Genesis 1:28-30 shows God addressing Adam and Eve and giving them specific instructions not included in the moral law written on their hearts. Genesis 2:16-17 shows God instructing Adam about the tree of knowledge of good and evil. Genesis 2:19 implies that God told Adam to name the animals. Genesis 3:8 implies that God appeared to Adam and Eve frequently for communion and communication. This is communication between God as Creator and man as creature; this was no doubt God's original intention and plan for special revelation as distinct from general revelation. From the very beginning, when God determined to create man in his own image and before the need for redemption entered the picture, he was designing man as man to be the recipient of his own face-to-face, mouth-to-mouth communication. Thus, making Christ the only revelation completely ignores the primacy of creation over redemption, and it ignores the original intention for special revelation as the means by which the Creator could engage in an on-going relation with man as the creature

117. Clark H. Pinnock, *Biblical Revelation: The Foundation of Christian Theology* (Chicago: Moody Press, 1971), p. 29. See also page 20: "Revelation is soteric in its intent."

made in his own image. Giving the revelation of Christ an epistemological primacy over all other forms of revelation results from the same oversight.

The second reason why we reject the approach to revelation described above is that the primary work of Jesus Christ is *redemption* as distinct from revelation. Of course we are not attempting an absolute separation between redemption and revelation. They necessarily go together. Without revelation Christ's redemptive work would be inaccessible to us, and without redemption even the most sublime revelation would be in vain. Nevertheless we must see that they are not the same thing, and we must see that the incarnation was required *not* by a need for revelation but by a need for *redemption*. Thus even though we may say that revelation was one of the purposes for which the Logos became incarnate, we must say that it was not the *compelling* purpose. If revelation were the only necessity, the incarnation would not have been required. We must not forget that revelation through visible presence was possible and had already been accomplished by means of some very significant theophanies in Old Testament times. But the one thing that could not be accomplished except through the incarnation was redemption through the death and resurrection of the God-man. *This* was Christ's primary purpose; this was his main work. As significant as his revelation was, it was separate and distinct from his redeeming acts. We reject completely the idea that these acts of redemption accomplished their purpose *by functioning as* revelation, e.g., a revelation of the loving heart of God, as the moral influence theory of atonement interprets the cross.

When we understand that redemption is Christ's primary purpose, we see that his *uniqueness* lies in this area and not necessarily in his revealing activity. There is a kind of uniqueness about Christ as a form of revelation, of course, since he is the only incarnate Son of God. But we do not have to exaggerate this uniqueness in order to preserve his uniqueness as such, since the latter lies in his redemptive work. Though his revelation truly outshines all others, it in no way impinges on the authority of the other forms of revelation. Christ did not nullify that which went before him, and he did not make other forms of revelation obsolete. As Kenneth Kantzer puts it, his uniqueness as Redeemer is absolute, but his uniqueness as Revealer is only relative.[118]

This leads us to the following conclusions. (1) Jesus Christ is not the *only* form of special revelation. There is valid special revelation outside of Jesus Christ, including the writings of the Old and New Testaments. (2) The revelation in Jesus is not a *higher* form of revelation in the sense that it has higher authority than other revelations from God. All revelation has the same authority since it all comes ultimately from the same source, namely, God himself. This does not mean that it is all equally applicable in every age; we must retain the distinction between the two covenant eras, for instance. With regard to inherent authority, though, the revelation in Christ is no different from the book of Isaiah or I Corinthians. Jesus Christ is not an epistemological norm for knowledge of God; this idea is the essence of the Christological fallacy. (3) Jesus Christ in his earthly ministry is not the *final* revelation. Revelation was given to apostles and prophets in the decades following the resurrection and ascension; indeed, Jesus promised his apostles that the Spirit would guide them into all truth, truth which was ultimately from him (John 16:13-14). Certain of the miraculous

---

118. Kenneth Kantzer, "The Communication of Revelation," p. 57.

spiritual gifts were revelatory in nature (e.g., prophecy and knowledge). The canonical writings known as the New Testament came into being after Christ's ministry on earth. These are all valid revelations and are equal in authority with Jesus' own words. They follow the revelation of the earthly Christ and are interpretive of his work. (We reject the concept of continuing revelation after the closing of the New Testament canon; the next revelation will be at Christ's second coming.) Finally, (4) Jesus Christ is not a higher form *than* word revelation (contra Brunner); he is simply the highest form *of* word revelation. We reject the idea that just the person and presence of Jesus and not his words constitute the revelation given in Christ. We also reject the idea that personal presence is a higher form of revelation than "mere" words. In fact, words in themselves constitute in a real sense the personal presence of their author. Words are not qualitatively different from personal presence but are one of its vital aspects. When God became personally present in visible form in Jesus Christ, a part of his personal presence was the words which Jesus spoke. The spoken words of Jesus are part (if not the *main* part) of the revelation received through him. The fact that he came and spoke to us in human speech does not make word revelation obsolete, but all the more validates it as a viable mode of revelation and source of knowledge about God.

Thus we conclude our discussion of the forms of special revelation. We have seen that these include mighty acts of God, spoken words of God, and the visible presence of God. Through any of these forms we receive true knowledge of God. We note, though, that in each case these forms are just that, namely, *forms*; also, every one of them is the form of something native to the created universe.

When the transcendent One comes to us in revelation, he condescends to use a creaturely medium. Thus revelation is always God breaking through the barrier of transcendence from his side into ours; it is never our act of penetrating that barrier and entering the divine dimension, contrary to most views of "mystical union" with the divine. Also, since God comes to us in creaturely forms which *mediate* his presence or his truth to us, there is no such thing as a "direct encounter" with God even by means of these forms. We stress this over against the encounter concepts of revelation, which posit a "direct confrontation with God" by means of the earthly carriers of revelation.[119] This is a kind of semi-mysticism which in fact involves a contradiction of terms, i.e., the concept of a *direct* encounter by some *means*. Contrary to all such ideas, the God who meets us and speaks to us in the revelation-forms is still the hidden and incomprehensible God.

The Content of Special Revelation

At this point we will present a brief survey of the content of special revelation, especially to see how it correlates with and complements general revelation. We note at the outset that the content of revelation is not just God himself in encounter, but also and primarily truth, yea even *truths* about God and his creation. This truth will be discussed in two main categories: first, truth about God and man; second, truth about sin and redemption.

119. Hendrikus Berkhof, *Christian Faith*, p. 52. He says, "The real event is an encounter in which the natural becomes the transparency of a divine word or act. The person perceiving that is thus by means of the natural brought to a direct confrontation with God."

Truth About God and Man

Special revelation contains first of all truth about God and man. Regarding the former, it gives us a rather detailed knowledge of God. We learn about his works, and we learn about his nature. We learn about his basic nature as the Creator, and we learn about his work of creation. It is significant that special revelation should give us some of the details of the creation of the universe. From general revelation we may learn the *fact* that this is a created world and that the invisible Creator produced it by a stupendous act of power. But general revelation could not convey to us the data of Genesis one and two. This knowledge of pre-human cosmic history could come to us only through verbal revelation. We find it ironic that some theologians who feel constrained to question the historicity of the first chapters of Genesis do so on the ground that there were, after all, no human observers there to record these events. It is said that origins have no history; thus our historical research draws a blank about the "stories" in early Genesis.[120] Now, obviously, Bible believers throughout history have been aware of the absence of a human observer during this period of origins, but by and large they have not felt it necessary to question the reality of the events on that account. Why not? Because they have recognized also the reality of word revelation. There is no reason why God could not have explained the details of creation first of all to Adam and Eve, and certainly to Moses. Special revelation is the key that unlocks the door to such knowledge of the Creator and his work of creation.

120. One expression of this idea is found in Bernard Ramm, *After Fundamentalism: The Future of Evangelical Theology* (San Francisco: Harper and Row, 1982), p. 82ff.

Also given through special revelation is more detailed knowledge about the Creator's will for his creatures. As we saw earlier, ethics is grounded in creation and has to do with the creature's relationship to his Creator. Through special revelation God tells us what he wants us to do and what he does not want us to do. In other words, he gives us law. Some of it is universally applicable (the moral law), and some of it is intentionally limited in scope (positive laws). Psalm 119 is a lengthy praise to God for the revelation of his precepts. Almost all of its 176 verses refer to God's specially-revealed will in terms of its law, testimony, way, precepts, statutes, commandments, judgments, word, or ordinances. According to II Timothy 3:16, all Scripture is profitable for training in righteousness.

We should note that data in these categories have been revealed both by general and by special revelation, some of the latter being given even before the entrance of sin. Even in the pre-Fall era, as we have seen, God did not intend to limit his revealing work merely to general revelation. Now that sin *has* entered the human situation, however, the need for special revelation is even more imperative. Even the data about God and man knowable through general revelation are re-published and clarified in the special forms and are complemented by the addition of more details. The special revelation given to man after the Fall has been adapted to man as sinner. It is more than simply *anthropic*—accommodated to man;[121] it is *peccatopic*, adapted to man as sinner. The following statement by Ramm is true of post-Fall special revelation:

121. Bernard Ramm, *Special Revelation and the Word of God*, pp. 33ff.

> Special revelation is remedial because it is God's means of reaching the *sinner* with saving, restorative truth. It is the knowledge of God adjusted for, and given for, sinners. It is the remedial crutch, and healing bandage, the corrective spectacles for crippled, wounded and blind sinners. . . .[122]

The fact that special revelation is adapted to sinners means that beyond the special revelation itself (e.g., the words of Scripture), no further special work of God is needed to enable the sinner to understand it and respond to it. The revelation itself impacts upon the sinner's heart and mind.[123] There is no special need for regeneration, illumination, or the internal testimony of the Spirit to enable this revelation to do its work. John says of the account in his gospel that "*these have been written* that you may believe that Jesus is the Christ" (John 20:31). "Faith comes by hearing," says Paul, "and hearing by the word of Christ" (Romans 10:17). God caused us to be born "by the word of truth," says James 1:18 (see I Peter 1:23-25).

Truth About Sin and Redemption

Special revelation also contains truth about sin and redemption. We may remember that general revelation alone convicts the lawbreaker of his sin against God and of his liability to God's wrath and punishment. But through special revelation the basic knowledge of sin and sinfulness also is clarified and complemented, and is adapted to the minds of sinners. If the sinner can be considered without excuse on the basis of general revelation alone, he is all the more inexcusable in the light of special revelation.

---

122. *Ibid.*, p. 20.

123. Perhaps we can say that general revelation impacts upon the mind only and not upon the heart, whereas special revelation touches the heart or will as well as the mind.

The one area where special revelation breaks new ground has to do with the subject of redemption. As we have seen, the creation-knowledge says nothing about God as Redeemer. This then becomes the main theme of the special revelation. Here we learn aspects of the nature of God not included in the general forms. Here we learn of his lovingkindness and his grace, his patience and his willingness to suffer pain in our place to save us from our own folly. We learn that even though he has been sinned against, he is willing to forgive the sinner and to receive him into fellowship anyway.

We also learn the truth about how this is all accomplished, namely, through the incarnate Logos, Jesus of Nazareth, the Son of God. From the very beginning of redemptive special revelation, the central theme is the gospel of salvation through Jesus Christ (Genesis 3:15). *Here* is the true centrality of Jesus Christ, namely, as the subject-matter of revelation, not the mode; as the main *content* of this revelation, not the main form. Christ as Redeemer (not Christ as Revealer) is the central *theme* of special revelation. Here is the glory of special revelation, as well as the glory of Jesus Christ. He is not the only content of this revelation, but he surely is its main theme. We glorify him when we honor him thus as the central content of the Bible.

One other point that should be mentioned is that from special revelation we also learn how to receive the benefits of Christ's saving work, and we learn how to love and serve God not just as Creator but as Redeemer, too. Specifically we learn to serve him through the new motive of loving gratitude in response to the grace he freely gives us.

As we conclude this chapter on our knowledge of God, we see very clearly that God has not remained completely hidden from us but has revealed himself, his mind, and his will to us even in our sinful state. Thus we have available for our edification a wealth of knowledge about God. At this point we should stress, though, that knowledge *about* God even in abundance is not an acceptable substitute for actually knowing God in personal relationship and submissive, obedient trust. Indeed, God gives us the former as a means to the latter. He wants us to know about him so that we may come to know him.[124] On the other hand we must stress that a personal knowledge of God can hardly be attained without a keen knowledge about God. Those who want us to "know God" without the discipline of learning about God run an awful risk of knowing only an idol of their own making. Let us not be guilty of pursuing a false choice here. Knowing about God and knowing God must be seen as not a matter of either/or but of both/and.[125]

---

124. In his book *Knowing God,* J. I. Packer stresses the importance of the latter. See especially chapters 2 and 3.

125. I believe the neo-Protestant concern for an encounter phase to revelation can be met by a proper attention to these concepts of knowing about God and knowing God, and the relationship between them. It is true that revelation (knowledge about God) does not accomplish its *ultimate* purpose until a positive response (knowing God) has been elicited. This hardly requires that we include this response in the very definition of revelation, however.

Chapter Eight

THE LIVING GOD

"The Lord lives"! Thus declares David in Psalm 18:46. Such a truth may seem so self-evident that it is regarded as unworthy of attention. At first we may be tempted simply to equate it with the fact of God's existence: "God lives" means "God exists." Certainly the fact that God lives includes the fact of his existence, but it means much more than this. It is a much richer and fuller affirmation. It refers to God's existence as Spirit, as a personal being who is dynamic and active. It refers not just to the fact that he exists but to the fact that he exists *for his people,* ready to come to their aid and to act in their defense and to bless them for his name's sake.

Thus the fact that God is the *living* God is one of the more profound characteristics of his nature, and it is also one of the more common themes of Scripture. According to R. T. France's count, God is called "the living God" fifteen times each in the Old and New Testaments. This includes John 6:57, where he is called "the living Father."[1] As the living God he is the source of life: "For with Thee is the fountain of life" (Psalm 36:9); the Lord is a "fountain of living waters" (Jeremiah 2:13; 17:13). Thus the living God alone can quench man's spiritual thirst: "My soul thirsts for God, for the living God" (Psalm 42:2). "My soul longed and even yearned for the courts of the Lord; my heart and my flesh sing for joy to the living God" (Psalm 84:2). It is no wonder that "we have fixed our hope on the living God" (I Timothy 4:10), the one who "has life in Himself" (John 5:26).

---

1. R. T. France, *The Living God* (Downers Grove, Ill.: InterVarsity Press, 1970), p. 12.

Also significant is the fact that one of the more frequent oaths used by Old Testament saints was "as the Lord lives," which meant "just as surely as the Lord lives, so is what I am about to say sure and true." This oath appears forty-three times (also France's count). For instance, King Saul pledges to spare David's life thus: "As the Lord lives, he shall not be put to death" (I Samuel 19:6). In the same way Zedekiah swears to protect Jeremiah: "As the Lord lives, who made this life for us, surely I will not put you to death nor will I give you over to the hand of these men who are seeking your life" (Jeremiah 38:16). God condemns those who take his name in vain: "And although they say, 'As the Lord lives,' surely they swear falsely" (Jeremiah 5:2). Pagan converts and repenting Israelites must cease to swear by false gods and must learn to swear exclusively, "As the Lord lives" (Jeremiah 4:1-2; 12:16). That this is the characteristic oath of the people of God shows that one of their most basic convictions was that Yahweh alone is the only true and living God.

This conviction was no doubt made all the more firm by the fact that God himself frequently gave his most solemn assurance with the oath, "As I live" (twenty-three times). In Numbers 14:21 he says, "But indeed, as I live, all the earth will be filled with the glory of the Lord." In Deuteronomy 32:40-41 he declares, "Indeed, I lift up My hand to heaven, and say, as I live forever, . . . I will render vengeance on My adversaries, and I will repay those who hate Me." France comments, "The veracity not only of the words of men, but of the very words of God, is staked on His being the living God. It is as basic as that."[2]

---

2. *Ibid.*

THE ONE TRUE GOD

Earlier we discussed the concept of God's *unity*, especially his unity of simplicity. This is the idea that God is one indivisible being, not composed of parts. We also mentioned his unity of singularity, which means that there is only one God. This is the point we are discussing now. There is only one true God, the God of the Bible. See Ephesians 4:6; I Timothy 1:17; 2:5. This is something recognized even by the demons (James 2:19). Our God is not like idols; he is "a living and true God" (I Thessalonians 1:9), "the only true God" (John 17:3). This is the meaning of the basic Israelite confession, "Hear, O Israel! The Lord is our God, the Lord is one!" (Deut. 6:4). When Jesus quotes this confession in Mark 12:29, the comment is then made, "Right, Teacher, You have truly stated that he is One; and there is no one else besides Him" (Mark 12:32). The Lord is our God; the Lord is *the* one, i.e., the one and only true God. See Romans 3:30 and Galatians 3:20.

" 'To whom then will you liken Me that I should be his equal?' says the Holy One" (Isaiah 40:25). Truly he has no equal; there is no one else in the category of deity at all, whether equal to or inferior to God. Unfortunately this is a lesson which mankind has had difficulty learning, since its most persistent inclination is toward idolatry.

The Vanity of Idols

Idolatry is the worship of a false god or of false gods. They may exist as tangible objects manufactured by human hands, or they may exist purely as mental images conjured up in the minds of men. This substitution of false gods for the one true God is a constant tendency of sinful man, since tailor-made deities are the handiest refuge from unwanted and uncomfortable truth. Paul speaks of this tendency in Romans 1:21ff., referring especially to pagans. Even though they knew God from general revelation, he says, "they became futile in their speculations, and their foolish heart was darkened." They "exchanged the glory of the incorruptible God for an image in the form of corruptible man and of birds and four-footed animals and crawling creatures." In this way they "exchanged the truth of God for a lie, and worshiped and served the creature rather than the Creator."

Thus one of the main themes of special revelation is the wickedness of idolatry. It is depicted not only as sinful but also as extremely foolish. Why should anyone want to forsake the only true God and serve idols? Only Yahweh is the *living* God; idols are lifeless nothings, things of vanity and emptiness.

Scripture constantly describes idols as worthless, as vanities, as nothings. A basic Old Testament word translated "idol" is *'elîl*, as in I Chronicles 16:26, "For all the gods of the peoples are idols." The root of this word is uncertain, but there are two main choices. Either it comes from a word which means literally "nothing," or it comes from a word meaning "weak, insufficient, feeble." Thus an idol is something feeble or worthless, a thing of nought, a vanity, a nothing. Another word sometimes used for idols is *hebel*, which means "vanity, emptiness, something unsubstantial or worthless." This word is used in Deuteronomy 32:21, "They have made Me jealous with what is not God; they have provoked Me to anger with their idols." See also Jeremiah 10:15, "They are worthless (*hebel*), a work of mockery." The same word occurs in Jeremiah 8:19; 14:22; 16:19; and also in Jeremiah 2:5, "They went far from Me and walked after emptiness and became empty." See II Kings 17:15, "They followed vanity and became vain." In Isaiah 41:24 the idols are literally called "nothings": "But you are less than nothing (*'ayin*) and your works are utterly worthless" (NIV). Isaiah 41:29 makes the same point in other terms: "Behold, all of them are false; their works are worthless, their molten images are wind and emptiness." In Acts 14:15 false gods are called *ta mataia*, "vain or useless things, vanities." The more common New Testament word for idols (*eidōlon*) was not generally used in classical Greek for images of the gods. It was used mostly for things which lacked substance or reality, e.g., phantoms, images in mirrors or water, and images or ideas in the mind. This is the term the Septuagint uses to translate about fifteen separate Hebrew words, and "it refers without exception to the images of the heathen gods and the deities represented by them."[3]

Lifeless Nothings

In terms of mockery the Bible stresses the lifelessness of idols in contrast with the living God. Breath, the most obvious sign of life, is missing: "For his molten images are deceitful, and there is no breath in them" (Jeremiah 10:14; 51:17; see Psalm 135:17; Habakkuk 2:19). Idols cannot do any of the things ordinary living beings can. They are but "the work of man's hands, wood and stone, which neither see nor hear nor eat nor smell" (Deut. 4:28). "They have mouths, but they cannot speak; they have eyes, but they cannot see;

---

3. Wilhelm Mundle, "Image, Idol, Imprint, Example," *The New International Dictionary of New Testament Theology*, ed. Colin Brown (Grand Rapids: Zondervan, 1976), II:284.

they have ears, but they cannot hear; they have noses, but they cannot smell; they have hands, but they cannot feel; they have feet, but they cannot walk; they cannot make a sound with their throat" (Psalm 115:5-7; see Psalm 135:15-18). I Corinthians 12:2 calls them dumb or voiceless. An idol cannot move, but depends on its worshipers to transport it: "They bow down, indeed they worship it. They lift it upon the shoulder and carry it; they set it in its place and it stands there. It does not move from its place" (Isaiah 46:6-7). See also Isaiah 46:1-2, where the images of the impotent Bel and Nebo (Babylonian deities) are mere loads for beasts of burden. Jeremiah 10:4 adds the point that an idol must be fastened down with nails and hammers "so that it will not totter."

The utter lifelessness and powerlessness of idols is graphically depicted in Jeremiah 10:5, "Like a scarecrow in a cucumber field are they, and they cannot speak; they must be carried, because they cannot walk! Do not fear them, for they can do no harm, nor can they do any good." The same futility and vanity are emphasized in Habakkuk 2:18-19,

> What profit is the idol when its maker has carved it, or an image, a teacher of falsehood? For its maker trusts in his own handiwork when he fashions speechless idols. Woe to him who says to a piece of wood, "Awake!" To a dumb stone, "Arise!" And that is your teacher? Behold, it is overlaid with gold and silver, and there is no breath at all inside it.

Immediately Habakkuk reminds us of the awesome reality of the living God, in contrast with inanimate images: "But the Lord is in His holy temple. Let all the earth be silent before Him" (2:20). The Psalmist has the same contrast in mind when he says, "But our God is in the heavens; He does whatever He pleases" (Psalm 115:3; see the citation of verses 5-7 above).

God's Challenge: Declare and Do!

Isaiah 40-48 is one long contrast between the impotent false gods of the nations and the omniscient and omnipotent God of Israel. God issues the challenge to all pretenders to deity to prove that they are gods. "'Present your case,' the Lord says. 'Bring forward your strong arguments,' the King of Jacob says" (Isaiah 41:21). If you are really gods, he says, then you should be omniscient. Time should be no barrier to your knowledge. You should be able to see the past and the future as clearly as the present. And if you are really gods, you should be able to do anything you want, and announce it ahead of time. So, present your case! Declare and do!

This challenge is clearly stated in Isaiah 41:22-23, where the tone of mockery is evident as well:

> . . . Let them bring forth and declare to us what is going to take place; as for the former events, declare what they were, that we may consider them, and know their outcome; or announce to us what is coming. Declare the things that are going to come afterward, that we may know that you are gods; indeed, do good or evil, that we may anxiously look about us and fear together.

Obviously they cannot, thus the following judgment: "Behold, you are of no account, and your work amounts to nothing; he who chooses you is an abomination" (verse 24). A similar challenge is given in Isaiah 43:8-9.

The challenge is given by way of contrast with God's own ability to declare past and future, and to accomplish whatever he purposes. Only God can do these things, so only *he* is truly God.

> . . . And who is like Me? Let him proclaim and declare it; yes, let him recount it to Me in order, from the time that I established the ancient nation. And let them declare to them the things that are coming and the events that are going to take place. Do not tremble and do not be afraid; have I not long since announced it to you and declared it? And you are My witnesses. Is there any God besides Me, or is there any other Rock? I know of none (Isaiah 44:7-8).

Similarly Isaiah 45:21 says, "Declare and set forth your case; indeed, let them consult together. Who has announced this from of old? Who has long since declared it? Is it not I, the Lord? And there is no other God besides Me."

Impotent to Save

The impotence of idols is most clearly seen in their inability to aid and to save their worshipers. The idol-maker expects such help from his god: "He falls down before it and worships; he also prays to it and says, 'Deliver me, for thou art my god'" (Isaiah 44:17). But such prayers are futile, and those who offer them are ignorant: "They have no knowledge, who carry about their wooden idol, and pray to a god who cannot save" (Isaiah 45:20). "Though one may cry to it, it cannot answer; it cannot deliver him from his distress" (Isaiah 46:7).

The gods of Egypt could not save the Egyptians from the plagues sent upon them by the Lord, and the gods of Canaan could not save the Canaanites from conquest by the Israelites. General Rabshakeh reminds Jerusalem that the gods of the nations had not been able to protect them against his Assyrian troops; why then should its residents expect their God to help them?

> . . . Beware lest Hezekiah misleads you, saying, "The Lord will deliver us." Has anyone of the gods of the nations

> delivered his land from the hand of the king of Assyria? Where are the gods of Hamath and Arpad? Where are the gods of Sepharvaim? And when have they delivered Samaria from my hand? Who among all the gods of these lands have delivered their land from my hand, that the Lord should deliver Jerusalem from my hand? (Isaiah 36:18-20)

Rabshakeh soon discovered the difference between the living God of Israel and the gods of the nations, but he was right about the latter: they were not able to save their worshipers.

The irony and the foolishness of worshiping impotent gods is highlighted in several Old Testament passages. In II Chronicles 25:14-15 we find that after King Amaziah had conquered the Edomites, "he brought the gods of the sons of Seir, set them up as his gods, bowed down before them, and burned incense to them." God sent a prophet to Amaziah, who pointedly emphasized the stupidity of these actions: "Why have you sought the gods of the people who have not delivered their own people from your hand?" When idolatrous Judah was carried away into captivity by the Babylonians, the people had to carry along with them the images of the gods who failed to save them (Isaiah 46:1-2). As the ultimate irony God declared that he would bring judgment upon idolaters and heap their remains upon the remains of their impotent idols (Leviticus 26:30), as a final and fitting "offering" to these lifeless nothings:

> . . . So your altars will become desolate, and your incense altars will be smashed; and I shall make your slain fall in front of your idols. I shall also lay the dead bodies of the sons of Israel in front of their idols; and I shall scatter your bones around your altars. In all your dwellings, cities will become waste and the high places will be desolate, that your altars may become waste and desolate, your idols may be broken and brought to an end, your incense altars may be cut down, and your works may be blotted out (Ezekiel 6:4-6).

In the time of judgment these idols will perish (Jeremiah 10:15); "the idols will completely vanish" (Isaiah 2:18). At the very time their help is needed the most, they will be discarded as useless: "In that day men will cast away to the moles and the bats their idols of silver and their idols of gold, which they made for themselves to worship" (Isaiah 2:20). And God will mock the idolaters and say, "Where are their gods, the rock in which they sought refuge?" (Deuteronomy 32:37). And the idolaters will be ashamed for their foolishness: "They shall be turned back and be utterly put to shame, who trust in idols, who say to molten images, 'You are our gods'" (Isaiah 42:17; see Psalm 97:7; Isaiah 44:9).

No Other Gods

Those who worship the God of Israel and the God of our Lord Jesus Christ will never have to be ashamed, because he is the one true and living God. This is his word of testimony to us: "I am the Lord your God and there is no other; and My people will never be put to shame" (Joel 2:27). "See now that I, I am He, and there is no god besides Me" (Deuteronomy 32:39). This claim is repeated again and again in the great challenge passage in Isaiah. "Understand that I am He. Before Me there was no God formed, and there will be none after Me. I, even I, am the Lord; and there is no savior besides Me" (Isaiah 43:10-11). "Thus says the Lord, of hosts: 'I am the first and I am the last, and there is no God besides Me. . . . Is there any God besides Me, or is there any other Rock? I know of none'" (Isaiah 44:6, 8). "I am the Lord, and there is no other; besides Me there is no God" (Isaiah 45:5). "To whom would you liken Me, and make Me equal and compare Me, that we should be alike? . . . For I am God, and there is no other; I am God, and there is no one like Me" (Isaiah 46:5, 9).

The first and second commandments affirm Yahweh's uniqueness as God and bind upon us exclusive worship of him. "You shall have no other gods before Me. You shall not make for yourself an idol, or any likeness of what is in heaven above or on the earth beneath or in the water under the earth. You shall not worship them or serve them" (Exodus 20:3-5). The second commandment excludes image-making either for the true God or for false gods. This further word is added: "You shall not make other gods besides Me; gods of silver or gods of gold, you shall not make for yourselves" (Exodus 20:23). *All* worship is to be reserved for the true God: "Hear, O Israel! The Lord is our God, the Lord is one! And you shall love the Lord your God with all your heart and with all your soul and with all your might" (Deuteronomy 6:4-5).

Those who are God's people will believe his testimony and obey his commandment; they will have "no other gods" besides him. This is Hannah's confession: "There is no one holy like the Lord, indeed, there is no one besides Thee. Nor is there any rock like our God" (I Samuel 2:2). And likewise David's: "For this reason Thou art great, O Lord God; for there is none like Thee, and there is no God besides Thee" (II Samuel 7:22). And King Hezekiah's: "O Lord, the God of Israel, who art enthroned above the cherubim, Thou art the God, Thou alone, of all the kingdoms of the earth" (II Kings 19:15). Jeremiah adds his praise: "There is none like Thee, O Lord; Thou art great, and great is Thy name in might. . . . But the Lord is the true God; He is the living God and the everlasting King" (Jeremiah 10:6, 10).

The Apostle Paul adds to the chorus: "We know that there is no such thing as an idol in the world, and that there is no God but one" (I Corinthians 8:4). David's question echoes with silence: "For who is God, but the Lord? And who is a rock, except our God?" (Psalm 18:31; see Psalm 83:18).

Certainly the angels are not to be thought of as in the same category with God. They surround him, but not as equals. He is Lord of all the angelic hosts.

> . . . For who in the skies is comparable to the Lord? Who among the sons of the mighty is like the Lord, a God greatly feared in the council of the holy ones, and awesome above all those who are around Him? O Lord God of hosts, who is like Thee, O mighty Lord? (Psalm 89:6-8).

Though the angels do not claim to be gods (see Revelation 19:10; 22:9), they do have reality. This cannot be said of the false gods represented by idols; they are simply not there. They have no reality. As we have seen, they are *nothings*. Paul speaks of the time when Gentile Christians were "slaves to those which by nature are no gods" (Galatians 4:8). Jeremiah 2:11 asks, "Has a nation changed gods, when they were not gods?" (Jeremiah 16:20). See also Jeremiah 5:7, "Your sons have forsaken Me and sworn by those who are not gods." Only in this sense is Yahweh spoken of as "above all gods" (Psalms 95:3; 97:9). This is not an expression of polytheism, as if there were many gods with Yahweh as their chief. Actually the Lord is above all gods because the others are only false gods; they are not really there. They are only idols, nothings. As Psalm 96:4-5 says, "For great is the Lord, and greatly to be praised; He is to be feared above all gods. For all the gods of the peoples are idols, but the Lord made the heavens."

The Apostle Paul makes this point in I Corinthians 8:4ff. when he says, "We know that there is no such thing as an idol in the world, and that there is no God but one." There may be "so-called gods," and in this sense we can say "there are many gods and many lords," but there is only one true God. In I Corinthians 10:19ff. Paul declares that an idol is nothing. The so-called gods which idolaters think they are worshiping do not exist. Paul does point out, though, that a sinister reality does lurk behind man-made idols, namely, demonic spirits who prey upon the ignorant pagans who think they are worshiping some deity. "No, but I say that the things which the Gentiles sacrifice, they sacrifice to demons, and not to God" (I Corinthians 10:20). The same connection between idols and demons is made in Deuteronomy 32:15ff.,

> . . . Then he forsook God who made him, and scorned the Rock of his salvation. They made Him jealous with strange gods; with abominations they provoked Him to anger. They sacrificed to demons who were not God, to gods whom they have not known, new gods who came lately . . . . They have made Me jealous with what is not God; they have provoked me to anger with their idols.

See also Psalm 106:36-37, "And served their idols, which became a snare to them. They even sacrificed their sons and their daughters to the demons."

Thus the violation of God's commandment to have no other gods besides him is fraught with many dangers. In the first place it is pure foolishness to forsake the living God for idols who cannot be of any help. "But they are altogether stupid and foolish in their discipline of delusion—their idol is wood! . . . Every man is stupid, devoid of knowledge; every goldsmith is put to shame by his idols; for his molten images are deceitful, and there is no breath in them" (Jeremiah 10:8, 14). Also, it brings the judgment of the true God upon the idolater: "And I will pronounce My judgments on them concerning all their wickedness, whereby they have forsaken Me and have offered sacrifices to other gods, and worshiped the works of their own hands" (Jeremiah 1:16). And finally, it places the idolater in the present danger of demonic intrusion. No wonder Paul and Barnabas told the pagans at Lystra to "turn from these vain things to a living God" (Acts 14:15). This is why Paul rejoiced that the Thessalonians had "turned to God from idols to serve a living and true God" (I Thessalonians 1:9). God's desire is that everyone should declare, "Nor will we say again, 'Our god,' to the work of our hands" (Hosea 14:3).

The God Who Acts

As the one true and living God, the God of Israel and the God of our Lord Jesus Christ is a God who *acts*. As suggested earlier, the very concept of "the living God" includes dynamic action. As Psalm 86:10 says, "For Thou art great and doest wondrous deeds; Thou alone art God." In fact, it is these very "wondrous deeds" that demonstrate the truth of God's claim to be the one true God. His works proclaim his deity and his lordship.

The God Who Creates Is Truly God

That the God of Israel, the God of our Lord Jesus Christ, is the Creator of heaven and earth is the first indication that he is truly God. Here the contrast between God and idols could not be any more extreme. Whereas God is the Maker of all things, idols are themselves made by men's hands.

This is one of the great ironies of idolatry: that a person should make something with his own hands and then fall down and worship it. This irony is scornfully noted in the frequent reference to idols as "the work of man's hands" (Deuteronomy 4:28; Psalms 115:4; 135:15). Isaiah 2:8 says, "Their land has also been filled with idols; they worship the work of their hands, that which their fingers have made." Idol worship is a delusion, since an idol is just "wood cut from the forest, the work of the hands of a craftsman with a cutting tool" (Jeremiah 10:3). See also Isaiah 40:18-20; Jeremiah 1:16; Hosea 13:2; Habakkuk 2:19. The point is put very succinctly in Hosea 8:6, "A craftsman made it, so it is not God."

The stupidity of worshiping something made by human hands is driven home in a lengthy passage in Isaiah 44:9-20. In the first place the one who makes the idol is himself a mere man, one who gets hungry and weary (verses 11-12). The implication is that the idol surely cannot be any greater than its maker. In fact, it is much less. At least the man is intelligent enough to make the tools with which he shapes the wood that is to be made into an idol (verse 12). But when the idol is made, even though it has the shape of a man, it just sits and does nothing (verse 13). From another perspective, the craftsman first plants a tree, then he cuts it down. Part of the wood he uses to build a fire, with which he bakes bread and roasts meat and warms himself. From the other part of the *same wood* he makes an image, falls down before it, and pleads, "Deliver me, for thou art my god" (verses 14-17). And he doesn't even have sense enough to recognize what he has done and to say, "I have burned half of it in the fire . . . . Then I make the rest of it into an abomination, I fall down before a block of wood!" (verse

19). He feeds on ashes, says Isaiah. His heart is deceived, and he does not realize he is holding a lie in his hands (verse 20).

By way of contrast the true and living God is not the product of human minds or hands; he is the one who has created all things. He alone is God, because he alone is Creator. This connection is noted frequently. Hezekiah in his prayer said, "O Lord, the God of Israel, who art enthroned above the cherubim, Thou art the God, Thou alone, of all the kingdoms of the earth. Thou hast made heaven and earth" (II Kings 19:15; see Isaiah 37:16). Psalm 95:3-5 says,

> . . . For the Lord is a great God, and a great King above all gods, in whose hand are the depths of the earth; the peaks of the mountains are His also. The sea is His, for it was He who made it; and His hands formed the dry land.

Psalm 96:4-5 adds, "For great is the Lord, and greatly to be praised; He is to be feared above all gods. For all the gods of the peoples are idols, but the Lord made the heavens." Nehemiah 9:6 says, "Thou alone art the Lord. Thou hast made the heavens, the heaven of heavens with all their host, the earth and all that is on it, the seas and all that is in them." The prophet Isaiah puts it thus: "For thus says the Lord, who created the heavens (He is the God who formed the earth and made it . . .), 'I am the Lord, and there is none else'" (Isaiah 45:18; see Isaiah 40:18-26). The pagans at Lystra were urged to turn from their idols "to a living God, who made the heaven and the earth and the sea, and all that is in them" (Acts 14:15).

The wisdom of serving the Creator rather than the passive products of human art is strongly set forth in Jeremiah

10:6-16. "There is none like Thee, O Lord; Thou art great, and great is Thy name in might" (verse 6). Those who worship idols are stupid; idols are just "the work of a craftsman and of the hands of a goldsmith" (verses 8-9). Only the Lord is the true and living God (verse 10). "The gods that did not make the heavens and the earth shall perish from the earth and from under the heavens." But God is the one "who made the earth by His power, who established the world by His wisdom" (verses 11-12). Idols are worthless and idolaters are stupid (verses 14-15), but "the portion of Jacob is not like these; for the Maker of all is He, . . . the Lord of hosts is His name" (verse 16).

In all these passages the point comes through very clearly, that the living and true God is the one who has acted in the creation of the universe.

The God Who Redeems Is Truly God

As we have seen, the vanity of idols is seen especially in their inability to rescue and redeem those who trust in them. But this is precisely where the God of Israel shows himself to be the true and living God, namely, in his mighty acts of redemption. In a way God's redeeming works are a more *immediate* evidence of his reality than his work of creation. This is true because we know the latter only after the fact, i.e., only by its effect and by his testimony. The works of redemption, on the other hand, have actually been witnessed by those involved. The works of redemption are also a more *specific* evidence that the God of Israel and the God of our Lord Jesus Christ is the one true God, rather than the gods of Assyria or the gods of Greece or the gods of India. This is true because these redeeming works are performed in the context of faith in this specific God. The God worshiped by the Israelites, not the Assyrians or the Egyptians, is the God who acts on behalf of his people. The God worshiped by the Israelites and by Christians, not the Greeks or Romans, is the God who raised Jesus Christ from the dead. That is to say, the works of redemption occur in a very specific context of faith, while the work of creation occurred in a real sense in no context at all.

One other thing that gives the works of redemption a greater evidential power is that God not only performs these mighty acts but *foretells* what he is going to do. Thus God's mighty power to save his people plus his transcendence of time (especially his foreknowledge) show him to be the one true God. This is of course the main point in God's challenge to the idols in Isaiah 40-48. "Present your case," he says. "Declare and do!" The false gods cannot; but he, the true and living God, can! "I am the Lord, that is My name," he says; "I will not give My glory to another, nor My praise to graven images. Behold, the former things have come to pass, now I declare new things; before they spring forth I proclaim them to you" (Isaiah 42:8-9).

> ". . . You are My witnesses," declares the Lord, "and My servant whom I have chosen, in order that you may know and believe Me, and understand that I am He. Before Me there was no God formed, and there will be none after Me. I, even I, am the Lord; and there is no savior besides Me. It is I who have declared and saved and proclaimed, and there was no strange god among you; so you are My witnesses," declares the Lord. "And I am God. Even from eternity I am He; and there is none who can deliver out of My hand; I act and who can reverse it?" (Isaiah 43:10-13).

"Do not tremble and do not be afraid; have I not long since announced it to you and declared it? And you are My witnesses. Is there any God besides Me, or is there any other Rock? I know of none" (Isaiah 44:8).

> . . . Declare and set forth your case; indeed, let them consult together. Who has announced this from of old? Who has long since declared it? Is it not I, the Lord? And there is no other God besides Me, a righteous God and a Savior; there is none except Me. Turn to Me, and be saved, all the ends of the earth; for I am God, and there is no other (Isaiah 45:21-22).

Remember that your idols are helpless; you cry to them, but they cannot deliver (Isaiah 46:6-7). But with the Lord it is very different.

> . . . Remember this, and be assured; recall it to mind, you transgressors. Remember the former things long past, for I am God, and there is no other; I am God, and there is no one like Me, declaring the end from the beginning and from ancient times things which have not been done, saying, 'My purpose will be established, and I will accomplish all My good pleasure'. . . . Truly I have spoken; truly I will bring it to pass. I have planned it, surely I will do it (Isaiah 46:8-11).

We should point out that God's power to "declare and do" applies to acts of judgment as well as to acts of redemption. Sometimes an act both judges and redeems at the same time. God sometimes delivers his people by destroying his enemies. For instance, Psalm 83 calls upon God to destroy his enemies, "that they may know that Thou alone, whose name is the Lord, art the Most High over all the earth" (Psalm 83:18).

Many examples of God's mighty acts of redemption may be cited. In the Old Testament the one that stands out is the deliverance of Israel from Egypt into Canaan. The Exodus and the Conquest of Canaan are considered as two phases of one complex event. The great miracles that brought the Israelites out of Egypt and across the Red Sea (mostly announced in advance, we should note) were in themselves ample evidence that the God of Israel is the only true God. This was their design. God told Moses to say to Pharaoh, "I will send all My plagues on you and your servants and your people, so that you may know that there is no one like Me in all the earth" (Exodus 9:14). At Sinai God prefaces the first commandment with this reminder: "I am the Lord your God, who brought you out of the land of Egypt, out of the house of slavery." This mighty act of redemption gave him the right to demand, "You shall have no other gods before Me" (Exodus 20:2-3). Just prior to their entrance into Canaan Moses reminds the Israelites of this deliverance and assures them of victories during the impending conquest; and he tells them that these mighty acts show that their God alone is God.

> . . . Because He loved your fathers, therefore He chose their descendants after them. And He personally brought you from Egypt by His great power, driving out from before you nations greater and mightier than you, to bring you in and to give you their land for an inheritance, as it is today. Know therefore today, and take it to your heart, that the Lord, He is God in heaven above and on the earth below; there is no other (Deut. 4:37-39).

In announcing the miracle that allowed the Israelites to cross the rain-swollen Jordan River, Joshua says, "By this you shall know that the living God is among you" (Joshua 3:10). King David sums up this point about the Exodus and the Conquest in these words:

> . . . For this reason Thou art great, O Lord God; for there is none like Thee, and there is no God besides Thee, according to all that we have heard with our ears. And what one nation on the earth is like Thy people Israel, whom God went to redeem for Himself as a people and to make a name for Himself, and to do a great thing for Thee and awesome things for Thy land, before Thy people whom Thou hast redeemed for Thyself from Egypt, from nations and their gods? (II Samuel 7:22-23).

See also Joshua 24:16-18 and I Chronicles 17:20-21.

Another example of a mighty act of deliverance that is at the same time a judgment is the destruction of the Assyrian army that threatened Jerusalem. We remember General Rabshakeh's taunts that the gods of other nations had not been able to save them, so the Israelites should not expect their God to help them, either (Isaiah 36:18-20). King Hezekiah was appalled that Rabshakeh should thus "reproach the living God" (Isaiah 37:4), and he prayed that God would vindicate his name: "And now, O Lord our God, deliver us from his hand that all the kingdoms of the earth may know that Thou alone, Lord, art God" (Isaiah 37:20). God's response was to destroy the whole Assyrian army in the night (Isaiah 37:36).

Two other specific acts of redemption in the Old Testament may be mentioned. On a small scale, when God delivered Daniel from the lions, this impressed King Darius in just the proper way. His response was,

> . . . I make a decree that in all the dominion of my kingdom men are to fear and tremble before the God of Daniel; for He is the living God and enduring forever, and His kingdom is one which will not be destroyed, and His dominion will be forever. He delivers and rescues and performs signs and

> wonders in heaven and on earth, who has also delivered Daniel from the power of the lions (Daniel 6:26-27).

On a larger scale, God accomplished the restoration of his people from the Babylonian captivity by raising up a sympathetic king, Cyrus by name, who let the people return to their land. What makes this significant is that God announced this act several hundred years in advance, calling Cyrus by name (Isaiah 44:28—45:1). God addresses the yet-to-come Cyrus in these words: "I am the Lord, and there is no other; besides Me there is no God. I will gird you, though you have not known Me; that men may know from the rising to the setting of the sun that there is no one besides Me. I am the Lord, and there is no other" (Isaiah 45:5-6).

The New Testament records God's climactic redeeming act, the resurrection of Jesus from the dead (announced in advance: John 2:19-22). In this mighty act God demonstrated that he, the God of Israel and the God of our Lord Jesus Christ, is truly the living God. By this act Jesus was declared to be the Son of God (Romans 1:4), and the God whose Son he is can be no other than Israel's Redeemer. Because of this mighty work he is known as the God "who gives life to the dead" (Romans 4:17), the "God who raises the dead" (II Cor. 1:9). Truly the one "who raised Jesus our Lord from the dead" (Romans 4:24) is the living God.

In contrast, then, with lifeless and impotent idols, the one true God shows himself to be God by his works of creation and redemption. He is the living God because he is a God who acts, and he acts because he is the living God.

A Jealous God

Only in the context of the living God versus idols can we properly understand the biblical concept of the jealousy of

God. This is an aspect of God's nature mentioned quite often in Scripture. "I, the Lord your God, am a jealous God," says God in the Decalogue itself (Exodus 20:5). He even applies it as a name to himself: "You shall not worship any other god, for the Lord, whose name is Jealous, is a jealous God" (Exodus 34:14). Moses reminds the Israelites of this fact: "For the Lord your God is a consuming fire, a jealous God" (Deuteronomy 4:24). Joshua does the same (Joshua 24:19).

At first when we read such statements as these, we think, "How can this be? How can the holy God be guilty of jealousy?" But this reaction is due to the fact that we often think of jealousy only in its sinful sense. Indeed, jealousy of a certain kind *is* sinful. The New Testament condemns it along with other sins; see Romans 13:13; I Cor. 3:3; II Cor. 12:20; Gal. 5:20; and James 3:14, 16. Sinful jealousy is very similar to envy. It is a spirit of ill will and envy toward other persons whose possessions, talents, or situation we covet. Packer describes it as "an expression of the attitude, 'I want what you've got, and I hate you because I haven't got it.' It is an infantile resentment springing from unmortified covetousness, which expresses itself in envy, malice, and meanness of action."[4] This is certainly not the kind of jealousy that is an aspect of God's nature.

Another kind of jealousy is characteristic of the marriage relationship, and here it may find either a good or bad expression. Sometimes one spouse is consumed by an inordinate sense of possessiveness toward the other, combined with an irrational suspicion of unfaithfulness. This is a common

---

4. J. I. Packer, *Knowing God* (Downers Grove, Ill.: InterVarsity Press, 1973), p. 153.

understanding of jealousy in a bad sense, and we do not connect this with God. But also in relation to marriage there is what Paul calls "a godly jealousy" (II Cor. 11:2), which is an earnest zeal to maintain the purity of the marriage relationship (or the betrothal in this case). It is a concern that one party in the covenant not be seduced and led astray into unfaithfulness. It is a spouse's zeal to protect the integrity of the relationship and to ward off all rivals to his or her exclusive claim to the affection of the other. *This* is the character of God's jealousy.

Both the Old Testament and the New Testament words for jealousy refer to an intense feeling of zeal or ardor, a fervor of spirit, a zealousness, a jealousy, even a jealous anger. When these words are used for God, the background always seems to be his relationship with his people understood figuratively as a marriage relationship. Like a husband, God is jealous for the welfare of his spouse and for the maintenance of her exclusive devotion toward himself. He is not indifferent about these things but has an intense concern about them. And what is the major threat to them both? Idolatry! Thus the biblical references to God as a jealous God most often appear in a context condemning idolatry. So it is in the Decalogue: "You shall have no other gods before Me. You shall not make for yourself an idol . . . . You shall not worship or serve them; for I, the Lord your God, am a jealous God" (Exodus 20:3-5). Also, "You shall not worship any other god, for the Lord, whose name is Jealous, is a jealous God" (Exodus 34:14). The same connection appears in Deuteronomy 6:14-15, "You shall not follow other gods, any of the gods of the peoples who surround you, for the Lord your God . . . is a jealous God" (see Deut. 4:22-24; 29:17-20). In Deuteronomy 32:21

the Lord declares, "They have made Me jealous with what is not God; they have provoked Me to anger with their idols" (see verse 16). In Joshua 24:19-20 the people are reminded that they cannot serve God and idols, too; for the Lord "is a jealous God." But this is exactly what Judah tried to do, and they "provoked Him to jealousy" with their false worship (I Kings 14:22-24). "For they provoked Him with their high places, and aroused His jealousy with their graven images" (Psalm 78:58). Paul warns Christians against any flirtation with idolatry, lest "we provoke the Lord to jealousy" (I Cor. 10:22).

False gods provoke God to jealousy because they are rivals to his exclusive claim to Godhood and to his exclusive right to the devotion of his creatures. This is where the concept of the marriage relationship enters. Those who are led astray by false gods are being unfaithful to their rightful spouse; they are guilty of spiritual adultery. This is why idolatry is so often spoken of as adultery or harlotry. For example, the Moabites are accused of enticing Israel to "play the harlot," because they "invited the people to the sacrifices of their gods, and the people ate and bowed to their gods" (Numbers 25:1-2). The Lord gave this message to Jerusalem through Jeremiah: "Your sons have forsaken Me and sworn by those who are not gods. When I had fed them to the full, they committed adultery and trooped to the harlot's house" (Jeremiah 5:7). Through Ezekiel he said, "You also took your beautiful jewels made of My gold and of My silver, which I had given you, and made for yourself male images that you might play the harlot with them" (Ezekiel 16:17; see the entire chapter; see 23:25-27).

Thus just as any husband would be hurt and indignant by his wife's unfaithfulness, God is provoked to jealousy when his people go after other gods. We should understand that the husband-wife-adultery situation is only an illustration of a truth that goes much deeper than this. God is not just a jealous husband forsaken by his wife; he is the sole Creator and absolute Lord of the universe aroused to righteous indignation by the fact that some "nothing" or something in the sphere of his own creation should so presumptuously be elevated to the role of deity alongside or above himself. Could there be a greater insult to the Maker of heaven and earth? No wonder he reacts with a jealousy for his glory. It is a natural expression of his nature as the only true and living God whenever his exclusiveness is violated by idolatry; it belongs to his very essence as God. The heart of the concept is revealed in Isaiah 42:8, "I am the Lord, that is My name; I will not give My glory to another, nor My praise to graven images." Packer says it well when he remarks that God's jealousy "is His zeal to maintain His own glory, which is jeopardized when images are used in worship."[5] He says also, "God seeks what we should seek—His glory, in and through men—and it is for the securing of this end, ultimately, that He is jealous."[6] We may recall that the ultimate end of creation itself is the praise of the glory of the Creator; thus God is jealous for the very purpose for which he created the universe in the first place. His jealousy is grounded in his nature as Creator, not in his covenant relationship with a particular people (contrary to Packer[7]). He is jealous for

5. *Ibid.*, p. 41.

6. *Ibid.*, p. 155.

7. *Ibid.* Packer says that God's jealousy "presupposes His covenant love," which is "the heart of God's plan for His world. And it is in the light of God's overall plan for His world that His jealousy must, in the last analysis, be understood." The only way to affirm this is to equate creation and covenant, which is to commit the Christological fallacy.

his rights as Creator, specifically his rightful claim to be the only true God. As he says in Ezekiel 39:25, "I shall be jealous for My holy name."

When this right is violated and devotion is given to false gods, God's reaction of jealousy includes an element of righteous anger against the idolater. Thus it is that jealousy and wrath are often mentioned together. God's declaration in the Decalogue implies this wrath when he says, "I, the Lord your God, am a jealous God, visiting the iniquity of the fathers on the children, on the third and the fourth generation of those who hate Me" (Exodus 20:5). In Deuteronomy 6:14-15 Moses warns the Israelites not to follow other gods, "for the Lord your God in the midst of you is a jealous God; otherwise the anger of the Lord your God will be kindled against you, and He will wipe you off the face of the earth." In Deuteronomy 29:20 he says that "the anger of the Lord and His jealousy will burn against" the idolater. These thoughts are also paralleled in Deuteronomy 32:21, "They have made Me jealous with what is not God; they have provoked Me to anger with their idols." But, says the Lord, when he metes out his judgment upon these spiritual adulterers, "so I shall calm My fury against you, and My jealousy will depart from you, and I shall be pacified and angry no more" (Ezekiel 16:42). (For other references to the connection between jealousy and wrath, see Psalm 79:5; Ezekiel 23:25; 36:6; 38:19; Zephaniah 1:18.) The intensity of this jealous wrath is seen in its equation with a consuming fire. "How long, O Lord? Wilt Thou be angry forever? Will Thy jealousy burn like fire?" (Psalm 79:5). "For the Lord your God is a consuming fire, a jealous God" (Deut. 4:24; see Hebrews 12:29). In Ezekiel 36:5 the Lord says, "Surely in the fire of My jealousy I have spoken against the rest of the nations." In Zephaniah 3:8 God declares his intention "to gather the kingdoms and to pour out my wrath on them—all my fierce anger. The whole world will be consumed by the fire of my jealous anger" (NIV; see also Zephaniah 1:18). Thus God's jealousy for his glory as the Creator and Lord of all and as the only true God cannot be taken lightly. Those who forsake the living God for idols do so at their own peril.

But there is another aspect of God's jealousy, one which also parallels his purpose for creation. We will remember that God created the universe not only for his glory but for the welfare of his people, especially those who are seeking to serve him and honor him as God. His wrath against the enemies of Israel is motivated at least in part by his desire to protect his people and to vindicate their trust in him before the scoffers. Thus he says to his captive people, "Thus says the Lord of hosts, 'I am exceedingly jealous for Jerusalem and Zion. But I am very angry with the nations who are at ease'" (Zechariah 1:14-15). Again he says, "I am exceedingly jealous for Zion, yes, with great wrath I am jealous for her" (Zechariah 8:2). When God sees the nations mocking Israel with the taunt, "Where is their God?" he will surely respond; "then the Lord will be zealous for His land, and will have pity on His people" (Joel 2:17-18). He will pour out the fire of his jealousy on the taunting nations (Ezekiel 36:5-6). We should note, however, that although God's jealousy for his people's welfare is real, it is subordinate to his jealousy for his own glory as the one true God. When he pours out judgment on his enemies and rescues his people, he is certainly vindicating the faith of the latter and blessing them by his almighty power. But at the same time, and more importantly, he is vindicating himself as the only true and living God. This is seen, for instance, in Ezekiel 39:25, which says, "Therefore thus says the Lord God, 'Now I shall restore the fortunes of Jacob, and have mercy on the whole house of Israel; and I shall be jealous for My holy name." In other words, when God's people are perceived as suffering misfortune, it reflects upon the God whom they worship. Thus when God rescues his people and judges the scoffers, he is glorifying his own name. As he says in Ezekiel 38:23, "And I shall magnify Myself, sanctify Myself, and make Myself known in the sight of many nations; and they will know that I am the Lord."

One final point to note about the jealousy of God is that it is a communicable attribute. That is to say, we can and should imitate this aspect of God's nature. We, too, should be jealous for God and his glory and his law and his purposes. We should be filled with zeal for the Lord of hosts and with indignation toward all rebelliousness against his lordship. We should be like Elijah, who said, "I have been very zealous for the Lord, the God of hosts" (I Kings 19:10, 14). Though we would not express it in the same way, we should be able to say with Jehu, "Come with me and see my zeal for the Lord" (II Kings 10:16), or have it said of us as the Lord said of Phinehas, "He was jealous with My jealousy among them" (Numbers 25:11). We should have the kind of zeal that Paul and other Jews had, though combined with proper knowledge so as not to be misdirected (Romans 10:2; Philippians 3:6). We should share Paul's godly jealousy for the purity of God's church (II Cor. 11:2), all to the praise of God's glory. In short we should have what Stumpff calls "a passionate, consuming zeal focused on God, or rather on the doing of His will and the maintaining of His honour in the face of the ungodly acts of men and nations."[8]

---

8. Albrecht Stumpff, "ζῆλος," *Theological Dictionary of the New Testament*, ed. Gerhard Kittel, tr. Geoffrey W. Bromiley (Grand Rapids: Eerdmans, 1964), II:878.

The First Commandment Today

The first commandment says, "You shall have no other gods before Me," and it still applies today. The Lord God who brought Israel out of Egypt with his mighty acts is the same God who raised Jesus Christ from the dead. He is the Maker of heaven and earth, the only God, the one true and living God; and he demands and deserves our full submission today no less than in other times. The words of Jesus in Matthew 4:10 express the eternal necessity: "You shall worship the Lord your God, and serve Him only."

This must be stressed because the tendency to idolatry—the tendency to worship false gods—is as prevalent today as it ever was. Most of the biblical teaching on idolatry occurs in the Old Testament, turning our minds toward the gods of Egypt or Philistia or Assyria or Babylon. These are the idolaters, we think to ourselves—these primitive, pagan, godless nations of ancient times. And of course there are still quite a few image worshipers around today, but only among the "primitives" and the heathen. There just isn't much application of this teaching about the living God versus idols in our "civilized" Western world. Or so we think. But we should remember this: idols can be made in the mind only, as well as by the hand. In our experience we may not know many people who worship physical images made of wood, metal, or plastic; but we know countless people whose lives are devoted to a deity manufactured by their own minds, consciously or unconsciously. In Romans 1:25 Paul speaks of those who exchange the truth of God for a lie. This includes false concepts of God as well as concrete images of God. For instance, a god who is all law and wrath without any grace is surely an idol who is a rival to the true and living God. (Compare the god of Islam.) Also, a god who is all love without any wrath is likewise an idol and a false god. (Compare the god of modernistic thought, or a god who will *always* say, "I forgive.")

We should also note that there are many objects of worship that are not called gods by their followers but which still function as such. After all, what does it mean to "have a god," in the sense of the first commandment? A person's god is simply that to which he gives supreme devotion, that which ultimately determines his decisions, that which takes first place in his life and thought. In this sense everyone "has a god," named or unnamed. This is implied in Jesus' statement, "You cannot serve God and mammon" (Matthew 6:24). "Mammon" was not a member of anybody's pantheon; it is simply a term that means money or riches. This is the god many people worship, as their whole life is devoted to this one end: the accumulation of this world's goods. The covetous man, says Paul, *is* an idolater (Ephesians 5:5; see Colossians 3:5). There are other such gods. Whatever is on the throne, whatever controls one's life is his idol. It may be personal pleasure (see Philippians 3:19, "whose god is their appetite"); it may be one's work or his family; it may be drugs; it may be "omnipotent" science; it may be just one's *self* (see Daniel 5:23, which says of Belshazzar, "You have exalted yourself against the Lord of heaven").

Self-examination is not out of order for anyone, even the devoutest of Christians. The Israelites knew that their God was the living God who had brought them out of the land of Egypt with mighty signs and wonders, but many of them turned to idols anyway. Certainly we know that our God is the living God who raised our Lord Jesus Christ from the dead; but we must remember that contemporary idols are very seductive, and we are not immune. "Take care, brethren, lest there should be in any one of you an evil, unbelieving heart, in falling away from the living God" (Hebrews 3:12).

The God of the Bible has amply demonstrated that he is the living and acting God. He has been such, he is such, and he will be such whether we acknowledge it or not. His name and his glory will be vindicated, whether we devote our lives to glorifying him or not. Nevertheless it is our purpose, our duty, and our privilege as his creatures to honor the Creator and worship him and glorify him as the one true God; and we should make it our life's sole aim to do just this.

PROOFS OF GOD'S EXISTENCE

According to Scripture God shows himself to be the one true and living God by his works. Our question now is, how does this relate to the traditional "proofs" for God's existence? As we have seen, to say that God *lives* and that God *exists* are not exactly the same thing. Nevertheless they are closely enough related to make the question of the theistic proofs relevant in this context. The idea that God is the living god certainly includes the fact of his existence.

There is another difference that is not quite so slight. The biblical concept is that God demonstrates his own existence[9] by his works. The theistic proofs, however, are considered to be a work of human reason alone. They ask the question whether it is possible for unaided human reason to demonstrate the existence of God. In terms of methodology these

---

9. Here the word *demonstrate* is not being used in the strict sense of absolute, demonstrative, syllogistic proof. It is used only in the sense of "give evidence for."

are two quite different enterprises. But as we shall see, they deal with the same phenomena and are quite similar in substance. We shall also see that in the final analysis the effectiveness of the theistic proofs depends on our seeing them more in terms of God's demonstration than man's rationalization.

Our purpose here is to give a basic summary of the main traditional proofs for God's existence, and to see how they relate to the biblical teaching about the living God.

The Ontological Argument

The ontological argument for God's existence is the only purely demonstrative proof. It is strictly logical, being based on the law of non-contradiction. It is an *a priori* proof, which means that it does not depend on the experience of any particular reality. It begins rather with only the *concept* of God as defined in a certain way. Given the particular concept or definition, it says simply that it is self-contradictory to deny that God exists. The very concept of God necessarily entails his existence.[10]

Forms of the Ontological Argument

The ontological argument was originated by Anselm (c. 1033-1109) and is found in his work called the "Proslogium."[11] There are actually two forms to the proof. The first begins with a certain *concept* of God and argues to the

10. For relevant texts and discussions relating to the ontological argument, see Alvin Plantinga, ed., *The Ontological Argument* (New York: Doubleday Anchor, 1965); see also John Hick and Arthur C. McGill, eds., *The Many-Faced Argument: Recent Studies on the Ontological Argument for the Existence of God* (New York: Macmillan, 1967).

11. Anselm, "Proslogium," *Saint Anselm: Basic Writings*, 2 ed., tr. S. W. Deane (La Salle, Ill.: Open Court, 1962), pp. 7-9.

existence of God. The argument proceeds like this: (1) God is a being than which nothing greater can be conceived, i.e., he is the greatest conceivable being. (2) God can be conceived of (i.e., thought about) in different ways. For instance, we can conceive of him as existing *only* in our minds, only as an idea. But we can also conceive of him as existing in *reality* as well as in our minds. (3) The latter is obviously greater than the former. I.e., it is greater to exist in reality than to exist only in the mind. (4) Therefore since God is the greatest conceivable being, he must exist in reality as well as in our minds. Otherwise he is not the greatest conceivable being.

The second form of Anselm's proof begins with the same concept of God but argues from it to the *necessary* existence of God. It goes as follows: (1) God is the greatest conceivable being. (2) It is possible to conceive of God as not existing, but it is also possible to conceive of him as not possibly not existing. (3) The latter is greater than the former. (4) Therefore since God is the greatest conceivable being, it is not possible for him not to exist. I.e., he exists necessarily.

The philosopher Descartes (1496-1650) gave the classic modern restatement of Anselm's first argument. Having already established to his own satisfaction the validity of what he called "clear and distinct ideas," Descartes proceeded to note the existence of two such clear and distinct ideas in his mind: (1) the idea of God as a supremely perfect being, and (2) the idea that actual and eternal existence belongs to the nature of God as one of his perfections or attributes. Thus existence is part of the very definition of God, just as three-sidedness is part of the definition of a triangle. So, Descartes concludes, "because I cannot conceive God unless as existing, it follows that existence is inseparable from him, and therefore that he really exists."[12]

There is considerable contemporary interest in the ontological argument, particularly by Charles Hartshorne and Norman Malcolm.[13] They develop the second form of Anselm's proof, focusing on *necessary* existence (rather than just existence) as part of the definition of the essence of God.

Criticisms of the Ontological Argument

The ontological argument has been subjected to quite rigorous criticism almost from its beginning. Most of its problems stem from its attempt to be a purely *a priori* argument in that it begins with a concept rather than with a certain experience of reality. The first criticism questions the very validity of the concept, i.e., the definition of God as a being than which nothing greater can be conceived (or the supremely perfect being). We may ask whether it is legitimate to *define* a being even before knowing whether such a being exists, and then argue for its existence from the definition. We may also note that not everyone is willing to grant this particular definition of God. Thomas Aquinas pointed this

12. René Descartes, *The Meditations and Selections from the Principles of René Descartes*, tr. John Veitch (La Salle, Ill.: Open Court, 1948), p. 79 (Meditation V).

13. Norman Malcolm, *Knowledge and Certainty* (Englewood Cliffs, N.J.: Prentice-Hall, 1963); Charles Hartshorne, *Man's Vision of God* (New York: Harper, 1941). See Hick and McGill, *The Many-Faced Argument*, pp. 301ff. See also John Hick, *Arguments for the Existence of God* (New York: Seabury, 1971), pp. 91-97, plus the bibliography on pp. 143-144. For another contemporary defense of this argument, see Sam M. Hamilton, "Natural Theology and the Ontological Argument," *The Seminary Review* (Winter 1961 and Spring 1961), 7:1-88.

out long ago,[14] and the current popularity of process philosophy's finite God is a good indication of it.

A second criticism, advanced by Immanuel Kant (1724-1804),[15] is that it is illegitimate to treat *existence* as a predicate or an attribute of anything. Whether a thing exists is simply a different kind of consideration from whether it is round or three-sided or sweet. G. E. Moore illustrates the difference by asking us to compare the statements, "Some tame tigers growl" and "Some tame tigers exist." That these are definitely not the same kind of statement can be shown by revising them thus: "Some tame tigers do not growl" and "Some tame tigers do not exist." The former statement is readily intelligible while the latter is not.[16]

A final criticism, also advanced by Kant,[17] is that it is impossible to argue simply from the *concept* of a thing to its *reality*. This applies to the concept of necessary existence as well as to the concept of existence. We may argue that the concept of God necessarily entails the *concept* of his existence, even the concept of his necessary existence. But we are still within the realm of concepts. The fact that there is a necessary connection between certain ideas in no way requires a transition from idea to reality. In other words, logical necessity does not imply ontological necessity. The most that can be concluded from the ontological argument is this: *if* God exists, he exists necessarily. But *whether* he exists must be determined on other grounds.

We conclude that the ontological argument has no validity.

---

14. Thomas Aquinas, *Summa Theologica*, I.ii1, *Basic Writings of Saint Thomas Aquinas*, ed. Anton Pegis (New York: Random House, 1945), I:20.

15. Immanuel Kant, *Critique of Pure Reason*, tr. J. M. D. Meiklejohn (New York: Willey Book Co., 1900), pp. 334-336.

16. G. E. Moore, "Is Existence A Predicate?" *The Ontological Argument*, ed. Alvin Plantinga (Garden City, N.Y.: Doubleday Anchor, 1965), pp. 74-78.

17. Immanuel Kant, *Critique of Pure Reason*, pp. 331-337.

The Cosmological Argument

The cosmological argument for God's existence is an argument from causality. It begins with an observed reality and therefore is an *a posteriori* type of proof. (Thus it differs fundamentally from the ontological argument.) It regards this observed reality as an *effect* which requires an explanation or a *cause*. Thus it argues backwards from effect to cause, not stopping until it arrives at an original, ultimate, primary cause—which is God.[18]

The form of the argument varies widely, and the observed reality varies from version to version. But in every case the cosmological argument includes these basic moves: (1) "X" exists as an observed effect. (2) Every effect has a cause sufficient to explain it. (3) There cannot be an infinite series or an infinite regress of causes. (4) Therefore there must be an ultimate or primary cause, which is God. William Craig expresses the point of this argument thus:

> Why *does* something exist instead of nothing? Unless we are prepared to believe that the universe simply popped into existence uncaused out of nothing, then the answer must be: Something exists because there is an eternal, uncaused being for which no further explanation is possible. . . .[19]

---

18. For relevant texts and discussions relating to the cosmological argument, see Donald R. Burrill, ed., *The Cosmological Arguments* (Garden City, N.Y.: Doubleday, 1967); and John Hick, ed., *The Existence of God* (New York: Macmillan, 1964).

19. William Lane Craig, *The Existence of God and the Beginning of the Universe* (San Bernardino, Cal.: Here's Life Publishers, 1979), pp. 37-38. See also the following works by Craig: *The Kalām Cosmological Argument* (New York: Barnes and Noble, 1979), and *The Cosmological Argument from Plato to Leibnitz* (New York: Barnes and Noble, 1980).

Forms of the Cosmological Argument

The cosmological argument is probably the most ancient and venerable of the theistic proofs, and over the centuries it has been formulated in many different ways. The variations in the argument are due mainly to the different beginning points adopted, or the different identifications of "X" as included in the above formula. Some of the forms of this argument are sometimes treated separately (e.g., the moral argument), but we include them all in one group because their fundamental structure is the same.

The point of reference in the history of the cosmological argument is Thomas Aquinas (1224-1274). Others had formulated the argument long before, however.[20] Both Plato and Aristotle argued from the existence of motion or change to the existence of a First Mover. For Plotinus the existence of a plurality of beings implied the existence of the One. Augustine argued that the existence of timeless, immutable truths requires a timeless, immutable Mind as their source. Anselm cited three observed realities which lead back to God: goodness, degrees of perfection, and "something." The Islamic thinker Alfarabi began with contingency or contingent beings and inferred the existence of a Necessary Being.

Thomas Aquinas, drawing upon the results of those who had preceded him, formulated his famous "five ways" to prove God's existence, four of which are forms of the cosmological argument.[21] His observed effects are motion, finite efficient causes, contingent beings, and degrees of

---

20. See the summary in Norman L. Geisler, *Philosophy of Religion* (Grand Rapids: Zondervan, 1974), pp. 163-173.

21. Thomas Aquinas, *Summa Theologica*, I:ii.3, *Basic Writings*, pp. 22-23.

perfection. Each of these four "ways" is basically the same in form. For instance, the first way begins with motion as the observed effect: we observe that some things are in motion. Now, whatever is in motion must have been set in motion by something else. But the sequence cannot go on forever; there can be no infinite regress. Therefore there must be a First Mover which is not itself set in motion but which has the principle of motion within itself. Everyone understands this to be God. For another example, Aquinas begins with contingency as the observed effect. That is, we observe that some things are contingent, i.e., it is possible for them not to exist. Now, whatever may possibly not exist at one time did not exist (otherwise it would be eternal and necessary, not contingent). But if everything were contingent, then at one time nothing at all would have existed, and therefore nothing would exist now, since from nothing comes nothing. Therefore something must exist which is non-contingent; i.e., it must exist eternally and necessarily. Everyone calls this God.

Since Aquinas' time a number of other forms of the cosmological proof have been set forth. For instance, Descartes began with two observed effects, namely the idea of God in the mind, and the existence of a thinking being who has the idea of God in his mind. Since causes must be greater than their effects, the only sufficient cause for each of these effects is God.[22] In more recent times C. S. Lewis has argued from the existence of reason as such to the existence of a rational Creator.[23] H. P. Owen has set forth a similar argument, beginning with the existence of morality or a moral

---

22. René Descartes, *The Meditations*, pp. 42ff. (Meditation III).

23. C. S. Lewis, *Miracles: A Preliminary Study* (New York: Macmillan, 1960), chapters 3-5.

sense in man.[24] Similar to this is the argument which begins with religious experience.[25] Mortimer Adler very recently has given us a version of the cosmological argument in which he says we must begin with the existence of the cosmos as a whole, the contingency of which requires the existence of an ultimate cause, which is God.[26] Finally we may note that two evangelical writers, Norman Geisler and William Craig, are staunch champions of the cosmological proof.[27]

Evaluation of the Cosmological Argument

An evaluation of this argument must begin with the notion of causality itself. Sometimes it is objected that the reality of causality cannot be proved.[28] But this is not a serious problem, since the process of rational thinking necessarily presupposes the existence of certain foundational principles or axioms of thought which we must assume to be true for even the first levels of reasoning to have validity. One such axiom is the principle of non-contradiction, without which all reasoning and communication are impossible. We assume it with every proposition or line of evidence. The principle of sufficient cause is also accepted in the same way. The concept of causality is something we recognize intuitively that we cannot do without, even if we cannot give a formal

---

24. H. P. Owen, *The Moral Argument for Christian Theism* (New York: Humanities Press, 1966).

25. See the section on A. E. Taylor in John Hick, ed., *The Existence of God*, pp. 153-164.

26. Mortimer J. Adler, *How To Think About God* (New York: Macmillan, 1980).

27. See footnotes 19 and 20 above.

28. This is usually attributed to David Hume. See Ronald Nash's remarks in *The Word of God and the Mind of Man* (Grand Rapids: Zondervan, 1982), pp. 18-19.

proof of it. Another objection related to causality is that it is improper to apply this concept to the universe as a whole in the same way that we apply it to individual items in the universe. In other words, it is one thing to say that a fossil or a crater must have a cause; but it is something altogether different to say that the totality of the universe is an effect that must have a cause. This supposedly begs the question of the existence of God. If the universe is assumed to have a cause, then we have already assumed God's existence. We reply that if this is true, then the opposite is also the case. To deny that the universe is an effect would also beg the question; it would amount to an *a priori* denial of God's existence. But the point is that the cosmological argument does not simply *assume* that the universe is an effect; it is an inference, e.g., from the concept of contingency. The very nature of contingent existence points to a non-contingent source.

Another major objection to the cosmological proof is that an infinite regress, an infinitely receding chain of causes, is not logically impossible. One might imagine, for instance, an infinite series of overlapping finite or contingent causes. Since the denial of infinite regress is crucial to this proof, this objection must be taken seriously. One way of responding to it is to distinguish between an originating cause and a sustaining cause, and to say that the objection applies only to the former. An originating cause would be the first or initial cause in a *temporal* series; some would grant that an infinite series in temporal sequence may be logically possible. But, they say, this is not the point of the cosmological argument, which is actually talking about a first or sustaining cause in a *hierarchical* series. That is to say, in the series of simultaneously existing causes and effects, there must be one highest cause on which all the others ultimately depend for their existence. Adler uses as an illustration the painting of a picture.[29] In this process the paint is applied to the canvas by a brush which is held by a hand which is controlled by a brain which is in turn controlled by a mind. This series of causes is operating simultaneously. So it is with the universe as a whole, we are told. The universe itself, being contingent, at any one moment depends for its existence on the non-contingent sustaining cause. The question of an infinite temporal regress is thus left open.

Another response to this objection is that we are not just *assuming* that an infinite temporal regress is impossible, but can actually offer *proof* that this is the case. This is what William Craig attempts to do in his defense of the cosmological argument. For instance, in his book, *The Existence of God and the Beginning of the Universe,* Craig offers two philosophical and two scientific arguments that the universe had a beginning and that an infinite temporal regress is impossible. These can only be summarized here. First, he says, there are different kinds of infinites; and an *actual* infinite cannot exist. But a beginningless series of events in time is an actual infinite. Therefore, a beginningless series of events in time cannot exist.[30] Second, a series of events in time is a collection formed by adding one member after another. A collection formed by adding one member after another cannot actually be infinite. Therefore, the series of events in time cannot be actually infinite.[31] Third, according to the best contemporary understanding of the cosmos,

29. Mortimer Adler, *How To Think About God,* pp. 41ff.

30. William Craig, *The Existence of God and the Beginning of the Universe,* pp. 39-48.

31. *Ibid.*, pp. 49-51.

at some past moment the entire known universe was contracted down to a single point. Something like a "big bang" caused it to begin to spread over infinite space. This could not be part of an eternal oscillation because there is not enough density in the universe to permit recontraction after expansion. Thus the universe must have had a beginning.[32] Finally, the second law of thermodynamics says that processes taking place in a closed system tend toward equilibrium; they run down. The universe is a giant closed system and thus in time will run down. But if the universe has existed forever, it would already have run down. Thus it must have had a beginning.[33]

A third objection to the cosmological argument is that even if we grant that there is a kind of "first cause" to the universe, this would not necessarily be the Christian God. Perhaps matter itself, or the laws of matter, could be this first cause. Antony Flew says, "No reason whatever has yet been given for considering that God would be an inherently more intelligible ultimate than—say—the most fundamental laws of energy and stuff."[34] John Hick cites this statement by Flew then responds to it. He grants that the cosmological argument is not capable of demonstrative proof; but he says that because of our own nature as conscious beings, it is just our natural and commonsense judgment that nonconscious existence (i.e., matter) is not self-explanatory, whereas on the other hand God as a conscious mental existence may well be self-explanatory.[35] He argues for the "explanatory

32. *Ibid.*, pp. 57-63. For an interesting secular perspective on this same point, see Robert Jastrow, *God and the Astronomers* (New York: W. W. Norton, 1978).

33. William Craig, *The Existence of God and the Beginning of the Universe*, pp. 63ff.

34. Antony Flew, *God and Philosophy* (New York: Hutchinson, 1966), p. 102.

35. John Hick, *Arguments for the Existence of God*, pp. 46-47.

ultimacy of mind for minds, or inevitable prejudice of mind in its own favour as an intrinsically intelligible kind of entity."[36] "Although no one is logically obliged to accept it, yet the principle is so entirely natural an expression of man's own self-awareness that to adopt it cannot be regarded as in any way irrational."[37] Hick concludes his discussion of this proof with this thoughtful remark:

> . . . And this, it seems to me, is where the cosmological argument leaves us. It points very clearly to the possibility of God as the ground of the ultimate intelligibility of the universe in which we find ourselves, and of ourselves as part of it. But in doing this it does not constitute a demonstration of God's existence. It leaves us with the alternatives that the universe is an inexplicable brute fact, or that its existence with the structure that it has is intelligible in the only way in which it could ever finally be intelligible to us, namely through its dependence upon a reality that is ultimate in the order of mind.[38]

Hick's point is well taken, namely, that the first cause is much more likely to be a living, rational being than inanimate matter. Thus we may well be justified in saying that the cosmological argument makes a fairly good case for the existence of God. But there is still some force remaining in this third objection, namely, that this God is not necessarily the God of the Bible. The First Mover may not necessarily be just *one*; Plato thought there would have to be at least two. Also the First Mover is not necessarily *all-good*; after all, are there not a lot of flaws and evils in the world? Some question whether this argument even requires an *infinite* cause. In other words, even if we grant the main

---

36. *Ibid.*, p. 50.
37. *Ibid.*
38. *Ibid.*, pp. 51-52.

point of the argument, we must recognize that the God of the Bible is not thereby proved. Something more is still needed.

In concluding our discussion of the cosmological argument, we may note that whenever this argument succeeds in convincing someone of God's existence, its success usually exceeds its inherent capacity as a purely rational argument. From a strictly logical, rational point of view, there are a few weaknesses that are not totally resolved as well as some ambiguities in the conclusion itself. Nevertheless the argument does have a power to convince, and Thomas Aquinas is not necessarily exaggerating when he says of his First Mover or First Cause that everyone understands it to be God. But how can this be? How can the argument accomplish more than it is inherently capable of accomplishing? I believe that it can and does do this because reason is not the only force at work in this "proof." Also at work is the impact of general revelation on the mind. Though we can properly distinguish these two forces conceptually, existentially it is impossible to distinguish them in the mental process of moving from the existence of the world as an effect to the existence of the Creator as its cause. The existence of the Creator is the basic datum of general revelation. The primary work by which the living God demonstrates his reality is the work of creation. The cosmological argument deals with exactly the same data as are involved in the general revelation of the Creator, but the direction of the process is reversed. In the former the movement is from man (via the reasoning process) to God; in the latter the movement is from God to man. When the former is considered in isolation from the latter, the argument has its weaknesses, though as Hick says it still clearly points at least to the *possibility* of God's existence. But when the rational argument is joined by the impact of the general revelation, the conclusion is much more satisfactory than this. Also, we may note that a total rejection of even the limited conclusion of the cosmological argument is more than likely just a rejection of the general revelation of the Creator, an act of rebellious suppression as described by Paul in Romans 1:18ff.

The Teleological Argument

The next proof for God's existence is the teleological argument. It is like the cosmological argument in that it is *a posteriori* and in that it is an argument from causality. But there is the following difference: whereas the cosmological argument begins with the simple *fact* of something's existence, the teleological proof begins with a certain *quality* in existing things, i.e., apparent design. The name itself is taken from the Greek *telos,* which means "end, goal, purpose." Certain things in the universe seem to be designed for a certain purpose or end. For instance, insect wings seem to have been designed for the specific purpose of enabling flight. They did not happen just accidentally. From this kind of observation the argument is formulated as follows. Premise A: whatever is designed must have a designer. Premise B: some things in the natural world are designed. Conclusion: therefore a designer exists, namely, God. We may note that this argument is based on an analogy between human artifacts and certain natural phenomena. We observe instances of design on the human level, and we apply the same mode of thought to natural things by analogy.[39]

---

39. For relevant texts and discussions relating to the teleological argument, see the sources listed in footnote 18 above.

Examples of the Teleological Argument

In presenting examples of the argument from design we may note in passing that Aquinas' "fifth way" was such an argument. It did not gain its full force, however, until the rise of the natural sciences in the seventeenth century. The more man learned about the details of the natural world, the more instances of design he seemed to uncover. In this context the classic statement of the argument is that of William Paley in his *Natural Theology.*[40] Paley reasoned that if one were crossing a meadow and found a watch, he would immediately recognize it as something which did not just happen to be there by an accident of nature. Even if he had never seen such an object before, he would be able to tell that it had been manufactured for a certain purpose, i.e., that it had a maker. In a way no less certain, said Paley, many of the natural phenomena in the universe give evidence of having been designed by a Maker to accomplish a specific end.

> . . . Every indication of contrivance, every manifestation of design, which existed in the watch, exists in the works of nature; with the difference, on the side of nature, of being greater and more, and that in a degree which exceeds all computation. I mean, that the contrivances of nature surpass the contrivances of art, in the complexity, subtilty, and curiosity, of the mechanism; and still more, if possible, do they go beyond them in number and variety; yet, in a multitude of cases, are not less evidently mechanical, not less evidently contrivances, not less evidently accommodated to their end, or suited to their office, than are the most perfect productions of human ingenuity.[41]

---

40. William Paley, "Natural Theology," *The Works of William Paley,* new ed. (Philadelphia: J. J. Woodward, 1841), pp. 387-487.

41. *Ibid.,* pp. 390-391.

One primary example of such design is the human eye, which Paley proceeded to describe to the limits of the current science.[42]

A more recent example of the design argument appears in the second volume of F. R. Tennant's *Philosophical Theology,*[43] published in 1930. Tennant tried to take account of prior criticisms of the argument. He did not focus so much on specific details as on the totality of things. Hence he presents a cosmic teleology with five main strands, which together produce a cumulative effect. John Hick summarizes these five strands thus:[44] (1) the mutual adaptation of *thought* and *things*; (2) the nature of the *process* of evolution, disregarding individual phenomena; (3) the fitness of the physical world to produce and sustain life, i.e., inorganic teleology; (4) the world as a bearer of *values*: nature produces beauty; and (5) the *moral* nature of man. The impact of these factors, as Hick summarizes it, is this:

> . . . The universe might have been a mere formless chaos; but it has form and order, and not only this but an evolving order in which one stage is built upon another to produce in man a consciousness of the universe which also looks beyond it to a transcendent purposive Mind. It is this total fact that demands explanation. . . .[45]

And the only sufficient explanation is a Creator God.

---

42. *Ibid.*, chapter 3.

43. F. R. Tennant, *Philosophical Theology,* 2 vols. (New York: Cambridge University Press, 1928-1930). The discussion of the teleological argument is found in Volume II, pp. 79ff.

44. John Hick, *Arguments for the Existence of God,* pp. 19-21.

45. *Ibid.*, p. 21.

Critique of the Teleological Argument

The classic critique of the argument from design was given by David Hume in his *Dialogues Concerning Natural Religion*, published in 1779.[46] His criticisms are limited, of course, to the forms the argument had received up to that point, and have been somewhat blunted by later discussions such as that of Tennant. Nevertheless there is still some force to the criticisms. Here we can only briefly summarize his main points and make a few relevant comments.

The first criticism is that the analogy between the world and a human artifact is weak. In the first place, how is it possible to compare the world as a whole to a single artifact? We have not even experienced the whole world. And even what we have experienced is really not very similar to any machine or contrived artifact with which we are familiar. It is in fact more like a plant or animal; so a better analogy for its origin may be animal generation or plant growth. One response to this criticism is that the argument usually does not compare the whole universe with an artifact, but rather focuses on individual natural phenomena such as the human eye and fetal circulation. Another response would be that of Tennant, who constructed his cosmic teleology specifically with a view to showing that the totality of the universe suggests design.

A second criticism is that alternative explanations may account for the apparent design as well as or better than the designer theory. Hume himself suggested a modified Epicurean hypothesis. In a universe composed of a finite number of particles of eternal duration, he said, we can expect every possible combination including the present one to appear by

---

46. David Hume, *Dialogues Concerning Natural Religion*, ed. Norman Kemp Smith (Indianapolis: Bobbs-Merrill, 1947).

chance any number of times, with no designer required. A later and more sophisticated version of this same suggestion is Darwinian evolution. The evidence suggests that Darwin developed his theory of natural selection as a deliberate alternative to Paley's argument.[47] How shall we respond to this criticism? Is it true that a chance system, particularly that of evolution, is a better explanation of apparent design than teleology? For one thing we may note that Tennant constructed his version of the design argument to include evolution. This is why he focuses on the cosmos as a whole rather than on specific natural phenomena. For another thing we may note that traditional teleology's very point is that chance is *not* a sufficient explanation for a multitude of presently existing phenomena. This is true especially of the inorganic realm (e.g., the marvel of water), an area unaffected by Darwinianism and emphasized by Tennant.[48] But even in the organic realm, we cannot lightly dismiss evidences of design in individual living species. This is especially true of organisms which depend for their very existence upon some apparently designed life-sustaining behavior or structure (used either for food-gathering or reproduction or defense).[49] The whole point of the teleological argument is that at times whole species are too dependent upon highly-specialized mechanisms to allow us to think that they might have occurred by chance.

---

47. Robert E. D. Clark, *Darwin: Before and After* (Exeter: Paternoster Press, 1966), pp. 80-97.

48. See Bernard Ramm, *The Christian View of Science and Scripture* (Grand Rapids: Eerdmans, 1956), pp. 147ff. See also Norman L. Mitchell, "Water of Life," *Ministry* (March 1980), 53:20-21.

49. Examples are numerous. We may cite only the defense mechanism of the bombardier beetle. For protection it discharges a repellant mist produced

(Continued on page 438.)

A final criticism is that the teleological argument, even if it is valid, does not demand the existence of a single perfect Creator. We cannot assume that the cause is greater than required by the effect. Some have pointed out that teleology would prove only an architect and not necessarily a Creator. Others point to the imperfections and evils in the world and insist that a designer has to be held accountable for these, too. Hence such a designer could not be everything the Christian God is supposed to be; he must lack some basic attribute such as love or omnipotence or wisdom. In response we may note that the problem of evil will be dealt with more fully in the next volume, but even a full accounting of it from the standpoint of Scripture cannot blunt the force of this criticism with respect to the teleological argument. In other words, this criticism seems to be valid. The argument may prove the existence of a designer, but this designer cannot be shown to be the God of the Bible from this argument alone. Something more is still needed.

On the other hand we may point out that the teleological argument is similar to the cosmological argument in that its effects often go beyond what is strictly warranted by reason alone. We would explain this in the same way as before, namely, by the unperceived concurrence of general revelation with the reasoning process. Thus the teleological

---

(Continued from page 437.)

internally by a chemical process so intense that by the time the fluid is ejected it has reached the boiling point and some has already vaporized. The beetle's spray gland has two chambers, each with its own chemical solution. When the beetle needs to spray, it squeezes some fluid from the inner chamber into the outer one, producing an immediate chemical reaction which ejects the boiling mixture with an audible pop (hence "bombardier"). The process is very similar to that used in some shaving-cream dispensers to produce heated lather. ("Hot Beetle," *Scientific American*, September 1969, 221:102.)

argument has a psychological and spiritual impact as well as a rational one, because it is simply an attempt to formulate in terms of reason what the Creator has already shown us by the work of his hands. John Hick would probably not state it in these terms, but still he recognizes the unusual power of this proof. The design argument, he says, does not really establish the probability of the Creator. "And yet . . . the response to the complex order of the world expressed in the design argument continues, relatively untroubled by the logical insufficiency of the argument itself." Why is this so? Because it "focuses our attention upon aspects of the world that evoke a sense of wonder and an awareness of mystery independently of the ratiocinative activity of the mind."[50] Even Immanuel Kant, a strong critic of this argument, felt it necessary to say, "Two things fill the mind with ever new and increasing admiration and awe, the oftener and more steadily we reflect on them: the starry heavens above me and the moral law within me."[51] That he was not discussing the teleological argument when he said this does not matter. At another time he said that the proof from design "always deserves to be mentioned with respect. It is the oldest, the clearest, and that most in conformity with the common reason of humanity." It would therefore be vain, he said, to attempt to diminish its authority. Whenever the mind is threatened with depression by the doubts suggested by subtle speculation, it is delivered from this state of uncertainty "the moment it casts a look upon the wondrous forms of nature and the majesty of the universe, and rises from height to height, from condition to condition,

50. John Hick, *Arguments for the Existence of God*, pp. 33-34.

51. Immanuel Kant, *Critique of Practical Reason*, tr. Lewis W. Beck (Indianapolis: Bobbs-Merrill, 1956), p. 166.

till it has elevated itself to the supreme and unconditioned author of all."[52]

The Historical Argument

The three theistic proofs discussed thus far are definitely limited with regard to their purely rational ability to establish the existence of the living God of the Bible. The ontological argument seems to lack validity altogether. The cosmological and teleological arguments seem to have a convincing power, but much of it appears to be due to the concurrent force of general revelation on the mind of the observer. Strictly from the standpoint of reason, these last two arguments fall short. They definitely establish the possibility of God's existence, but this is not saying very much. Some would insist that they show that God's existence is probable. But even if this is the case, the *identity* of this "god" is by no means clear. As we have seen, even if the arguments succeed in their main point of proving God's existence, the God whose existence is proved thereby is not necessarily the God of the Bible. Thus something more is needed, not only to prove God's existence with greater certitude but also to establish his identity as the God of Israel and the God of our Lord Jesus Christ. This "something more" is the historical proof.

The historical proof, which can only be described briefly here, centers around the historical claim that Jesus of Nazareth was raised from the dead by the God of Israel who is also the God of the Christian Church. This is a historical argument and not a biblical one as such, because its methodology deliberately excludes any presupposition about the inspired

52. Immanuel Kant, *Critique of Pure Reason*, p. 349.

nature of the Bible. For the sake of the argument it approaches the biblical writings as a historian would approach any other ancient documents, with a view to assessing their claims rationally, i.e., using only the accepted canons of historical research. The argument moves through two stages: first, what proves the resurrection? and second, what does the resurrection prove?[53]

In the first stage the point is to establish the fact that the resurrection of Jesus actually occurred. The key factor in the proof is the principle of sufficient cause. The contention is that there are certain established historical facts for which the only sufficient cause is the bodily resurrection of Jesus Christ. These facts are as follows: the disciples' report that Jesus' tomb was empty; the disciples' report that Jesus appeared bodily to them after his death and burial; the unshakable faith of the apostles; the conversion of Saul of Tarsus; the establishment and rapid growth of the Christian Church; and the transition from Saturday to Sunday as the Church's special day. No other historical explanation can satisfactorily account for these indisputable facts; the resurrection must indeed have occurred.

But this is only the first half of the historical argument. So Jesus rose from the dead: what does that prove? It proves basically the integrity of Jesus as a teacher and the truth and authority of his teaching. This includes among other things his implicit and explicit acceptance of the Old Testament's testimony to the exclusive reality of the God of Israel, as well as his own teaching concerning the reality

---

53. See Jack Cottrell, *The Authority of the Bible* (Grand Rapids: Baker, 1979), chapter 7: "Jesus' Resurrection and Its Implications." See also Gary Habermas, *The Resurrection of Jesus: An Apologetic* (Grand Rapids: Baker, 1980).

and nature of Yahweh. The fact that the resurrection occurred in this particular historical context and in connection with these particular teachings establishes the validity of this specific view of God. Thus the historical argument supplies what the cosmological and teleological proofs lack. When taken together, these three proofs establish the rational probability that the God of the Bible truly exists.

We conclude this chapter by pointing out once again how these theistic proofs converge and overlap with God's own demonstration of his reality as the one true and living God through his works of creation and redemption. God's demonstration via his works is the primary basis for our faith in him as the living God. The theistic proofs, by taking the same data (i.e., creation and resurrection) and casting them in the form of rational arguments, serve to augment and support and confirm this faith. They also have a limited value in the dialogue with unbelievers, as expressed by Louis Berkhof:

> . . . They are important as interpretations of God's general revelation and as exhibiting the reasonableness of belief in a divine Being. Moreover, they can render some service in meeting the adversary. While they do not prove the existence of God beyond the possibility of doubt, so as to compel assent, they can be so construed as to establish a strong probability and thereby silence many unbelievers.[54]

---

54. Louis Berkhof, *Systematic Theology* (London: Banner of Truth Trust, 1939), p. 28.

Chapter Nine

THE FEAR OF GOD

In this volume our goal has been to set forth the biblical doctrine of God as Creator. We have discussed the meaning of creation itself, that mighty act by which God brought into existence out of nothing the whole material universe as well as the realm of created spirits. We have discussed the nature of the God who is capable of such an incomparable deed. We have seen that he alone is Uncreated Spirit, the holy and exalted one who transcends the whole of his creation. We have seen that he is infinite in his existence, his knowledge, and his power; and he is unlimited by space and time. He is the hidden and incomprehensible God, yet he has chosen to make himself known to his creatures through his deeds and words. He is the Living God, the only true God, the one who rightfully demands and deserves our exclusive worship and service.

A theme that has run throughout this book is that creation is the primary work of God, and that our relationship to God as creature to Creator is the fundamental fact of our existence. In this final chapter our question is this: What is the basic response which the Creator expects from us, his creatures? This should be a matter of urgent concern to all of us. Since creatureliness is our elemental essence, we should want to know the nature of our primary obligation to our Maker, for herein lie the foundation and the key to our authentic existence. What, then, is the answer? It is this: *the fear of God.* As soon as we are aware of ourselves as creatures made by the hand of the almighty God, our hearts should be filled with an overwhelming sense of fear, awe, and reverence toward the one who has made us.

THE GREATNESS AND GLORY OF GOD

Quite often the biblical writers express their praise and adoration for the Creator in general terms. They are not concerned with emphasizing any one particular attribute of God; they just want to declare how great he is. Their purpose is similar to that of the person who wrote the gospel song, "We've got a great big wonderful God!" There are several biblical words which accomplish this purpose. They are words of a general nature, words which embrace the totality of God's transcendent holiness, the fullness of his deity, the entirety of his incomparable Being. They are words which bring all of the Creator's attributes together and magnify them in their infinite grandeur. The two basic terms are *greatness* and *glory,* along with the words *splendor* and *majesty.*

Sometimes these words of praise appear in clusters along with others, as in David's blessing of the Lord in I Chronicles 29:10-11,

> Blessed art Thou, O Lord God of Israel our father, forever and ever. Thine, O Lord, is the greatness and the power and the glory and the victory and the majesty, indeed everything that is in the heavens and the earth; Thine is the dominion, O Lord, and Thou dost exalt Thyself as head over all.

In Psalm 145:5 David praises "the glorious splendor of Thy majesty." Psalm 104:1 multiplies the praise: "Bless the Lord, O my soul! O Lord my God, Thou art very great; Thou art clothed with splendor and majesty." Psalm 96:4-8 includes these words:

> . . . For great is the Lord, and greatly to be praised . . . . Splendor and majesty are before Him, strength and beauty

> are in His sanctuary. Ascribe to the Lord, O families of the peoples, ascribe to the Lord glory and strength. Ascribe to the Lord the glory of His name . . . .

We are left with the impression that there are just not enough words to describe and declare the greatness and glory of the Creator.

God Is Great

A familiar childhood prayer begins with the affirmation that "God is great." The Bible makes this same affirmation many times, using the ordinary words for "great" and "greatness," words which connote greatness in size or greatness in importance. When applied to God these terms declare that God is what he is in the most exalted and superlative sense, and that there is no one who can compare with him. "Thou art great, O Lord God; for there is none like Thee, and there is no God besides Thee" (II Samuel 7:22). "For I know that the Lord is great, and that our Lord is above all gods," says the psalmist (Psalm 135:5). "His name is great" (Psalm 76:1). "Great is the Lord, and highly to be praised; and His greatness is unsearchable" (Psalm 145:3). He deserves praise because of his "excellent greatness" (Psalm 150:2). He is "the God of gods and the Lord of lords, the great, the mighty, and the awesome God" (Deuteronomy 10:17; see Nehemiah 1:5; 9:32). Those who observed Jesus' divine power at work "were all amazed at the greatness of God" (Luke 9:43).

The greatness of God is evidenced especially in his works. In the words of Moses, "O Lord God, Thou hast begun to show Thy servant Thy greatness and Thy strong hand; for what god is there in heaven or on earth who can do such works and mighty acts as Thine?" (Deuteronomy 3:24). This is true of his works in general, and it is especially true of his work of creation. Psalm 96:4-5 says, "Great is the Lord, and greatly to be praised; He is to be feared above all gods. For all the gods of the people are idols, but the Lord made the heavens." Psalm 104 begins with a declaration of the greatness of God, and continues with a rehearsal of the mighty act of creation and God's continuing involvement in nature. The first two verses say, "Bless the Lord, O my soul! O Lord my God, Thou art very great; Thou art clothed with splendor and majesty, covering Thyself with light as with a cloak, stretching out heaven like a tent curtain." "O Lord, our Lord, how majestic is Thy name in all the earth, who hast displayed Thy splendor above the heavens!" (Psalm 8:1). When the Lord himself stoops to rebuke the presumptuousness of Job, he magnifies his own greatness by emphasizing his power and wisdom as Creator: "Where were you when I laid the foundations of the earth! Tell Me, if you have understanding, who set its measurements, since you know? Or who stretched the line on it? . . . Or who laid its cornerstone?" (Job 38:4-6). "Do you give the horse his might? . . . Is it by your understanding that the hawk soars?" (Job 39:19, 26). Truly, "His splendor covers the heavens, and the earth is full of His praise" (Habakkuk 3:3). "Great are the works of the Lord; they are studied by all who delight in them. Splendid and majestic is His work" (Psalm 111:2-3). The redeemed will forever sing, "Great and marvelous are Thy works, O Lord God, the Almighty" (Revelation 15:3).

God Is Glorious

The word which best sums up the collective greatness of God is the term *glory*. He is the "King of glory" and the

"Lord of glory" (Psalm 24:7-10; I Corinthians 2:8).[1] He is also called the "Father of glory" (Ephesians 1:17) and the "God of glory" (Acts 7:2). "Great is the glory of the Lord," says Psalm 138:5. "His name alone is exalted; His glory is above earth and heaven" (Psalm 148:13). See Psalms 57:5; 108:5.

The principal Old Testament word for glory (*kābōd*) in its adjective form literally means great, heavy, or weighty. It is used often in a figurative sense to mean significant, important, noteworthy, impressive, or severe. In this figurative sense it refers to God and is usually translated "glorious" or "glory." The glory of God thus is his infinite significance, the totality of his perfections, the fullness of his deity compressed into a single concept.

But there is another connotation that makes the glory of God something special. God *is* infinitely great and perfect; this remains true whether or not his greatness is ever displayed or manifested in any way. However, he does choose to manifest his greatness, displaying the majesty of his perfections in visible ways. Most specifically, the *glory* of God is his greatness as it is manifested and as it shines forth for all to see. "Glory is displayed excellence," as J. D. Pentecost says.[2] It is "Jehovah Himself in the manifestation of His majesty"; it is "the external manifestation of the eternal God who is the Creator of heaven and earth," as Klaas Runia puts it.[3] Bavinck elaborates that it "indicates the

1. These passages refer specifically to Jesus Christ as God the Son. Psalm 24:7-10 is a prophetic picture of the ascension.

2. J. Dwight Pentecost, *The Glory of God* (Portland, Oregon: Multnomah Press, 1978), p. 8.

3. Klaas Runia, "Glory, Glorification," *The Encyclopedia of Christianity*, Volume IV, ed. Philip E. Hughes (Marshallton, Del.: The National Foundation for Christian Education, 1972), p. 345.

splendor and brilliancy that is inseparably connected with all of God's virtue and with his self-revelation in nature and grace, the luster of his manifestation to creatures."[4]

God's glory is associated with his visible presence, as in the case of the Old Testament theophanies. The glory of God appeared in the cloud which guided Israel and indwelt the temple (Exodus 16:7, 10; 40:34-35; I Kings 8:10-11). "O Lord," declared David, "I love the habitation of Thy house, and the place where Thy glory dwells" (Psalm 26:8). It was the "glory of the Lord" that rested on Mount Sinai; "and to the eyes of the sons of Israel the appearance of the glory of the Lord was like a consuming fire on the mountain top" (Exodus 24:16-17). The similarity to fire indicates that the glory of God in his visible presence to man is like a radiant and shining light (see I Timothy 6:16). Ezekiel's visions of God emphasize this point. As he describes it, "Then the glory of the Lord went up from the cherub to the threshold of the temple, and the temple was filled with the cloud, and the court was filled with the brightness of the glory of the Lord" (Ezekiel 10:4). Also, "the glory of the God of Israel was coming from the way of the east. And His voice was like the sound of many waters; and the earth shone with His glory" (Ezekiel 43:2). Sometimes even the angels who appeared to men reflected this brightness of God's glory. For instance, when the angel appeared to the shepherds, "the glory of the Lord shone around them" (Luke 2:9). In Revelation 18:1, when an important angel appeared, "the earth was illumined with his glory."

---

4. Herman Bavinck, *The Doctrine of God*, tr. William Hendriksen (Grand Rapids: Eerdmans, 1951), p. 249. See also Emil Brunner, *The Christian Doctrine of God: Dogmatics, Volume I*, tr. Olive Wyon (Philadelphia: Westminster Press, 1950), pp. 285-287.

When God became present to man in Jesus Christ, the glory of his divine nature shone through the human nature of the man of Galilee. In the prophetic words of Isaiah 60:1-2, "Arise, shine; for your light has come, and the glory of the Lord has risen upon you. For behold, darkness will cover the earth, and deep darkness the peoples; but the Lord will rise upon you, and His glory will appear upon you." As John 1:14 puts it, "And the Word became flesh, and dwelt among us, and we beheld His glory, glory as of the only begotten from the Father, full of grace and truth." Jesus was the very radiance of the glory of God (Hebrews 1:3). At his resurrection and ascension even his human nature, being changed into an immortal form, began to reflect the glory of his divine nature (John 7:39; Philippians 3:21).

The spiritual theophany of God in heaven is a continual manifestation of his glory; Stephen was privileged to see it just before his death (Acts 7:55). Following the day of judgment God will transfer his glorious presence to the New Jerusalem and will dwell with the redeemed upon the new earth (Revelation 21:1-3, 11). "And the city has no need of the sun or of the moon to shine upon it, for the glory of God has illumined it" (Revelation 21:23; see Isaiah 60:19). The Christian's "hope of glory" (Colossians 1:27; Romans 5:2) is his expectation of seeing the glory of God and of dwelling in its presence for eternity; it is also his expectation of receiving a new and immortal body which reflects God's glory just as the new human body of Jesus Christ does. See Romans 8:17-18, 29-30; 9:23; Philippians 3:21.

But there is another aspect of the glory of God which must be emphasized here. Not only is his glory manifested in his visible presence; it is also displayed in a more indirect way in his many marvelous works. Indeed, his glory and his works are equated with one another in the poetic couplet of I Chronicles 16:24, "Tell of His glory among the nations, His wonderful deeds among all the peoples." See also Psalm 66:1-5,

> Shout joyfully to God, all the earth; sing the glory of His name; make His praise glorious. Say to God, "How awesome are Thy works! Because of the greatness of Thy power Thine enemies will give feigned obedience to Thee. All the earth will worship Thee, and will sing praises to Thee; they will sing praises to Thy name." Come and see the works of God, who is awesome in His deeds toward the sons of men.

His great deeds of redemption on behalf of Israel are specifically mentioned as manifestations of his glory: "For the Lord has redeemed Jacob and in Israel He shows forth His glory" (Isaiah 44:23; see Numbers 14:22). Works of judgment also display his glory (Ezekiel 39:13).

No work of God displays his glory more intensely than his work of creation. When God rebukes Job by magnifying his role as Creator, he hints that the original creation was observed by an audience of angels. When he laid the earth's foundation and cornerstone, says God, "the morning stars sang together, and all the sons of God shouted for joy" (Job 38:4-7). The "morning stars" and "sons of God" probably are the angels. Pentecost suggests that God wanted the angels to witness the creation so that they could behold his glory. He says,

> . . . God planned creation in part to be an object lesson to angels so that angels would know just how glorious, how powerful a God He is. God spoke a word and out of nothing

> this vast expanse of the universe came into existence. When the angels beheld the power of God in creation, all the angelic chorus sang together and the sons of God shouted with joy. This was not because they had been given a place to dwell in, but because creation had revealed to the angels how great God was. In response, they sang, shouted and praised God, because creation had demonstrated that God is a God of limitless power who could call things into existence out of nothing.[5]

In terms of the sheer magnitude of glory, it is difficult to imagine a more impressive event than creation. (May we be pardoned for envying the angels at this point?) Even though we as human beings were not privileged to witness the original act itself, we do see its results in the general revelation around us; and there the glory of the Creator still shines. "The heavens are telling of the glory of God; and their expanse is declaring the work of His hands" (Psalm 19:1). This is the "glory of the incorruptible God" seen through the things he has made, the very glory rebellious man rejects and replaces with finite objects of worship (Romans 1:20-23). The twenty-ninth Psalm begins with a proper response to God's glory: "Ascribe to the Lord, O sons of the mighty, ascribe to the Lord glory and strength. Ascribe to the Lord the glory due to His name" (vv. 1-2). The following verses are a celebration of the glory of God displayed in nature:

> . . . The voice of the Lord is upon the waters; the God of glory thunders, the Lord is over many waters. The voice of the Lord is powerful, the voice of the Lord is majestic. The voice of the Lord breaks the cedars; yes, the Lord breaks

5. J. D. Pentecost, *The Glory of God*, p. 21.

> in pieces the cedars of Lebanon. And He makes Lebanon skip like a calf, and Sirion like a young wild ox. The voice of the Lord hews out flames of fire. The voice of the Lord shakes the wilderness; the Lord shakes the wilderness of Kadesh. The voice of the Lord makes the deer to calve, and strips the forests bare, and in His temple everything says, "Glory!" (vv. 3-9).

It is possible that "His temple" is used here figuratively for the whole earth, which exults in the presence of the Creator and cries out "Glory!" Or it could be the angels continuing to shout for joy as they observe the mighty power of God in the ongoing creation (see Job 38:7). In either case the glory of God is displayed throughout the earth.

Considering the abundance and magnitude of the works of God, we are not surprised that the seraphim who attend the Lord call out to one another, "Holy, Holy, Holy, is the Lord of hosts, the whole earth is full of His glory" (Isaiah 6:3). God himself has promised, "Indeed, as I live, all the earth will be filled with the glory of the Lord" (Numbers 14:21). See Psalm 72:18-19.

THE FEAR OF GOD

In view of the biblical teaching about the nature and work of the Creator, especially as summed up in the concepts of the greatness and the glory of God, there is only one proper response from the creature, namely, *fear.* Here we need to be very careful, because the biblical words for fear have two main connotations. First, there is fear in the sense of terror or dread, fear in the sense of *being afraid* of God. This is not the original fear of God, the fear of creatures before their Creator. It is rather a fear that comes upon men when they have sinned, and when they know they stand before God not just as Creator but also as Judge. It is the fear of sinners before the all-knowing God of wrath and judgment. It is certainly appropriate and natural for sinners to have such fear. As Hebrews 10:31 says, "It is a terrifying thing to fall into the hands of the living God." Jesus said, "Do not fear those who kill the body, but are unable to kill the soul; but rather fear Him who is able to destroy both soul and body in hell" (Matthew 10:28).

The Old Testament gives us several examples of the fear of terror. The sailors who witnessed the judgment of God against Jonah "feared the Lord greatly, and they offered a sacrifice to the Lord and made vows" (Jonah 1:16). By his mighty deeds God instilled the "dread of the Lord" in the hearts of Israel's enemies (I Samuel 11:7; II Chronicles 20:29). The prospect of God's judgment has this effect on the nations: "They will come trembling out of their fortresses; to the Lord our God they will come in dread, and they will be afraid before Thee" (Micah 7:17). "So they will fear the name of the Lord" (Isaiah 59:19). In the time of judgment "men will go into the caves of the rocks, and into holes of the ground before the terror of the Lord, and before the splendor of His majesty, when He arises to make the earth tremble" (Isaiah 2:19; see vv. 10, 21). This is true even of the sinners among the Israelites: "Sinners in Zion are terrified; trembling has seized the godless" (Isaiah 33:14).

Given the fact of sin, the fear of terror is a legitimate fear as experienced by the rebellious and unbelieving sinner. But this is *not* the kind of fear which God originally intended man to have, nor is it the fear which he wants to engender toward himself. There is another kind of fear which is more basic and more natural than terror, and which is the proper response of the creature to the Creator. The latter will be the focus of our attention in this final section of this volume.

Reverence and Awe

The creaturely fear of God may be defined as a sense of reverence, respect, and awe. This is definitely a valid connotation of the biblical terms, as seen in their usage in other contexts. For instance, in Leviticus 19:3 children are commanded to fear their parents; modern translations usually render this as "reverence." Also, I Peter 3:2 may be understood as admonishing wives to fear their husbands, though only in terms of reverence and respect. Ephesians 6:5 says, "Slaves, be obedient to those who are your masters according to the flesh, with fear and trembling." Again this is the fear of respect. We may note finally that Isaiah 11:2-3 prophesies that the Messiah will be filled with "the spirit of knowledge and the fear of the Lord" and that "He will delight in the fear of the Lord." Certainly this cannot be construed as any kind of terror or dread.

In relation to God, the idea is that the great and glorious Creator is a Being so fearsome and awesome that we cannot help but be overwhelmed with an inner sense of awe at the very thought of him. "For great is the Lord, and greatly to be praised; He is to be feared above all gods" (Psalm 96:4). He is described as "awesome" ("terrible" and "fearful" in the King James Version). "Who is like Thee among the gods, O Lord? Who is like Thee, majestic in holiness, awesome in praises, working wonders?" (Exodus 15:11). "For the Lord your God is the God of gods and the Lord of lords, the great, the mighty, and the awesome God" (Deuteronomy 10:17); therefore you must "fear this honored and awesome name, the Lord your God" (Deuteronomy 28:58). "Come and see the works of God, who is awesome in His deeds toward the sons of men" (Psalm 66:5; see Psalm 65:5). "The Fear of Isaac" is a name ascribed to God in Genesis 31:42, 53. As

Isaiah 8:13 says, "It is the Lord of hosts whom you should regard as holy. And He shall be your fear, and He shall be your dread." Given the fact that God is who he is, how could it be otherwise? John Murray aptly says,

> . . . If we know God we must know him in the matchless glory of his transcendent majesty, and the only appropriate posture for us is prostration before him in awe and reverence. To think otherwise is to deny the transcendent greatness of God, and that is infidelity. The pervasive emphasis of Scripture upon the fear of God as the determinative attitude of heart in both religion and ethics and as the characteristic mark of God's people is exactly what must have been if the Bible is consistent with itself. The doctrine of God could know nothing else. . . . Our consciousness is not biblical unless it is conditioned by the fear of God.[6]

How can we describe this reverential fear of God? Rudolf Otto calls it "creature-consciousness" or "creature-feeling." As he says, "It is the emotion of a creature, abased and overwhelmed by its own nothingness in contrast to that which is supreme above all creatures." It contains "the note of self-abasement into nothingness before an overpowering, absolute might of some kind."[7] Otto is on the right track here, though the concept of nothingness is probably too extreme. It would be better to say that the creature-feeling is a sense of smallness and weakness in the presence of the all-great and all-powerful Creator. Brunner calls it "an incomparable sense of distance" before the all-holy

6. John Murray, *Principles of Conduct* (Grand Rapids: Eerdmans, 1957), p. 241.

7. Rudolf Otto, *The Idea of the Holy*, revised ed., tr. John W. Harvey (New York: Oxford University Press, 1926), p. 10.

one.[8] "The creature should bow the knee in reverence before the Holy God. This humble recognition of the infinite distance between God and man is the 'fear of the Lord.'"[9] It is a profound sense of awe which causes even the angelic beings to cover their faces in God's presence and to cry out, "Holy, Holy, Holy" (Isaiah 6:2-3). It causes us all to say with Jeremiah, "There is none like Thee, O Lord; Thou art great, and great is Thy name in might. Who would not fear Thee, O King of the nations? Indeed it is Thy due!" (Jeremiah 10:6-7).

Since man's primary relationship to God is that of creature to Creator, the fear of God must be regarded as the most basic and essential of human attitudes. In the total picture it may not be the most important (cf. Matthew 22:37), but it is certainly foundational for all the rest. Thus the fear of the Lord is called "the beginning of knowledge" (Proverbs 1:7) and "the beginning of wisdom" (Psalm 111:10; Proverbs 9:10). It is the key to life (Proverbs 10:27; 14:27; 19:23), and it is the key to peace and well-being. Regarding the latter, Ecclesiastes 8:12 says that "it will be well for those who fear God, who fear Him openly." Proverbs 15:16 says, "Better is a little with the fear of the Lord, than great treasure and turmoil without it." Even the vaunted covenant relationship presupposes an attitude of reverential fear: "The secret of the Lord is for those who fear Him, and He will make them know His covenant" (Psalm 25:14). This is why Murray calls it "the determinative attitude of heart in both religion and ethics and . . . the characteristic mark of God's people."[10]

---

8. Emil Brunner, *The Christian Doctrine of God*, p. 162. He is not thinking in terms of *spatial* distance.

9. *Ibid.*, p. 163.

10. John Murray, *Principles of Conduct*, p. 241.

I must confess that when I first read this statement many years ago, I put a question mark in the margin. But now I see that Murray is absolutely right. The fear of God is basic; the primacy of creation demands it.

Murray's statement includes the idea that the fear of God is "the characteristic mark of God's people." That is, in the Bible those who are seeking to honor and serve God are called "God-fearing." Thus it is with Abraham (Genesis 22:12), Job (Job 1:1), and Cornelius (Acts 10:2, 22). According to the way Paul addressed his audience in Acts 13:16, 26, there must have been a number of Gentiles who feared the true God as the result of the faithful testimony of the faithful Jews. The church itself is described as "going on in the fear of the Lord and in the comfort of the Holy Spirit" (Acts 9:31). On the other hand, the Bible describes the ungodly as being devoid of the fear of the Lord. "Transgression speaks to the ungodly within the heart; there is no fear of God before his eyes" (Psalm 36:1; Romans 3:18). See Deuteronomy 25:18; Ecclesiastes 8:13; Jeremiah 2:19.

Though reverential fear is a natural response to the creature, the passages just cited show that it will not occur automatically and without exception. Thus we must be commanded to fear God, even in this sense of reverence and awe. According to the Mosaic law, "You shall fear the Lord your God; you shall serve Him and cling to Him" (Deuteronomy 10:20; see Leviticus 19:14; 25:17). David admonished, "O fear the Lord, you His saints; for to those who fear Him, there is no want. . . . Come, you children, listen to me; I will teach you the fear of the Lord" (Psalm 34:9, 11). "Live in the fear of the Lord always," says Proverbs 23:17. Peter says simply, "Fear God" (I Peter 2:17; see Ecclesiastes 5:7; Revelation 14:7). "Work out your salvation with fear and trembling," says Paul in Philippians 2:12.[11] In Psalm 33:6-9 the exhortation to fear God comes as a natural consequence of the fact of creation:

> By the word of the Lord the heavens were made, and by the breath of His mouth all their hosts. He gathers the waters of the sea together as a heap; He lays up the deeps in storehouses. Let all the earth fear the Lord; let all the inhabitants of the world stand in awe of Him. For He spoke, and it was done; He commanded, and it stood fast.

Thus God's desire for Israel was that they should fear the "honored and awesome name" of the Lord God (Deuteronomy 28:58), that they should fear him all the days of their lives on earth and that they should teach their children to do the same (Deuteronomy 4:10). Thus David prayed that God would strengthen his heart "to fear Thy name" (Psalm 86:11). This should be the prayer of every human being. "How blessed is the man who fears the Lord" (Psalms 112:1; 128:1). "How great is Thy goodness, which Thou hast stored up for those who fear Thee" (Psalm 31:19; see Psalm 33:18ff.). The Messianic Covenant is grounded on the fear of God (Jeremiah 32:39-40), and those who fear his name will receive an eternal reward (Revelation 11:18).

Is it possible for a God-fearing person today to be filled only with reverential awe, with no mixture of terror and dread? Probably not. This is not because God wants us to be terrified of him, because he does not. The exhortation to "fear not" occurs frequently in the Bible.[12] Its use in

---

11. "Fear and trembling" does not necessarily mean terror. See I Corinthians 2:3; II Corinthians 7:15; Ephesians 6:5.

12. See Genesis 15:1; Isaiah 41:10; 43:1, 5; 44:2; Matthew 17:6-7; Luke 1:13, 30; Revelation 1:17. See also Romans 8:15.

Exodus 20:20 shows the ideal which God desires: "Do not be afraid; for God has come in order to test you, and in order that the fear of Him may remain with you." That is, he does not want us to be afraid (in the sense of terror), but he wants us to fear him (in the sense of awe). Realistically, however, it is extremely difficult for anyone who is conscious of his sinfulness to overcome all terror in the presence of the God of all righteousness. Isaiah's reaction to his vision of the holy God was certainly mixed with dread: "Woe is me, for I am ruined! Because I am a man of unclean lips, and I live among a people of unclean lips; for my eyes have seen the King, the Lord of hosts" (Isaiah 6:5). Gideon and Samson's parents reacted similarly when they realized they were standing before the Angel of Yahweh (Judges 6:22-23; 13:22). The pious psalmist says, "My flesh trembles for fear of Thee, and I am afraid of Thy judgments" (Psalm 119:120). When the church beheld the judgment of God upon Ananias and Sapphira, "great fear" came upon them all (Acts 5:5, 11).

The idea seems to be that whenever we consider the fact of the judgment of God upon sin, it is impossible not to tremble in terror at such a prospect. It would not be unreasonable to think that Adam and Eve even before the Fall experienced such fear when God warned them not to eat of the tree of the knowledge of good and evil lest they die. Even though a believer is completely forgiven by the blood of Jesus Christ and is not under condemnation, it is appropriate for pangs of terror to strike his heart at the merest thought of apostasy or falling away. Thus Paul says, "Do not be conceited, but fear"—because God will not hesitate to cut you off if you fall into unbelief (Romans 11:20ff.).

This is the underlying warning of the whole book of Hebrews: "Therefore, let us fear lest, while a promise remains of entering His rest, any one of you should seem to have come short of it" (Hebrews 4:1). Willful apostasy carries with it "a certain terrifying expectation of judgment" (Hebrews 10:27; cf. verse 31). This seems to be Jesus' point also in Matthew 10:28.

On the other hand, as redeemed and justified believers we must not forget the cleansing and protecting power of the blood of Christ. We must remember that his death has fully paid the penalty for our sins, and that "there is therefore now no condemnation for those who are in Christ Jesus" (Romans 8:1). In our present relation to God, and in prospect of our firm intention to remain faithful to our Lord and Savior, there is no reason for us to harbour a continuing sense of terror and dread. Indeed, it is inconsistent with our love for the one who has redeemed us, according to I John 4:17-18. The more we love him, the less we will fear him, for "perfect love casts out fear." John is obviously talking about the fear of terror, since reverential fear should and will continue to increase along with our love. As John Murray says,

> . . . God's dread majesty can never be dissolved and neither can the sense of it in those who serve him. The deeper the apprehension of God's glory the more enhanced will be our wonderment. It will not be the wonderment of perplexity or horror but of reverential and exultant adoration.[13]

It is in this sense that the fear of God continues to be a motive for obedience and Christian service. God's work of

13. John Murray, *Principles of Conduct*, p. 242.

redemption has modified our motivation to the extent that grateful love should now be our primary motive for serving him. However, this does not altogether exclude the fear of God as an incentive for avoiding sin and doing good. But here we are not talking about the dread of punishment, but rather the reverence and respect we should have for the Creator-God and thus also for the holy majesty of his laws. One who truly stands in awe of God will also stand in awe of his commandments and will seek to obey them. One whose heart is filled with reverence for the Creator will be opposed to whatever displeases him. Here is a principal difference between the two kinds of fear: terror hates punishment (I John 4:18), but reverence hates evil itself. Proverbs 8:13 says, "The fear of the Lord is to hate evil." So "by fear of the Lord one keeps away from evil" (Proverbs 16:6). When the fear of God is in us, we will not sin (Exodus 20:20). "Fear God and keep His commandments," says Ecclesiastes 12:13; these naturally go together. "How blessed is the man who fears the Lord, who greatly delights in His commandments" (Psalm 112:1; see Psalm 128:1). The Christian should be "perfecting holiness in the fear of God" (II Cor. 7:1), and conducting himself in fear during his time on earth (I Peter 1:17). How could we do otherwise, in view of the majestic greatness and transcendent glory of God? Another quote from Murray sums it up well:

> The fear of God could be nothing less than the soul of rectitude. It is the apprehension of God's glory that constrains the fear of his name. It is that same glory that commands our totality commitment to him, totality trust and obedience. The fear of God is but the reflex in our consciousness of the transcendent perfection which alone could

> warrant and demand the totality of our commitment in love and devotion. . . . It is the transcendent perfection of God, the fact that he is God and there is none else, that validates this totality demand. The fear of God in us is that frame of heart and mind which reflects our apprehension of who and what God is, and who and what God is will tolerate nothing less than totality commitment to him. The commandments of God are the concrete expressions to us of God's glory and will. If we are committed to him in devotion and love, we shall love his commandments, too. The fear of God and the love of God are but different aspects of our response to him in the glory of his majesty and holiness . . . .[14]

To Magnify and To Glorify

The fear of God is an inner sense, an attitude of the heart. However, it cannot remain a purely inward attitude, but must find expression in open praise and testimony. Those who stand in awe before the greatness and glory of God must in turn magnify and glorify his name. Matthew 9:8 expresses this natural sequence: "But when the multitudes saw this, they were filled with awe, and glorified God." As Revelation 14:7 admonishes, "Fear God, and give Him glory." Indeed, "who will not fear, O Lord, and glorify Thy name?" (Revelation 15:4). See Luke 5:26; 7:16.

Our task, then, is to magnify and glorify God. Psalm 34:3 exhorts, "O magnify the Lord with me, and let us exalt His name together." "Let all who seek Thee rejoice and be glad in Thee; let those who love Thy salvation say continually, 'The Lord be magnified!'" (Psalm 40:16; see Psalms 35:27; 70:4). Moses invites us to join him in magnifying God: "For I proclaim the name of the Lord; ascribe

14. *Ibid.*

greatness to our God!" (Deuteronomy 32:3). We must "praise Him according to His excellent greatness" (Psalm 150:2). We must "give Him glory," says Revelation 14:7. As Psalm 29:1-2 says, "Ascribe to the Lord, O sons of the mighty, ascribe to the Lord glory and strength. Ascribe to the Lord the glory due to His name; worship the Lord in holy array." Psalm 66:2 adds, "Sing the glory of His name; make His praise glorious." That Romans 1:21 condemns even the heathen for failing to glorify God and give him thanks, even though they know him only through general revelation, shows the basic character of this obligation.

What does it mean to magnify and glorify God? Is it possible for us in any way to increase God's greatness and glory? Of course not. His greatness and his glory are infinite; nothing we do can add to them. What we *can* do, however, is *acknowledge* his greatness, and work to cause others to do the same. Thus his greatness is magnified in the minds and hearts of men. The same is true of his glory. We can recognize and acknowledge his glory, and work to cause others to do the same. Thus his glory is reflected to an even greater extent throughout his creation.

Thus the fear of the Lord will cause us to magnify and glorify our God first of all by simply acknowledging his greatness and glory in praise and worship and thanksgiving. In prayer and song and testimony, we will offer up to God our "sacrifice of praise" and "the fruit of lips that give thanks to His name" (Hebrews 13:15). As God says, "He who offers a sacrifice of thanksgiving honors Me" (Psalm 50:23). Examples of such acknowledgement of God's glory are found throughout the Bible. One of the most intense is David's great hymn of praise before the assembly of Israel, as given in I Chronicles 29:10-13,

> Blessed art Thou, O Lord God of Israel our father, forever and ever. Thine, O Lord, is the greatness and the power and the glory and the victory and the majesty, indeed everything that is in the heavens and the earth; Thine is the dominion, O Lord, and Thou dost exalt Thyself as head over all. Both riches and honor come from Thee, and Thou dost rule over all, and in Thy hand is power and might; and it lies in Thy hand to make great, and to strengthen everyone. Now therefore, our God, we thank Thee, and praise Thy glorious name.

Another hymn of praise was led before an assembly by a group of Levites and is recorded in Nehemiah 9:5-7,

> Arise, bless the Lord your God forever and ever! O may Thy glorious name be blessed and exalted above all blessing and praise! Thou alone art the Lord. Thou hast made the heavens, the heaven of heavens with all their host, the earth and all that is in it, the seas and all that is in them. Thou dost give life to all of them and the heavenly host bows down before Thee. Thou art the Lord God . . . .

As the psalmist says, "Great is the Lord, and greatly to be praised" (Psalms 48:1; 96:4; 145:3).

In the New Testament the gospel writers inform us that as a result of the great works of Jesus Christ, the people were continually glorifying God, i.e., they were praising him and giving him the honor and credit for the wonderful things they were experiencing and witnessing. The angels' song at the announcement of Christ's birth set the pattern: "Glory to God in the highest" (Luke 2:14). The shepherds who heard it and saw the Lord were "glorifying and praising God for all that they had heard and seen" (Luke 2:20). When the paralytic was healed, he rose up and glorified God; and the people who witnessed it "were all seized with astonishment and began glorifying God" (Luke 5:25-26). This was repeated many times, e.g., Luke 7:16; 13:13; 17:15; Matthew 15:31.

The rest of the New Testament contains a number of doxologies which ascribe glory to God. They are fine examples of praise: "For from Him and through Him and to Him are all things. To Him be the glory forever. Amen" (Romans 11:36). "To Him be the glory in the church and in Christ Jesus to all generations forever and ever. Amen" (Ephesians 3:21). "Now to our God and Father be the glory forever and ever. Amen" (Philippians 4:20). "Now to the King eternal, immortal, invisible, the only God, be honor and glory forever and ever. Amen" (I Timothy 1:17). See Galatians 1:5; Revelation 1:6.

The book of Revelation shows us how to glorify God through praise to his name, since it contains several examples of such praise as it is being offered to God before his throne by the angelic beings and by the redeemed themselves. The four living creatures "give glory and honor and thanks to Him who sits on the throne," and the twenty-four elders worship him saying, "Worthy art Thou, our Lord and our God, to receive glory and honor and power; for Thou didst create all things, and because of Thy will they existed, and were created" (Revelation 4:9-11). The whole angelic host praises the Redeemer with a loud voice. "Worthy is the Lamb that was slain to receive power and riches and wisdom and might and honor and glory and blessing." Every creature joins in the praise in order to say, "To Him who sits on the throne, and to the Lamb, be blessing and honor and glory and dominion forever and ever" (Revelation 5:11-13). The angels also say, "Amen, blessing and glory and wisdom and thanksgiving and honor and power and might, be to our God forever and ever. Amen" (Revelation 7:12). The praise continues: "Hallelujah! Salvation and glory and power belong to our God; because His judgments are true and righteous . . . . Give praise to our God, all you His bond-servants, you who fear Him, the small and the great. . . . Hallelujah! For the Lord our God, the Almighty, reigns. Let us rejoice and be glad and give the glory to Him" (Revelation 19:1-7).

If we want to magnify and glorify God today, we will express our praise to him in terms such as these. We will sing the songs of praise from our hymnbooks with sincerity and fervor. We will include in our prayers, public and private, words of adoration and thanksgiving.

In addition to our own expressions of worship, our fear of God will elicit from us attempts to cause others to join us in magnifying and glorifying God. This can be done by direct testimony, by giving praise to God among the unbelievers (see Romans 15:9); or it can be done indirectly through an upright, God-honoring life of obedience. We should glorify God in our bodies, says Paul (I Cor. 6:20); everything we do should be to the glory of God (I Cor. 10:31). If we have special gifts or talents or offices, we should acknowledge them as being from God "so that in all things God may be glorified" (I Peter 4:10-11). Whether it be ordinary obedience or special service, when we live godly and sincere lives in the sight of others, they have reason to be impressed with our God. As Jesus puts it, "Let your light shine before men in such a way that they may see your good works, and glorify your Father who is in heaven" (Matthew 5:16). Peter repeats this admonition thus: "Keep your behavior excellent among the Gentiles, so that in the thing in which they slander you as evildoers, they may on account of your good deeds, as they observe them, glorify God in the day of visitation" (I Peter 2:12). If we bear much fruit, whether that be the fruit of the Spirit (Galatians 5:22-23) or the fruit of converts won to the Lord, God is glorified thereby (John 15:8). Every Christian should strive to be able to say with Paul, "And they were glorifying God because of me" (Galatians 1:24).[15]

There is something paradoxical about our reverential fear toward our awesome Creator. On the one hand, it leads us necessarily to praise and magnify his name with our hearts and voices. But, as the writer of Ecclesiastes says, there is a time to speak and a time to be silent (Eccles. 3:7). Thus it is that meditation on the greatness and the glory of God also has the effect of stilling our voices and of making all our attempts to vocalize his transcendent majesty seem so woefully inadequate. Then the most appropriate thing to do is to bow in silent adoration before him. In the words of Habakkuk 2:20,

> The Lord is in His holy temple,
> Let all the earth be silent before Him.

---

15. See Romans 2:23-24 for the opposite effect: hypocritical living causes unbelievers to blaspheme God.

Bibliography

Abbott, Edwin A. *Flatland: A Romance of Many Dimensions*. 5 ed. New York: Barnes and Noble, 1963.

Acton, H. B. "Dialectical Materialism," *The Encyclopedia of Philosophy*, ed. Paul Edwards. New York: Macmillan, 1967. II:389-397.

Adler, Margot. *Drawing Down the Moon: Witches, Druids, Goddess-Worshippers, and Other Pagans in America Today*. Boston: Beacon Press, 1979.

Adler, Mortimer J. *How To Think About God*. New York: Macmillan, 1980.

Allen, Alexander V. G. "The Continuity of Christian Thought," *American Protestant Thought: The Liberal Era*, ed. William R. Hutchison. New York: Harper Torchbook, 1968. Pp. 57-68.

Althaus, Paul. *The Theology of Martin Luther*, tr. Robert C. Schultz. Philadelphia: Fortress Press, 1966.

Altizer, Thomas J. J. "The Anonymity of God," *Is God GOD?* ed. Axel D. Steuer and James W. McClendon, Jr. Nashville: Abingdon, 1981. Pp. 19-35.

__________. *The Gospel of Christian Atheism*. Philadelphia: Westminster, 1966.

Ames, Edward Scribner. *The Divinity of Christ*. Chicago: Bethany Press, n.d.

Anderson, Ray S. *Historical Transcendence and the Reality of God*. Grand Rapids: Eerdmans, 1975.

Anselm. "Proslogium," *Saint Anselm: Basic Writings*, tr. S. W. Deane. 2 ed. La Salle, Ill.: Open Court, 1962. Pp. 1-34.

Armstrong, A. H. *Plotinus*. New York: Collier Books, 1962.

Ashcraft, Morris. *Rudolf Bultmann*. Waco: Word Books, 1972.

Athanasius. "On the Incarnation of the Word," tr. Archibald Robertson. *Christology of the Later Fathers*, ed. Edward

R. Hardy. "Library of Christian Classics," Volume III. Philadelphia: Westminster, n.d. Pp. 55-110.

Athenagoras. "On the Resurrection of the Dead," tr. B. P. Pratten. *The Ante-Nicene Fathers,* Volume II, ed. Alexander Roberts and James Donaldson. New York: Charles Scribner's Sons, 1913. Pp. 149-162.

_________. "A Plea for the Christians," tr. B. P. Pratten. *The Ante-Nicene Fathers,* Volume II, ed. Alexander Roberts and James Donaldson. New York: Charles Scribner's Sons, 1913. Pp. 129-148.

Augsburger, Myron S. "Christian Pacifism," *War: Four Christian Views,* ed. Robert Clouse. Downers Grove, Ill.: InterVarsity Press, 1981. Pp. 81-97.

_________. "A Christian Pacifist Response," *War: Four Christian Views,* ed. Robert Clouse. Downers Grove, Ill.: InterVarsity Press, 1981. Pp. 58-63.

Augustine. "The City of God," tr. Marcus Dods. *Basic Writings of Saint Augustine,* Volume II, ed. Whitney J. Oates. New York: Random House, 1948. Pp. 1-663.

_________. "The Enchiridion," tr. J. F. Shaw. *The Works of Aurelius Augustine,* Volume IX, ed. Marcus Dods. Edinburgh: T. & T. Clark, 1873. Pp. 173-260.

_________. "On the Trinity," *The Works of Aurelius Augustine,* Volume VII, ed. Marcus Dods, tr. A. W. Haddan. Edinburgh: T. & T. Clark, 1878. Pp. 1-440.

_________. "Reply to Faustus the Manichaean," *The Works of Aurelius Augustine,* Volume V, ed. Marcus Dods, tr. Richard Stothert. Edinburgh: T. & T. Clark, 1877. Pp. 145-559.

Aulen, Gustaf. *The Faith of the Christian Church,* tr. Eric H. Wahlstrom and G. E. Arden. 4 ed. Philadelphia: Muhlenberg Press, 1948.

Baillie, John. *The Idea of Revelation in Recent Thought.* New York: Columbia University Press, 1956.

__________. *Our Knowledge of God.* London: Oxford University Press, 1939.

Bambrough, Renford. "Demiurge," *The Encyclopedia of Philosophy,* ed. Paul Edwards. New York: Macmillan, 1967. II:337-338.

Barr, James. *Old and New in Interpretation.* New York: Harper and Row, 1966.

__________. "Revelation Through History in the Old Testament and in Modern Theology," *New Theology No. 1,* ed. Martin E. Marty and Dean Peerman. New York: Macmillan, 1964. Pp. 60-74.

Barth, Karl. *Church Dogmatics, Volume I: The Doctrine of the Word of God, Part 1,* tr. G. T. Thomson. Edinburgh: T. & T. Clark, 1936.

__________. *Church Dogmatics, Volume I: The Doctrine of the Word of God, Part 2,* tr. G. T. Thomson and Harold Knight. Edinburgh: T. & T. Clark, 1956.

__________. *Church Dogmatics, Volume II: The Doctrine of God, Part 1,* tr. T. H. L. Parker et al. Edinburgh: T. & T. Clark, 1957.

__________. *Church Dogmatics, Volume III: The Doctrine of Creation, Part 1,* tr. J. W. Edwards et al. Edinburgh: T. & T. Clark, 1958.

__________. *Church Dogmatics, Volume III: The Doctrine of Creation, Part 2,* tr. Harold Knight et al. Edinburgh: T. & T. Clark, 1960.

__________. *The Epistle to the Romans,* tr. Edwyn C. Hoskyns. 6 ed. New York: Oxford University Press, 1933.

__________. *The Humanity of God,* tr. J. N. Thomas and T. Weiser. Richmond: John Knox Press, 1960.

__________, and Emil Brunner. *Natural Theology*, tr. Peter Fraenkel. London: Geoffrey Bles, 1946.

Basak, Radhagovinda. "The Hindu Concept of the Natural World," *The Religion of the Hindus*, ed. Kenneth Morgan. New York: Ronald Press, 1953. Pp. 83-116.

Bavinck, Herman. *The Doctrine of God*, ed. and tr. William Hendriksen. Grand Rapids: Eerdmans, 1951.

__________. *Our Reasonable Faith*, tr. Henry Zylstra. Grand Rapids: Eerdmans, 1956.

Berkhof, Hendrikus. *Christian Faith: An Introduction to the Study of the Faith*, tr. Sierd Woudstra. Grand Rapids: Eerdmans, 1979.

Berkhof, Louis. *Systematic Theology*. London: Banner of Truth Trust, 1939.

Berkouwer, G. C. *General Revelation*. Grand Rapids: Eerdmans, 1955.

__________. *The Triumph of Grace in the Theology of Karl Barth*, tr. Harry R. Boer. Grand Rapids: Eerdmans, 1956.

Blaikie, Robert J. *"Secular Christianity" and God Who Acts*. Grand Rapids: Eerdmans, 1970.

Bockmühl, Klaus. "God and Other 'Forgotten Factors' in Theology," *Christianity Today* (February 19, 1982), 26:48-49.

Bonhoeffer, Dietrich. *Letters and Papers from Prison*, tr. Reginald H. Fuller. New York: Macmillan, 1962.

Borland, James A. *Christ in the Old Testament*. Chicago: Moody Press, 1978.

Braaten, Carl. *New Directions in Theology Today, Volume II: History and Hermeneutics*. Philadelphia: Westminster, 1966.

Brown, Colin. *Karl Barth and the Christian Message*. London: Tyndale Press, 1967.

Brunner, Emil. *The Christian Doctrine of Creation and Redemption: Dogmatics, Volume II,* tr. Olive Wyon. Philadelphia: Westminster, 1952.

__________. *The Christian Doctrine of God: Dogmatics, Volume I,* tr. Olive Wyon. Philadelphia: Westminster, 1950.

__________. *Revelation and Reason,* tr. Olive Wyon. Philadelphia: Westminster, 1946.

Bultmann, Rudolf. "New Testament and Mythology," *Kerygma and Myth: A Theological Debate,* ed. Hans Werner Bartsch, tr. Reginald H. Fuller. New York: Harper Torchbook, 1961. Pp. 1-44.

Buri, Fritz. "How Can We Still Speak Responsibly of God?" *Andover Newton Quarterly* (November 1967), 8:127-139.

Burrill, Donald R., ed. *The Cosmological Arguments.* Garden City, N.Y.: Doubleday, 1967.

Buswell, James O., Jr. *A Systematic Theology of the Christian Religion.* 2 vols. Grand Rapids: Zondervan, 1962.

Calvin, John. *Institutes of the Christian Religion,* ed. John T. McNeill, tr. Ford Lewis Battles. 2 vols. "Library of Christian Classics," Volumes XX-XXI. Philadelphia: Westminster, 1960.

Campbell, Alexander. "An Address on Colleges," *The Millennial Harbinger,* Fourth Series, Volume IV (February 1854), pp. 61-79.

__________. "Theology, Natural and Revealed," *The Millennial Harbinger,* Fourth Series, Volume III (May 1853), pp. 285-292.

Campbell, Keith. "Materialism," *The Encyclopedia of Philosophy,* ed. Paul Edwards. New York: Macmillan, 1967. V:179-188.

Casey, John W. "Liberty, Legalism, or License?" *Christian Standard* (April 8, 1967), 102:211-212.

Cauthen, Kenneth. *The Impact of American Religious Liberalism*. New York: Harper and Row, 1962.

Chafer, Lewis Sperry. *Systematic Theology*. 8 vols. Dallas: Dallas Seminary Press, 1947.

Charnock, Stephen. *The Existence and Attributes of God*. Grand Rapids: Kregel reprint, 1958.

Chatterjee, Satis Chandra. "Hindu Religious Thought," *The Religion of the Hindus,* ed. Kenneth W. Morgan. New York: Ronald Press, 1953. Pp. 206-261.

Christian, James L. *Philosophy: An Introduction to the Art of Wondering*. 3 ed. New York: Holt, Rinehart and Winston, 1981.

Clark, Robert E. D. *Darwin: Before and After*. Exeter: Paternoster Press, 1966.

Clark, Ronald W. *Einstein: The Life and Times*. New York: World, 1971.

Clarke, Arthur C. "The Nine Billion Names of God," *Science Fiction Hall of Fame,* ed. Robert Silverberg. Garden City, N.Y.: Doubleday, 1970. I:424-430.

Clarke, William Newton. *An Outline of Christian Theology*. 3 ed. Edinburgh: T. & T. Clark, 1899.

Clement of Alexandria. "The Stromata, or Miscellanies," *The Ante-Nicene Fathers,* Volume II, ed. Alexander Roberts and James Donaldson. New York: Charles Scribner's Sons, 1913. Pp. 299-568.

Clement of Rome. "To the Corinthians," *The Apostolic Fathers,* ed. J. B. Lightfoot and J. R. Harmer. Grand Rapids: Baker, 1962. Pp. 13-41.

Cobb, John B., Jr., and David Ray Griffin, eds. *Process Theology: An Introductory Exposition*. Philadelphia: Westminster, 1976.

Collins, James. *God in Modern Philosophy*. Chicago: Henry Regnery, 1959.

Cone, James H. "The Story Context of Black Theology," *Theology Today* (July 1975), 32:144-150.

Cook, Stuart D. "Making Christ Central," *Christian Standard* (April 19, 1981), 116:12-14.

Copleston, Frederick. *A History of Philosophy, Volume I: Greece and Rome*. New revised edition, in two parts. Garden City, N.Y.: Doubleday Image, 1962.

__________. *Religion and the One: Philosophies East and West*. New York: Crossroad, 1982.

Cornford, F. M. *Plato's Cosmology*. New York: Humanities Press, 1952.

Cosser, William. *Preaching the Old Testament*. London: Epworth Press, 1966.

Cottrell, Jack. *The Authority of the Bible*. Grand Rapids: Baker, 1979.

__________. "Conditional Election," *Grace Unlimited*, ed. Clark Pinnock. Minneapolis: Bethany Fellowship, 1975. Pp. 51-73.

__________. "The Errors of Pacifism," *Christian Standard* (August 8/15, 1982), 117:4-6/6-8.

__________. *His Way*. 2 ed. Cincinnati: Standard Publishing, 1979.

__________. "Theology and the Church," *Christian Standard* (February 7, 1982), 117:4-5.

__________. "The Transcendence of God," *The Seminary Review* (Spring 1968), 14:59-69.

Cousins, Ewert H., ed. *Process Theology: Basic Writings*. New York: Newman Press, 1971.

Cox, Harvey. *On Not Leaving It to the Snake*. New York: Macmillan, 1969.

__________. *The Secular City*. Revised edition. New York: Macmillan, 1966.

Craig, William Lane. *The Cosmological Argument from Plato to Leibnitz.* New York: Barnes and Noble, 1980.

__________. *The Existence of God and the Beginning of the Universe.* San Bernardino, Cal.: Here's Life Publishers, 1979.

__________. *The Kalām Cosmological Argument.* New York: Barnes and Noble, 1979.

Crawford, C. C. *Survey Course in Christian Doctrine.* Volume I. Joplin, Mo.: College Press, 1962.

Cullmann, Oscar. *Salvation in History,* tr. Sidney Sowers et al. New York: Harper and Row, 1967.

Daly, Mary. "Theology After the Demise of God the Father: A Call for the Castration of Sexist Religion," *Sexist Religion and Women in the Church,* ed. Alice Hageman. New York: Association, 1974.

Davies, E. O. *Prolegomena to Systematic Theology.* London: Hodder and Stoughton, 1909.

DeGroot, Alfred T. *The Restoration Principle.* St. Louis: Bethany Press, 1960.

Demarest, Bruce. *General Revelation: Historical Views and Contemporary Issues.* Grand Rapids: Zondervan, 1982.

Denzinger, Henricus, and Adolfus Schönmetzer, eds. *Enchiridion Symbolorum.* 32 ed. Freiburg: Verlag Herder, 1963.

Descartes, René. *The Meditations and Selections from the Principles of René Descartes,* tr. John Veitch. La Salle, Ill.: Open Court, 1948.

Dewart, Leslie. "God and the Supernatural," *Commonweal* (February 10, 1967), 85:523-528.

Dewey, Edward R. "Cycles," *Science of Mind* (June 1973), 46:54-55.

DeWolf, L. Harold. *A Theology of the Living Church.* New York: Harper and Brothers, 1953.

Dickinson, Curtis. "What's Happened to God?" *The Witness* (May 1976), 16:1-2.

Dillenberger, John. *God Hidden and Revealed.* Philadelphia: Muhlenberg Press, 1953.

__________. *Protestant Thought and Natural Science.* Nashville: Abingdon, 1960.

"Dogmatic Constitution on the Church," *Documents of Vatican II,* ed. Austin P. Flannery. Grand Rapids: Eerdmans, 1975.

Dowey, Edward A., Jr. *The Knowledge of God in Calvin's Theology.* New York: Columbia University Press, 1952.

Drescher, John. "Why Christians Shouldn't Carry Swords," *Christianity Today (November 7, 1980), 24:15-23. Drummond, Henry. The Ascent of Man.* 7 ed. New York: James Pott & Co., 1898.

Duddington, John W. "The Red Herring of a Three-Story Universe," *Christianity Today* (November 5, 1971), 16:13-16.

Ehrhardt, Arnold. *The Beginning: A Study in the Greek Philosophical Approach to the Concept of Creation.* Manchester: Manchester University Press, 1968.

Ellwood, Robert S., Jr. *Alternative Altars.* Chicago: University of Chicago Press, 1979.

"Eternity—A Different Concept," *The Cable* (October 1979), 5:2.

Feibleman, James K. *The New Materialism.* The Hague: M. Nijhoff, 1970.

Ferre, Nels F. S. *Christ and the Christian.* New York: Harper and Brothers, 1958.

__________. *The Living God of Nowhere and Nothing.* Philadelphia: Westminster, 1966.

Flew, Antony. *God and Philosophy.* New York: Hutchinson, 1966.

France, R. T. *The Living God.* Downers Grove, Ill.: Inter-Varsity Press, 1970.

Geisler, Norman L. *Philosophy of Religion.* Grand Rapids: Zondervan, 1974.

Gilkey, Langdon. *Maker of Heaven and Earth.* Garden City, N.Y.: Doubleday Anchor, 1965.

Gill, Jerry. "Transcendence: An Incarnational Model," *Encounter* (Winter 1978), 39:39-44.

Grant, Robert M. *Gnosticism and Early Christianity.* Revised edition. New York: Harper and Row, 1966.

"Greek vs. Hebraic Concepts," *Journal of the American Scientific Affiliation* (June 1979), 31:128.

Guthrie, Shirley C., Jr. "Theology and Metaphysics," *America and the Future of Theology,* ed. William A. Beardslee. Philadelphia: Westminster, 1967. Pp. 127-135.

Habermas, Gary. *The Resurrection of Jesus: An Apologetic.* Grand Rapids: Baker, 1980.

Hall, Roland. "Monism and Pluralism," *The Encyclopedia of Philosophy,* ed. Paul Edwards. New York: Macmillan, 1967. V:363-365.

Hamilton, Sam M. "Natural Theology and the Ontological Argument," *The Seminary Review* (Winter 1961 and Spring 1961), VII:1-88.

Hancock, Roger. "Metaphysics, History of," *The Encyclopedia of Philosophy,* ed. Paul Edwards. New York: Macmillan, 1967. V:289-300.

Hardesty, Nancy. Book review, *Christianity Today* (June 6, 1975), 19:39-41.

Hartshorne, Charles. *The Divine Relativity.* New Haven: Yale, 1948.

_________. *Man's Vision of God.* New York: Harper, 1941.

__________, and William L. Reese, eds. *Philosophers Speak of God*. Chicago: University of Chicago Press, 1953.

Hartwell, Herbert. *The Theology of Karl Barth: An Introduction*. Philadelphia: Westminster, 1964.

Heinze, Max. "Pantheism," *The New Schaff-Herzog Encyclopedia of Religious Knowledge*, ed. Samuel M. Jackson et al. Grand Rapids: Baker, 1964 reprint. VIII:328-332.

Henry, Carl F. H. *God, Revelation and Authority, Volume I: God Who Speaks and Shows, Preliminary Considerations*. Waco: Word Books, 1976.

__________. *God, Revelation and Authority, Volume II: God Who Speaks and Shows, Fifteen Theses, Part One*. Waco: Word Books, 1976.

__________. *God, Revelation and Authority, Volume III: God Who Speaks and Shows, Fifteen Theses, Part Two*. Waco: Word Books, 1979.

Hepburn, Ronald. "Creation, Religious Idea of," *The Encyclopedia of Philosophy*, ed. Paul Edwards. New York: Macmillan, 1967. II:252-256.

Heppe, Heinrich. *Reformed Dogmatics*, ed. Ernst Bizer, tr. G. T. Thomson. London: Allen and Unwin, 1950.

Hick, John. *Arguments for the Existence of God*. New York: Seabury, 1971.

__________. *Philosophy of Religion*. 2 ed. Englewood Cliffs, N.J.: Prentice-Hall, 1973.

__________, ed. *The Existence of God*. New York: Macmillan, 1964.

__________, and Arthur C. McGill, eds. *The Many-Faced Argument: Recent Studies on the Ontological Argument for the Existence of God*. New York: Macmillan, 1967.

Hocking, William E. *Science and the Idea of God*. Chapel Hill: University of North Carolina Press, 1944.

Hodge, Charles. *Systematic Theology.* 3 vols. Grand Rapids: Eerdmans reprint, n.d.

Hodgson, Peter C. *New Birth of Freedom: A Theology of Bondage and Liberation.* Philadelphia: Fortress Press, 1976.

"Hot Beetle," *Scientific American* (September 1969), 221:102.

Houston, James M. *I Believe in the Creator.* Grand Rapids: Eerdmans, 1980.

Hughes, H. Maldwyn. *The Christian Idea of God.* London: Duckworth, 1936.

Humanist Manifestos I and II. Buffalo: Prometheus Press, 1973.

Hume, David. *Dialogues Concerning Natural Religion,* ed. Norman Kemp Smith. Indianapolis: Bobbs-Merrill, 1947.

Jastrow, Robert. *God and the Astronomers.* New York: W. W. Norton, 1978.

Jeans, James. *The Mysterious Universe.* New York: Macmillan, 1930.

Jenkins, David E. *The Glory of Man.* New York: Charles Scribner's Sons, 1967.

Johnson, H. Eugene. *Simple Principles.* Tampa: author, 1977.

Jonas, Hans. *The Gnostic Religion.* 2 ed. Boston: Beacon Press, 1963.

__________. "Gnosticism," *The Encyclopedia of Philosophy,* ed. Paul Edwards. New York: Macmillan, 1967. III:336-342.

Justin Martyr. "Dialogue of Justin, Philosopher and Martyr, with Trypho, a Jew," *The Ante-Nicene Fathers,* Volume I, ed. Alexander Roberts and James Donaldson. New York: Charles Scribner's Sons, 1913. Pp. 194-270.

Kant, Immanuel. *Critique of Practical Reason,* tr. Lewis W. Beck. Indianapolis: Bobbs-Merrill, 1956.

__________. *Critique of Pure Reason,* tr. J. M. D. Meiklejohn. New York: Willey Book Co., 1900.

Kantzer, Kenneth. "The Communication of Revelation," *The Bible: The Living Word of Revelation,* ed. Merrill C. Tenney. Grand Rapids: Zondervan, 1968. Pp. 51-80.

Kaufman, Gordon D. "Constructing the Concept of God," *Is God GOD?* ed. Axel D. Steuer and James McClendon, Jr. Nashville: Abingdon, 1981. Pp. 111-143.

__________. *The Religious Imagination: Constructing the Concept of God.* Philadelphia: Westminster, 1981.

Kerr, Hugh T. "What's the Story?" *Theology Today* (July 1975), 32:129-132.

Ketcherside, W. Carl. *The Death of the Custodian.* Cincinnati: Standard Publishing, 1976.

Kierkegaard, Soren. *Concluding Unscientific Postscript,* tr. David Swenson and Walter Lowrie. Princeton: Princeton University Press, 1941.

Kittel, Gerhard. "αἴνιγμα," *Theological Dictionary of the New Testament,* ed. Gerhard Kittel, tr. Geoffrey Bromiley. Grand Rapids: Eerdmans, 1964. I:178-180.

Kleinknecht, Hermann. "θειότης," *Theological Dictionary of the New Testament,* ed. Gerhard Kittel, tr. Geoffrey Bromiley. Grand Rapids: Eerdmans, 1965. III:123.

Kuen, Alfred. *I Will Build My Church,* tr. Ruby Lindblad. Chicago: Moody, 1971.

Kuhn, Harold B. "Relationalism: Principle or Slogan?" *Christianity Today* (February 28, 1975), 19:49-50.

Kuitert, H. M. *The Reality of Faith,* tr. Lewis B. Smedes. Grand Rapids: Eerdmans, 1968.

Lactantius. "The Divine Institutes," tr. William Fletcher. *The Ante-Nicene Fathers,* Volume VII, ed. Alexander Roberts and James Donaldson. New York: Charles Scribner's Sons, 1913. Pp. 9-223.

LaHaye, Tim. *The Battle for the Family.* Old Tappan, N.J.: Revell, 1981.

__________. *The Battle for the Mind.* Old Tappan, N.J.: Revell, 1980.

__________. *The Battle for the Public Schools.* Old Tappan, N.J.: Revell, 1982.

Lee, Francis Nigel. *Communist Eschatology.* Nutley, N.J.: Craig Press, 1974.

Lewis, C. S. *The Abolition of Man.* New York: Macmillan, 1947.

__________. *Miracles: A Preliminary Study.* New York: Macmillan, 1960.

Lightner, Robert P. *The First Fundamental: God.* Nashville: Thomas Nelson, 1973.

Long, Charles H. *Alpha: The Myths of Creation.* New York: Collier Books, 1969.

Lovett, C. S. *Jesus Wants You Well!* Baldwin Park, Cal.: Personal Christianity, 1973.

__________. "Why You Should Minister to the Lord!" *Personal Christianity* (October 1978), 18:2-5.

MacIntyre, Alasdair. "Pantheism," *The Encyclopedia of Philosophy,* ed. Paul Edwards. New York: Macmillan, 1967. VI:31-35.

Mackintosh, H. R. *The Christian Apprehension of God.* New York: Harper and Brothers, 1929.

Malcolm, Norman. *Knowledge and Certainty.* Englewood Cliffs, N.J.: Prentice-Hall, 1963.

Martensen, H. *Christian Dogmatics,* tr. William Urwick. Edinburgh: T. & T. Clark, 1898.

Martin, Walter. *The New Cults*. Santa Ana, Cal.: Vision House, 1980.

Mascall, E. L. *Christian Theology and Natural Science*. New York: Ronald Press, 1956.

__________. *He Who Is: A Study in Traditional Theism*. London: Darton, Longman & Todd Libra edition, 1966.

Matthews, W. R. *God in Christian Experience*. New York: Harper and Brothers, 1930.

McComiskey, Thomas E. "bārā'," *Theological Wordbook of the Old Testament*, ed. R. Laird Harris et al. Chicago: Moody Press, 1980. I:127-128.

Mellert, Robert. *What Is Process Theology?* New York: Paulist Press, 1975.

Merlan, Philip. "Plotinus," *The Encyclopedia of Philosophy*, ed. Paul Edwards. New York: Macmillan, 1967. VI: 351-359.

Michalson, Carl. "Theology as Ontology and as History," *The Later Heidegger and Theology*, ed. James M. Robinson and John B. Cobb, Jr. New York: Harper and Row, 1963.

Milligan, Robert. *An Exposition and Defense of the Scheme of Redemption*. St. Louis: Bethany Press, 1962 printing.

Miranda, Jose P. *Marx and the Bible: A Critique of the Philosophy of Oppression*, tr. John Eagleson. Maryknoll, N.Y.: Orbis Books, 1974.

Mitchell, Norman L. "Water of Life," *Ministry* (March 1980), 53:20-21.

Molnar, Thomas. *Theists and Atheists: A Typology of Non-Belief*. New York: Mouton Publishers, 1980.

Moody, Dale. *The Word of Truth: A Summary of Christian Doctrine Based on Biblical Revelation*. Grand Rapids: Eerdmans, 1981.

Moore, G. E. "Is Existence a Predicate?" *The Ontological Argument,* ed. Alvin Plantinga. Garden City, N.Y.: Doubleday Anchor, 1965. Pp. 71-85.

Morris, Leon. *I Believe in Revelation*. Grand Rapids: Eerdmans, 1976.

Mott, Stephen Charles. *Biblical Ethics and Social Change*. New York: Oxford University Press, 1982.

Mundle, Wilhelm. "Image, Idol, Imprint, Example," *The New International Dictionary of New Testament Theology,* ed. Colin Brown. Grand Rapids: Zondervan, 1976. II: 284-286.

Murch, James D. *The Free Church*. N.p.: Restoration Press, 1966.

Murray, John. *Principles of Conduct. Grand Rapids: Eerdman, 1957.*

Nakamura, Hajime. *Ways of Thinking of Eastern Peoples: India, China, Tibet, Japan,* ed. and tr. Philip Wiener. Honolulu: East-West Center Press, 1964.

Nash, Ronald. *The Word of God and the Mind of Man.* Grand Rapids: Zondervan, 1982.

Oepke, Albrecht. "διά," *Theological Dictionary of the New Testament,* ed. Gerhard Kittel, tr. Geoffrey Bromiley. Grand Rapids: Eerdmans, 1964. II:65-70.

Origen. "Commentary on John," tr. Allan Menzies. *The Ante-Nicene Fathers,* Volume IX, ed. Allan Menzies. New York: Charles Scribner's Sons, 1912. Pp. 297-408.

__________. "De Principiis," tr. Frederick Crombie. *The Ante-Nicene Fathers,* Volume IV, ed. Alexander Roberts and James Donaldson. New York: Charles Scribner's Sons, 1913. Pp. 239-382.

Orr, James. *Sidelights on Christian Doctrine*. London: Marshall Brothers, 1909.

Otto, Rudolf. *The Idea of the Holy,* tr. John W. Harvey. Revised edition. New York: Oxford University Press, 1926.

Owen, H. P. *Concepts of Deity.* New York: Herder and Herder, 1971.

__________. *The Moral Argument for Christian Theism.* New York: Humanities Press, 1966.

Packer, J. I. *Knowing God.* Downers Grove, Ill.: Inter-Varsity Press, 1973.

Paley, William. *The Works of William Paley.* New edition. Philadelphia: J. J. Woodward, 1841.

"The Pastor of Hermas," tr. F. Crombie. *The Ante-Nicene Fathers,* Volume II, ed. Alexander Roberts and James Donaldson. New York: Charles Scribner's Sons, 1913. Pp. 9-55.

Pentecost, J. Dwight. *The Glory of God.* Portland, Ore.: Multnomah Press, 1978.

Petersen, William J. *Those Curious New Cults.* 2 ed. New Canaan, Conn.: Keats, 1975.

Phillips, J. B. *Your God Is Too Small.* New York: Macmillan, 1961.

Pieper, Francis. *Christian Dogmatics.* 4 vols. St. Louis: Concordia, 1950.

Pinnock, Clark H. *Biblical Revelation: The Foundation of Christian Theology.* Chicago: Moody Press, 1971.

__________. "God Made in the Image of Man," *Christianity Today* (September 3, 1982), 26:35.

Plantinga, Alvin, ed. *The Ontological Argument.* New York: Doubleday Anchor, 1965.

Pohle, Joseph. *God: The Author of Nature and the Supernatural,* ed. Arthur Preuss. St. Louis: B. Herder, 1912.

Prenter, Regin. *Creation and Redemption,* tr. Theodor Jensen. Philadelphia: Fortress Press, 1967.

Pritchard, James B., ed. *Ancient Near Eastern Texts Relating to the Old Testament.* Princeton: Princeton University Press, 1950.

Rajneesh, Bhagwan Shree. *A Rajneesh Reader: The Great Challenge.* New York: Grove Press, 1982.

Ramm, Bernard. *After Fundamentalism: The Future of Evangelical Theology.* San Francisco: Harper and Row, 1983.

__________. *The Christian View of Science and Scripture.* Grand Rapids: Eerdmans, 1956.

__________. *Special Revelation and the Word of God.* Grand Rapids: Eerdmans, 1961.

Redmond, Howard A. *The Omnipotence of God.* Philadelphia: Westminster, 1964.

Robinson, James M. "The German Discussion of the Later Heidegger," *The Later Heidegger and Theology,* ed. James M. Robinson and John B. Cobb, Jr. New York: Harper and Row, 1963. Pp. 3-76.

__________, and John B. Cobb, Jr., eds. *The Later Heidegger and Theology.* "New Frontiers in Theology," Volume I. New York: Harper and Row, 1963.

Robinson, John A. T. *Honest to God.* London: SCM Press, 1963.

Robson, James. "God, Concept of (Islam)," *A Dictionary of Comparative Religion,* ed. S. G. F. Brandon. London: Weidenfeld and Nicolson, 1970. Pp. 306-307.

Rowley, Peter. *New Gods in America.* New York: David Mackay, 1971.

Runia, Klaas. "Glory, Glorification," *The Encyclopedia of Christianity,* Volume IV, ed. Philip E. Hughes. Marshallton, Del.: The National Foundation for Christian Education, 1972. Pp. 345-348.

Russell, Bertrand. "A Free Man's Worship," *Mysticism and Logic*. Garden City, N.Y.: Doubleday Anchor, n.d. Pp. 44-54.

Schaff, David S. (completing the work begun by Philip Schaff). *History of the Christian Church, Volume V: The Middle Ages*. Grand Rapids: Eerdmans, reprint of 1907 edition.

Schaff, Philip. *History of the Christian Church, Volume II: Ante-Nicene Christianity*. Grand Rapids: Eerdmans, 1959 reprint of 1910 edition.

__________. *History of the Christian Church, Volume IV: Medieval Christianity*. Grand Rapids: Eerdmans, reprint of 1910 edition.

Scheffczyk, Leo. *Creation and Providence*, tr. Richard Strachan. New York: Herder and Herder, 1970.

Schleiermacher, Friedrich. *The Christian Faith*, English translation edited by H. R. Mackintosh and J. S. Stewart. 2 vols. New York: Harper Torchbook, 1963.

A Secular Humanist Declaration. Buffalo: Prometheus Press, 1980.

Seebass, Horst. "Holy, Consecrate, Sanctify, Saints, Devout," *The New International Dictionary of New Testament Theology*, ed. Colin Brown. Grand Rapids: Zondervan, 1976. II:223-238.

Shedd, William G. T. *Dogmatic Theology*. 3 vols. Grand Rapids: Zondervan, 1969 reprint.

"The Shorter Catechism," *The School of Faith*, ed. and tr. T. F. Torrance. London: James Clarke & Co., 1959. Pp. 261-278.

Silvester, Hugh. *Arguing with God*. Downers Grove, Ill.: InterVarsity Press, 1971.

Smart, Ninian. "Gods, Hindu," *A Dictionary of Comparative Religion*, ed. S. G. F. Brandon. London: Weidenfeld and Nicolson, 1970. Pp. 308-309.

__________. "Indian Philosophy," *The Encyclopedia of Philosophy*, ed. Paul Edwards. New York: Macmillan, 1967. IV:155-169.

__________. "Sankara," *The Encyclopedia of Philosophy*, ed. Paul Edwards. New York: Macmillan, 1967. VII: 280-282.

Smith, Morton H. "God, The Attributes of," *The Encyclopedia of Christianity*, Volume IV, ed. Philip Hughes. Marshallton, Del.: The National Foundation for Christian Education, 1972. Pp. 366-375.

__________. "God, The Names of," *The Encyclopedia of Christianity*, Volume IV, ed. Philip Hughes. Marshallton, Del.: The National Foundation for Christian Education, 1972. Pp. 356-366.

Smith, Ronald Gregor. *Secular Christianity*. London: Collins, 1966.

Snaith, Norman. *The Distinctive Ideas of the Old Testament*. New York: Schocken Books, 1964.

Sproul, Barbara, ed. *Primal Myths: Creating the World*. San Francisco: Harper and Row, 1979.

Sproul, R. C. "The Relativity Blitz and Process Theology," *Christianity Today* (April 23, 1982), 26:50-51.

Staton, Knofel. *Spiritual Gifts for Christians Today*. Joplin: Mo.: College Press, 1973.

Steuer, Axel D. "The Supposed Incoherence of the Concept of God," *Is God GOD?* ed. Axel D. Steuer and James E. McClendon, Jr. Nashville: Abingdon Press, 1981. Pp. 86-107.

Strong, Augustus H. *Systematic Theology*. 3 vols. in 1. Valley Forge, Pa.: Judson Press, 1907.

Stroup, George W., III. "A Bibliographical Critique," *Theology Today* (July 1975), 32:133-143.

Stumpff, Albrecht. "ζῆλος," *Theological Dictionary of the New Testament*, ed. Gerhard Kittel, tr. Geoffrey W. Bromiley. Grand Rapids: Eerdmans, 1964. II:877-888.

Talmage, James E. *A Study of the Articles of Faith*. 13 ed. Salt Lake City: The Church of Jesus Christ of Latter-Day Saints, 1924.

Tawney, R. H. *The Acquisitive Society*. London: G. Bell, 1924.

Temple, William. *Nature, Man and God*. London: Macmillan and Co., 1934.

Tennant, F. R. *Philosophical Theology*. 2 vols. New York: Cambridge University Press, 1928-1930.

Tertullian. "The Prescription Against Heretics," tr. Peter Holmes. *The Ante-Nicene Fathers*, Volume III, ed. Alexander Roberts and James Donaldson. New York: Charles Scribner's Sons, 1908. Pp. 243-265.

Theophilus. "To Autolycus," tr. Marcus Dods. *The Ante-Nicene Fathers*, Volume II, ed. Alexander Roberts and James Donaldson. New York: Charles Scribner's Sons, 1913. Pp. 89-121.

Thielicke, Helmut. *The Evangelical Faith, Volume Two: The Doctrine of God and of Christ*, tr. and ed. Geoffrey W. Bromiley. Grand Rapids: Eerdmans, 1977.

Thiessen, Henry Clarence. *Introductory Lectures in Systematic Theology*. Grand Rapids: Eerdmans, 1949.

Thomas Aquinas. *Basic Writings of Saint Thomas Aquinas*, ed. Anton Pegis. 2 vols. New York: Random House, 1945.

Thomas, W. H. Griffith. *The Principles of Theology: An Introduction to the Thirty-Nine Articles*. London: Longmans, Green and Company, 1930.

Tillich, Paul. *Systematic Theology.* 3 vols. Chicago: University of Chicago Press, 1951-1963.

Torrance, T. F. *Divine and Contingent Order.* New York: Oxford University Press, 1981.

Tresmontant, Claude. *Christian Metaphysics,* tr. Gerard Slevin. New York: Sheed and Ward, 1965.

__________. *The Origins of Christian Philosophy,* tr. Mark Pontifex. New York: Hawthorn Books, 1963.

"UFOs: Is Science Fiction Coming True?" *SCP Journal,* Volume I (August 1977).

Von Weizsäcker, C. F. *The Relevance of Science: Creation and Cosmogony.* London: Collins, 1964.

Weidner, Revere F. *Theologia, or the Doctrine of God.* New York: Revell, 1902.

Whale, J. S. *Christian Doctrine.* Cambridge: Cambridge University Press, 1941.

Whalen, William J. *Strange Gods: Contemporary Religious Cults in America.* Huntington, Ind.: Our Sunday Visitor, 1981.

Whitehead, Alfred North. *Process and Reality.* New York: Macmillan, 1929.

Widengren, Geo. *Mani and Manichaeism,* tr. Charles Kessler. New York: Holt, Rinehart and Winston, 1965.

Wiley, H. Orton. *Christian Theology.* 3 vols. Kansas City, Mo.: Beacon Hill Press, 1940.

Williams, Gardner. "Humanistic Theism," *The Humanist Alternative,* ed. Paul Kurtz. Buffalo: Prometheus Press, 1973. Pp. 67-69.

Wilson, Clifford. *The Chariots Still Crash.* Old Tappan, N.J.: Revell, 1975.

__________. *Crash Go the Chariots.* New York: Lancer Books, 1972.

__________. *Gods in Chariots and Other Fantasies.* San Diego: Creation-Life, 1975.

Wilson, R. McL. "Mani and Manichaeism," The *Encyclopedia of Philosophy,* ed. Paul Edwards. New York: Macmillan, 1967. V:149-150.

Wingren, Gustaf. *Creation and Law,* tr. Ross Mackenzie. Edinburgh: Oliver and Boyd, 1961.

Wright, G. Ernest. *God Who Acts.* London: SCM Press, 1952.

Zaehner, R. C. *Hindu and Muslim Mysticism.* London: University of London Athlone Press, 1960.

__________. *Hinduism.* 2 ed. New York: Oxford University Press, 1966.

Zahrnt, Heinz. *The Question of God: Protestant Theology in the Twentieth Century,* tr. R. A. Wilson. New York: Harcourt Brace Jovanovich, 1969.

Zwingli, Huldreich. "Commentary on True and False Religion," *The Latin Works of Huldreich Zwingli,* tr. for S. M. Jackson, ed. C. N. Heller. Philadelphia: Heidelberg Press, 1929. III:43-343.

__________. "An Exposition of the Faith," *Zwingli and Bullinger,* tr. G. W. Bromiley. "The Library of Christian Classics," Volume XXIV. Philadelphia: Westminster, 1953. Pp. 245-279.

Index of Names

Index of Subjects

Index of Scriptures

(Psalms)

Proverbs

(Isaiah)

Jeremiah

(This index of Scripture passages was prepared by Viola Malek.)